NATIONAL WILDLIFE FEDERATION

WHERE
THE BIRDS
ARE

NATIONAL WILDLIFE FEDERATION.

WHERE THE BIRDS ARE

The 100 Best Birdwatching Spots in North America

ROBERT M. BROWN • SHEILA BUFF

TIM GALLAGHER • KRISTI STREIFFERT

A GRAND CENTRAL PRESS BOOK

LONDON, NEW YORK, SYDNEY, DELHI, PARIS,
MUNICH AND JOHANNESBURG

SENIOR EDITOR: Jill Hamilton
ART EDITOR: Megan Clayton
EDITORIAL DIRECTOR: LaVonne Carlson
ART DIRECTOR: Tina Vaughan
PUBLISHER: Sean Moore
PRODUCTION DIRECTOR: David Proffit

PRODUCED BY GRAND CENTRAL PRESS
EXECUTIVE EDITOR: Judy Pray
CONSULTING EDITOR: Nick Viorst • DIRECTOR: Paul Fargis
PROJECT EDITOR: Sarah Scheffel • FACTCHECKER: Justine Gardner
COPYEDITOR: Carol Healy • DESIGNER: Wendy Palitz
PRODUCTION DESIGN: Smythtype • MAPS: Natasha Perkel
PHOTO RESEARCH: Lauren Weinberger for Steven Diamond, Inc.
ABOUT THE BIRDS TEXT: George O. Miller

First American Edition, 2001
2 4 6 8 10 9 7 5 3 1
Published in the United States by
Dorling Kindersley Publishing, Inc.
95 Madison Avenue
New York, New York 10016

Dorling Kindersley Publishing, Inc. offers special discounts for bulk
purchases for sales promotions or premiums. Specific, large-quantity
needs can be met with special editions, including personalized covers,
excerpts of existing guides, and corporate imprints.
For more information, contact Special Markets Department,
Dorling Kindersley Publishing, Inc.,
95 Madison Avenue, New York, NY 10016
Fax: 800-600-9098.

Where the birds are / by Robert M. Brown…[et al.].
p. cm.
ISBN 0-7894-7169-8 (alk.paper)
1. Birding sites—North America—Guidebooks. 2. Bird watching—
North America—Guidebooks.
3. Birds—North America. 4. North America—Guidebooks. I. Brown,
Robert M. (Robert Musser), 1918-

QL681.W53 2001
598'.07'2347—dc21   00-058935

Reproduced by Colourscan, Singapore.
Printed and bound by R. R. Donnelley & Sons Co.
in the United States.

See our complete catalog at
www.dk.com

CONTENTS

BRITISH COLUMBIA

Black-billed Magpies *flock over farms and open woodlands.*

MAN

The Great Egret *is widespread in wetlands throughout the U.S.*

| 79 | 80 |

WASHINGTON

77

73

72

50

51 | NORTH DAK

MONTANA

OREGON

70

71 | IDAHO

82

WYOMING

56 | SOUTH DA

75

78

81

64

NEVADA

68

49

NEBRASI

UTAH

COLORADO

48

P

A

C

I

F

I

C

CALIFORNIA

74

40

67

KANSAS

65

54

ARIZONA

NEW MEXICO

O

66

76

O

C

E

A

N

62

63

TEXAS

M E X I C O

59

ALASKA

61

69

HAWAII

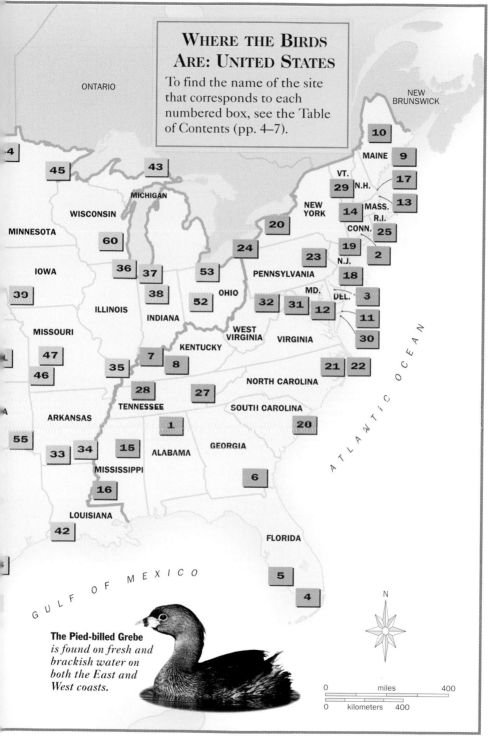

United States

WHERE THE BIRDS ARE: UNITED STATES

To find the name of the site that corresponds to each numbered box, see the Table of Contents (pp. 4–7).

ONTARIO

NEW BRUNSWICK

4

45

43

MICHIGAN

WISCONSIN

MINNESOTA

60

36 37

IOWA

39

ILLINOIS

MISSOURI

47

46

35 7 8

28 27

ARKANSAS

55

33 34 15

MISSISSIPPI

16

LOUISIANA

42

38

52

INDIANA

53

24

20

NEW YORK

PENNSYLVANIA

OHIO

32 31 12

WEST VIRGINIA

KENTUCKY

VIRGINIA

NORTH CAROLINA

SOUTH CAROLINA

26

ALABAMA

GEORGIA

6

FLORIDA

MAINE 9

VT. 29 N.H. 17

14 MASS. 13

R.I.

CONN. 25

19 2

23 N.J.

18

MD. DEL. 3

11

30

21 22

10

GULF OF MEXICO

5

4

ATLANTIC OCEAN

N

The Pied-billed Grebe *is found on fresh and brackish water on both the East and West coasts.*

0   miles   400

0   kilometers   400

9

Canada

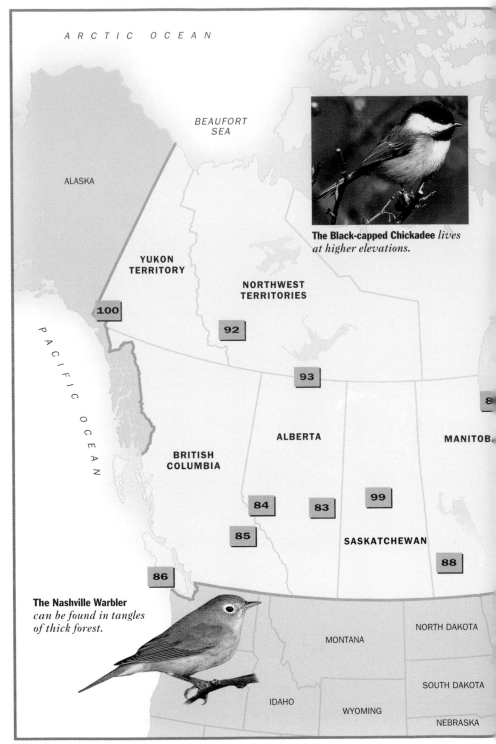

ARCTIC OCEAN

BEAUFORT
SEA

ALASKA

The Black-capped Chickadee *lives at higher elevations.*

YUKON
TERRITORY

NORTHWEST
TERRITORIES

100

92

93

8

ALBERTA

MANITOB

BRITISH
COLUMBIA

84 83 99

85

SASKATCHEWAN

86 88

The Nashville Warbler
can be found in tangles of thick forest.

PACIFIC OCEAN

MONTANA NORTH DAKOTA

SOUTH DAKOTA

IDAHO

WYOMING

NEBRASKA

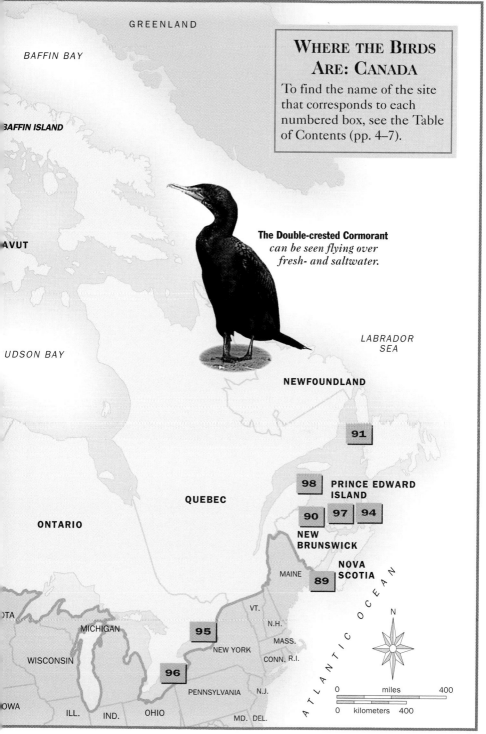

GREENLAND

BAFFIN BAY

BAFFIN ISLAND

WHERE THE BIRDS ARE: CANADA
To find the name of the site that corresponds to each numbered box, see the Table of Contents (pp. 4–7).

AVUT

The Double-crested Cormorant *can be seen flying over fresh- and saltwater.*

UDSON BAY

LABRADOR SEA

NEWFOUNDLAND

91

98 **PRINCE EDWARD ISLAND**

QUEBEC

90 97 94

ONTARIO

NEW BRUNSWICK

NOVA SCOTIA

MAINE

89

MICHIGAN

95

VT.

N.H.

MASS.

ATLANTIC OCEAN

N

OTA

WISCONSIN

NEW YORK

CONN. R.I.

96

PENNSYLVANIA N.J.

0   miles   400

OWA

ILL.   IND.   OHIO

MD. DEL.

0   kilometers   400

11

WHERE THE BIRDS ARE

Norgh America is enriched with a bevy of dazzling birds. Look up to see them soaring and shimmering all around. From bright bluebirds to wind-riding hawks, these amazing creatures adorn the United States and Canada like feather jewelry. New birdwatchers are often astounded when they realize the diversity of bird life inhabiting our national parks, refuges, and other natural areas – more than 900 species in all. From countryside to urban areas, travel anywhere in North America and see a wide array of birds, many unique to that location.

BIRD FINDING

The art of birdwatching provides extra incentive to visit some of the most beautiful natural areas in North America: *Where the Birds Are* features 100 of these biologically rich, bird-filled places. From the rainforests of Olympic National Park in Washington state to the Rio Grande river, which sets the stage for the Bosque del Apache National Wildlife Refuge in New Mexico, this book represents an impressive parade of wetlands, deserts, forests, seacoasts, and more, all home to an equally impressive range of bird life.

Not to be missed are the airborne river of fall migrating raptors at Hawk Mountain Sanctuary in Pennsylvania, the confetti of spring warblers migrating through New York's Central Park, and the noisy congregation of wintering waterfowl at Florida's J.N. "Ding" Darling National Wildlife

Concentrations of winter waterfowl, such as these Snow Geese, can reach into the tens of thousands at some of the featured wildlife refuges and parks.

The Scarlet Tanager *is a brightly colored songbird that graces North America's deciduous forests.*

Refuge. The Swan Days festival at Mattamuskeet National Wildlife Refuge in North Carolina and spring bird-banding days at Long Point Bird Observatory in Ontario are also well worth attending.

Discovering not only where to look for birds but when, why, and for what species is an essential part of birding. *Where the Birds Are* also offers inside information, gathered from biologists, refuge managers, and local experts that will give a new dimension to weekend excursions, family vacations, and any type of travel. Users of this book will learn to watch for Harlequin Ducks not on rural ponds with Mallards and geese, but on the swift, mountain streams such as those found in Glacier National Park in Alaska. Likewise, they'll learn that Colorado's Monte Vista National Wildlife Refuge is the stage for the early dancing grounds of Sandhill Cranes.

Most birdwatchers keep a life list where they record all the species they have seen since they first began noticing birds – and write their dreams. How many new birds might I see if I visit Texas? Where can I observe Arctic Terns? *Where the Birds Are* not only helps answer these questions, but suggests precisely where in Texas to look for southern rarities – Bentsen-Rio Grande Valley State Park – and where to see a variety of far-northern birds – the Churchill area in Manitoba.

TRAVEL GEAR AND SAFETY

Birdwatchers need two basic tools to get started: high-quality binoculars and a field guide. Choose binoculars that are designed especially with birders in mind (try bird-watching stores or advertisements in birding magazines). Keep in mind that quality of optics increases dramatically with price. The oft-heard advice from seasoned birdwatchers is "Buy the most expensive birding binoculars you can afford."

Many birders buy several field guides to determine which system of bird identification works best for them. Field

The Northern Cardinal *and other familiar backyard birds are often the first birds on a birdwatcher's life list. Visit the sites featured in this book to add hundreds of other species to that list.*

guides, by definition, provide illustrations, range maps, and identification information for all the birds in a given area. Some emphasize comparisons, others rely more on photographs and color keys, while still others provide more detailed written descriptions.

Most birdwatchers eventually invest in a spotting scope, which is invaluable for viewing waterfowl, shorebirds, perched birds of prey, and for up-close feather-by-feather views of cooperative birds of any species.

Other handy items include a camera with a telephoto lens; up-to-date road maps; relevant state atlases; a carrying pouch for field guides; field bird list; a notebook (worn around the waist for easy access); and a daypack for water, mosquito repellent, and extra clothes. Long-sleeved pants, shirts, hat, and hiking boots (break in the boots at home!) are also recommended.

Sprained or broken ankles and wrists are not unknown injuries among birdwatchers, who sometimes forget to watch where they walk. In addition, birders should be aware of their fitness level before undertaking strenuous hikes or any high-elevation

Good binoculars are a must, and a spotting scope is great for long-distance viewing.

activity. When driving pay attention to the road; pull well off to the side of the road before stopping, even if the bird of a lifetime is within viewing distance.

BIRDS UP CLOSE

Unobtrusive birders who approach birding areas slowly and quietly usually find it quite easy to observe birds close-up. Patient birdwatchers (especially those dressed in earth-tones) are rewarded with intriguing natural behaviors – the sight of a Northern Harrier eating a mouse at Snake River Birds of Prey National Conservation Area in Idaho, perhaps, or a pelican catching a fish at Pea Island National Wildlife Refuge in North Carolina.

The Brown Pelican *and a host of other large water-dependent birds can be observed along North America's coasts.*

Although birds are often quite unconcerned by human presence, take care not to disturb them. Birders are getting too close if the bird looks at them and begins acting agitated. Be especially cautious around feeding, resting, and nesting birds. Never, never frighten a parent bird from the nest. When possible, use a car as a viewing blind, since birds are often undisturbed by automobiles. Be conscientious about staying on established roads, though.

To see the most birds – both in variety and number – heed the birdwatchers admonition: "The magic is over by 8 a.m." If there are no hotels within a half-hour or so of the intended birding site, consider camping. With practice a birder can learn to identify dozens of species by sound alone before even leaving the tent.

The National Wildlife Federation (NWF) is committed to fighting the habitat destruction and loss that threatens waterfowl, such as this Mallard, and all other bird life.

WILD PLACES, WILD BIRDS

For over 100 years – starting in 1900 with the Christmas Bird Count, an annual census conducted by volunteers – birdwatchers have been sending an urgent message: our birds are under threat. Birders have seen firsthand the effects of habitat fragmentation and degradation. They've watched favorite birding sites drained, paved, plowed, overgrazed, and chemically polluted. Often their voices were the first ones raised in protest. Rachel Carson, author of *Silent Spring*, the book that spawned the modern environmental movement, was not surprisingly a birdwatcher.

Many others eventually joined the battle to save habitat, and today conservation is a concept held dear to most residents of North America. The sites included in this book – from Indiana Dunes National Lakeshore on Lake Michigan to the Chincoteague National Wildlife Refuge on the Atlantic shore – represent hard-won battles by an array of people committed to providing places for wildlife.

The National Wildlife Federation is one of the oldest and largest of these member-supported environmental organizations, with a long-term mission to educate and inspire conservation of places like those listed in this book. Since its inception in 1936, the NWF has worked with conservation-minded people to make a place for wildlife in our modern world. From the

The Red-tailed Hawk *is a common raptor that can be seen soaring over the United States and Canada relatively undisturbed.*

Endangered Species Act to its own Backyard Wildlife Habitat Program, from International Migratory Bird Day to PBS's *Birdwatch*, National Wildlife Federation's participation in the conservation movement has made it possible for these wild places and wild birds to thrive.

HOW TO USE THIS BOOK

Where the Birds Are is organized so that readers can easily find the best places to birdwatch in their region of choice, whether that's the Eastern, Central, or Western United States, or Canada. The states or provinces within each region are organized alphabetically, then numbered 1 through 100. The page numbers where the sites appear in the book are listed in the table of contents, pages 4–7. A map of the United States (see pp. 8–9) and one of Canada (see pp. 10–11) shows each region and displays the location of each site.

Each site is accompanied by two maps – one locates the site within North America and the other illustrates directions to the site. These are accompanied by written directions, which in most cases are for road travel from the nearest large city. Some sites can only be reached by airplane or ferry; in those cases phone numbers for service providers are listed.

Each site also includes a boxed section titled Birds to Look For, which lists 12 to 15 of the birds found at the site. The organization of these bird names follows the sequence found in the *Checklist of North American Birds* (7th Edition, 1998) of the American Ornithologists' Union (A.O.U.). This checklist arranges bird species according to what is understood of their natural and evolutionary relationships, and is widely followed by ornithologists and birdwatchers throughout North America.

To find out more about swans and other waterfowl species, start with the About the Birds section at the back of the book.

Other practical information includes each site's hours of operation, entrance and parking fees, and special access for the disabled. Listings for campgrounds, on-site or nearby lodging, and licensed guides are also provided. Many sites are closed on national holidays, and other information can change without notice, so it's a good idea to call ahead for details before visiting any of the sites in this book.

The final section of the book, About the Birds, serves as a miniature field guide to the birds most commonly found at these 100 sites. This guide highlights birds that are widespread (such as the Canada Goose and Black-and-white Warbler), or very rare (including the Golden Eagle and Piping Plover). About the Birds is arranged in A.O.U. order, and each entry lists the sites where the featured bird is discussed. Readers who want to add a particular species to their life list should consider starting their search for information here.

How to Use the Maps

KEY

———(45)——— Interstate Highway

——(45)—— U.S. Federal Highway

——(45)—— State, County, Local or Other Road

■/■ Featured Wildlife Site

Other Forest, Park, Wilderness Area

Urban

✪ State Capitol

ABBREVIATIONS

AVE. .... Avenue
BLVD. .... Boulevard
HWY. .... Highway
N.P. .... National Park
N.F. .... National Forest
N.C.A. .... National Conservation Area
N.W.R. .... National Wildlife Refuge
PKWY. .... Parkway
RD. .... Road
S.F. .... State Forest
S.P. .... State Park
ST. .... Street
TPKE. .... Turnpike
W.A. .... Wildlife Area
W.M.A. .... Wildlife Management Area

Map Site and Information Icons

🚗 = Getting there

◻ = Open

⬤ = Closed

ℹ = Visitor information

☎ = Telephone number and URL

⑤ = Entrance fees

♿ = Disabled access

🅰 = Camping

🚹🚹 = Outfitters and/or guide services

🏨 = Accommodations

Eastern United States

Alabama
Connecticut
Delaware
Florida
Georgia
Kentucky
Maine
Maryland
Massachusetts
Mississippi
New Hampshire
New Jersey
New York
North Carolina
Pennsylvania
Rhode Island
South Carolina
Tennessee
Vermont
Virginia
West Virginia

WHEELER NATIONAL WILDLIFE REFUGE

This northern Alabama refuge wears a colorful cape of waterfowl in the winter and a crazy-quilt of warblers in the spring.

Wheeler National Wildlife Refuge, administered by the U.S. Fish and Wildlife Service, is a 35,000-acre gem surrounded by some of the most urban landscape in Alabama. The much-beloved refuge has an extensive interpretive and observation program to serve this large population. The refuge covers the middle third of the Tennessee Valley Authority's Wheeler Reservoir and stretches along the Tennessee River from west of Decatur east nearly to Huntsville.

HABITAT

Wheeler National Wildlife Refuge is on the eastern edge of the lower Mississippi flyway. It supports one of the southernmost concentrations of wintering Canada Geese and also serves as winter habitat for the largest duck population in the state. The refuge is managed primarily for migrating waterfowl and attracts an average of 60,000 ducks and several thousand geese each winter. The extensive forests on the refuge are a haven to migrating songbirds.

BIRD LIFE

Many birdwatchers start at the western entrance to the White Springs Unit, just north of Decatur. Park at the locked gate (but do not block it) and walk in 200 yards for views of waterfowl ranging from Green-winged Teal to Northern Shovelers. A dike runs along the area for several miles; those who love long walks will want to hike, perhaps taking a picnic.

To explore new territory, however, take I-565 west. Exit 2 leads to Mooresville, and then a right (at the first light) on Old Highway 20 leads to a left – Arrowhead Landing Road – in less than a mile. This country road passes through some of the best birdwatching territory in the area. The first gated road on the left leads to a cemetery. Park at the gate and walk up the dirt track: from this high vantage point, visitors can see many geese and Sandhill Cranes.

Continuing on Arrowhead Landing Road, there are several other spots that offer great looks at waterfowl. Visitors should stop when they first see water – it will be Limestone Bay – on the left. In the summer this area is filled with shallow water but in the fall and winter, the water is lowered, revealing extensive mudflats and water-filled

The Cerulean Warbler's plumage, bluish above with dark streaks and white below, makes this woodland bird easy to identify.

BIRDS TO LOOK FOR

Snow Goose • Canada Goose • American Wigeon • Green-winged Teal • Sharp-shinned Hawk • Cooper's Hawk • Sandhill Crane • Semipalmated Sandpiper • Dunlin • Short-billed Dowitcher • Barred Owl • Yellow Warbler • Pine Warbler • Cerulean Warbler • Black-and-white Warbler • Worm-eating Warbler

Black-and-white Warblers, plus 19 other warbler species, find refuge in Wheeler's forests.

channels. Fall shorebirds attracted to the mudflats include Dunlins, Semipalmated Sandpipers, Short-billed Dowitchers, and many others.

In the winter, both here and at the boat landing about a mile farther, birdwatchers have a chance of seeing four different species of goose and one morph, or color phase. Look for large numbers of Canada Geese (those that winter here nest at James Bay, Ontario), Snow Geese (white morph), and a few Ross's and Greater White-fronted Geese. Of the 4,000 or so Snow Geese that winter on the refuge, 75 percent are of the blue form: they have the typical white head of Snow Geese, but their bodies are gray-blue.

When they aren't feeding elsewhere on the refuge, Mallards, Northern Pintails, American Black Ducks, Hooded

Mergansers, and several other species of ducks are found here, too.

The other side of the Tennessee River also has much to offer. Just south of Decatur (on State Route 67), the Visitor Center offers not only educational displays, but also a state-of-the-art observation building overlooking a wetland and pond. One-way glass means that birdwatchers can get very close looks at Gadwall, American Wigeon, and many other duck species (including an occasional Eurasian Wigeon), plus geese and Sandhill Cranes.

Very close by, the Flint Creek Trail (go east on Route 67 and take the next right) provides quick and easy access

Short-billed Dowitchers *and other shorebirds can be seen on the mudflats near Limestone Bay in fall.*

21

to the spring songbirds. For those with a bit more time, the less accessible Dancy Bottoms Trail provides even better habitat for migrants. The 100-year-old-woods (about 20 minutes from the Visitor Center, accessed by going east on 67, right on Indian Hills Road, and right on Redbanks Road) is known as a local migrant magnet. On a good spring morning, look for 20 species of warblers, including Blackburnian, Black-and-white, Cerulean, Nashville, Palm, Pine, Yellow, and Worm-eating. Go before dawn to hear the incomparable chorus of thrushes, tanagers, thrashers, and more.

VISITING

No waterfowl hunting is allowed on Wheeler National Wildlife Refuge, so all areas remain open in the winter. The best time to see waterfowl is November through January. Fall brings good shorebird-watching; spring is best for warblers; and summer is best avoided by all but die-hard mosquito-watchers.

HIGHLIGHTS

Local birdwatchers love exploring the White Springs area by mountain bike. Ride the eight-mile dike along Wheeler Reservoir to check out the many waterfowl. Biker-birders should also investigate the several gravel tracks and trails next to the dike. The woods here harbor Sharp-shinned, Cooper's, Red-tailed, and Broad-winged Hawks, as well as Barred Owls.

Site Map and Information

WHEELER NATIONAL WILDLIFE REFUGE

🚗 From nearby Huntsville, take I-565 west to I-65 south to Highway 67 (the Priceville exit). Go 2.5 miles west and turn left to reach the Visitor Center.

🗓 Daily, sunrise to sunset, year-round.

🚫 Never.

ℹ️ Wheeler National Wildlife Refuge, 2700 Refuge Headquarters Road, Decatur, AL 35603. The Visitor Center is open daily, 9 a.m.–5 p.m., October through February, and 9 a.m.–4 p.m., Tuesday through Saturday, March through September.

📞 (256) 350-6639

💲 None.

♿ The Visitor Center, Atkeson Trail, and Observation Building Trail are wheelchair accessible.

⛺ Available at Point Mallard Park in Decatur; call (256) 351-7772 for details.

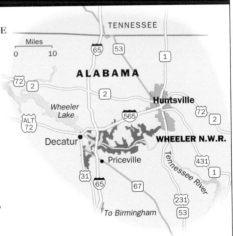

🚶 Several times each winter refuge volunteers lead field trips to the White Springs area; call the Visitor Center for dates.

🏨 Hotels, motels, and bed-and-breakfasts are available in nearby Decatur; call the Decatur Chamber of Commerce at (256) 353-5312 for listings.

HAMMONASSET BEACH STATE PARK

This small seashore refuge contains a wider variety of bird life and habitat than any other site in Connecticut.

Bound by the Long Island Sound on its southern side, this waterfront territory has served a wide variety of human purposes over the ages. Its first documented inhabitants were Native Americans of the Hammonasset tribe, who grew crops here. During World Wars I and II, the land was under the control of the U.S. Army, which used it to test ammunition. But since war's end, the park's 923 acres have been enjoyed by visitors who come to swim, boat, picnic, and watch birds.

HABITAT

Glacial ice covered the the present site of Hammonasset Beach State Park for some 3,000 years. During its retreat, the glacier widened the Hammonasset River, which forms the park's northern boundary, and dug out the course of stream beds that still show their ancient outlines today. The glacier's other legacy was a distinctive ground cover featuring sand, silt, clay, pebbles, and boulders.

Salt marsh is the dominant habitat, occupying approximately 45 percent of the park's acreage. Cord grass,

Yellow-bellied Sapsuckers *may be seen drilling rows of holes in trees, later returning for the sap and insects they attract.*

marsh hay, reed grass, and spike grass or spike rush grow here, providing ideal habitat for waterbirds. The habitat picture is completed by a beach composed of sand and a pebbly stretch created from glacial till.

BIRD LIFE

The range of bird life (both migratory and permanent) is readily apparent in the latest birding checklist, available at the park's Nature Center. Included among the park's 286 species are 20 species of sparrows, 15 varieties of warbler, 26 different ducks, and multiple species of thrushes, herons, sandpipers, gulls, terns, and more.

To see a variety of these birds, follow the Willard Island Self-Guided Trail, three-quarters of a mile long and completely surrounded by salt marsh. Thirteen designated stops provide opportunities to

BIRDS TO LOOK FOR

Snowy Egret • Glossy Ibis • Mute Swan • Osprey • Willet • Semipalmated Sandpiper • Bonaparte's Gull • Great Horned Owl • Northern Saw-whet Owl • Yellow-bellied Sapsucker • Gray Catbird • Northern Mockingbird • Blue-winged Warbler • Yellow Warbler • Saltmarsh Sharp-tailed Sparrow • Seaside Sparrow

Populations of Mute Swans along the East coast are on the rise.

watch birds and other wildlife in a diversity of habitats along the way.

Station Number 1 on the self-guided trail looks out over an expanse of common reeds that are home to the Marsh Wren, one of four wren species found at the park. Station Number 2 is at the edge of the salt marsh, a food-rich habitat that attracts a variety of different birds. Look here for the Saltmarsh Sharp-tailed Sparrow and the Seaside Sparrow, which nest on the island and feed on what is for sparrows a somewhat unique diet – snails, insects, seeds, and an occasional small crab. A generous variety of wading birds, including Green Herons, Snowy Egret, and Glossy Ibis, and sandpipers, such as Willets and Semipalmated Sandpipers, are also well represented here. Look also for Northern Harriers flying overhead.

The Northern Mockingbird *is a notable singer that often imitates the songs and calls of others.*

Continuing through the salt marsh, Willard Island Trail passes through low-growing thickets of bayberry, poison ivy (watch out!), Virginia creeper, and eastern red cedars. Stop at Station Number 3 to look and listen for a variety of songbirds, including the Song Sparrow, Yellow Warbler, Carolina Wren, Gray Catbird, Northern Mockingbirds, and Brown Thrasher.

At Station Number 5, a cedar grove draws 29 bird varieties, which feast on the grayish-blue fruit of the female tree during fall and winter. The exquisite songs of thrushes – Swainson's, Hermit, and Wood – are melodic mainstays here during migration. Thanks to the Hammonasset Beach reforestation program, many other songsters also use these cedars for breeding or migratory resting sites. Northern Saw-whet, Eastern Screech-, and Great Horned Owls also roost in this cedar grove during daylight hours.

Station Number 6 is Eastern Bluebird territory. A stand of sassafras trees near Station Number 8 sometimes hosts as many as eight kinds of warblers, while the ancient apple tree at Station Number 9 is investigated regularly by the Yellow-bellied Sapsucker. The viewing platform is a fine place to observe the bird life along the Hammonasset River and in the marshland. As many as 25 species of duck are found here.

VISITING

Spring, summer, and fall are all very productive times for bird observation at Hammonasset Beach State Park.

Warblers sport their colorful breeding plumage in the spring, particularly in late April and May; many of them, including Common Yellowthroats and Blue-winged and Black-and-white Warblers, nest in the park. In the summer the park offers some of the best sightings of nesting Ospreys in the United States. The reason? Fish are plentiful in the sound and there are few visitors to disturb them.

HIGHLIGHTS

Be sure to enjoy a walk along the boardwalk. Terns wheel overhead, sharing air rights and beach with the heavier Black-headed Gull (a rare bird) and other more common gull species, including Bonaparte's, Ring-billed, Great Black-backed, and Herring Gulls.

Site Map and Information

HAMMONASSET BEACH STATE PARK

🚗 From New Haven take I-95 north 25 miles to Exit 62 and follow the turnpike connection south to reach the park entrance. From New London take I-95 south 30 miles to reach the turnpike.

🕐 Daily, 8 a.m. to sunset, year-round.

⬤ Never.

ℹ️ Hammonasset Beach State Park, P.O. Box 271, Madison, CT 06443. The park has no Visitor Center, but during high season maps and bird checklists are available at the Nature Center near the park entrance.

📞 (203) 245-2785

💲 Residents of CT: $7 weekends, $5 weekdays; nonresidents: $12 weekends, $8 weekdays.

♿ The Nature Center and boardwalk are wheelchair accessible.

⛺ Nearby William F. Miller Campground has more than 550 sites for trailers and tents; call (877) 668-2267 for reservations.

🚻 None.

🏨 Motels are plentiful in Madison and Clinton, just minutes away.

BOMBAY HOOK NATIONAL WILDLIFE REFUGE

This Delaware refuge offers a dazzling sight: Snow Geese, moving fast from far northern habitats, dropping down by the thousands.

It was no dashing Indian raja who suggested Bombay Hook's name, but a stolid Dutch settler, who in 1697 called this land off Delaware Bay *"Bompies Hoeck,"* or "Little Tree Point." More than 300 years later, visitors come to Bombay Hook in numbers the Dutchman could never have foreseen. They come to drive over a 12-mile refuge road and walk along three information-packed trails where they may observe one of the largest, most diverse concentrations of birds in the eastern United States.

The Ruddy Duck *often uses its long stiff tail feathers as a rudder to direct its underwater course.*

The most popular visiting period runs from October through November, when migrating ducks and Snow Geese – over 150,000 of them – come in for landings on the marshes, ponds, tidal flats, and rivers of the refuge. Shorebirds arrive in May, timing migrations of hundreds of miles so that their arrival will coincide exactly with the annual frenzy of horseshoe crabs mating and egg-laying along the Delaware Bay shore. The birds gobble up most of the exposed eggs.

HABITAT

Almost two-thirds of Bombay Hook's 15,978 acres spill out into tidal salt marsh and cordgrass meadows, broken up by creeks and small rivers. However, the remaining third contains a generous mix of croplands, grass-covered fields, brushlands, swamps, and woods. The main custodial objective of this large refuge is still the protection of migrating waterfowl, but the area is also host to many songbirds, including the lovely Indigo Bunting. The largest tract of tidal salt marsh in Delaware also welcomes shore and wading birds, and swift-flying ducks of all descriptions.

BIRD LIFE

The best cumulative views of Bombay Hook's avian activity are found on three walking trails and the carefully managed expanses of water and land that are useful legacies of Civilian Conservation Corps muscle and creativity.

One of these, the mile-long Parson Point Trail, passes through an isolated forest with many tall trees that nesting Bald Eagles prefer. (The trail is sometimes closed when young eagles

BIRDS TO LOOK FOR

Horned Grebe • Black-crowned Night-Heron • Snow Goose • Gadwall • Green-winged Teal • Ruddy Duck • Bald Eagle • Northern Bobwhite • American Coot • Semipalmated Sandpiper • Barred Owl • Chimney Swift • Bank Swallow • Brown Creeper • Black-and-white Warbler • Swamp Sparrow • Indigo Bunting

Fall migration brings the largest concentration of Snow Geese in the United States.

are hatching in March.) One of the prime viewing spots on this trail is at Shearness Pool – a favored watery expanse for Mallards, Northern Pintails, Ruddy Ducks, and Snow and Canada Geese. Raymond Pool, a smaller pond much favored by painted turtles, is also a roosting area for the Black-crowned Night-Heron, whose late-night, nerve-rattling squawk is distinctive.

The trail also passes through damp woods, where the leaves and berries of jack-in-the-pulpit attract Wild Turkeys and Ring-necked Pheasants in the fall. A champion ant-eater, the Northern Flicker, as well as the Red-bellied Woodpecker, are both common along the route. Many warblers, including the Black-and-white Warbler, share this wooded space with them.

Boardwalk Trail, a half-mile, 30-minute walk, passes through or by four separate habitats: woodlands, fresh-water and brackish ponds, and salt marsh. Wood Ducks and their fluff-covered ducklings frequent these

The Northern Bobwhite *takes its name from the male's call, a whistled* bob-white.

ponds beginning in May. Wetlands along this trail, viewed from an encircling boardwalk, are prime nesting and resting havens for American Black Ducks, Gadwalls, Mallards, and Green-winged Teal.

Bear Swamp Trail boasts a 30-foot observation tower from which to view the spectacular fall arrivals of Snow Geese, the largest concentration of this bird in the entire United States. Binocular scans will turn up Glossy Ibis, Black-necked Stilts, Avocets,

Semipalmated and Least Sandpipers, Killdeer, and different species of herons in company with Snowy and Great Egrets. Yellow-rumped Warblers, always a birder's favorite, are especially visible in September, when bayberry yields up its fruits.

VISITING

Key birding months for the refuge are October, November, April, and May. October and November are the months when waterfowl populations are heaviest. October is also American Avocet month. Spring waterfowl migrations peak in March. April is when early songbird migrations begin; May is the month for peak concentrations of shorebirds along ponds and marshes. June is when Black-necked Stilts build their nests in specially designed impoundments. Even bleak January has its specialties – Red-tailed and Rough-legged Hawks are active, and Bald Eagles begin putting together their stick nests in trees near the water.

Upon arrival at Bombay Hook, stop by the Visitor Center to pick up a map, bird list, and up-to-date information about seasonal birds.

HIGHLIGHTS

Although staff interaction with visiting birders takes place year-round, it intensifies during special observances. These include celebrations on Earth Day, Migratory Bird Day, National Wildlife Refuge Week, and an annual Field Day. Call the Visitor Center for details.

Site Map and Information

BOMBAY HOOK NATIONAL WILDLIFE REFUGE

🚗 Take Route 9 north through Leipsic, then take the first right, Whitehall Neck Road, which leads directly to the refuge.

🕐 Daily, sunrise to sunset, year-round.

🌑 Never.

ℹ Refuge Manager, Bombay Hook National Wildlife Refuge, 2591 Whitehall Neck Road, Smyrna, DE 19977. Visitor Center is open weekdays, 8 a.m.–4 p.m., and weekends, 9 a.m.–5 p.m.; closed weekends during the summer and winter.

☎ (302) 653-6872

$ $4 per car. Annual individual passes are sold at the Visitor Center.

♿ The Visitor Center and Bear Swamp Trail are wheelchair accessible.

🅰 Camping not permitted on-site, but available in nearby Lums Pond and Killens Pond State Parks.

🚶 Nature walks, habitat studies, and tours are available to groups by advance request.

🏨 Accommodations in nearby Dover. Or call the Kent County Tourism Office at (800) 233-KENT for listings.

EVERGLADES NATIONAL PARK

Conservationists are working hard to restore the freshwater quality and quantity of these immense wetlands at Florida's southern tip, home to a wealth of birds.

Everglades National Park was dedicated in December 1947 by President Harry S. Truman, who vowed that the nation would work to safeguard this valuable habitat. Now recognized internationally, this national park protects just over 1.5 million acres, including 230,000 acres of mangrove forest, vast expanses of 15-foot-high sawgrass, and the 99-mile Wilderness Waterway.

HABITAT

Known to the Native Americans who once lived in this region as "a river of grass," the Everglades feature immense swaths of sawgrass swayed by barely moving currents that slide gently southward toward the Florida Bay. The stately cypress tree serves as a launching pad for the large raptors that hunt in the park; mangrove swamps shelter large populations of wading birds and other marsh birds.

This spectacular national park is unlike any other worldwide. The only subtropical preserve on the North American continent, it contains the largest mangrove ecosystem in the entire Western Hemisphere, and its 572,000-acre sawgrass prairie is North America's largest. The area is also home to more than 1,000 different seed-bearing plants, including 120 species of trees.

Clapper Rails *are common, although elusive, in this immense salt marsh.*

BIRD LIFE

Where to start? Should one spend the entire morning exploring the park's ponds and riverbanks in search of an endangered Wood Stork? Or train binoculars on a hardwood hammock in search of such local specialties as Mottled Ducks, Great Egrets, Purple Gallinules, and Swallow-tailed Kites?

The park's generous songbird population offers almost unlimited sightings, too. Look for five wren species and 31 species of warblers, from Cape May and Bay-breasted to the rarely seen Blue-winged and Golden-winged Warblers. The abundant Savannah Sparrow and a greenish morph of the Seaside Sparrow, plus Painted Buntings and Yellow-billed Cuckoos are found here.

Whatever habitat is selected, no birdwatcher leaves the Everglades

BIRDS TO LOOK FOR

American White Pelican • Double-crested Cormorant • Anhinga • White Ibis • Roseate Spoonbill • Wood Stork • Mottled Duck • Swallow-tailed Kite • Purple Gallinule • Common Moorhen • White-rumped Sandpiper • Caspian Tern • Yellow-billed Cuckoo • Cape May Warbler • Seaside Sparrow • Painted Bunting

Visit the Anhinga Trail to observe its namesake bird and many other rare birds.

disappointed. It boasts an astounding 400 species, many of which are rare. Highlights along the Anhinga Trail include the Anhinga, the White Ibis and the Roseate Spoonbill. The trail begins as a boardwalk at the Royal Palm Visitor Center in the southeastern part of the park.

Those who kayak or canoe into the Ten Thousand Islands sector in the northwestern corner of the park will be richly rewarded. Here are feeding grounds for a great variety of waders, including ibis, both White and Scarlet (a South American species), which interbreed to create offspring that are various shades of pink. This is also good terrain for heron spotting; look for Great Blue, Green, Little Blue, and Tricolored, as well Black-crowned and Yellow-crowned Night-Herons. Brown Pelicans live here and sometimes Bald Eagles and Ospreys fish these waters. The Double-crested Cormorant and American White Pelicans also winter here.

Even the heavily traveled Tamiami Trail (Route 41), which follows the northern border of Everglades National Park, offers large groups of birds, including rare ones.

The Swallow-tailed Kite *is a graceful bird that drops down to catch snakes or flying insects.*

Just off this road are mating and feeding areas used by three kinds of egrets: Great, Snowy, and Reddish Egrets. Look also for White-crowned Pigeons, Clapper Rails, and Common Moorhen, plus other waterfowl.

The wetlands near the seaside edges of the park host 11 species of terns, including Caspian, Gull-billed, and Royal Terns. Shorebirds and gulls are plentiful near Flamingo Bay Visitor Center. Over 20 species of sandpipers are also found, including Ruddy Turnstones and Western, Least, and White-rumped Sandpipers.

VISITING

Most birdwatchers visit Everglades National Park between December and April, when the sighting opportunities are richest. The park boasts 82 miles of surfaced roads; 156 miles of walking and canoe trails; and five miles of surfaced trails, plus a mile-long elevated boardwalk.

HIGHLIGHTS

Visit the Shark Valley Observation Tower, conveniently located along the Wilderness Waterway, which offers prime views of the birds living in the park's sawgrass prairie. Tour guides can be hired in Everglades City, or paddlers with strong arms and good maps might want to rent a canoe or kayak and explore the waterway themselves.

Site Map and Information

EVERGLADES NATIONAL PARK

🚗 From Miami, approximately 50 miles away, take the Florida Turnpike south to the last exit, where it merges with U.S. Highway 1, and continue south to the main entrance.

🕐 Daily, 24 hours, year-round.

🔴 Never.

ℹ Everglades National Park, 40001 State Road 9336, Homestead, FL 33034. Ernest F. Coe Visitor Center, located at the main entrance, is open daily, 8 a.m.–5 p.m.

📞 (305) 242-7700; www.nps.gov/ever

💲 $10 per vehicle for a 7-day pass. Bicyclists and individual hikers, $5 for a 7-day pass. No entrance fee is charged at the Gulf Coast entrance in the northwestern corner of the park.

♿ All major trails are wheelchair accessible. Boarding assistance is provided for tram tours and boat trips.

🅰 Campgrounds are available on-site at Long Pine Key, Flamingo, and Chekika. The Flamingo and Gulf Coast Visitor Centers issue back-country camping permits from November through mid-April.

👥 Check the Ernest F. Coe Visitor Center for news of ranger-conducted programs and tours.

🛏 Lodgings are available on-site through the Flamingo Visitor Center; call (941) 695-3101 for reservations. Motels, hotels, and bed-and-breakfasts are also available in Everglade City and nearby Homestead, Florida City, and Miami.

J. N. "DING" DARLING
NATIONAL WILDLIFE REFUGE

On a good winter's day, birdwatchers can expect to spot dozens of species from among the more than 230 that inhabit or visit this Florida treasure.

Occupying approximately half of the beautiful barrier island of Sanibel off the southern Gulf Coast, this national wildlife refuge represents a significant commitment to the preservation of Florida's native creatures and natural habitats. The 6,000-plus-acre oasis was launched by J. N. "Ding" Darling, America's most popular newspaper cartoonist during the 1930s, who was also an ardent advocate for the conservation of the nation's wildlife.

HABITAT
The refuge's prodigal mix of Florida sunshine, ocean, mangrove thickets, marshes and wetlands, and upland forest draws almost a million visitors each year. Three species of mangrove – black, red, and white – dominate the landscape. The tough roots of these trees shelter fish that are hunted by shore and wading birds, while upland forests serve as part-time homes for thousands of migrating songbirds.

BIRD LIFE
"Ding Darling" Refuge is an ideal place to see birds that are difficult to spot anywhere else. The American Bittern is here, although this master of camouflage makes itself difficult to pick out. A Wood Stork may materialize anywhere along the

refuge's main road or interior trails, and a drumming in the woods probably signifies that a Pileated Woodpecker is up and about. Pre-dawn early risers can head to the marsh flats to watch flocks of White Ibis feeding.

The Tricolored Heron *is a common inhabitant of the mangrove swamps and saltwater marshes of this refuge.*

The exquisite pink plumage of Roseate Spoonbills was once so popular for use in women's fans that this wader was threatened by extinction – but no longer. Wintertime visitors may witness a flock of as many as a hundred of these birds

BIRDS TO LOOK FOR

American White Pelican • Brown Pelican • Anhinga • Magnificent Frigatebird • American Bittern • Tricolored Heron • Reddish Egret • Yellow-crowned Night-Heron • Roseate Spoonbill • Wood Stork • Mangrove Cuckoo • Palm Warbler

A pair of Roseate Spoonbills performs a graceful air ballet.

feeding in the tidal flats. Afterward, these birds stand motionless on long, thin legs until an almost imperceptible dip of a leader's spatula-shaped bill signals them to take to the air all at once.

This might be the first opportunity for many birders to see the Anhinga, whose ungainly shape seems like a throwback to prehistoric times. Four species of egret also inhabit the island, including the infrequently seen Reddish Egret. The Brown Pelican is abundant here during all seasons, while the American White Pelican is active primarily during fall and winter.

Although water and wading birds, such as the elegant Tricolored Heron, attract the attention of most birdwatchers, numerous songbirds,

Brown Pelicans, *distinguished by their truly gigantic bills, are abundant at the refuge in all seasons.*

including 20 warbler species, flit through the refuge's hardwood forests in search of insects, seeds, and berries. Songbirds such as the Mangrove Cuckoo and Great Crested Flycatcher are birds for all seasons, while the Chimney Swift can be spotted most of the year except in winter.

VISITING

Wintertime – November through April – is the best season for birdwatching at the "Ding Darling" Refuge, and morning, evening, and low tide are the most productive times of day. Expect temperatures in the mid- to upper 70s during daylight hours, which fall to the mid-50s at night. Remember that no one can spot the more than 230 species of birds that live on or visit the refuge in a day, but a slightly longer stay can produce gratifying results.

The refuge staff sums up its advice in just four words: "Drive slowly, watch carefully." The backbone of the refuge is Wildlife Drive, a one-way, five-mile-long main road (speed limit: 15 mph) that loops and winds through it, with great bird-viewing opportunities all along the way.

Even more intimate access to the birdlife can be enjoyed by following two canoe and kayak routes through fresh, brackish, and saltwater waterways or by exploring the three well-marked foot trails through forested areas that are the ideal habitat for the many migrant songbirds wintering here.

The refuge offers many information markers for those going it on their own, but volunteer and staff guides also offer frequent group tours. The Tarpon Bay area concession offers tram, canoe, and kayak tours as well. Boat rentals are also available, and biking around the refuge is encouraged.

HIGHLIGHTS

The refuge's observation tower, located just past the crossdike, provides sweeping views of water, beach, forest, marshes, and mud flats – the entire site from a single vantage point, two stories high. It is open daily except Friday, from one hour before sunrise to a half-hour before sunset. Admission is free.

Site Map and Information

J. N. "Ding" Darling National Wildlife Refuge

🚗 From Fort Myers, a 3-mile causeway leads directly onto Periwinkle Way, which deadends onto Tarpon Bay Road. Take a right, then a left onto Sanibel-Captiva Road; the Visitor Center is 2 miles away, on the right.

🕐 Daily, sunrise to sunset, year-round.

◉ Wildlife Drive is closed on Fridays.

🏢 J. N. "Ding" Darling National Wildlife Refuge, One Wildlife Drive, Sanibel, FL 33957. Visitor Center is open daily, 9 a.m.–5 p.m.

📞 (941) 472-1100

💲 For Wildlife Drive only: $5 per vehicle, $1 for hikers and bicyclers.

♿ Wildlife Drive, the Visitor Center, Shell Mound Trail, Mangrove Overlook, and Tarpon Bay Recreation Area are all wheelchair accessible.

🅰 None on-site. One campground is available on Sanibel Island, four on nearby Fort Myers Beach, and one at Fort Myers, 10 miles away.

🔭 Birdwatching tours are conducted by refuge staff and volunteers. Canoe rentals are also available; call (941) 472-5218.

🛏 Call Sanibel-Captiva Chamber of Commerce at (941) 472-1080 for lodging listings.

OKEFENOKEE NATIONAL WILDLIFE REFUGE

Many birdwatchers have dreams of rediscovering the Ivory-billed Woodpecker still surviving somewhere deep within the swamps of this vast Georgia refuge.

Founded in 1937, this refuge contains the most ecologically intact swampland in all of North America. Inhabited as early as 2,500 B.C., this swampy region was formed by successive layers of peat (plant matter that has decomposed in water) built up over many years, where a variety of grasses, trees, and shrubs took root. Early Seminole Indian residents gave it the name Okefenokee or "Land of the Trembling Earth," because they noticed that when they stamped on the hard peat, the water rippled, grasses shook, and the earth trembled. Today this refuge consists of almost 700 square miles of protected land.

HABITAT

This enormous peat-filled bog, based in Georgia but spilling over into Florida, is brimming with life-supporting vegetation and freshwater. It is home to a huge assembly of birds that swim, wade, and fly through its watery terrain, which features stands of cypress trees and pine uplands, many a half century or more old.

Suwannee River, which serves as the swamp's principal drainage river, passes through the northwestern side of the refuge and then winds its way south to the Gulf of Mexico. The smaller Saint Marys River drains the southeastern section of Okefenokee then empties into the Atlantic Ocean, 50 miles to the east. However, 80 percent of the refuge's water is circulated through evaporation and transpiration rather than drainage.

BIRD LIFE

Visitors should bring their binoculars so they can scan this bird-rich terrain. A resting place for many

Prothonotary Warblers *and a host of other warblers are found at this refuge in September.*

wintering birds and summer breeding ground for others, Okefenokee National Wildlife Refuge is bursting with surprises almost guaranteed to fill up birding checklists any time of year.

One specialty is the three-foot-long Anhinga, a year-round resident that uses its long pointed bill to spear frogs, young alligators, fish, and water snakes. This species is joined by an array of herons, egrets, and related waders, many of whom find this swampy terrain an ideal nesting and brooding ground for their young.

BIRDS TO LOOK FOR

Anhinga • Cattle Egret • Green Heron • White Ibis • Wood Duck • Red-shouldered Hawk • King Rail • Purple Gallinule • Sandhill Crane • Yellow-billed Cuckoo • Red-cockaded Woodpecker • Pileated Woodpecker • Northern Parula • Pine Warbler• Prothonotary Warbler

Cattle Egrets are just one of the many wading birds found in this huge swampland.

Green Herons, Cattle Egrets, and White Ibis are also common here year-round, seen fanning out over the marshes in early morning to hunt for food. The American Bittern is primarily a winter resident.

Waterfowl may be seen wintering in this mild southern refuge. Look in and along the rivers and in the marshes for Mallards, Ring-necked Ducks, Wood Ducks, Hooded Mergansers, and Green-winged and Blue-winged Teal. Other winter visitors include Tree Swallows, American Robins, and Eastern Phoebes. Spring replaces these songbirds with Prothonotary Warblers, Pine Warblers, Northern Parulas, and Eastern Kingbirds, as well as Yellow-billed Cuckoos and White-Eyed Vireos.

Early dawn brings the King Rail, which at 15 inches long is the largest North American rail. Other marsh birds found at Okefenokee include the Purple Gallinule, which skips over lily pads in search of food. In winter as many as 1,000 Sandhill Cranes make Okefenokee's freshwater marshes their home; this number includes a small resident breeding population and the northern relatives that join them.

Red-shouldered Hawks and Osprey also breed and raise their young at the refuge; in fact, the latter begins building its nests in the cypress trees as early as February. Woodpeckers, including Pileated and the endangered Red-cockaded, are year-round residents in

The King Rail *is identified primarily by its* kek kek kek *call and freshwater habitat.*

the swampland's pine trees, but alas, no one has sighted even a single Ivory-billed Woodpecker in the last 50-plus years. Alligator sightings are much more reliable; in fact, the refuge's cypress swamps reportedly host the largest population of these primitive reptiles anywhere – 10,000 to 12,000 in all!

VISITING

The management of Okefenokee National Wildlife Refuge does not declare any time optimum for bird viewing. Instead they note that, from a birdwatcher's point of view, there is plenty of action year-round. Visitors can plan their trips according to when their bird of choice is likely to be present.

The refuge is accessible by a driving trail and several hiking trails. In addition its swamps can be explored via canoe or kayak, which can be rented from Okefenokee Adventures located at the east entrance of the refuge.

HIGHLIGHTS

There's no question that the unrestrained courtship dance of the Sandhill Crane is one of the most notable sights at Okefenokee. The dances take place in spring on the refuge's marshes where the bird's mating grounds are located. In winter these cranes are joined by others from the north, which come to share the pleasant climate.

Site Map and Information

OKEFENOKEE NATIONAL WILDLIFE REFUGE

🚗 From Jacksonville, FL (approximately 50 miles away), take 295 north to Route 1 and continue north to Folkston. Turn left on Main Street, then take Okefenokee Drive left and continue 11.7 miles to reach the refuge entrance. Folkston can also be reached via I-40 west from Kingsland (approximately 20 miles).

🕐 Daily, November through February, one-half hour before sunrise to 5:30 p.m.; March through October, one-half hour before sunrise to 7:30 p.m.

🌑 Closed Christmas Day.

ℹ️ Okefenokee National Wildlife Refuge, Route 2, Box 338, Folkston, GA 31537. The Visitor Center is open daily, 9 a.m.–5 p.m.

📞 (912) 496-7836; http://okefenokee.fws.gov

💲 $5 per vehicle.

♿ The Visitor Center is wheelchair accessible. For TTD, call (912) 496-7836.

🅰️ Kingfisher Wilderness Campground is 13 miles north of Folkston; call (912) 496-2186. Okefenokee Pastimes is near the refuge's eastern entrance; call (912) 496-3412.

🔭 To arrange a birdwatching tour, call (912) 496-7156.

🏨 Call the nearby Western Hotel at (912) 496-4711 or The Inn at Folkston at (912) 496-6256 for reservations.

JOHN JAMES AUDUBON STATE PARK

A walk along northwestern Kentucky's Warbler Road offers the opportunity to follow in the footsteps of John James Audubon.

The Blue-Gray Gnatcatcher's *scolding* pwee *can be heard at the park in summer.*

America's most famous painter of birds spent his struggling-artist years in Henderson, Kentucky. His troubles served to refine his art and his resolve, and after leaving Henderson in 1819, Audubon began work on his masterpiece, a book of paintings titled *The Birds of America*.

John James Audubon State Park preserves the woods where the naturalist walked. It is home to a museum, which houses the largest collection of Audubon's oil paintings, engravings, and personal memorabilia, and a nature center featuring a wildlife observatory and a variety of displays.

HABITAT

The upland and bottomland hardwood forests found south of the Ohio River in western Kentucky provided many opportunities for Audubon to pursue his passion. Today the 692-acre state park's mature habitat is a distinctive assemblage of beech, sugar maple, and other hardwood trees. Its location near the junction of the Ohio and Green Rivers makes it a major highway for

BIRDS TO LOOK FOR

Green Heron • Wood Duck • Pileated Woodpecker • Eastern Wood-Pewee • Eastern Kingbird • Red-eyed Vireo • Carolina Chickadee • Blue-gray Gnatcatcher • Northern Mockingbird • American Redstart • Hooded Warbler • Scarlet Tanager • Northern Cardinal • Rose-breasted Grosbeak • Indigo Bunting

migrating songbirds. Over 20 species of warbler pass through each spring and fall. The park is also home to two man-made lakes, Wilderness Lake and Recreational Lake, which attract a variety of birds year-round.

BIRD LIFE

The observation center enclosed in the gothic-looking museum building makes a great starting place for a tour. Established feeding stations and native plant gardens outside the center's windows draw Northern Cardinals, Downy and Red-bellied Woodpeckers, White-breasted Nuthatches, and more. In the spring, migrating Rose-breasted Grosbeaks are the biggest crowd pleasers, but in this setting birdwatchers savor the more commonplace Tufted Titmice and Carolina Chickadees, too. Outside the museum, birders can spot nectar-sipping Ruby-throated Hummingbirds.

Of the seven miles of trails through the park's nature preserve, the two-mile Wilderness Lake Loop Trail

Abundant woodlands and lakes attract American Redstarts, among other wood-warblers.

covers the most habitat and provides the most bird variety. The beginning of the trail follows Warbler Road, a paved section surrounded by woods that is very popular during spring migration. In spring, migrant warblers fly about 40 miles each night, timing their arrival in their breeding grounds with the first appearance of new leaves. Unlike ducks or shorebirds, they travel in mixed flocks, and birders can see more than 10 species on a good late-April day. Look especially for American Redstarts, Hooded Warblers, Black-and-white Warblers, and Kentucky Warblers. The males will be showing off bright, butterflylike colors, and the females follow in their more conservative plumage.

Fall migration is an event, too, occurring in some cases a mere seven weeks after spring migration. Other migrating songbirds to look for in the forested section of the Wilderness Lake Loop include Baltimore Orioles and Scarlet Tanagers. Year-round, Northern Mockingbirds and Brown Thrashers can be spotted in the undergrowth. In the summer, flycatchers – Eastern Wood Pewees, Eastern Phoebes, and Eastern Kingbirds – can be found in the areas around Wilderness Lake.

Wilderness Lake itself harbors Great Blue Herons and Green Herons. Look for waterfowl too, including Canada Goose, Green-winged Teal, Wood Ducks, and occasional Mute Swans, all of which spend winter at the park. Smaller birds to see in the Wilderness Lake area include

The Hooded Warbler *is common here, although its often difficult to spot among the undergrowth and low branches.*

Prothonotary Warblers, Indigo Buntings, and Belted Kingfishers.

The additional five miles of trails offer abundant opportunity to see many of the 170 species of birds that occur in the park. Gray Catbirds mew and skulk in the underbrush, Mourning Doves coo from tree limbs, and Pileated Woodpeckers drum on dead snags. In the summer, listen for the Red-Eyed Vireo's continuous, whiny *Where am I? Here am I. Look, up here. Where am I?* Blue-gray Gnatcatchers scold from holly thickets until fall migration, and in the winter, it is easy to watch Carolina Chickadees and Brown Creepers searching for food.

VISITING

Spring and early summer are the seasons to observe the migrating and nesting species. Fall migration is good for those who wish to challenge their identification skills, and winter brings waterfowl to the park's two lakes.

HIGHLIGHTS

To take the Audubon-country experience farther afield, go birdwatching along western Kentucky's John James Audubon Birding Trail. Call the Kentucky Department of Fish and Wildlife Resources at (800) 858-1549 for a birding guide, map, and bird list.

Site Map and Information

JOHN JAMES AUDUBON STATE PARK

🚗 From Henderson, take US 41 north about 4 miles to reach the park entrance, which is half a mile prior to the US 41 bridge over the Ohio River.

◻ Daily, sunrise to sunset, year-round.

◼ The park, including museum/nature center, is closed for one week at Christmastime.

ℹ John James Audubon State Park, P.O. Box 576, Henderson, KY 42419. The museum and nature center, located in the same building, are open daily, 10 a.m.–5 p.m.

☎ (270) 826-2247 (park information); (270) 827-1893 (museum/nature center); www.jaudubon@henderson.net

⑤ No fees to explore the park; museum is $4 per adult, $2.50 per child (ages 12 and under), or $10 per family.

♿ The museum is wheelchair accessible and Warbler Road is asphalt-topped and wheelchair-friendly. To reach TTY, call (800) 325-8388.

🅰 Contact the park naturalist at (270) 826-4424 for a schedule

of birdwatching tours and other interpretive events.

🏕 The 69-site campground functions on a first-come, first-served basis.

🛏 Five 1-bedroom cottages and 1 wheelchair-accessible 2-bedroom cottage, with linens and fully equipped kitchens, available on-site; call (270) 826-2247 for reservations. For information about other area lodging, contact the Kentucky Tourist Offices's nearby Welcome Center at (270) 826-3128.

MAMMOTH CAVE NATIONAL PARK

Like the many woodland birds attracted to this fine Kentucky park, 18th-century folk hero Daniel Boone would have felt right at home here.

In the 1790s a Kentucky bear-hunter discovered an entrance to the vast network of underground passages that would come to be known as Mammoth Cave. The ownership of this geological marvel was fiercely contested for many decades, and it wasn't until well into the 20th century that much attention was paid to the forested areas that lie above the caves. However, fueled by a national conservation movement, the area (both above and below ground) was officially founded as Mammoth Cave National Park in 1941. Today the park is a birdwatcher's paradise and a testament to naturalist John Muir's claim that "the clearest way into the Universe is through a forest wilderness."

HABITAT

Besides the marvelous caves, the predominant feature of this national park is its bird-rich hardwood forests, which include beech, sugar maple, white and black oak, hickory, and magnolia trees. The sandstone gorges in the northern portion of the park also attract woodland birds, due to the hemlock, yellow birch, and holly trees they sustain. The sandstone bluffs above offer a clear view of soaring raptors, including Red-tailed Hawks.

The Green and Nolin Rivers both run through the park, intersecting near its southwestern border. Their clean waters attract plentiful waterfowl and wading birds. The park also has numerous small ponds, stream banks, and sinkholes (limestone hollows that connect to caverns) attractive to birds and other wildlife.

The Ruby-crowned Kinglet *may be spotted flicking its wings and calling out a scolding* je-ditt.

BIRD LIFE

The diversity and accessibility of habitats at Mammoth Cave National Park attract both birds and birdwatchers. The Whip-poor-will can easily find plenty of suitable dry soil on which to build its nest. And, close by, the rivers and ponds attract plentiful big-winged insects for it to feed on. At night birdwatchers can spot the Whip-poor-will in either habitat, and should also be on the lookout for Common Nighthawks, another night-hunter of large-winged insects, albeit a higher flyer.

BIRDS TO LOOK FOR

Great Blue Heron • Green Heron • Red-tailed Hawk • Wild Turkey • Solitary Sandpiper • Common Nighthawk • Whip-poor-will • Ruby-crowned Kinglet • Tennessee Warbler • Kentucky Warbler • Hooded Warbler • Summer Tanager • Indigo Bunting • Eastern Meadowlark

Hardwood forests draw abundant woodland birds, including Summer Tanagers.

A range of warblers can be found in the park's moist, secluded woodlands and other habitats each spring; many of them stay to breed. Look for the state's namesake warbler – the Kentucky Warbler, common in the park's deciduous forests. Other warblers found with regularity include Black-throated Green, Hooded, Prairie, Prothonotary, Tennessee, and Worm-eating Warblers. The Black-throated Blue Warbler is rarer.

Look for Scarlet and Summer Tanagers, both of which nest within the park. Its dramatically colored plumage is not a match to the brilliant blue sported by the male Indigo Bunting, however. His persistent, if not particularly melodic, tunes continue into late summer, when many other songbirds have left the park. Another songbird to look

and listen for is the Eastern Meadowlark, which conceals its dome-shaped nest in patches of weeds and grass at the edges of the woods, fields, pastures, and meadows. Winter brings the Ruby-crowned Kinglet to the park's woodlands.

The two rivers and ponds attract their own bird constituency each year, although many of these are rare or transient visitors. The Belted Kingfisher, found along the riverbanks during nesting season, is one of the most common birds in this habitat. Other water-dependent

The Common Nighthawk *roosts on the ground, as well as higher up, on posts and branches.*

birds found in the park include a wide range of ducks, wading birds, such as Great Blue and Green Herons, and shorebirds, including Solitary Sandpipers.

Wild Turkeys were reintroduced to Mammoth Cave National Park in the mid-1980s. Listen for the males' mating call, a gobble that resounds in the woodlands in spring.

Visiting

Spring through mid-autumn is the preferred period to watch birds here. Unfortunately, this is the same period favored by that devilish scourge of the South known as the chigger. Tick repellent is recommended. Staying on trails and avoiding shrub or grassy areas will also help avoid chiggers.

The good news is that the park offers 73 miles of interconnecting trails – a network largely completed by the Civilian Conservation Corps. Leafy riverbank vistas can also be scanned from canoes in relatively chigger-free comfort. Driving also facilitates select viewing. Stop at the Visitor Center to pick up a map.

HIGHLIGHTS

Even the most single-minded birder can't pass up the opportunity to explore the underground wonders of Mammouth Cave. Tours of some of Mammoth Cave's 360 miles of known passages are offered every day except Christmas. For tour reservations, call NPRS at (800) 967-2283.

Site Map and Information

Mammoth Cave National Park

🚗 The park is almost equidistant from Louisville and Nashville, TN. From Louisville, follow I-65 about 85 miles south to Exit 53 and turn west to reach park entrance. From Nashville, follow I-65 approximately 85 miles north to Exit 48; turn north to reach park entrance.

⏲ Daily, 24 hours, year-round.

⬤ Never.

ℹ Mammoth Cave National Park, PO Box 7, Mammoth Cave, KY 42259. The Visitor Center, located in the middle of the park, is open daily, 7:30 a.m.–7 p.m., from late June through Labor Day and daily, 9 a.m.–6 p.m., off season.

☎ (270 758-2328; www.nps.gov/maca/home.htm

⑤ None.

♿ The Visitor Center and several trails are wheelchair accessible.

⛺ Three on-site campgrounds are available on a first-come, first-served basis. Two

group campgrounds, Maple Springs and Headquarters Campground, accepts reservations; call (800) 967-2283.

🚣 A 1-hour scenic boat cruise on the Green River is offered from April through October, river conditions permitting; call (270) 758-2243 for reservations.

🏨 The Mammoth Cave Hotel is on-site; call (270) 758-2225 for reservations.

ACADIA NATIONAL PARK

This Maine treasure is the summer home of over 70 species of land birds,
plus a rich mix of birds that thrive in its coastal waters.

The most stunning view of this glorious park, which is situated on Mount Desert Island, is from the top of Cadillac Mountain, the highest elevation along America's Atlantic coast. From this windswept pinnacle of 1,530 feet, the birder's eye can sweep over the park's rock-rich coastline, green forestland, and glacier-scoured terrain.

The gifts of a number of summer residents who visited during the early years of the 20th century were what made this national park, officially founded in 1919, a reality. Benefactors included John D. Rockefeller Jr., retired Harvard University president Charles W. Eliot, and Boston millionaire George B. Dorr. Rockefeller funded the building of 45 miles of carriage roads and 16 bridges.

The Blue-winged Teal *male has prominent white crescents below its eyes.*

HABITAT

Acadia's 41,000-plus acres boast ocean-battered coastline; five large freshwater lakes and a generous sprinkling of salt marshes, ponds, and streams; extensive tracts of pine-scented evergreen forests; and more than a dozen ancient mountains. Northern and temperate zones overlap here, which helps account for the diversity of plant and bird life.

It is difficult to comprehend the mighty forces that shaped Acadia National Park's terrain, particularly because its mountains look so peaceful today. Yet these granite-littered peaks were sculpted by glaciers thousands of years ago, and the tidepools are the work of the churning ocean.

BIRD LIFE

With a checklist of 273 birds, many of them nesters, wonderful sightings are everywhere, but it is probably appropriate that the first bird most visitors see upon entering the park is the familiar Black-capped Chickadee, Maine's state bird.

From then on, warbler lovers will be kept busy looking and listening for the 21 species of warblers found in the park – in volume representing almost *half* the total number of species of these songbirds in the United States.

BIRDS TO LOOK FOR

Great Cormorant • Wood Duck • Blue-winged Teal • Common Eider • Surf Scoter • Bald Eagle • Broad-winged Hawk • Peregrine Falcon • Purple Sandpiper • Northern Saw-whet Owl • Ruby-throated Hummingbird • Hairy Woodpecker • Hermit Thrush • Cedar Waxwing • Northern Parula • Chestnut-sided Warbler • Black-throated Green Warbler

The park's woodlands draw Broad-winged Hawks, among other raptors.

Some of them, including the Northern Parula and Tennessee, Nashville, and Yellow Warblers, nest here in a range of habitats. Blackburnian and Black-throated Green Warblers nest among the evergreens, while the Chestnut-sided Warbler prefers deciduous woodlands for its nests.

Acadia is also the breeding ground of four species of liquid-voiced thrushes – the Veery, plus Hermit, Swainson's, and Wood Thrushes. Old reliables that show up every year include the Red-winged Blackbird, Red-eyed Vireo, Gray Catbird, Cedar Waxwing, and Winter Wren. The tiny Ruby-throated Hummingbird builds its nest in shrubs or the low branches of trees.

Many species of waterfowl can be seen at Acadia, but along the coastline and in the saltwater back bays the one commonly seen in summertime is the Common Eider. Its numbers increase in fall, when it is joined by other ducks, including Surf Scoters and White-winged, Common Goldeneyes and Buffleheads. Look for Blue-winged Teal and Wood Ducks on the park's interior ponds.

Cormorants are also present off the park's coast – the Double-crested in summer and the Great in winter. Although the Scootic Peninsula is more notable for scenery than for birdwatching, patient birdwatchers can pick out gulls, gannets, and shearwaters on the coastal rocks. Along the beaches look for migrant sandpipers and plovers (Ruddy

Great Cormorants *winter off the park's coast, while the Double-crested Cormorant can be spotted in summer.*

Turnstones, Least Sandpipers, Semipalmated and Black-bellied Plovers, and more), which arrive in mid-August. The Purple Sandpiper is the only one to stay the winter.

In all seasons listen for the *rat-a-tat* signals of Downy and Hairy Woodpeckers, easily outdone by the vigorous drumming of the Ruffed Grouse, whose courtship booming can last all night and day. The island's rugged terrain is also ideally suited to raptors such as the Osprey, Broad-winged and Red-tailed Hawks, the American Kestrel, and five species of owls, including the Northern Saw-whet. Today, with increasing frequency, the massive shadow of the Bald Eagle glides over Acadia.

VISITING

Although the park is open year-round (with some roads closed in winter), the best birdwatching is from May through September. The park boasts paved roads and parking areas, as well as the carriage roads Rockefeller laid out years ago, now open to foot and bike traffic.

HIGHLIGHTS

In the summer, park staff lead bird walks; call the Visitor Center to sign up. From late August through mid-October the park hosts a daily hawk watch on top of Cadillac Mountain. In May and mid-August, the park also hosts organized Peregrine Falcon watches.

Site Map and Information

ACADIA NATIONAL PARK

From Ellsworth, take Route 3 east approximately 10 miles until the road forks, then take the left fork, toward Bar Harbor; continue 3 miles to reach the Visitor Center.

Daily, 24 hours, year-round. Some roads, usually including the steep and winding climb up Cadillac Mountain, may be shut down temporarily due to heavy snowfalls, ice, or thick ocean fog.

Never.

Acadia National Park, PO Box 177, Bar Harbor, ME 04609. The main Visitor Center, located at the park entrance, is open daily, 8 a.m.–4:30 p.m.

(207) 288-3338; (voice/TDD); www.nps.gov/acad

$10 park user fee

Much of the carriage trail network is suitable for wheelchair travel. Some of the hiking trails in the park's lowlands are also navigable by wheelchair users and people with limited walking abilities.

]Blackwoods Campground is open May to mid-September; call (800) 365-2267 for reservations. Seawall Campround is open May through September on a first-come, first-served basis.

The park offers bird walks and watches; call the general number for information.

Bed-and-breakfasts, motels, and lodges are available in nearby Bar Harbor and Northeast and Southwest Harbor.

BAXTER STATE PARK

*The vast park, commanded by the most magnificent mountain in Maine,
has become a favorite birdwatching destination.*

It is probable that no land grant to the American people has come close to matching the generosity of Percival P. Baxter's 1930 gift. A former governor of Maine and great lover of the outdoors, Baxter donated the first 6,000 acres to establish the park. Thanks to the governor's subsequent land grants and financial donations, Baxter State Park is now more than 200,000 acres in size. Central to Baxter's gift and to the park's fame is the great, hulking mass called Mount Katahdin, which forms the northern terminus of the Appalachian Trail and at 5,267 feet is the highest elevation in all of Maine.

Bohemian Waxwings, *which winter irregularly in the northeast, are found in Baxter every year.*

The park is not terrain for the timid. Its mountain ridges are buffeted by electric storms, and snow falls on Mount Katahdin every month of the year. But as Baxter so enthusiastically wrote: "Man is born to die, his works are short-lived. / Buildings crumble, monuments decay, / Wealth vanishes. / But Katahdin in all its glory, / Forever shall remain the mountain of the People of Maine."

HABITAT
The great beauty of this park is undeniable. Over 40 peaks and ridges are home to an abundance of pristine ponds, lakes, streams, and forests attractive to a magnificent range of birds that in some cases have migrated directly from distant arctic tundra and waterways.

However, all of Baxter State Park is dominated by Mount Katahdin, a peak so massive and tall that it contains four distinct vegetation zones, each drawing its own bird specialties. Most Katahdin trails begin in mixed hardwood forests of birch, maple, and white pine. Higher up they pass through boreal forests of balsam fir, spruce, and white birch. Near the treeline, stunted fir and spruce take over, growing between boulders that are covered with lichen and moss. From 4,000 feet to the mountain's peak, the terrain consists of treeless tundra, frequently whipped by fierce wind, rain, and snow squalls alternating with brilliant sunshine.

BIRDS TO LOOK FOR

Ring-necked Duck • Common Merganser • Hooded Merganser • Broad-winged Hawk • Spruce Grouse • Three-toed Woodpecker • Eastern Wood-Pewee • Gray Jay • Boreal Chickadee • Gray-cheeked Thrush • American Pipit • Bohemian Waxwing • Wilson's Warbler • Rusty Blackbird • Pine Siskin

Spruce Grouse feed on pine needles in the winter months.

BIRD LIFE

The range of bird life found in the park is suggested during the 20-mile drive from the town of Millinocket to the park's southern entrance. Look for an abundance of mergansers, both Hooded and Common; American Black and Ring-necked Ducks; Rusty Blackbirds and Olive-sided Flycatchers; Three-toed Woodpeckers; and warblers, including Nashville, Palm, and Wilson's. This checklist, all found within Baxter State Park, only hints at the incredible avian diversity found here.

The Eastern Wood-Peewee *got its name from its call, a clear pee-a-wee.*

Mount Katadhin's forest-covered mass looms at the southern entrance to the park, offering wonderful birdwatching opportunities at every elevation. The American Pipit, usually considered a far northern songbird, may be found in the mountain's tablelands

Thrushes, including the Wood and Hermit Thrush, are sufficiently hardy to nest at 3,000-foot levels or higher on Mount Katahdin; listen for their exquisite evening songs.

Other forest birds to look for include the Bohemian Waxwing, Gray Jay, Pine Siskin, and Eastern Wood-Pewee. Broad-winged Hawks may be seen soaring above, and Spruce Grouse may be seen strutting in the coniferous forests.

Although a car is especially handy (some would say critical) to get from site to site, this behemoth of a park possesses 175 hiking trails that pass through just about every habitat and region in it. Another site worth visiting is the Great Basin area, where a camping is permitted. Red and White-winged Crossbills are active here, especially in early morning and evening, along with Golden-crowned Kinglets, Bay-breasted and Blackpoll Warblers, Boreal Chickadees, and Swainson's and Gray-cheeked Thrushes.

VISITING

The staff of Baxter State Park reminds visitors to make their personal safety a priority, especially when the weather gets bad. Travel above tree line may be particularly treacherous, and rescues are sometimes delayed due to heavy snow or ice buildup, so exercise appropriate caution.

All hikers are advised to stay on trails and avoid direct confrontations with bears or moose. Full water bottles, multilayered clothing, comfortable footwear, flashlights, and first aid kits are also recommended. Above the tree line, sunglasses are essential. And, as enchanting as summer birding may be, be prepared for Maine's infamous mosquitos and blackflies.

HIGHLIGHTS

Baxter State Park offers the unsurpassable opportunity of walking a portion of the Appalachian Trail; its northern entrance is on Mount Katahdin. The effort will be rewarded by magnificent scenery and a wealth of bird life, from thrushes to raptors to woodpeckers. Stop by the Visitor Center for a map and checklist.

Site Map and Information

BAXTER STATE PARK

🚗 From Bangor, drive north on I-95 to Medway, then west on Routes 11/157 to Millinocket (70 miles in all). Continue on Routes 11/157 20 miles northwest to reach the park's southern entrance, where the Visitor Center is located.

🕐 Daily, 24 hours, year-round.

⬤ Some areas are closed seasonally during bad weather.

ℹ Baxter State Park, 64 Balsam Drive, Millinocket, Maine 04462. The Visitor Center is open daily, 7 a.m.–3 p.m., Memorial Day through October 15.

📞 (207) 723-5140

💲 Free for Maine residents. $8 per motor vehicle per day or $25 for a season's pass for nonresidents.

♿ The Visitor Center, campgrounds, and picnic grounds are wheelchair accessible. Call (207) 723-9905 to reach TTY.

⛺ Ten on-site campgrounds offer a range of spaces, from cabins and bunkhouses to lean-tos, tent sites, and group camps. Call the Visitor Center for a schedule and rates. Reservations are required.

🍽 None.

🏨 Motels, hotels, and bed-and-breakfasts are available in the nearby towns of Millinocket and Patten; call the Millinocket Chamber of Commerce at (207) 723-4443 for listings.

ASSATEAGUE ISLAND NATIONAL SEASHORE

This constantly changing barrier island refuge offers some of Maryland's best birdwatching, including a rich variety of waterfowl, waders, and songbirds.

Winter storms and hurricanes moving in from the Atlantic Ocean often bring radical changes to the landscape of Assateague Island, a 37-mile-long coastal barrier island, but these changes are part of a natural cycle of renewal. Assateague Island National Seashore became part of the National Park System in 1965, joining two miles of the island to the north that had already gained protection as Assateague State Park in 1963. These were joined in 1979 by Chincoteague National Wildlife Refuge on the south part of the island in Virginia territory.

The Belted Kingfisher *may be seen fishing in Assateague's marshlands.*

BIRDS TO LOOK FOR

Common Loon • Green Heron • Piping Plover • American Oystercatcher • Willet • Whimbrel • Ruddy Turnstone • Herring Gull • Great Black-backed Gull • Forster's Tern • Black Skimmer • Belted Kingfisher • Eastern Kingbird • Fish Crow • Common Yellowthroat • Field Sparrow • Eastern Meadowlark

HABITAT

A representative of native barrier island habitat, Assateague Island National Seashore was built by ocean waves and sand. Each of its habitats – dune, forest, and marsh – is accessible via a nature trail. These sandy and ever-windy habitats are ideal places to look for animal tracks. Fox and raccoon tracks are often seen, along with some of the almost 300 species of birds found on the island.

BIRD LIFE

Assateague National Seashore's main road, Bayberry Drive, leads to all three of the park's nature trails and is also a good place to spot Northern Bobwhites. The Bayside Campground and adjacent Life of the Marsh Nature Trail can be covered in the same walk. Look throughout the trail and along the campground loops for Yellow-rumped Warblers, which occur here year-round.

During winter check the trees for Great Horned Owls, and the shrubs and thickets for Eastern Towhees, Chipping Sparrows, and White-throated Sparrows. Spring through fall the marshes host Tricolored and Little Blue Herons, and Great and Snowy Egrets can be seen stalking minnows. The marsh trail is also one of the best places in the park to hear, and maybe even see, Brown Pelicans, Clapper Rails, Ospreys, and Forster's Terns.

Summer days are filled with the ringing *whitchity-whitchity-whitchity* calls of the Common Yellowthroat. At dusk and dawn Chuck-will's-widows will be

American Oystercatchers feed in small, noisy flocks along Assateague's beaches.

repeating their names, and persistent birders may even see one of these well-camouflaged birds. In the winter Common and Red-throated Loons loaf in Tom's Cove.

The trail to hike is the Life of the Forest Trail. If it is summer, birdwatchers will merely want to hurry through the forest, which may be mosquito filled, to get to the breezy overlook, which offers the most varied birding in the park. Here, with their scopes, birders can spot forest birds and the marsh and Sinepuxent Bay habitat below. Song Sparrows, Northern Cardinals, and Gray Catbirds call from the thickets, while Green Herons and Belted Kingfishers may be seen hunting from snags in the marsh. Eastern Meadowlarks often sing in the distance, and Eastern

Kingbirds feed on the throngs of flying insects. Noisy but well-camouflaged Willets nest here.

The third nature trail, Life of the Dunes, and the adjacent beach round out the Assateague experience. Here, it seems, many of the birds are black: Red-winged Blackbirds, both Common and Boat-tailed Grackles, and two species of crows may be seen easily here. The odd, nasal *ca-hah* of the Fish Crow is the only reliable way to separate this smaller species from the more common American Crow. Field Sparrows and Brown Thrashers are common in the beach heather.

Anywhere in the park the four most common gulls can be seen in action. The Herring and Ring-

Ruddy Turnstones *have slender bills that they use to flip aside debris in the search for food.*

51

billed Gulls might steal a sandwich right from a visitor, while the Great Black-backed Gull is shy around people. The Laughing Gull's behavior falls in between the two extremes.

From the parking area at the northern end of the park, the hearty birdwatcher can take a two-mile hike north along the beach to endangered Piping Plover nesting grounds. From mid-March through August hikers are restricted to walking only along the intertidal zone indicated by the fencing around the nesting areas. Other birds to look for include Brown Pelicans, American Oystercatchers, Black Skimmers, and Common Terns.

VISITING

Summer may be considered prime time by most visitors, but mid-April to mid-May is the best month for birders: the Piping Plovers and other nesters have arrived, but the summer crowds and mosquitoes have not. September through October offers surprising numbers of migrating songbirds.

HIGHLIGHTS

Canoe or kayak the tiny coves and inlets of Sinepuxent Bay, where waders, ducks, and shorebirds are protected enough to ignore human presence. Either join a park ranger for a guided trip (daily in summer, most weekends in spring and fall) or rent a canoe at the end of Bayside Drive. At migration time, spring and late summer, go during low tide to see shorebirds such as Red Knots, Ruddy Turnstones, and Whimbrels.

Site Map and Information

ASSATEAGUE ISLAND
NATIONAL SEASHORE

🚌 From Ocean City, MD, take US 50 west less than 1 mile to Maryland 611 and follow 7 miles south to reach the Barrier Island Visitor Center, just north of the entrance to Assateague National Seashore.

🕐 Daily, 24 hours, year-round.

⬤ Never.

ℹ️ Assateague Island National Seashore, 7206 National Seashore Lane, Berlin, MD 21811. The Barrier Island Visitor Center is open daily, 9 a.m.–5 p.m.

📞 (410) 641-1441; www.nps.gov/asis

💲 $5 per vehicle, valid for 7 days. An additional $2 fee is charged during summer to use the adjacent Assateague State Park.

♿ Visitor Center and two trails, Marsh Nature Trail and Life of the Forest Trail, are wheelchair accessible.

🅰️ The National Park Service offers various naturalist-led activities, including bird walks. Schedules are available at the Visitor Center.

🏕️ Both the state park and national seashore offer camping. (RVs are accommodated, but there are no hookups.) For state park reservations call (888) 432-2267; for the national seashore call (800) 365-CAMP.

🏨 Nearby Ocean City offers many accommodations.

CHESAPEAKE AND OHIO CANAL NATIONAL HISTORIC PARK

Along the towpath of the C&O Canal, on the Maryland side of the Potomac River, birders find an abundance of birds – from warblers to waterfowl.

It is providential for birders that Supreme Court Justice William O. Douglas decided to undertake the preservation of the Chesapeake and Ohio Canal. The canal along the Potomac River was completed in 1850 as a commercial trade waterway, but had been deteriorating since it was made obsolete by railroads at the turn of the century.

By the 1950s the canal was slated to be transformed into a new parkway. Justice Douglas, who cherished the natural habitat along the waterway, was horrified by the idea and invited the editors of the Washington, D.C., newspapers to hike the canal with him. The ensuing hoopla resulted in the conservation of the canal.

HABITAT

The C&O Canal National Historic Park now preserves 184.5 miles of bottomland woods along one of the continent's most important migratory flyways. From late April through June the music of migration and breeding season presents an irresistible call to birders. Those who come to stroll on the towpath between the river and the canal find a bevy of swallows, vireos, flycatchers, thrushes, and warblers.

The towpath area, and the narrow strip of land beside it, form a distinct environmental zone known as the floodplain. Eastern box turtles, two-lined salamanders, and copperhead snakes join Red-headed Woodpeckers and Carolina Chickadees in making use of this fertile habitat.

The Green Heron, *a chunky short-legged wader bird, is often seen foraging alone for food.*

BIRD LIFE

Although some birdwatchers hike and/or cycle to explore the entire towpath on camping trips, the way to birdwatch at the canal in just a few days is to drive from the urban Washington, D.C., area, working into the various access points until reaching

BIRDS TO LOOK FOR

Green Heron • Black-crowned Night Heron • Wood Duck • Osprey • Red-shouldered Hawk • Yellow-billed Cuckoo • Barred Owl • Ruby-throated Hummingbird • Red-bellied Woodpecker • Great Crested Flycatcher • Swainson's Thrush • Cerulean Warbler • Scarlet Tanager • Baltimore Oriole

The Scarlet Tanager's red and black breeding plumage is hard to miss.

the canal's western terminus in Cumberland, Maryland. Frequent mile markers, also indicated on the National Park Service visitor map, help locate various points along the way.

About two miles north of Georgetown (which is considered Mile 0), Fletcher's Boathouse off Canal Road offers natural habitat in the city. The picnic area is home to nesting Orchard and Baltimore Orioles. Look along the river for nesting Turkey and Black Vultures, too. A one-mile hike on the towpath leads to Chain Bridge, and from there birders can scan adjacent ponds and the river for Tree Swallows, Ospreys, ducks, and Ring-billed Gulls.

Prime habitat increases as the lands become less urban west of the Capital Beltway (I-495). Look along the canal for Barred Owls, Belted

Great Crested Flycatchers *breed along the Potomac, beginning in mid-spring.*

Kingfishers, Red-bellied and Pileated Woodpeckers, and Brown Creepers. Breeding all along the river, starting in mid-spring, are Yellow-billed Cuckoos and Great Crested and Acadian Flycatchers.

Wood Ducks, a favorite among the canal's breeding birds, start nesting in March, high in the sycamores all along the canal. Wood Ducks are a uniquely North American species, and their range barely leaves the U.S. The male's vivid green-and-white pattern draws even the most jaded eye. And the species' habit of nesting up to fifty feet above the ground in tree cavities astounds birders, who often observe known nests in hopes of seeing the one-day-old young flutter to the ground and toddle to the nearest water.

The middle section of the C&O Canal, between Pennyfield Lock (at Mile 20) and Sycamore Landing Road, is especially good for birding. During migration, the 1.5-mile hike between Pennyfield Lock and Blockhouse Point often features Black-throated Blue Warblers, Swainson's Thrushes, and Rose-breasted Grosbeaks. Scarlet Tanagers and Red-eyed Vireos nest here. Other towpath birds include Ruby-throated Hummingbirds and Yellow-rumped Warblers.

For deep forest habitat, visit Little Orleans (Mile 141). Some say that walking north along the towpath in this area provides the very best birdwatching along the canal. Look for Cerulean Warblers, Wood Thrushes, and Black-capped Chickadees. In addition, the Potomac River at the western terminus of the canal (Mile 185) features Great Blue Herons, Black-crowned Night-Herons, and a variety of dabbling ducks.

VISITING

If you want to be overwhelmed by the sight and sound of spring migrants, arrive at dawn. By 9 a.m. the show has settled down to merely interesting.

HIGHLIGHTS

Bird the old-fashioned way – by canal boat. Tours through the park on the Canal Clipper are offered from mid-April through mid-October. Look for Northern Rough-winged Swallows and Green Herons. For information about trips, call (301) 767-3714.

Site Map and Information

CHESAPEAKE AND OHIO CANAL NATIONAL HISTORIC PARK

🚗 From Washington, D.C., the 185-mile-long canal follows the Potomac River along the state lines of Maryland, Virginia, and West Virginia. No road follows the entire length directly; instead, various points are accessed via feeder roads. Major highways leading to canal access are – from east to west – I-495, I-270, and US Route 40.

⌷ Daily, sunrise to sunset, year-round.

⬤ Never.

🛈 Chesapeake and Ohio Canal National Historic Park, PO Box 4, Sharpsburg, MD 21782. There are 6 Visitor Centers, but the primary one is Great Falls Tavern Visitor Center in Potomac. It's open daily, 9 a.m.–5 p.m., year-round.

📞 (301) 299-3613; www.nps.gov/choh

💲 $4.00 per vehicle is charged at the Great Falls Tavern entrance; cyclists and walkers pay $2.00.

♿ The canal towpath is generally passable to wheelchairs, but it is not paved.

⛺ Many National Park Service campgrounds serve both overnight hikers and drive-in campers on a first-come, first-served basis.

👥 Ranger-led tours are held monthly throughout the park; contact the Visitor Center for details.

🛏 Many accommodations are available in the larger towns near the towpath, including Washington, D.C., Hagerstown, and Cumberland.

PARKER RIVER NATIONAL WILDLIFE REFUGE

The Piping Plover is treated like royalty at this Massachusetts refuge, which reserves more than six miles of beach for its nesting and brooding activities.

Conveniently situated along the Atlantic flyway, Parker River National Wildlife Refuge was established in 1942 as a feeding, resting, and nesting haven for migrant waterfowl, shorebirds, and songbirds. The key element of this 4,662-acre refuge is Plum Island, a barrier island between the Atlantic Ocean and Broad Sound, where the Parker River empties. The island is nothing less than a bird magnet. The refuge in its entirety attracts more than 300 species of birds.

The Eastern Phoebe *spreads its tail and bobs it up and down when perching.*

pans (shallow saltwater basins), not to mention a creek and Parker River itself, which feeds into Broad Sound.

Increasing the richness of this natural landscape are several man-made enhancements. A portion of land is mowed in the summer to provide food and habitat for American Woodcocks and Bobolinks, both of which breed at the refuge. Water levels are lowered to expose additional mud flats for migrant shorebirds and to allow the germination of wetland areas to produce food for waterfowl. Refuge management supplies nest boxes for Purple Martins and elevated platforms for Osprey.

HABITAT

This diversity of bird life can be explained in part by the variety of habitats that Plum Island's eight-mile stretch encompasses. A mix of uplands and wetlands, this island consists of sandy beaches and dunes, low-growing thickets, freshwater and saltwater marshes, mud flats and salt

BIRDS TO LOOK FOR

Snowy Egret • Glossy Ibis • Canada Goose • Blue-winged Teal • White-winged Scoter • Common Goldeneye • Sharp-shinned Hawk • American Kestrel • Piping Plover • Greater Yellowlegs • Sanderling • Eastern Phoebe • Purple Martin • Tree Swallow • Yellow-rumped Warbler • Pine Warbler • Palm Warbler

BIRD LIFE

Parker River National Wildlife Refuge maintains incomparable records of the arrival and departure times of migrating bird populations, as well as wonderful sites from which visitors can view the spectacle.

In spring wood-warblers – including Palm, Pine, Chestnut-sided, Magnolia, and Yellow-rumped Warblers – are among the first migrants, arriving as soon as early April. Warbler species are numerous at the refuge by late May and early June, and again from mid-August to early September when waves of migrants return. Beginning in

Once hunted close to extinction, the Snowy Egret is easily found at Parker River.

mid-April Purple Martins nest, forming the largest martin colony in the state. The Eastern Phoebe is another refuge nester. Tree Swallows are visible singly or in small groups through the summer, and they form large flocks from mid-August through mid-September, in preparation for their flight south.

Migrant ducks, sometimes as many as 30 different species in March and April, abound at the refuge in early spring and late fall. Some of the best places to watch them are Salt Pannes, Stage Island, Bill Forward, and North Pools (the Visitor Center can provide directions). These ducks, from American Black Ducks to Blue-winged Teal, are joined by migrant geese, including Canada and Snow Geese and the smaller Brant. At the Merrimac River Seawall, just north of the

refuge, the Common Goldeneye is joined in fall and winter by loons, grebes, and the White-winged Scoter.

Among the migrant shorebirds, the Piping Plover and Killdeer are refuge nesters, while two other plovers – the Semipalmated and Black-bellied – stop over in spring and fall only. Beginning in July and peaking in August, other migrant shorebirds arrive, including Greater and Lesser Yellowlegs, Whimbrel, Sanderlings, Semipalmated and Least Sandpipers, and Short-billed Dowitchers. These and others may be spotted combing over the refuge's marshes, ponds, and salt pans for food.

The Pine Warbler *forages for food on low branches or on the ground.*

Waders, including Great and Snowy Egrets, Glossy Ibis, and herons, are regular nesters at the refuge. Raptors such as the American Kestrel and the larger Sharp-shinned Hawk are visible in large numbers in spring. The best place to spot them is from the Hellcat Observation Tower.

VISITING

A wonderful introduction to Parker River's wealth is a slow drive along the 6.3-mile Refuge Road. The road begins at the refuge's gatehouse and runs the length of Plum Island, to Emerson Rocks at the southern tip. It passes by the salt pans and two hiking trails – Hellcat Interpretive Trail and Pines Trail – allowing birders to scope out marshes (both fresh- and saltwater), thickets, and dunes for more in-depth exploration later. An early morning drive turns up the most songbirds, from warblers to sparrows.

HIGHLIGHTS

Although April through October is the most popular time to visit Parker River National Wildlife Refuge, the wintertime sight of a Snowy Owl flying in the refuge's salt marshes or roosting in tree boughs along Refuge Road is unforgettable. Migrants from the winter darkness of the arctic circle, these impressive raptors are found on the refuge from late November through February.

Site Map and Information

PARKER RIVER NATIONAL WILDLIFE REFUGE

🚗 From Newburyport, take Route 1A southeast 3.5 miles to Rolfe Lane, turn left and continue ½ mile to reach Plum Island Turnpike. Turn right onto turnpike and continue over the bridge onto the island, then turn right onto Sunset Drive and follow it ⅓ mile to reach park entrance.

⬜ Daily, sunrise to sunset, year-round.

⬤ Plum Island occasionally closes in the summer when parking lots are full to avoid visitor overload.

ℹ Parker River National Wildlife Refuge, 261 Northern Boulevard, Plum Island, Newburyport, MA 01950. The Visitor Center is open weekdays, 8 a.m.–4:30 p.m.

📞 (978) 465-5753; http://northeast.fws.gov

💲 $5 per automobile and $2 per biker or walker to visit the Plum Island section. Annual passes are also available.

♿ The Visitor Center and boardwalk are wheelchair accessible.

🏕 None on-site, but campsites are available at nearby Salisbury Beach State Reservation; call (978) 462-4481 for details.

🚻 None.

🛏 Motels and bed-and-breakfasts are available in nearby Newburyport; call the Chamber of Commerce at (978) 462-6680 for listings.

PLEASANT VALLEY WILDLIFE SANCTUARY

Woodland and wetland birds attract thousands of birdwatchers to this hardwood forested valley in the Berkshires of western Massachusetts.

This truly pleasant valley was established as a wildlife sanctuary by the Lenox Garden Club in 1929. Some 20 years later the club turned it over to the Massachusetts Audubon Society's permanent protection to ensure that the site's plentiful birds, beavers, and other wildlife would continue to thrive.

Ruby-throated Hummingbirds are the only hummers regularly found in the East.

Today Pleasant Valley Wildlife Sanctuary's 1,400 acres boast seven miles of hiking trails; one of them, the Ledges Trail, climbs 814 feet up Lenox Mountain, the 2,126-foot-tall peak situated along the sanctuary's western border. Striated gouges on rocky outcrops along this trail are evidence of the advance and retreat of the mile-thick layer of ice that covered this region in prehistoric times.

HABITAT

Contained within what appears as just a dot on Massachusett's map are extensive hardwood forests, as well as uplands, fields, ponds, swamps, hedgerows, and thickets. Water is retained by clay-rich earth below the topsoil, promoting tree growth and health. Most of the valley is second-growth timber, which secured footholds in the second half of the 19th century after many small New England farms were abandoned because the large-acre, rich-soil farms of the Midwest were growing in numbers and output. Maples, beeches, oaks, and birches returned to this land. So did the birds.

BIRD LIFE

The diversity of birds attracted to this beautifully wooded sanctuary underscores nature's ability to rejuvenate itself if given the opportunity. The current species count has climbed to 163, including 80 species that breed here. Before hiking, stop by the site's feeding station, which routinely draws backyard favorites, including Black-capped Chickadee, Dark-eyed Junco, and American Goldfinch.

The rich terrain attracts a wide range of warblers – 31 recorded species, 15 of them breeders – including American Redstarts and

BIRDS TO LOOK FOR

Great Blue Heron • Ruby-throated Hummingbird • Belted Kingfisher • Yellow-bellied Sapsucker • Alder Flycatcher • Eastern Phoebe • Hermit Thrush • Wood Thrush • Chestnut-sided Warbler • Yellow-rumped Warbler • American Redstart • Scarlet Tanager • Swamp Sparrow • Dark-eyed Junco • Rose-breasted Grosbeak

The sanctuary's hardwood forests are home to the Yellow-bellied Sapsucker.

Black-and-white, Blackburnian, and Black-throated Blue Warblers. The most easily identified call among them is the Chestnut-sided Warbler's *pleased-to-meetcha* greeting, sung over and over again. Almost as plentiful is the inelegantly (but accurately) named Yellow-rumped Warbler, which features distinctive yellow patches on its side and crown as well as its rump.

All of the singing is not performed by warblers, however. The lovely, steady song of the Rose-breasted Grosbeak can be heard in and around the woodlands that it favors. In addition, listen for Eastern Phoebes, Scarlet Tanagers, Hermit and Wood Thrushes, and Gray Catbirds.

The Yellow-bellied Sapsucker can be spotted in the hardwoods, where it drills small openings and extracts sap with its fine-haired tongue. Other woodpeckers found here include Northern Flickers, plus Downy, Hairy, and Pileated Woodpeckers.

The sanctuary is also a welcome destination to migrant Ruby-throated Hummingbirds, the only hummingbird species regularly found east of the Mississippi. Almost always spotted while hovering around flowers, this tiny bird's metabolism is so high that it must feed on nectar all day long just to stay alive.

Pleasant Valley's wetlands and ponds are not

The Rose-breasted Grosbeak's *call is a squeaky* eek!

large, but they offer sufficent food and cover for the Belted Kingfisher, Alder Flycatcher, and other wetland birds that frequent them. The Swamp Sparrow, which builds a side entrance to further conceal the whereabouts of its nest, is dwarfed in size by the Wood Duck, Hooded Merganser, and Great Blue Heron that share this moisture-rich habitat.

VISITING

The beginning of May through the end of July is the best time for birdwatchers to visit, and foot traffic is the rule here. All trails are color-coded (blue leading away from the headquarters and yellow for the return), and signs identify all trail intersections.

After a successful day of birdwatching, the scenic Berkshires offer ample pleasures. These include traditional New England inns, which promise good regional dining and a pleasant night's rest.

HIGHLIGHTS

More of a bonus than a highlight, Canoe Meadows Wildlife Sanctuary, Pleasant Valley's smaller sister sanctuary, is within easy driving distance. The 262-acre preserve is composed of cultivated and uncultivated fields, mixed hardwoods, flood plains, and wetlands, frequented by Bobolinks, Alder and Willow Flycatchers, several kinds of sparrows, and various wetland species.

Site Map and Information

PLEASANT VALLEY WILDLIFE SANCTUARY

■ From Lenox, MA, 2 miles away, drive north on US 7 until it intersects with US 20. Continue 3 miles north to West Dugway Road and follow it 1.6 miles east to reach the sanctuary entrance.

◻ Daily, sunrise to sunset, from the beginning of July through Columbus Day; daily, 24 hours, Tuesday through Sunday, from Columbus Day through the end of June.

◉ Mondays, from Columbus Day through the end of June.

ℹ Pleasant Valley Wildlife Sanctuary, 472 West Mountain Road, Lenox, MA 01240. Headquarters, which functions as a Visitor Center, are open weekdays, 9 a.m.–5 p.m., and weekends, 10 a.m.–4 p.m.

◖ (413) 637-0320; www.massaudubon.org

⑤ $3 per adult; $2 for children (3–15 years old) and seniors.

♿ No special facilities.

🅰 Prohibited on-site. Nearby Bear Town

State Forest has campgrounds; call (877) 422-6762 for reservations.

👥 Occasional naturalist-led walks and programs. Call the sanctuary for a schedule.

🏨 Bed-and-breakfasts, inns, and motels are available in nearby Lenox, Stockbridge, and Lee; call (800) 237-5747 for area listings.

NOXUBEE NATIONAL WILDLIFE REFUGE

*The endangered Red-cockaded Woodpecker enjoys sanctuary
within the pine forests of this eastern Mississippi refuge.*

Walking through Noxubee National Wildlife Refuge's lush forests today, it isn't easy to visualize the condition of the area at the beginning of the 20th century. Intensively farmed and overgrazed, the timber-stripped, water-depleted land had become virtually useless to wildlife, especially to birds. Fortunately, in 1940 the U.S. Fish and Wildlife Service founded the refuge, with the goal of restoring the pine and hardwood wilderness that once flourished in the area.

The Great Crested Flycatcher *feeds high in the forest's canopy.*

Today about 125,000 visitors drive and hike through the refuge's 48,000 acres each year. These include birdwatchers drawn to the site's now plentiful bird count – 253 species in all. These birds share the refuge with an abundance of other wildlife, including river otters, bobcats, and alligators.

BIRDS TO LOOK FOR

Great Blue Heron • Cattle Egret • Wood Stork • Wood Duck • American Wigeon • Blue-winged Teal • Ring-necked Duck • Golden Eagle • Killdeer • Red-headed Woodpecker • Red-cockaded Woodpecker • Great Crested Flycatcher • Bank Swallow • Prothonotary Warbler • Scarlet Tanager

HABITAT

The principal natural bodies of water are the Noxubee River, which gives the refuge its name, and two large lakes – Bluff Lake and Loakfoma Lake. "Manipulate" is a word refuge management employs to describe how it uses Noxubee's 15 wetland impoundments to create ideal habitats for birds and other wildlife. Waterfowl especially benefit from low levees constructed to encourage winter flooding of part of the refuge's hardwood bottomland forests.

Water levels in other refuge impoundments create good growth conditions for native wetland plant species, resulting in not only seeds but a bumper crop of mollusks, crustaceans, and insects for wading birds, shorebirds, and migratory waterfowl to feed on. The refuge also boasts a lush mix of woodlands, where tracts of oak, hickory, and loblolly pine grow in abundance.

BIRD LIFE

Refuge management is determined to get the Red-cockaded Woodpecker, once abundant in the upland pines of this area, off the endangered species list. This bird, which nests only in the cavities that it excavates in mature southeastern pine trees, has suffered a devastating decline in its population from loss of its pine forest habitat. The best estimates are that this woodpecker's population in

*The Killdeer's call is easy to recognize – listen for a piercing **kill-dee**.*

the United States has dwindled to 1,200; approximately 100 of these birds live and nest at Noxubee – and this number is on an upswing. By living in the refuge year-round, the Red-cockaded Woodpecker unwittingly helps the refuge in its conservation efforts.

The refuge's forests are home to many other birds as well. The Red-cockaded Woodpecker's kin – including Red-headed, Downy, Hairy, and Pilcated Woodpeckers – are busy in wooded areas year-round. Four kinds of owls make their home here as well. Thousands of neotropical songbirds arrive from Central and South America in the spring and some stay through the summer to breed. Nesters include the Scarlet Tanager, the Great Crested Flycatcher, Bank and Barn Swallows, and plenty of warblers, including Prothonotary, Hooded, Black-and-white, and Pine Warblers.

Fall also attracts impressive numbers of migrating waterfowl and shorebirds to the refuge's abundant wetlands; most stay until spring, when they become migrants again. Look for Mallards, Wood Ducks, Ring-necked Ducks, Gadwall, American Wigeon, and both Green-winged and Blue-winged Teal. Keeping company with the ducks are a variety of shorebirds, including Greater and Lesser Yellowlegs, Spotted Sandpipers, Killdeer, and Semipalmated Plovers.

The Red-headed Woodpecker *is just one of several species of woodpeckers that makes its home in Noxubee's hardwood forests.*

Visit the 200-yard-long Bluff Lake Boardwalk and observation platform for a good vantage point from which to watch waterfowl and shorebirds, as well as a variety of egrets and other wading birds that make their home in the refuge's wetlands. These include the Great Blue and Little Blue Herons, a scattering of White Ibis, and more than a scattering of Snowy Egrets. The area also harbors a Cattle Egret rookery that boasts more than 5,000 nesting pairs.

Visitors to the refuge in the fall and winter can see both Bald and Golden Eagles in flight. The two raptors, which face vigorous hunting competition from each other, can be best observed from the refuge's two observation platforms, the Bluff Lake Boardwalk, and several walking trails. Stop by refuge headquarters to pick up a map of these landmarks.

VISITING

The best times to birdwatch at Noxubee are spring (March through May) and fall (September through November), although birdwatching opportunities are plentiful year-round. Summers are hot and insects are out in full force, but late summer, when water levels are low, provides the chance to see hundreds of Wood Storks active in the swamps and marshes. Visitors should bring insect repellent and bottled water.

HIGHLIGHTS

To enhance the endangered Red-cockaded Woodpecker's chance of surviving, refuge management drills extra nesting holes in the pines of the upland forests. Look for the tree trunks designated by white bands, but take care not to disturb the birds.

Site Map and Information

NOXUBEE NATIONAL WILDLIFE REFUGE

🚌 From Louisville, MS, take Route 25 north 15 miles to reach the western entrance, or from Starkville take Route 25 south 12 miles. The refuge's eastern entrance is 18 miles west of Brooksville off Route 388.

🚪 Daily, 24 hours, year-round.

⦿ Never.

ℹ Noxubee National Wildlife Refuge, Route 1, Box 142, Brooksville, MS 39739. Refuge headquarters, which function as a Visitor Center, are open weekdays, 8 a.m.–4:30 p.m.

☎ (662) 323-5548; http://noxubee.fws.gov

Ⓢ None.

♿ Bluff Lake Boardwalk and refuge headquarters are wheelchair accessible.

Ⓐ None on-site. Public campgrounds are available at John Starr Memorial Forest; call (662) 325-2191 for reservations.

🍴 None.

🛏 Motels are available in nearby Starkville, Brooksville, and Louisville; call the Oktibbeha County Chamber of Commerce at (662) 323-5783 for listings.

St. Catherine Creek National Wildlife Refuge

Busy as ever, the beaver is the architect of some of the ponds used by the thousands of ducks and wading birds found on this peaceful Mississippi refuge.

St. Catherine Creek National Wildlife Refuge was established in 1990 to provide suitable habitat for the abundant waterfowl attracted to the lower Mississippi Valley. Although creating a home for ducks such as the Mallard, Northern Pintail, Blue-winged Teal, and Wood Duck was the primary impetus, the refuge never intended a "members only" policy. Today, in addition to waterfowl, the refuge is the year-round home or an important stopover to 14 species of shorebirds, 16 wading birds, and as many as 50 other species, primarily songbirds.

The Eastern Bluebird *is a musical bird – listen for its* chur chur-lee chur-lee *song.*

Habitat

The Mighty Mississippi, which forms the refuge's western boundary, helps dictate the habitats that compose its 24,442 acres. A portion of the refuge is upland forest – oak, gum, elm, ash, and cottonwood – and cypress swampland is found in the bottomlands. Five permanent bodies of water help make the refuge a very wet place. These are St. Catherine Creek and 4 lakes – Butler, Gilliard (the largest at 500 acres), Salt, and Swamp Lakes. The remainder of the refuge is fallow field that Old Man River periodically invades; when the flooding subsides dozens of temporary ponds are created and immediately appropriated by waterfowl.

Bird Life

Birdwatchers will probably spend most of their time at St. Catherine Creek National Wildlife Refuge identifying and studying ducks, shorebirds, and wading birds, for there are sizeable numbers of all three groups in action during much of the year.

Ducks in particular seek out the many ponds created when the Mississippi River floods the area. They also can be found dependably along St. Catherine Creek and in the refuge's lakes. Besides the big four – Mallards, Northern Pintail,

BIRDS TO LOOK FOR

Anhinga • Snowy Egret • Wood Stork • Wood Duck • American Wigeon • Blue-winged Teal • Mississippi Kite • King Rail • Killdeer • Black-necked Stilt • Lesser Yellowlegs • Barred Owl • Eastern Bluebird • Yellow Warbler • Summer Tanager • Blue Grosbeak

The King Rail, a freshwater bird, makes its home in this very wet refuge.

Blue-winged Teal, and Wood Duck – all found in abundance, keep an eye out for Canvasbacks, American Wigeon, and Common Goldeneye. This wet place also attracts grebes, which stay through the winter.

All ducks and grebes are possible food for the Barred Owl, a skillful hunter common in the refuge's cypress swamps and upland woods. Another raptor to watch for is the **Wood Storks** Mississippi Kite, *walk sedately* which breeds at *and soar and* the refuge. *circle slowly.* Marvelous fliers, these birds sometimes climb so high that they are mere specks in the sky; they can be spotted more easily in the refuge's forests, perched in pairs on a tree branch.

A variety of shorebirds may be observed along the the refuge's shorelines and wetlands any time of year. Keep an eye out for the rare Piping Plover and the Black-necked Stilt. A host of sandpipers are found here, including the Solitary Sandpiper, Short-billed Dowitcher, Lesser Yellowlegs, and Killdeer.

A variety of fascinating wading birds are found in the cypress swamps and other wetlands year-round.

Common on the refuge are King Rail, Snowy Egrets, Little Blue Herons, and Black-crowned Night-Herons. Lucky birdwatchers might spot the more exotic (and very large) Anhinga, Glossy Ibis, Roseate Spoonbill, or Wood Stork.

Local farmers who set aside a portion of their crops to feed the birds are welcome allies in St. Catherine Creek's efforts to attract songbirds (which like the seeds) and waterfowl (which eat the plants). Songbirds include familiar backyard birds, such as the Eastern Bluebird, Northern Cardinal, and Baltimore Oriole, and less often seen gems, such as the Blue Grosbeak, Summer Tanager, and Yellow Warbler.

VISITING

The best times to see waterfowl are from October to February (winter residents) and March to October (migrants). The best viewing months for shorebirds run from August through December and March through October – practically year-round. Raptors are active throughout the year, and scores of wading birds are refuge residents.

Stop at the headquarters to pick up a bird checklist and site maps. The refuge roads offer good vantage points from which to birdwatch, or walk along Whitetail Ridge Trail, a quarter-mile trail that is closed to hunting. Look for the big riverboats, which can be seen "comin' round the bend" of the Mississippi several times a day.

HIGHLIGHTS

Every August the Natchez Birding Festival is held at the refuge. Highlights of this one-day celebration include birdwatching tours featuring the Cloverdale Unit, a bird-rich portion of the refuge usually closed to the public. Call the general information number below for details.

Site Map and Information

St. Catherine Creek National Wildlife Refuge

From Natchez, take Route 61 south 12 miles to Sibley. Turn right on York Road (just before reaching the Sibley post office) and continue 2 miles to Pintail Lane. Turn left; refuge headquarters are just .7 mile away.

Daily, sunrise to sunset, year-round.

Some areas may be closed occasionally because of flooding.

St. Catherine Creek National Wildlife Refuge, PO Box 117, Sibley, MS 39165. Refuge headquarters, which function as a Visitor Center, are open weekdays, 7:30 a.m.–4 p.m.

(601) 442-6696; www.SaintCatherineCreek@fws.gov

$5 for a day-use pass; $12.50 for an annual public-use permit. Admission for visitors who are under 16, over 65, or wheelchair-dependent is free.

Refuge headquarters are wheelchair accessible.

None on-site.

None.

Several hotels and motels are available in nearby Natchez. For listings of bed-and-breakfasts in the area, call the Pilgrimage Garden Club at (601) 445-4420.

Odiorne Point State Park

No need to brave summer seacoast crowds – New Hampshire's best birds are winter residents and spring migrants, many found at this state park.

Was it sweeping views of the Atlantic Ocean and rocky shores at Odiorne Point that attracted Englishman David Thompson to establish New Hampshire's first permanent settlement here in 1623? For the 10,000 years previous, this coastal wilderness drew the people of the Pennacook and Abnaki tribes only during the summers. However, with the advent of Europeans, the Native American way of life died out, replaced by farming and commercial fishing. European settlement spread along the coast and up the Piscataqua River for 400 years, gradually developing into summer estates and large seaside resorts.

The Semipalmated Plover *visits Odiorne's beaches during migration.*

World War II again brought drastic change to the area, when the federal government purchased all Odiorne Point property, closed off access, and built massive bunkers and supply structures. For the next 20 years, Odiorne Point became known as Fort Dearborn. In 1961 the 330-acre Fort Dearborn site was sold to the state of New Hampshire for $91,000 and Odiorne Point State Park was born.

Habitat

Just 18 miles long, the New Hampshire seacoast is the shortest of all the coastal states', but it has much to offer. Although the coast is home to a number of public beaches and parks, Odiorne Point State Park provides the greatest array of habitats – from tide pools to forestland. Remnants of formal gardens, overgrown military bunkers, and a man-made cattail marsh only add to the variety. An ocean jetty, some small pebbled beaches, and a saltmarsh complete the mosaic. Popular creatures here include the hermit crabs, sea stars, and snails of the intertidal zone. The avian representatives range from sea ducks to gulls to songbirds.

Bird Life

At the southern end of Odiorne Point State Park, just south of the main parking lot, lies a tidepool-filled inlet known as Sunken Forest. Here, at low

---

BIRDS TO LOOK FOR

Red-throated Loon • Horned Grebe • Red-necked Grebe • Common Eider • White-winged Scoter • Black Scoter • Oldsquaw • Sharp-shinned Hawk • Merlin • Peregrine Falcon • Semi-palmated Plover • Semipalmated Sandpiper • Purple Sandpiper • Black Guillemot • Yellow-billed Cuckoo • Magnolia Warbler

Waterfowl such as the Oldsquaw may be observed along the park's rocky coastline.

tide, children love to search for mussels, rock crabs, and other sea life. Also on the hunt are Black-crowned Night-Herons, Herring Gulls, and, in winter, Purple Sandpipers.

Along the rocky coast directly in front of the Seacoast Science Center, rafts of wintering waterfowl, including scoters (Surf, Black, and White-winged), loons (Common and Red-throated), and grebes (Horned and Red-necked), are a major winter attraction, starting in October. Look among the offshore groups for Common Eider, Oldsquaw, and Black Guillemots, too. During migration the contiguous shore attracts shorebirds that include Ruddy Turnstones, Semipalmated Plovers, and Semipalmated Sandpipers.

North of the science center a maze of trails leads through some of the best habitat for songbird migrants along the seacoast. Throughout the month of May, Magnolia Warblers, Blackpolls, and

American Redstarts, along with Blue-headed Vireos and both Yellow-billed and Black-billed Cuckoos, captivate the many birdwatchers who come for the spring migration.

In the fall hawk migration is never a disappointment here. Less than a mile north of the main parking lot, what looks like a hill is actually an overgrown military bunker called the Seaman Battery. From the top of this bunker, from September through October, hawks fly by at eye level, sometimes hundreds in a day. Look for Osprey, Northern Harriers, Sharp-shinned and Cooper's Hawks, Peregrine Falcons, Merlins, and American Kestrels.

The Red-throated Loon *is found intermingling here with the Common Loon and other waterbirds.*

From the hawk-watching spot, a freshwater marsh is also visible. A hike to the marsh in summer often yields Marsh Wrens and nesting Virginia Rails. But for mud flat and saltmarsh habitat, visit the boat launch site, about one mile north on Route 1A. This is a good place to look for Lesser and Greater Yellowlegs and Black-bellied Plovers during low tide. A trail leads along the saltmarsh area, which in the winter often shelters ducks including Buffleheads and Common Goldeneyes.

VISITING

The New Hampshire seacoast fills with crowds in the summer, and the birding is not at its most productive in June and July. Many birdwatchers cannot resist August, however, when shorebird migration begins. Birding along the park's seacoast is productive from the beginning of shorebird migration in August through the songbird migration in May.

HIGHLIGHTS

Learn about the habitats that sustain the birds of Odiorne Point at the on-site Seacoast Science Center. Exhibits feature both natural and human history. The center is open daily, 10 a.m.–5 p.m.; admission is just $1, and children under 5 enter for free.

Site Map and Information

ODIORNE POINT STATE PARK

🚗 The Seacoast Science Center is located 3 miles south of Portsmouth on Route 1A. From the Portsmouth traffic circle, follow the Route 1 Bypass toward "Beaches and Hampton." Drive south 1.9 miles, past Yokens Restaurant. Turn left at the stoplight onto Elwyn Road. Continue for about 1.5 miles to the stop sign at the Foyes Corner intersection with Route 1A. Take Route 1A south. After 1.1 miles, look for the Odiorne Point State Park north parking area and boat launch on the left. The park's main entrance and the Seacoast Science Center are 0.7 mile farther south.

🚪 Daily, sunrise to sunset, year-round.

⬤ Never.

ℹ️ Odiorne Point State Park, New Hampshire Division of Parks, P.O. Box 606, Rye Beach, NH 03871. The Seacoast Science Center, open daily, 10 a.m.–5 p.m., functions as a Visitor Center.

📞 (603) 436-1552 (park information); (603) 436-8043 (Seacoast Science Center);

www.nhparks.state.nh/us or www.seacentr.org

💲 $2.50 per adult; free for seniors and children 12 and under.

♿ Seacoast Science Center and a number of paved paths are wheelchair accessible.

🅰 Contact the Seacoast Science Center for information about naturalist-led programs.

🏕 No camping on-site.

🏨 Hotels, motels, and bed-and-breakfasts available in nearby Portsmouth. Contact the Greater Portmouth Chamber of Commerce at (603) 436-1118 for listings.

EDWIN B. FORSYTHE
NATIONAL WILDLIFE REFUGE

This haven for waterbirds along southern New Jersey's coast is situated only eleven miles northeast of the bright lights and gambling palaces of Atlantic City.

Still known by veteran birdwatchers as Brigantine, its original name, this 43,000-acre coastal refuge was established in 1939 for a very specific purpose – to save two splendid waterfowl species from likely extinction. The fast-flying American Black Duck was expiring because of loss of coastal habitat, and a freak blight of eel grass in coastal locales had deprived the Brant goose of its primary food. The establishment of the Brigantine refuge saved the day for both species. In 1984 it was combined with the nearby Barnagat refuge to form the Edwin B. Forsythe National Wildlife Refuge. Today, as many as 200,000 birdwatchers visit this site annually to observe the more than 290 species seen in the area.

HABITAT

Salt meadow and salt marsh interspersed with ponds and shallow bays are the key components of the Forsythe habitat. Plants provide food for the thousands of waterfowl that drop down from the Atlantic flyway during spring and fall migration periods. And 5,000 acres of upland woods are the temporary or permanent home for a variety of land birds.

The management of Edwin B. Forsythe National Wildlife Refuge has helped create this bird-friendly terrain. Water levels in the almost 1,500 acres of water impoundments (both freshwater and brackish) are

controlled, ensuring optimum food supplies for visiting waterfowl and creating mud flats in the spring that attract a host of shorebirds.

The Savannah Sparrow *is one of a dozen sparrow species that may be spotted along the Woodland Trail.*

BIRD LIFE

One of the distinguishing aspects of Edwin B. Forsythe National Wildlife Refuge is that the needs of birders have been addressed just as carefully as the needs of the birds themselves. Even in winter months management has established special viewing locations from which to watch the Brant, Snow Geese, diving ducks, and raptors that remain on the refuge.

BIRDS TO LOOK FOR

Glossy Ibis • Snow Goose • Brant • Gadwall • American Black Duck • Blue-winged Teal • Semipalmated Plover • Greater Yellowlegs • Ruddy Turnstone • Short-billed Dowitcher • Black Skimmer • Red-bellied Woodpecker • Savannah Sparrow • Northern Cardinal •

This coastal park appeals to a range of water birds, such as the Black Skimmer.

They also have created the Wildlife Drive, an eight-mile auto tour loop, with 15 recommended stopping points that cover many of the refuge's key habitats. This wide road, which begins near refuge headquarters, is built over a system of dikes. Eventually the roadway passes by a 900-acre freshwater pond and an adjacent 700-acre brackish impoundment that are managed to attract an abundance of migrant waterfowl and shorebirds, as well as resident waders like the Glossy Ibis. The freshwater pond is alternately deepened or partially drained to achieve maximum growth of spikerush, which Blue-winged Teal, Gadwall, and Bufflehead, among others, feed on before going south for the winter.

Farther along the Wildlife Drive is Turtle Cove, where an observation tower affords the astounding view of breeding horseshoe crabs in April and May.

Their eggs become food for the refuge's sandpipers, 13 species in all, who are always on time for this annual event. These sandpipers include Ruddy Turnstones, Greater Yellowlegs, Short-billed Dowitchers, and Dunlins; four species of plovers, including Semipalmated and Black-bellied Plovers, are found at Edwin B. Forsythe National Wildlife Refuge as well. These shorebirds can also be seen probing the refuge's mud flats for food in late summer and early fall. Some gulls and terns, including Black Skimmer, nest here.

The salt marsh supports thousands of Brants and thousands more Snow Geese, which gather in large flocks to feed in November.

The Northern Cardinal *sings almost year round – listen for its loud whistling* cue cue cue *and* purty purty purty *songs.*

Although Forsythe was founded to provide habitat for waterfowl, its forests draw songbirds, from swallows to larks to vireos. A walk along the Woodland Trail provides good opportunities to study the refuge's warblers (25 species in all), including Yellow, Prairie, and Blackpoll Warblers. Other sightings in this forest habitat may include the Red-bellied Woodpecker; sparrows, such as Savannah and Seaside; and standbys like the Northern Cardinal.

VISITING

Spring and fall are the optimum birdwatching seasons at Edwin B. Forsythe National Wildlife Refuge. Unfortunately, they are also times when biting insects are busy. Bring insect repellant and stay on the trails to avoid ticks, especially during summer, when they are most active. The speed limit on the Wildlife Drive is 15 mph and no bikes or motorized vehicles are allowed on the trails – regulations that encourage careful observation and discourage habitat damage.

HIGHLIGHTS

The refuge's most breathtaking event is surely the arrival of thousands upon thousands of migrant Snow Geese and Brant. Visit in late fall to see this spectacle, which is more than worth the effort.

Site Map and Information

EDWIN B. FORSYTHE NATIONAL WILDLIFE REFUGE

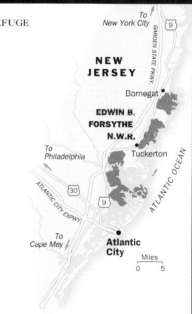

🚗 From Atlantic City take Rt. 30 west to its intersection with Rt. 9, then follow Rt. 9 north to reach refuge headquarters and the entrance.

🕐 Daily, sunrise to sunset, year-round.

⬤ Never.

ℹ️ Edwin B. Forsythe National Wildlife Refuge, Great Creek Road, P.O. Box 72, Oceanville, NJ 08231-0072. Refuge headquarters, open daily, 9 a.m.–5 p.m., functions as a Visitor Center.

📞 (609) 652-1665

$ Entrances fees for Wildlife Drive and the associated foot trails are collected at two self-service sites.

♿ Refuge headquarters, the Wildlife Drive (explored by car), and the first 700 yards of Leeds Eco-Trail are wheelchair accessible.

🅰 Not allowed on-site, but commercial campgrounds are available along Rt. 9, to the north and south.

🚻 None.

🏨 Plenty of hotels and motels are available in nearby Atlantic City.

CENTRAL PARK

An abundance of birds and birdwatchers happily coexist in New York City's Central Park, amidst concerts, ball games, horse-drawn carriages, and more.

"Revolutions are all caused by poets," according to England's Percy Bysshe Shelley. Poet (and Evening Post editor) William Cullen Bryant supported this claim when in 1844 he raised the call for a vast public park in New York City. The idea caught hold, and in 1853 a 750-acre site above 59th Street was selected for the park, north of where Manhattan's 300,000 residents lived at the time.

Architect Frederick Law Olmsted and his partner, Calvert Vaux, won the public competition for a park design, and the majestic but welcoming pastoral park was completed by 1873. Today the Central Park Conservancy manages the park under a contract with the City of New York Parks and Recreation Department, and the park's green acres have become a vital part of this energetic city and a refuge to more than 200 species of birds.

The Scarlet Tanager *adds a dash of color to the urban park.*

HABITAT

Central Park spans 643 acres, from 59th Street on the south to 110th Street on the north; Central Park West and Fifth Avenue form its western and eastern borders. Enclosed within this sanctuary are widely varying habitats that draw a truly astounding number of birds year-round. The park's freshwater habitats, including the Lake, Turtle Pond, the Jacqueline Kennedy Onassis Reservoir, and two streams, provide fish and aquatic plants for food and small islands for safe nesting. The open grassy expanses and field edges of areas such as the Great Lawn and woodlands like the Ramble attract their own bird constituencies.

Central Park's most distinguishing marks were made 18,000 years ago, when the last ice age glacier rolled over the area. It piled ice as high as some of the city's tallest skyscrapers, leaving behind grooves and striation marks still visible on rocky outcroppings.

BIRDS TO LOOK FOR

Great Egret • Black-crowned Night-Heron • Mute Swan • Northern Shoveler • Red-tailed Hawk • Long-eared Owl • Blue-headed Vireo • Veery • Hermit Thrush • Magnolia Warbler • Black-and-white Warbler • Scarlet Tanager • Song Sparrow • Red-winged Blackbird

BIRD LIFE

New Yorkers love to share good birdwatching news about Central Park; in fact, there are those who have made it their life's hobby to identify and study the park's birds. A case in point is the special relationship between an owl and a man. For the

The Magnolia Warbler is one of the birds to enjoy in Frederick Law Olmsted's park.

last five years, this Long-eared Owl has claimed a branch of a Norway spruce near a busy footpath, just south of the Metropolitan Museum of Art. For the same length of time, Merrill Higgins has used his weekends to focus a scope on the silent owl and invite passersby to take a look.

Farther south two Red-tailed Hawks nest on a sculptured ledge above an elegant Fifth Avenue apartment. This pair of hawks soar over Central Park so often and appear on the news so frequently that local birdwatchers can recognize them immediately.

Consult the volunteers at any of the Visitor Centers for information about sitings. They may suggest checking out Turtle Pond, where a circle of Northern Shovelers are beating their wings, or the Lake, where a pair of Mute Swans and their young have been sighted. Black-crowned Night-Herons are year-round residents, but adept at screening their

movements, while Great and Snowy Egrets are easier to spot on the park's waters. In spring and fall, Snow Geese and Brant may be sighted flying over the park, but they rarely descend.

The perimeter of open fields attract the familiar but no less welcome Red-winged Blackbird and 11 species of sparrows, including Chipping and Song Sparrows, which coexist with the noisy crow. The Northern Mockingbird's forever-changing songs announce its whereabouts throughout the park. Other insect-eaters include the Chimney Swift, Tree Swallow, and Northern Rough-winged Swallow.

Northern Shovelers *and a variety of other waterfowl may be observed at Turtle Pond.*

Wooded areas, most notably the North Woods and the Ramble, draw a host of migrant songbirds, including the Black-billed Cuckoo, Hermit Thrush, Veery, Red-eyed and Blue-headed Vireos, Scarlet Tanager, and many warblers, including Black-and-White and Magnolia Warblers. The Kentucky, Prothonotary, and Cerulean Warblers are the first of the spring warblers, while the Connecticut Warbler makes an arrival in the fall.

VISITING

Although spring and fall are the prime birdwatching seasons, Central Park's species mix makes any time of year rewarding. Most importantly, leave your car at home. Public transportation to the park's many access points is fast and plentiful, and walking is the best way to enjoy its bird life.

HIGHLIGHTS

From mid-August through September, birders should spend time hawk-watching with the staff at Belvedere Castle. With a spotting scope, visitors can observe Sharp-shinned and Broad-winged Hawks, Bald Eagles, Turkey Vultures, and Osprey.

Site Map and Information

CENTRAL PARK

🚗 Cabs are plentiful and city buses and subways stop at or near all park entrances. Parking spaces are available along Fifth Avenue, but they fill rapidly, so public transportation is advised.

🕐 Daily, sunrise to 9 p.m., year-round.

⬤ Never.

ℹ️ Central Park, c/o Central Park Conservancy, 14 E. 60th St., 8th floor, New York, NY 10022. The Park has 4 Visitor Centers: the Dairy in mid-park at 65th Street; Belvedere Castle in mid-Park at 79th Street; North Meadow Recreation Center in mid-Park at 97th Street; and the Charles A. Dana Discovery Center at 110th Street near Fifth Avenue. These are open Tuesday through Sunday, 10 a.m.–5 p.m.

☎ (212) 310-6600; www.centralparknyc.org

Ⓢ None.

♿ All Visitor Centers except the Dairy are wheelchair accessible, as are many of the park's trails and walkways. To reach the TTY, call (800) 281-5722.

⛺ No camping permitted on-site.

🚶 The Urban Park Rangers sponsor tours, nature center talks, and an annual hawk watch; call (212) 360-2774. The Central Park Conservancy conducts monthly bird walks; call (212) 360-3444. Free

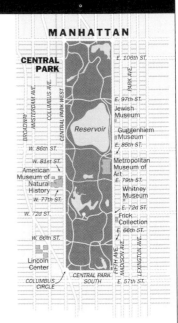

birdwatching kits are available at Belvedere Castle; call (212) 772-1210 for details.

🏨 Hotels, motels, and bed-and-breakfasts are abundant in Manhattan and surrounding boroughs. Call the New York Convention and Visitors Bureau at (212) 484-1232 for listings.

MONTEZUMA NATIONAL WILDLIFE REFUGE

The deep serenity of the New York Finger Lakes region is felt in this resting place for migrant birds – often many thousands strong.

This central New York haven, north of Cayuga Lake and about midway between the cities of Rochester and Syracuse, was conceived in 1938 as a refuge and breeding ground for migratory birds and other wildlife.

In the 1970s the Bald Eagle was succumbing to new pesticides, loss of habitat, and illegal killings and it faced extinction across the United States. The refuge was selected by the New York State Department of Environmental Conservation (acting jointly with the U.S. Fish and Wildlife Service) to initiate programs that would take young, nesting-age Bald Eagles into captivity to prepare them for life in a more benign, pesticides-controlled environment. Thanks to these efforts, the Bald Eagle is again riding the skies above Montezuma, healthy and free.

The Baltimore Oriole *male has a black hood and back with a bright orange rump and chest; females are brownish-olive on top and orange underneath.*

BIRDS TO LOOK FOR

American Bittern • Great Blue Heron • Canada Goose • Tundra Swan • Wood Duck • Blue-winged Teal • Green-winged Teal • Osprey • Bald Eagle • Red-tailed Hawk • Killdeer • Belted Kingfisher • American Pipit • Cerulean Warbler • Baltimore Oriole

HABITAT

Montezuma National Wildlife Refuge is set in the beautiful Finger Lakes, which stretch north and south across central New York like an extended hand. Its 7,400 acres are broken up by diked pools in which submergent and emergent vegetation thrives. This food source acts like a magnet, attracting thousands of ducks and geese traveling the lanes of the Atlantic flyway overhead. Bald Eagles find good nesting sites in this lake country. The refuge also possesses grass, brush, and wooded sections that suit the lifestyles of a variety of migrant songbirds.

BIRD LIFE

Eagles, understandably, are the primary draw for many birdwatchers who choose to visit Montezuma, but this small refuge supports incredible numbers of waterbirds as well, which are present in peak numbers from mid-September until temperatures drop and the ice forms. During this time, 50,000 Canada Geese and as many Mallards may be on hand, as well as 25,000 Black Ducks. A mid-September peak is registered by Killdeer and Greater and Lesser Yellowlegs, who remain on guard for hungry hawks while they forage in marshes and mud flats for food. Green-winged and Blue-winged Teal, as well as that sleek

A juvenile Bald Eagle (left) takes four or five years to achieve its full adult plumage.

and colorful swimmer, the Wood Duck, are also plentiful.

Waders of interest include nesting colonies of Great Blue Herons and Black-crowned Night-Herons, which draw their share of visitors. True to its name, the latter squawks unmusically all night long. Egrets and American Bitterns are also busy hunters throughout the summer.

Songbirds are abundant at this hospitable refuge too. Warblers are always welcome and Montezuma has 27 different species lending dabs of color to its woods and grasslands. It's almost certain that an Eastern Wood-Pewee will make birders' sightings lists, although it takes sharp eyes to follow the aerial dartings of these small birds. Look for Baltimore Orioles too. Somehow, the ubiquitous House Sparrow has not invaded the refuge, but less aggressive sparrow species – 13 in all – have filled that gap, including the Fox Sparrow. The White-throated Sparrow stays on through the winter, sometimes singing all night long when the moon is full.

The Canada Goose *is easily identified by its black head and neck and the distinctive white "strap" under its chin.*

Ospreys are another sure bet at Montezuma. The watery terrain suits these raptors, which find plentiful fish in the diked ponds. Seven different hawks also hunt throughout the refuge, but only the Red-tailed Hawk is present in good numbers.

VISITING

The spring migrations of waterfowl to the refuge start in late February and continue through the end of April.

Songbird arrival time is generally from the end of April through the third week in May, and early morning viewing is rewarded by sightings of a large warbler population visible from various points along Esker Brook Trail. The broods of several duck species appear by early May and swim with confidence as the summer wears on. The Main Pool is a favorite heron haunt, particularly because the adjacent wooded area is good for nesting. Shorebird watching is best in mid-September.

The 3.5-mile Wildlife Drive provides an excellent overview of the refuge, and the site's numerous walking trails can be traveled easily in all but the most inclement weather. Since the recent restoration of the marshlands, visitors can view the

bounty enjoyed by the Iroquois natives and early white settlers who fished and hunted in this region.

Winter is generally quiet as far as bird life is concerned. Most of the shallow pools quickly freeze over, forcing most of the overwintering birds to move to nearby Cayuga and Seneca Lakes. The Visitor Center shuts down in November.

HIGHLIGHTS

The pride and joy of Montezuma National Wildlife Refuge is its success in reintroducing the Bald Eagle to New York State. Therefore, a climb up the refuge's observation tower to witness these great raptors in flight is an essential feature of any trip to this site.

Site Map and Information

MONTEZUMA NATIONAL WILDLIFE REFUGE

From Syracuse or Rochester, take the New York State Thruway (I-90) to Route 414 south (exit 41). Follow it for about 200 yards, then make a left onto Route 318 east. Continue for just over 5 miles, then turn east onto Routes 5 and 20 East; follow for 1.25 miles to refuge entrance.

Daily, sunrise to sunset, year-round.

Never.

Montezuma National Wildlife Refuge, 3395 Routes 5 and 20 East, Seneca Falls, NY 13148. Visitor Center open April through November, generally 10 a.m.–3 p.m. weekdays and until 4 p.m. on weekends. Call ahead for exact schedule.

(315) 568-5987; www.fws.gov/r5mnwr

None.

Wheelchair-accessible buildings and parking facilities.

None on-site. Campgrounds available in nearby Cayuga State Park.

None.

Bed-and-breakfasts and motels are available in nearby Waterloo, Seneca Falls, and Auburn.

MATTAMUSKEET NATIONAL WILDLIFE REFUGE

Fifteen miles long, and only a swan's neck deep, Lake Mattamuskeet in eastern North Carolina is perfect winter quarters for thousands of waterfowl.

Nature writer Rachel Carson never forgot her mid-1940s stay at Mattamuskeet National Wildlife Refuge. She wrote in a letter to friends about the constant haunting music of the geese. Carson was not alone in being moved; every fall, visitors to North Carolina's largest natural lake are touched by the abundance of wintering birds at the 50,180-acre refuge, which was designated a national wildlife refuge in 1934.

HABITAT

The Mattamuskeet National Wildlife Refuge lies only a few feet above sea level, inland from the Outer Banks of North Carolina, and in the midst of extensive farmlands. In addition to the 40,000-acre lake, the refuge covers more than 10,000 acres of marsh, timber, and agricultural lands. Loblolly pine, bald cypress, and mixed hardwoods dominate the forests. This rich habitat is home to gray foxes, white-tailed deer, muskrats, raccoons, and an occasional American alligator.

BIRD LIFE

During early winter, Mattamuskeet becomes one of the premier birdwatching hot spots on the southeast coastal plain. Since it lies in the middle of the Atlantic flyway, the refuge draws large numbers of Canada Geese, Snow Geese, Tundra Swans and 18 species of ducks to overwinter on the refuge.

The five-mile-long causeway that transects the lake (State Highway 94) provides some of the best views of waterfowl you're ever likely to have.

Before reaching the water, stop at the pine trees at the refuge boundary to check for Brown-headed Nuthatches, which are present year-round on the refuge. Their characteristic "rubber ducky" squeak makes this southeastern specialty easy to spot.

Continuing on NC 94 just a bit, check the marsh to the left for Wood Ducks, Ring-necked Ducks, and Hooded Mergansers in the winter. In spring listen for the unmistakable ringing *zweet* notes of Prothonotary Warblers. Look for their nests – the

Orchard Orioles *nest at Mattamuskeet; look for them in the shrubby areas along Wildlife Drive.*

BIRDS TO LOOK FOR

Pied-billed Grebe • Tundra Swan • Wood Duck • Gadwall • American Black Duck • Lesser Scaup • Hooded Merganser • Pileated Woodpecker • Red-eyed Vireo • Brown-headed Nuthatch • Prothonotary Warbler • Ovenbird • Orchard Oriole

The large Pileated Woodpecker may be seen, and heard, in marshes and swamps.

Prothonotary is the only eastern warbler to nest in tree cavities, and they prefer them to be near water.

Out on the causeway proper, prepare to see a large number of winter duck and goose species, especially in mid-November though mid-December. Birdwatchers may be able to check off Mallards, American Black Ducks, Gadwall, Green-winged Teal, American Wigeon, Northern Pintail, and Northern Shovelers. In addition, numerous species of diving ducks will be found – including Canvasbacks, Ruddy Ducks, and Lesser Scaup. Tundra Swans are another big attraction along the refuge's causeway.

There is more to the refuge than the causeway in winter, of course. Wildlife Drive runs beside either marsh or lake for most of its length and provides good birdwatching in any season. Look for Pied-billed Grebe in the marshy areas, and for a variety of songbirds in the shrubby areas. During breeding season, watch for Eastern Kingbirds and Orchard Orioles. Near the beginning of Wildlife Drive, a new boardwalk trail loops through a marsh and cypress swamp, where you should look for Pileated and Red-Bellied Woodpeckers, American Black Ducks, Wood Ducks, and a resident Great Horned Owl.

A common sound heard on summer walks near the wooded areas along Wildlife Drive is a hollow, wooden *kuk-kuk-kuk*, ending with a *kowlp, kowlp!* The caller is the Yellow-billed Cuckoo, a member of a bird family that is widespread in other parts of the world but is represented in the United States by only a few species, including the Greater Roadrunner.

Pied-billed Grebes *feature a bold black ring around a white bill during the breeding season.*

At the west end of the refuge, near Rose Bay Canal, a mature pine and hardwood forest is home to several Barred Owls and Red-shouldered Hawks. To reach the area, follow US 264 west from headquarters and turn right onto SR 1304. After about five miles, the road crosses Rose Bay Canal; the parking area here is surrounded by woods. Exploring the edge of this area can yield big results. Early in breeding season, look for Ovenbirds, Wood Thrushes, and Red-eyed Vireo.

VISITING

Summer is hot and humid, with temperatures occasionally climbing above 95°F. Spring, best for migrating songbirds and nesting specialties, is pleasant, as is fall. Winter visitors will find mild, oftenff rainy weather, but temperatures seldom go below 30°F.

HIGHLIGHTS

On the first weekend in December the refuge and the nearby community of Swan Quarter celebrate the Swan Days Festival. Craft and food vendors populate the historic lodge/pumping station at headquarters, and van tours leave every morning to birdwatch in areas of the refuge normally off-limits to visitors. Write the refuge for tour reservations (a small fee is charged).

Site Map and Information

MATTAMUSKEET NATIONAL WILDLIFE REFUGE

🚗 From Washington, NC, take US 264 east 70 miles to refuge entrance. From Williamston, take Highway 64 east 45 miles to Highway 94, then continue south 35 miles to refuge entrance.

🚻 Daily, sunrise to sunset, year-round.

⬤ During December and January, Wildlife Drive is closed until 1 p.m. on Tuesdays, Wednesdays, Fridays, and Saturdays. However, the causeway that transects Lake Mattamuskeet is open for birdwatching at these times.

ℹ️ Mattamuskeet National Wildlife Refuge, 38 Mattamuskeet Road, Swan Quarter, NC 27885. Refuge headquarters, which functions as a small Visitor Center, is open weekdays, 7:30 a.m.–4 p.m. The lodge/pumping station located adjacent to headquarters is a national historic building that houses displays of interest to birdwatchers; it is open Tuesday through Saturday, 8 a.m.–4:30 p.m.

📞 (252) 926-4021; www.fws.gov/mattamuskeet

💲 None

♿ Refuge headquarters, all observation platforms, and the boardwalk trail near headquarters are wheelchair accessible.

🏕️ Gull Rock Campground is nearby; call (252) 925-4641 for information.

🚌 Mattamuskeet Wildlife Tours, (252) 926-1881

🏨 Hotel Engelhard is within ten minutes of refuge headquarters; call (800) 290-5311. Or call the Greater Hyde County Chamber of Commerce at (252) 925-5201 for additional listings.

PEA ISLAND NATIONAL WILDLIFE REFUGE

No more than a speck on the map, this peaceful North Carolina sanctuary is the winter home to thousands of migrant birds.

One of the densest bird populations in the United States might never have developed were it not for a small pink-and-lavender-flowered plant. Called "dune peas" by fishermen and the few local inhabitants, this plant produces nutritious beans that have been a key food for the thousands of Snow Geese that have wintered on this coastal island for years. Human efforts, including the manipulation of water levels in refuge impoundments, have also contributed to an environment that is attractive to more than 300 species of birds found at Pea Island National Wildlife Refuge throughout the year.

The Parasitic Jaeger, *a predatory seabird, takes four years to reach adult plumage.*

HABITAT
This 5,915-acre island refuge off the Atlantic Coast contains a profuse mix of beachfront, freshwater and brackish ponds, salt marshes, tidal creeks, and small bays. Pamlico Sound, an estuary between the barrier islands and the mainland, is an important breeding and resting area for birds and, in addition to the island's interior ponds and wetlands, an important food supply.

Pea Island is of modest proportions, with widths ranging from a few hundred yards to just half a mile and elevations varying from sea level to 17 feet. Sand dunes were built to protect manmade features such as the impoundments, which could easily have been destroyed by high tide.

BIRD LIFE
This tiny refuge offers year-round birdwatching pleasures. In spring and fall, witness the ducks, geese, and warblers that stop over. Summer is nesting time for herons, egrets, ibis, terns, Piping Plovers, and gulls, and migrant ducks and geese winter here by the thousands.

In short, Pea Island deserves the nickname "Catch-up Island." Here birders can fill their notebooks with new sightings not featured at even some of the largest parks and reserves.

For those hoping to add waterfowl to their life lists, Pea

BIRD TO LOOK FOR

Common Loon • Snow Goose • Tundra Swan • American Black Duck • Northern Shoveler • Surf Scoter • Red-breasted Merganser • Peregrine Falcon • Piping Plover • Greater Yellowlegs • Dunlin • Parasitic Jaeger • Bonaparte's Gull • Great Black-backed Gull • Black Skimmer • Seaside Sparrow

Occasional Surf Scoters can be spotted from the beaches of this island refuge.

Island attracts more than 30 species to its wetlands, impoundments, and sounds. American Black Ducks, Northern Pintail, Buffleheads, Red-breasted Mergansers, and Ruddy Ducks are abundant; also seen are Green-winged and Blue-winged Teal, American Wigeon, and Northern Shovelers. Occasionally Black and Surf Scoters can be spotted from the beaches as well. Snow Geese are best seen from mid-November to early March. Tundra Swans are also found here; look in the refuge's ponds and marshy areas.

Birdwatchers without much access to northern waters can make up for that void here. Both the Common and Red-throated Loon may be seen offshore, leaving northern lakes long before they freeze over. Common Loons use the ponds from time to time, and Red-throated Loons may be spotted flying over the refuge, but only rarely.

This refuge is a sandpiper mecca, boasting more than 30 overwintering species. Easily spotted are Dunlins, Greater Yellowlegs, Sanderlings, Western and Least Sandpipers, and Red and Wilson's Phalaropes. American Avocets and Black-necked Stilts are regulars on the refuge's beaches.

Bonaparte's Gull *is one of many gulls that display a dark hood in summer.*

Many gulls and terns are residents and can be found in the island's marshes, sand flats, and beaches. Look for the refuge's dozen species of gulls, including Great Black-backed, Bonaparte's, and Herring Gulls, plus Black Skimmers, Least Terns, and five other species of terns.

The absence of dense foliage in this sea-washed haven makes binocular sweeps rewarding. Look for raptors such as the Northern Harrier and Peregrine Falcon in flight. Seaside Sparrows are common. Spotting scopes turned seaward may spy large seabirds, from the hard-to-locate shearwaters to Northern Gannets and Pomarine, Parasitic, and Long-tailed Jaegers, although these birds often spend their time on open ocean.

VISITING

Birdwatchers are welcomed to Pea Island year-round, but they are asked to respect the refuge's primary mission: to create optimum conditions for the birds and other wildlife that inhabit the island.

HIGHLIGHTS

Every fall, usually in early November, Pea Island National Wildlife Refuge hosts "Wings over Water," a three-day event dedicated to its rich and varied bird life. Field trips and workshops are offered. At a recent celebration more than 200 species were identified over the weekend. For details call the general information number below.

Site Map and Information

PEA ISLAND NATIONAL WILDLIFE REFUGE

From Nags Head, take Route 12 south 26 miles to reach the Visitor Center; from Buxton, take Route 12 north 37 miles.

Daily, sunrise to sunset, year-round.

Never.

Pea Island National Wildlife Refuge, PO Box 1969, Manteo, NC 27954. The Visitor Center is open daily, 9 a.m.–4 p.m., May through October, and Thursday through Sunday, 9 a.m.–4 p.m., November through April.

(252) 473-1131; www.outer-banks.com/coastal-wildlife

None.

The Visitor Center and North Pond Wildlife Trail are wheelchair accessible. Wheelchairs may be borrowed at the Visitor Center.

Not permitted on Pea Island. Campgrounds are available March through November at Cape Hatteras KOA Campground, which is on the mainland nearby; call (800) KOA-5268 for details.

Birdwatching tours are offered in summer and fall; call the Visitor Center for details.

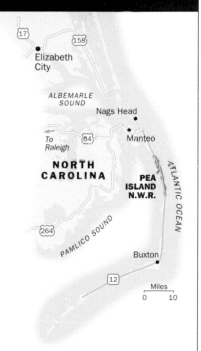

None on-site, but lodgings are available in nearby Buxton, Nags Head, Manteo, Kill Devil Hills, and Ocracoke; call the Outer Banks Chamber of Commerce at (252) 441-8144 for listings.

HAWK MOUNTAIN SANCTUARY

Every fall this central Pennsylvania bird sanctuary provides a deeply satisfying experience: the chance to watch thousands of migratory raptors passing overhead.

Hawk Mountain Sanctuary straddles Kittatinny Ridge, a 300-mile-long mountain chain that forms the southeastern spine of the central Appalachian Mountains. Founded in 1934, this rugged 2,400-acre nature preserve was the world's first refuge for predatory birds. Many birdwatchers still consider it the very best spot in the United States from which to view raptors in their migratory flights.

The Northern Goshawk *hunts its prey from a perch or by flying low over the ground.*

HABITAT

What makes Hawk Mountain so special, even to veteran bird watchers? It's the accommodating winds that visit it daily. For 65 years naturalists have recognized the importance of this busy spot on the Appalachian flyway, where crosswinds roll head-on into Kittatinny Ridge, creating updrafts and thermals that act as an invisible stairway. The winds lift raptors thousands of feet before the birds continue soaring south again to warmer lands and fresh food. Singly or in groups, they travel over Hawk Mountain's eastern deciduous forest, the Little Schuykill River, and a boulder field that is 15,000 years old. But the prime viewing spot is North Lookout, a 1,521-foot-tall vantage point just one mile from the Visitor Center, where much of the best hawk watching takes place.

BIRD LIFE

Three of the fall raptor migrants take obvious advantage of the powerful updrafts and air "pools" that form on Kittatinny Ridge. When a raptor sails by, making two successive flaps with its wings, followed by a glide, then another two-and-one sequence, it is probably a Sharp-shinned Hawk, a Cooper's Hawk, or a Northern Goshawk. A somewhat reluctant fellow-traveler to South America is the Osprey, which must leave behind the collection of old muskrat skulls and lost car keys that it busily crams into its large, untidy nest for decoration.

Often before its migration begins from Hawk Mountain, the Northern Harrier enchants visitors with its marital antics. With unerring marksmanship and a heads-up cry to alert his mate waiting expectantly below, he tosses a choice food morsel to

---

BIRD TO LOOK FOR

Black Vulture • Osprey • Bald Eagle • Northern Harrier • Sharp-shinned Hawk • Cooper's Hawk • Northern Goshawk • Broad-winged Hawk • Red-tailed Hawk • American Kestrel • Merlin • Peregrine Falcon • Scarlet Tanager • Indigo Bunting

---

The Merlin is just one of many raptors observed passing over during migration.

her from on high. For sheer flying chutzpah, top honors belong to the young Broad-winged Hawks, some of which have had only four or five hours of flying before starting out on their two month trip to another continent. Look for Black Vultures, which are sanctuary residents, scavenging in open areas or, from time to time, in the garbage.

The parade of raptors heading south above Kittatinny Ridge begins in earnest about mid-September. Broad-winged Hawks, the most numerous of the migrating raptors, begin active and heavy migrations in mid-September, flaunting their conspicuous white tail bands as they pass over. Ospreys, Bald Eagles, American Kestrels, and Merlins also get busy then. Late September

The American Kestrel *has a shrill call that sounds like* **killy killy killy.**

and early October is migrating time for Sharp-shinned Hawks, and in early November the Red-tailed Hawk finally heads south.

The migrations-in-progress over the sanctuary are so concentrated that biologists come here from all over to compare notes and study the annual counts kept by a dedicated staff, including some volunteers skilled in deciphering various plumages, wing spans, and silhouettes.

VISITING

Raptor watchers, like the strong birds they study, are apparently a hardy bunch, coming to Hawk Mountain in both fair weather and foul. Visitors sometimes have to battle stiff winds on their way to the best observation points, and hike up and down rocky and ungraded pathways. The

87

sanctuary's trails are clearly marked, however, although the staff strongly suggests allowing enough time to arrive back at the Visitor Center before darkness falls.

The rewards for these climbs are tremendous panoramic views of the Appalachian ridges, and a visibility range of up to 70 miles. The Scenic Lookout Trail, a one-mile hike to the North Lookout, offers a great view of fall-raptor activity. Those with stout hearts and good hiking shoes will find additional challenges in the round trip River of Rocks Trail, which passes by

bogs, the ice age boulder field, and large stands of tulip poplars. It's a rough four-mile trip, out and back, but the songbird sightings along the way are well worth the effort.

HIGHLIGHTS

Although raptors are the stars of Hawk Mountain Sanctuary, migrating passerines pass through in spring. Look for bright beauties such as Indigo Bunting and Scarlet Tanager, plus a host of warblers during the first two weeks of May.

Site Map and Information

Hawk Mountain Sanctuary

🚗 From Reading take Route 61 north 4.5 miles to Molino. Turn right on Route 895 and continue 2.5 miles to Drehersville, then turn right again onto Hawk Mountain Road and follow it into the sanctuary.

🕐 Daily, sunrise to sunset, year-round.

🌑 Never.

ℹ️ Hawk Mountain Sanctuary Association, 1700 Hawk Mountain Road, Kempton, PA 19529. The Visitor Center is open daily, 9 a.m.–5 p.m., from December through August, and 8 a.m.–5 p.m., from September through November.

📞 (610) 756-6000; www.hawkmountain.org

💲 $4 for adults; $3 for seniors; $2 for children (6–12); and free for children under 6. Weekends from September through November, admission is $6 for adults; $4 for seniors; and $3 for children (6–12).

♿ The South Lookout is wheelchair accessible and only one-third of a mile from the Visitor Center.

🅰️ Five sites are available nearby: Appalachian Campsites (in Shartlesville), Blue Rocks Campground (near

Lenhartsville), Christmas Pines Campground (near Auburn), Pine Hill Campground (near Krumsville), and Robin Hill Camp Resort (near Lenhartsville).

👥 School and other groups can arrange weekday tours; call the Visitor Center for details.

🛏️ Motels and bed-and-breakfasts are available in nearby Schuylkill Haven; call the Visitors Bureau at (800) 765-7282 for listings.

PRESQUE ISLE STATE PARK

This lakeside western Pennsylvania park shelters more threatened, endangered, and rare birds than the balance of this expansive state.

The 3,200-acre peninsula known as Presque Isle juts out from Pennsylvania northeast into Lake Erie about seven miles. This strip of land is remembered as the site of a small but significant event in American history. Here, using local lumber, U.S. Admiral Oliver Hazard Perry supervised the building of an 11-ship fleet, which he used to destroy British control of the Great Lakes. After winning the fierce Battle of Sandusky on April 10, 1813, Perry and his ships remained in Presque Isle Bay, guarding against further British attacks, until after the War of 1812.

Today Presque Isle State Park continues its own battle: the fight to halt beach erosion of this fragile peninsula, exceptional for its abundant bird life. More than 325 species have been identified at Presque Isle State Park, with shorebirds representing the largest numbers.

HABITAT

It is a little hard to believe that this relatively small peninsula, composed primarily of sand, encompasses six different habitats. These include Lake Erie and its shorelines and bays, sand dunes and ridges, and ponds, sand plains, and marshes. The area also possesses thickets and forest, including the red oak and cottonwood trees visible soon after passing through the park entrance.

The Long-billed Dowitcher *uses its long straight bill to feed in the muddy waters of Presque Isle State Park.*

However, no habitat can be considered permanent that's in close proximity to a lake as large and volatile as Lake Erie. Storm action makes fast and dramatic inroads into the park's shorelines, contributing to Presque Isle's reputation as "a peninsula that wants to be an island." Fifty-eight breakwaters, and sand rejuvenation of badly pummeled beach after storms, help maintain this beautiful, bird-rich peninsula near the port city of Erie.

BIRDS TO LOOK FOR

Least Bittern • Tundra Swan • Common Moorhen • Semipalmated Plover • Greater Yellowlegs • Least Sandpiper • Dunlin • Long-billed Dowitcher • Bonaparte's Gull • Great Black-backed Gull • Great Horned Owl • Red-eyed Vireo • Hermit Thrush • Swainson's Thrush • Cedar Waxwing • Scarlet Tanager

Many sandpipers, such as this Dunlin, are attracted to this park on the Great Lakes.

BIRD LIFE

Although there are 11 miles of hiking trails winding through Presque Isle State Park, birdwatchers will be forgiven if they make a beeline to the paved 1.5-mile-long Gull Point Trail, which passes through great bird habitat and ends up at the northernmost tip of the peninsula, where an observation platform is located. Although the Gull Point Natural Area is closed from April through November, this platform provides great views of the park's shoreline, and forests and ponds as well.

Many sandpipers can be observed combing the shoreline for food; these include Greater Yellowlegs, Long-billed Dowitcher, Ruddy Turnstone, Dunlin, Sanderling, Whimbrel, Least Sandpiper, and others. Spring is plover time on the beaches; look for the Semipalmated Plover, the most often seen, and Black-bellied Plover, among others. As expected gulls of many species fish off this peninsula, most notably Herring, Bonaparte's, Ring-billed, and Great Black-backed Gulls. In summer they spend much of their time on sand spits in Lake Erie.

Birdwatchers should explore the park's ample forests and wetlands as well, where they may see seven species of

The Least Bittern's *call is a harsh* kek *sound; its song is a softer* ku.

90

woodpeckers, including the Pileated Woodpecker and Yellow-bellied Sapsucker. The peninsula's woods are home to more than eight species of owls, including the Eastern Screech-Owl and Great Horned Owl, although these are never present in large numbers. Other woodland birds include Hermit and Swainson's Thrushes, Cedar Waxwings, Red-eyed Vireos, Scarlet and Summer Tanagers, and a large roster of warblers.

Presque Isle's ponds and marshes, especially dominant in the eastern portion of the park, are easily accessed via the park's extensive network of trails. Look for both the American and Least Bittern, the Great Blue Heron, and marsh birds such as the American Coot and Common Moorhen. Other sightings may include waterfowl, such as the Northern Pintail, Hooded Merganser, Wood Duck, and Tundra Swan; the Common Loon is likely to be heard but not seen.

VISITING

Internationally known to the birdwatching fraternity, Presque Isle State Park is cherished by vacationers and weekenders as well. Although birdwatchers will have lots of company in peak seasons, there is still plenty of space for their pursuit. The best times for birdwatchers are during fall migration (September through October) and spring migration (March through May). Stop by the Visitor Center to pick up a bird list and map of Presque Isle State Park's 11 miles of hiking trails.

HIGHLIGHTS

Songbirds, from Hermit Thrushes to Scarlet Tanagers, congregate at Fry's Landing, which is located near Misery Bay. On a good spring day, lucky visitors can spot more than 20 species of warblers here in the pine forests.

Site Map and Information

PRESQUE ISLE STATE PARK

🚗 From Erie, take U.S. Grant Highway (Buffalo Road) southwest to Route 832 and follow it northeast to reach the park's entrance.

🕐 Daily, sunrise to sunset, year-round.

🌑 Never.

ℹ️ Presque Isle State Park, P. Box 8510, Erie, PA 16505-0510. The Visitor Center is open daily, 9 a.m.– 5 p.m.

📞 (814) 833-7424; www.dcnr.state.pa.us

💲 None.

♿ Stull Interpretive Center is wheelchair accessible, and the multipurpose National Recreational Trail is paved.

🅰️ No camping on-site.

🚸 None.

🏨 Motels are available off the interstate, within 2 miles of the park.

BLOCK ISLAND CONSERVATION PROPERTIES

In spring, and especially in fall, this small island off Rhode Island's southern coast is brimming with migrant songbirds.

With good reason, this lovely island has been called "the jewel of southern New England." In summer the fragrance of its famous wild beach roses seems to be everywhere, as are the sounds of male songbirds singing to their mates. Various twists and turns in Block Island's roads and trails reveal some of the most striking ocean views found along the entire Atlantic Coast.

Efforts to conserve this 12-square-mile island and its wildlife began about a century ago when a school teacher named Elizabeth Dickens mistakenly shot a swan instead of a goose for her dinner. On the spot she vowed to spend the rest of her life studying natural habitats and bird life. The Block Island conservation effort is her legacy. It includes the Block Island National Wildlife Refuge, which encompasses 37 percent of the island at the northern tip.

HABITAT

Block Island was formed about 12,000 years ago by the same Ice Age glacier that created Massachusett's Cape Cod, Nantucket, and Martha's Vineyard, and New York's Long Island – all islands off the Atlantic coast. At Block Island the glacier left behind an intriguing mix of beaches, sand dunes, coastal bluffs, maritime scrubland, grasslands, and kettle hole ponds. This wide variety of habitats, plus the fact that Block Island lies on the fringe of the great Atlantic flyway, have made it one of the prime spots to see migrant birds in the eastern United States.

The Wood Thrush's song consists of liquid phrases that end in a complicated trill.

BIRDS TO LOOK FOR

Common Loon • Sooty Shearwater • Northern Gannet • Black-crowned Night-Heron • Common Eider • Bufflehead • Northern Harrier • Northern Saw-whet Owl • Red-eyed Vireo • Tree Swallow • Wood Thrush • Yellow Warbler • Black-throated Green Warbler • Common Yellowthroat • Eastern Towhee • Rose-breasted Grosbeak

BIRD LIFE

Spring, summer, and fall are all good times to birdwatch at Block Island Conservation Properties. Some especially hardy birders also visit in winter to see sea ducks, such as Common Eiders, and Bufflehead, and Great Cormorants offshore.

Spring on the island is usually ushered in by strong southwesterly winds, and riding in on them are songbirds galore. Colorful mating

Songbirds, including the Eastern Towhee, abound in this island park.

plumages announces such varied arrivals as the Ruby-throated Hummingbird, Veery, Wood Thrush, Red-eyed Vireo, and thousands of warblers, including Black-throated Green, Black-and-white, Blackpoll, Magnolia, Chestnut-sided, and Nashville Warblers. Look for larger songsters, too, including Baltimore Orioles, Indigo Buntings, and Rose-breasted Grosbeaks.

Two key locations for spring and summer songbird viewing are Clay Head, on the northeastern end of the island, and Nathan Mott Park (also known as the Enchanted Forest), in the center of the island. Also, Tree Swallows hunt winged insects above the ponds; Barn Swallows are busy for the same reason over open fields. And bird songs are pervasive. The Yellow Warbler trills its *sweet*

sweet sweet I'm so sweet, the Common Yellowthroat calls its *wichity wichity wich*, and the Eastern Towhee's *drink your tea* call sounds throughout the island.

As might be expected in this ocean setting, seabirds are plentiful offshore. Shearwaters – Sooty, Greater, and Cory's – are regular summer offshore visitors, as are Double-crested Cormorants, Northern Gannets, and Common Loon. Watch these birds with a spotting scope from high on Mohegan Bluffs on the southeastern part of the island or from Sandy Point on the north end. Ducks are abundant on the

The Red-eyed Vireo *is just one of many spring migrants that visit Block Island annually.*

island's freshwater ponds and saltwater bays. Look for Ring-necked Ducks, Greater and Lesser Scaup, Common Goldeneye, and Red-breasted and Common Mergansers.

Block Island's birdwatching crescendo comes in the fall, beginning in the third week of September and culminating in the first week of November, when a strong wind is often blowing. Ducks, warblers, cuckoos, wrens, tanagers, thrushes, and sparrows stop to rest on the island during their long migration south from northern New England and Canada.

Local birdwatchers pay special attention to three species – the Black-crowned Night-Heron, Northern Saw-whet Owl, and Northern Harrier – to ensure that their numbers are holding.

VISITING

Although birdwatching is good all over Block Island, four locations within Block Island Conservation Properties are considered the very best. These are the already mentioned Clay Head and the Enchanted Forest (for songbirds) and Sachem Pond and Andy's Way (for waterbirds).

HIGHLIGHTS

The 800 year-round residents and veteran birdwatchers agree that some of the most majestic ocean views between Maine and Florida are found near the northern end of Block Island. Be sure to visit Clay Head and Mohegan Bluffs to experience the beauty of this vantage point.

Site Map and Information

BLOCK ISLAND CONSERVATION PROPERTIES

🚢 Ferries to Block Island run daily, year-round, from Point Judith, RI (a 1-hour ride). In the summer other ferries leave from New London, CT, and Montauk, NY. For RI and CT ferries, call (401) 783-4613. For the NY ferry, call (516) 668-5700. For Point Judith and New London ferries (which carry cars as well as people), make reservations 4 months in advance during peak season and at least 1 month in advance off season.

◻ Daily, sunrise to sunset, year-round.

◼ Never.

ℹ Block Island Conservation Properties, c/o The Nature Conservancy, P.O. Box 1287, Block Island, RI 02807. Nature Conservancy Headquarters, located at 352 High Street, serve as a Visitor Center; open weekdays, 9 a.m.–5 p.m., May through September.

☎ (401) 466-2129 (The Nature Conservancy)

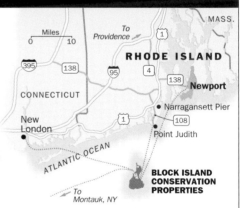

⑤ None.

♿ No special facilities.

⛺ No camping on the island.

👥 Guided walking tours are offered in spring, summer, and fall. Check the local newspaper for schedule.

🛏 Bed-and-breakfasts, rental cottages, and hotels are all available. Contact the Block Island Chamber of Commerce at (401) 466-2982 for listings.

HUNTINGTON BEACH STATE PARK

Least Bitterns and Purple Gallinules slip in and out of the grasses and reeds of coastal South Carolina's premier birding location.

Colonial ships began to bring settlers to the east coast of South Carolina in the 17th century. Today, a leisurely drive along the coast takes visitors past the sites of Revolutionary War encampments, vanished plantation mansions, Civil War battles, and slave quarters. Now the landscape is filled with booming retirement communities and golf courses, but, thankfully, there is still some natural habitat left, in various parcels protected by state, federal, and private owners. Huntington Beach State Park is one of the best of these. Boasting 2,500 acres of rich natural habitat, it has become known as one of the best birdwatching spots on the East Coast.

HABITAT

Huntington Beach State Park, only 17 miles south of Myrtle Beach, contains fresh- and saltwater marshes, lagoons, and dunes. Of these habitats, the highly productive salt marsh – a veritable food factory – is the star. Because this habitat is rich in dense plant growth such as salt marsh cord grass, it is a bountiful nursery to fish and invertebrates, which in turn provide food for birds.

In addition to the thriving saltwater marsh, the park has one of the best-preserved examples of natural

coastline beaches on the Carolina coast, plus a freshwater lagoon and maritime forest. Several short nature trails and boardwalks quickly immerse birdwatchers in these habitats, which support such an amazing variety of wildlife that birdwatchers have recorded a total of nearly 300 species.

Summer Tanagers *add a splash of rosy red (males) and mustard yellow (females).*

BIRD LIFE

The causeway road coming into the park provides an opportunity to observe the freshwater lagoon on the south side and a salt marsh on the other. The lagoon side is home to

BIRDS TO LOOK FOR

Northern Gannet • Least Bittern • Tricolored Heron • Green Heron • Wood Stork • Bufflehead • Ruddy Duck • Clapper Rail • Purple Gallinule • Wilson's Plover • Purple Sandpiper • Black Skimmer • Brown-headed Nuthatch • Summer Tanager • Eastern Towhee • Indigo Bunting • Painted Bunting

The Least Bittern is one of 300 species that may be seen in this coastal park.

Least Bitterns, Purple Gallinules, and in the winter, Tundra Swans, American Wigeon, and many other species of waterfowl. From July through October look for Wood Storks, too.

Although many birds use the park's salt marshes as grocery stores, few conduct their entire lives there. The elusive Clapper Rail is one exception; in June it parades in full view with the newly hatched young. The Salt Marsh Boardwalk (found at the end of the causeway to the left) showcases many of the other birds that feed in the marsh. Look for Snowy and Great Egrets and Tricolored and Green Herons, along with Black Skimmers (in summer) and Northern Harriers (in fall and winter).

The Purple Gallinule *may be observed in the park's freshwater lagoon.*

The Sandpiper Pond Trail wanders through even more diverse habitat, including maritime forest, sand dunes, and a brackish pond that is heavily used by waterfowl and shorebirds in the winter. On the muddy pond edges look for Willets, Wilson's Plovers, and Greater and Lesser Yellowlegs. Waterfowl usually include Gadwall, Northern Pintail, Buffleheads, and Ruddy Ducks. This easy two-mile loop brings birders into contact with forest birds – among them, Eastern Towhees, Brown-headed Nuthatches, and Brown Thrashers year-round, and Summer Tanagers and Painted and Indigo Buntings in the summer.

In the beach and dune areas look for Sanderlings and Piping Plovers (in winter). Overhead look for Laughing Gulls (in summer, fall, and spring) and Bonaparte's Gulls (in winter). Other winter gulls include Herring and Ring-billed Gulls.

Another short trail, the Kerrigan Nature Trail, is found by turning right at the end of the causeway. The trail ends at the lagoon, which harbor winter waterfowl, including Red-breasted Mergansers. Purple Martins breed here, and Tree Swallows are common during migration.

A short hike from the picnic area (at the opposite end of the park from the campground) leads to the Murrells Inlet Jetty, a hot spot for rarities such as Wilson's Storm-Petrels and other seabirds. In the winter Northern Gannets, Purple Sandpipers, Red-throated Loons, and Horned Grebe may be spotted.

VISITING

Huntington Beach offers good birdwatching year-round, especially in late fall and early spring, when migrants mix with residents. During these times it is possible to see more than 100 species in a day. Bird activity calms in the summer, when many of the birds that reside at the park head north for their brief nesting season.

HIGHLIGHTS

Huntington Beach State Park holds the Tidelands Birding and Wildlife Festival annually, the third weekend in February. Field trips, seminars, and special speakers feature the many habitats and creatures that are influenced by tides. Call (843) 234-1421 for details.

Site Map and Information

HUNTINGTON BEACH STATE PARK

- Take US 17 south 17 miles from Myrtle Beach or north 160 miles from Charleston to reach park entrance.

- Daily, 6 a.m.–10 p.m. from March through November; daily, 6 a.m.–6 p.m. from December through February.

- Never.

- Huntington Beach State Park, Murrells Inlet, SC 29576. The park office, open daily, 9 a.m.–5 p.m., functions as a Visitor Center.

- (803) 237-4440; www.southcarolinaparks.com

- $4 per adult, $2 per child (ages 6–12).

- Boardwalks and campground facilities are wheelchair accessible.

- Daily nature programs, including several naturalist-led birdwalks each week, are included with the price of admission. Call ahead for schedule.

- Huntington Beach State Park has a 186-site campground with water and electric hookups, primarily available on a first-come, first-served basis.

- Hotels, motels, and bed-and-breakfasts abound in nearby Myrtle Beach; call Grand Strand Tourism at (843) 546-8502 for listings.

GREAT SMOKY MOUNTAINS NATIONAL PARK

*This magnificent expanse of varied mountain woodlands, straddling
North Carolina and Tennessee, is home to equally magnificent bird life.*

This much-loved and heavily visited national park was created in response to a growing danger: the rapid increase of logging and lumbering operations, which threatened to decimate the area's forests and wildlife. Authorized by Congress in 1926 and formally established in 1934, Great Smoky Mountains National Park was purchased with funds contributed by its parent states (Tennessee and North Carolina) and private citizens. The park's numerous mountain peaks and verdant valleys are accessible by 800 miles of foot and horse trails and 270 miles of good paved and gravel roads.

Red Crossbills *use their distinctive bills to pry open pine cones in the park's coniferous forests.*

HABITAT

One clue to the varied bird life of Great Smoky Mountains National

Park is the range of forest habitats that exist within it. Beneath the blue haze that softens the outlines of the 6,000-foot-high mountains and gave this haven its name, are stands of pine and oak, hemlock, cove and northern hardwoods, spruce and fir – each habitat attractive to a different collection of bird life. Fast-flowing streams fed by mountain springs provide relief for wildlife, as does the long sprawl of Fontana Lake, or the park's southern boundary.

BIRD LIFE

There are few more promising sites in North America to spot hard-to-find bird species than this forest preserve. Spring migrations begin in late March with the arrivals of the Blue-headed Vireo, Yellow-throated and Black-and-white Warblers, and Louisiana Waterthrush. In April come the Ruby-throated Hummingbird, Veery, Wood Thrush, Yellow-throated Vireo, Scarlet Tanager, and the Chestnut-sided, Blackburnian, and Canada Warblers. All of these are breeding and nesting through the summer, and by September Broad-winged Hawks are sailing past Clingman's Dome in their southern migration.

Fall migration, beginning as early as August, means an exodus of the park's songbirds. These departures slow to a

BIRDS TO LOOK FOR

Wild Turkey • Black-capped Chickadee • Eastern Screech-Owl • Common Raven • Winter Wren • Cedar Waxwing • Yellow-throated Warber • Pine Warbler • Black-and-white Warbler • Worm-eating Warbler • Louisiana Waterthrush • Scarlet Tanager • Red Crossbill

The Black-capped Chickadee's call is a low, slow chick-a-dee-dee-dee.

halt in early November, leaving the woods to the Ruffed Grouse, Cedar Waxwing, Yellow-rumped Warbler, Red-breasted Nuthatch, Black-capped Chickadee, American Goldfinch, and Wild Turkey.

The variety of birds inhabiting this national park is staggering; however, birdwatchers must seek out the appropriate habitat to find their bird of choice. Mountain terrain is sighting ground for such day-time predators as Sharp-shinned and Cooper's Hawks. Five species of owls also find deep-wooded terrain to their liking. The largest, the Great Horned Owl, is seldom seen. The Eastern Screech-Owl and the Barred Owl are more likely to be spotted.

Great Smoky Mountains National Park has a good representation of wood warblers during the spring and summer breeding season. In the lower-elevation pine and oak forests, the Pine Warbler and Black-and-white Warbler are most easily spotted. In the hemlock forests, the Black-throated Green Warbler can be seen. In the northern hardwoods, spruce, and firs, the Blackburnian Warbler is a neighbor of the Common Raven, and Winter Wrenl. The banks along the park's streams are inviting to the Louisiana Waterthrush, another warbler.

Cades Cove, a mountain set among former pasturelands, is another incentive to drive the mountain's one-way looping road. Be sure to look in

Wild Turkeys *are ground-walkers, strong fliers, and, at night, they roost in trees.*

the grasslands for Eastern Meadowlarks, Eastern Kingbirds, and Eastern Bluebirds.

VISITING

Some birdwatchers prefer the fall, when the whole park seems ablaze with the colors of changing leaves, but to sight the most species, come in the spring, which sometimes begins as early as March, or in early summer. Midsummer (when it tends to be hot, hazy, and humid) and the month of October are the times when the park tallies most of its nine million annual visitors. Visitors from November through February should be prepared

for snowy weather as well as the possibility of sunny days, with temperatures as warm as 65°F.

Stop by one of the Visitor Centers to pick up a bird checklist and maps, and for more detailed information, the book *Birds of the Smokies* by Fred Alsop.

HIGHLIGHTS

A trip to Great Smoky Mountains National Park may prove a once-in-a lifetime opportunity to hike a 2-mile section of the famous 2,000-mile-long Appalachian Trail. This stretch offers stunning views of the Smokies, and birds are abundant all along the route.

Site Map and Information

GREAT SMOKY MOUNTAINS NATIONAL PARK

🚗 A number of roads lead to or near the park, including I-75 from Atlanta, GA; I-40 west from Nashville, TN; I-40 east from Asheville, NC; and I-81 from Roanoke, VA. US 441 leads directly into the park from Knoxville, TN.

⭕ Daily, 24 hours, year-round.

◐ High-altitude roads, including Clingmans Dome Road, are closed in winter. Others may be closed temporarily during bad weather.

🛈 Great Smoky Mountains National Park, 107 Park Headquarters Road, Gatlinburg, TN 37738. The Sugarlands (main) and Oconaluftee Visitor Centers are open daily, 8 a.m.–4:30 p.m., year-round. Cades Cove Visitor Center is open daily, 8 a.m.–4:30 p.m., except in winter, when it is open only on weekends.

📞 (865) 436-1200; http://nps.gov/grsm

⑤ None.

♿ All Visitor Centers are wheelchair accessible. The Sugarlands Valley Nature Trail is an all-access trail along the Newfound Gap Road.

🅰 There are 10 campgrounds on-site; reservations are accepted at 3 of them (Elkmont, Smokemont, and Cades Cove). Call (865) 436-1200.

👥 Two nonprofit groups, Great Smoky Mountains Institute at Tremont and the Smoky Mountains Field School, offer day trips and week-long excursions. For details call (865) 435-1200.

🛏 A wide range of accommodations is available in nearby towns. LeConte Lodge, the only on-site accommodations, is reached via a 5-mile trail walk; call (865) 429-5704 for reservations.

TENNESSEE NATIONAL WILDLIFE REFUGE

From Bald Eagles in winter to songbirds in spring, birdwatching along the shores of northern Tennessee's large reservoirs is always in season.

L oud complaints of "Socialism!" accompanied the 1933 legislation that created the Tennessee Valley Authority, but the dams and reservoirs built on the Tennessee River provided one of the nation's most poverty-stricken river basins with electric power and flood and erosion control. Although the 1945 establishment of a national wildlife refuge in the newly formed wetland and riparian habitat didn't cause as much of a stir, the long-term effects have been beneficial – to wildlife and humans alike.

Palm Warblers *may be observed wagging their tails as they forage for food.*

HABITAT

Tennessee National Wildlife Refuge was formed with waterfowl (and waterfowl hunters) in mind, and its 25,000 acres of waterways attract abundant geese and ducks – more than 100,000 and 200,000, respectively, in peak winter months. However, the preservation of 20,000 acres of forest, mostly upland hardwoods, has been an unintended bonus. In recent years wildlife managers have begun conscious efforts to improve and increase the

refuge's forest habitat for the migrant and breeding songbirds that flourish there – particularly for the Cerulean and Swainson's Warblers.

BIRD LIFE

Tennessee National Wildlife Refuge lies along the Mississippi flyway, a major migratory route for waterfowl, songbirds, and shorebirds. In the spring and fall, shorebirds can be seen from the observation platform at the Duck River Bottoms entrance. In addition to Greater and Lesser Yellowlegs, look for Solitary, Pectoral, and Least Sandpipers. Ring-billed Gulls and Herring Gulls pass through as well.

This same platform offers visitors good looks, in the winter, at many of the 20-plus species of ducks that migrate to the refuge. Mallards, Gadwall, and American Black Ducks are abundant here. Canada Geese abound, too and several hundred nonmigratory birds nest on the refuge. To see more waterfowl, visit the V. L. Childs Overlook at the Big Sandy Unit off Swamp Creek Road. This area adds

BIRDS TO LOOK FOR

Canada Goose • American Black Duck • Ring-necked Duck • Ruddy Duck • Bald Eagle • Greater Yellowlegs • Lesser Yellowlegs • Least Sandpiper • Pectoral Sandpiper • Ring-billed Gull • Herring Gull • Wood Thrush • Blackpoll Warbler • Worm-eating Warbler • Kentucky Warbler • Hooded Warbler

Lesser Yellowlegs may be seen along the shores of the refuge's man-made reservoirs.

diving ducks to the mix, including Canvasbacks, Ruddy Ducks, and Ring-necked Ducks.

For spring birdwatching, return to Duck River Bottoms, where migrating songbirds, including Blackpoll Warblers and Palm Warblers, rest in the trees. The best birdwatching is near the observation platform and along the gravel roads and levees. Wood Thrushes and Worm-eating, Kentucky, and Hooded Warblers are all found here. Look in the trees and willow thickets along the shorelines for other resting migrants, including Orchard Orioles, Indigo Buntings, and Blue-gray Gnatcatchers.

To see the largest forested area in the refuge, visit the Big Sandy Peninsula. It contains 4,000 acres of forest in one tract alone. To get there, follow County Road 69A north from the town of Big

Sandy; refuge signs guide visitors to the entrance. From here, a gravel refuge road loops left several miles out to the tip of the peninsula and back.

All along the Big Sandy Peninsula Road, upland forest, old fields, and a few small wetlands yield an array of birds year-round. During the summer, Northern Bobwhites call from the fields and Common Snipe are known to hide in the wetlands. Up to five species of swallows – Tree, Northern Rough-winged, Bank, Cliff, and Purple Martins – hawk insects. Eastern Kingbirds and Great Crested Flycatchers perch on limbs on the

The Solitary Sandpiper *can be found in freshwater habitat, bobbing its head and tail.*

edges of forest and field, also preying on the insects.

The end of the peninsula – Pace Point – is known to local birdwatchers as a rarities hot spot. Experts have spotted Red-throated Loons and Long-tailed Jaegers across the waters of the reservoirs, but visitors are more likely to see spring migrants, returning fall shorebirds, and winter waterfowl.

Birdwatchers who remain in the Big Sandy Peninsula area until dusk in summer have a good chance of encountering three different species of a group of night hunters – the Caprimulgidae. Common Nighthawks, Chuck-will's-widows, and Whip-poor-wills all have wide, gaping mouths, designed to snare flying insects.

VISITING

The refuge's several units are not contiguous and stretch for 65 miles, so plan on driving time. Winter waterfowl season begins in November and remains until February. Mid-April is the beginning of spring migration for songbirds. Fall migration for both shorebirds and songbirds begins as early as the beginning of August.

HIGHLIGHTS

From December through February, park at the Robins Creek Hollow on the Big Sandy Peninsula at night to see 30 to 40 Bald Eagles come home to roost. The roost is about two miles north of the refuge entrance.

Site Map and Information

TENNESSEE NATIONAL WILDLIFE REFUGE

🚗 Tennessee National Wildlife Refuge is approximately 130 miles northeast of Memphis; area access is via I-40. The two units mentioned in the text are about 40 miles apart. The Big Sandy Unit entrance is near the refuge headquarters in Paris, reachable via County Route 69A. The Duck River Unit lies nearer I-40 and is reached from US 70.

◻ Daily, sunrise to sunset, year-round.

◑ Never, although sections are closed seasonally to protect waterfowl.

ℹ Tennessee National Wildlife Refuge, 3006 Dinkins Lane, Paris, TN 38242. Refuge headquarters, open 7 a.m.–3:30 p.m. weekdays, functions as a Visitor Center.

☎ (901) 642-2091; http://southeast.fws.gov

Ⓢ None.

♿ Refuge headquarters and select observation blinds are wheelchair accessible.

🅰 No camping on-site.

🏕 Nathan Bedford Forrest State Park near Camden has a number of primitive campsites, available on a first-come, first-served basis; call (901) 584-6356 for details.

🏨 Paris Landing State Park, 18 miles east of Paris on US 79, has both a 130-room resort inn and cabins for rent; call (800) 250-8614 for reservations. Additional hotels and motels are available in nearby Paris, Waverly, and Camden.

Dead Creek Wildlife Management Area

A migrating throng of Snow and Canada Geese makes an annual visit to this site along one of Vermont's most famous autumn foliage routes.

Dead Creek is a tiny, 12-mile-long tributary of the great Lake Champlain, renowned since 1609, when French explorer Samuel de Champlain canoed the lake's 120 miles, discovering what was to become an important transportation route. In 1806 the Champlain Transportation Company began regular steamship service on Lake Champlain, and beginning in 1823 the Champlain Canal, from the town of Whitehall to the Hudson River, brought ships carrying products to cities along the Atlantic Coast. Today tourism plays a key role in the economic vitality of the area, and Dead Creek Wildlife Management Area, located along the southern end of the lake, makes its contribution by drawing thousands of birdwatchers each fall to see the annual goose migration.

Eastern Meadowlarks *are one of many nesting grassland birds found in the park's fields in spring and summer.*

Birds to Look For

Least Bittern • Green Heron • Black-crowned Night-Heron • Snow Goose • Canada Goose • Wood Duck • Rough-legged Hawk • American Kestrel • Ruffed Grouse • Common Moorhen • American Woodcock • Great Horned Owl • Vesper Sparrow • Bobolink • Eastern Meadowlark

Habitat

Although the oak and sugar maple forests set the Vermont leaf-peeper scene in the Dead Creek area, the cattail-dominated wetlands and agricultural lands play a more important role in attracting geese to the center stage. Dead Creek, so named because of its slow-flowing nature, lies on the Atlantic flyway, a major migratory route for waterfowl. The wildlife management area was established in 1950 by the Vermont Department of Fish and Wildlife to provide more habitat for these birds. This was accomplished in part by the construction of several impoundments, or diked pools, along the stream to enhance the marshy nature of Dead Creek and its branches. In addition to field and wetlands, the protected area's nearly 3,000 acres of wildlife habitat also includes forest and grassland – attracting more than 200 bird species.

Bird Life

The yearly convergence of geese is no secret. The show – best viewed from the 2,200-foot observation area and visitor kiosk off Route 17, less than two miles west of Addison – begins with Canada Geese in September, and continues as they are joined by nearly 20,000 Snow Geese by mid-October.

Geese are grassland grazers. The fields adjacent to the observation area are planted with alfalfa, clover, and corn to provide the migrants with fuel

From the park's observation deck, visitors can observe American Kestrels.

for their journey south. Although some of the Canada Geese are resident nesters, many more arrive from northern Quebec. The Snow Geese come from their nesting grounds in the eastern Canadian arctic.

Fortuitously, the greatest goose concentration usually coincides with the peak of fall foliage in the Champlain Valley – in mid-October. The geese leave Vermont and continue on to their wintering grounds in early November. They aren't going far: the Canada Geese will head for the Chesapeake Bay, and the Snow Geese will winter along the Atlantic from New Jersey to North Carolina.

The observation area overlooks the designated refuge portion of the wildlife management area, which is off-limits to humans. These fields offer great raptor habitat, too. American Kestrels, Red-tailed Hawks, and Northern Harrier are common in all seasons except the winter. Rough-legged Hawks are common during fall migration, especially in late October, and through the winter. In spring and summer nesting grassland birds such as Bobolinks, Eastern Meadowlarks, and Vesper Sparrows may be observed in these fields.

To access the marshes where ducks are found, take the first left past the observation area (just after crossing over Dead Creek). In the fall, drive slowly down this marsh-bordered dead-end road looking for ducks resting along their migration route, including American Black Duck,

The Great Horned Owl, *chiefly a nocturnal bird, is recognized by its call, a series of three to eight loud but deep hoots.*

Green-winged Teal, and Northern Pintail. In the summer, look for nesting ducks including Wood Duck, Blue-winged Teal, and Hooded Merganser. Visitors who arrive early on a June or July morning may witness these ducklings on parade. Other marsh birds to look for include many waders – Great Blue Herons, Green Herons, and Black-crowned Night-Herons among them. Birdwatchers might also spot Least and American Bitterns and Common Moorhens in this habitat.

Continue down this road to a refuge parking area surrounded by woods. Look here for American Woodcocks and Ruffed Grouse. Great Horned Owls may be found in the tall trees.

VISITING

During the goose migration in late September and October, mornings and late afternoons are the best times to see large flocks. Early afternoon can be good because the geese often feed near the observation area then. Spring and summer visits yield nesting birds, but winter is only for the hearty.

HIGHLIGHTS

From the seat of a canoe, a paddler can enjoy close encounters with the wetland waders and ducks of Dead Creek. But take care not to approach nests or broods too closely. Canoes can be rented from the Alpine Shop in South Burlington; call (802) 862-2714.

Site Map and Information

DEAD CREEK WILDLIFE MANAGEMENT AREA

🚗 Dead Creek Wildlife Management Area is just 30 miles south of Burlington. Take Route 7 south to Route 22A to reach the small town of Addison. At the intersection of Routes 22A and 17, turn west on Route 17 and drive 2 miles to reach the observation area.

◻ Daily, 24 hours, year-round.

◉ Never. Restricted areas are clearly marked by signs.

ℹ Dead Creek Wildlife Management Area, c/o Vermont Department of Fish and Wildlife, 111 West Street, Essex Junction, VT 05452. There is a visitor kiosk in the observation area, but it is unmanned.

📞 (802) 878-1564; http://anp.state.vt.us/fw

Ⓢ None.

♿ The observation area adjacent to Route 17, including the visitor kiosk, is wheelchair accessible.

🅰 None on-site. Call Rivers Bend

Campground at (888) 505-5159 or Button Bay State Park at (802) 475-2377 for reservations.

🔭 The Vermont Institute of Natural Sciences conducts occasional natural history tours of the area; call (802) 457-2779 for information.

🛏 Lodging is available in the nearby towns of New Haven, Vergennes, and Middlebury, as well as in Burlington, Vermont's largest city.

CHINCOTEAGUE NATIONAL WILDLIFE REFUGE

Washed by the sea and protected by dunes, this peaceful island refuge off the Virginia mainland is perhaps the northernmost place to find the Brown-headed Nuthatch.

For several years Chincoteague Island, a barrier island positioned along the East Coast just below the great Atlantic flyway, was known for its tremendous numbers of migratory waterfowl. However, in the early years of the 20th century these numbers showed an alarming decrease. Wetlands once ringing with the clamor of ducks and geese were being transformed into housing and industrial sites. Waterfowl poaching was on the rise.

The American Coot *has a white bill, blackish head, and small, reddish-brown shield on its forehead.*

In 1943 the federal government established the Chincoteague National Wildlife Refuge to preserve a piece of this island for migratory birds, with an emphasis on conserving Snow Geese. Today the site encompasses almost 14,000 acres and serves as the permanent or temporary home for an astounding 320 species of birds.

HABITAT

Any drive, bicycle ride, or hike through this refuge reveals why so many migratory birds drop down from the Atlantic flyway to explore its treasures. Extensive expanses of freshwater and brackish marshes, ponds, and saltwater estuaries form its principal habitats. On higher ground maritime forests, composed primarily of oak and loblolly pine, attract woodland birds and other wildlife. Fifteen miles of trails provide visitors access to all of the refuge's rich environments.

BIRD LIFE

Concentrations of species on Chincoteague Island are so plentiful – over 20 species of familiar sandpipers, for example, including Pectoral and Stilt Sandpipers – that the experienced birdwatcher may want to focus on adding birds to his or her personal birding list. Duck varieties? As many as 26 species – including the common Bufflehead, Gadwall, and Northern Pintail – can be sighted on the marshes and ponds. Geese? There are four species, including the strong-flying Greater Snow Goose, which sometimes makes a carefully executed landing, other times, a wild, zigzagging dive.

The warbler population in the refuge's woodlands is large and varied,

---

BIRDS TO LOOK FOR

Common Loon • Glossy Ibis • Snow Goose • Tundra Swan • Gadwall • Bufflehead • Peregrine Falcon • American Coot • Black-bellied Plover • American Avocet • Pectoral Sandpiper • Stilt Sandpiper• Royal Tern • Brown-headed Nuthatch • Carolina Wren • Winter Wren • White-throated Sparrow• Red-winged Blackbird

The Glossy Ibis uses its long, curved bill to feed in the freshwater or brackish marshes.

consisting of nearly 30 species, including a half dozen species that breed here. Eighteen varieties of sparrows – 10 common, 8 rare – also can be spotted in the woodlands.

A novice setting forth in a first pair of wading boots or heavy-duty walkers can have just as stimulating a time at Chincoteague National Wildlife Refuge as the seasoned birder. A Glossy Ibis or graceful American Avocet may emerge from among the water grasses in a refuge marsh. Beginner's luck may lead to the American Bittern, a large wader so adept at hiding that it ripples and sways to imitate grasses waving on the shorelines. The American Coot may be spotted in freshwater marshes or ponds.

Common songbirds are abundant in the woodlands. Look for American Robins, Red-winged Blackbirds, Northern Cardinals, and Gray Catbirds. In the oak and

pine tracts sharp eyes may also pick out the small Carolina Wren collecting grasses, stems, and bark to build her nest, all the while singing as many as 27 different duets with the nearby male. A Peregrine Falcon may be spotted flying far above.

A bonus spectacle awaiting visitors is the scores of wild ponies found on Chincoteague Island. The romantically inclined say these ponies are descended from equine survivors of a Spanish galleon shipwrecked well before the United States came into being. Pragmatists say they are the descendants of farm horses that settlers brought to the island to graze in the 17th century.

The Royal Tern, *like all terns, can be distinguished from gulls by its forked tail and long, pointed wings and bill.*

VISITING

The refuge draws well over a million visitors annually, including a fair number of visitors in the wintertime. In blustery January and February, wintering waterfowl are dominant, including thousands of Greater Snow Geese. After April, when many of the migrant waterfowl leave, the great influx of shorebirds and songbirds begins. Early May is an exceptional time to see near-peak numbers of migrating songbirds, as well as some lingering waterfowl. In summer months, great numbers of herons and egrets can be seen fishing from along the island's Beach Road, and as fall approaches, the Common Loon becomes easier to spot.

Fall is migration time for hawks and falcons. When the winter months bring harsh winds again, Greater Snow Geese drop down from the Atlantic flyway to begin their seasonal stay at the refuge.

HIGHLIGHTS

Special days and weeks observed at the refuge include an international migratory bird celebration on Mother's Day weekend; National Wildlife Refuge Week, beginning on Columbus Day weekend; and a popular Eastern Shore Birding Festival, also in October. Call the Chincoteague Chamber of Commerce at (757) 336-6161 for details.

Site Map and Information

CHINCOTEAGUE NATIONAL WILDLIFE REFUGE

🚗 From Ocean City, MD, take Route 113 to Route 12, which connects with Route 679 in VA. Continue to junction with Route 175 and follow 175 to Chincoteague Island. Turn left on Main Street, then right on Maddox Boulevard to reach the Visitor Center.

◻ Daily, sunrise to sunset, year-round (call for exact hours).

⬤ Never.

🅗 Chincoteague National Wildlife Refuge, 8231 Beach Road, P.O. Box 62, Assateague Island, Chincoteague, VA 23336. Visitor Center is open 9 a.m.–5 p.m., Memorial Day weekend through Labor Day weekend, and 9 a.m.–4 p.m. all other times.

☎ (757) 336-6122

⑤ $5 for 7-day-pass. An annual pass costs $12.

♿ Vistor Center and several trails are wheelchair accessible.

🅐 None on-site, but camping is available on Chincoteague Island. Call the Chamber of Commerce at (757) 336-6161 for listings.

👪 Contact the Visitor Center about walks, tours, and family activities.

🏨 Motels and bed-and-breakfasts available on Chincoteague Island in nearby Ocean City, Berlin, Snow Hill, and Pocomoke City.

GREAT FALLS PARK

*An abundance of warblers and other bird life grace this spectacular
riverside park, just 12 miles from the nation's capital.*

As the Potomac River passes by this 800-acre area, it tumbles over a series of steep, jagged rocks, creating the waterfalls that gave Great Falls Park its name. These truly great falls drop an astounding 78 feet in less than a mile, offering views that are worthy of a special trip just minutes from Washington, D.C.

Because the nation's capital is just 12 miles away, it's hard to believe that more than 160 different species of birds can be found here each year.

The American Robin's cheerily cheer-up cheerio *song is sure to cheer even the most dour birder.*

Disbelief fades fast, however, after a visitor sights a Bald Eagle or Cooper's Hawk or hears a Pileated Woodpecker drumming in yet another beautiful morning.

HABITAT

Great Falls Park lies within the Potomac River floodplain. The dominant feature of the park is, of course, its famous boulders and waterfalls. Other habitats include a swamp and a pond, deciduous forests, and bedrock terraces. Its woodland thickets shelter numerous warblers and other songbirds, and the pond and quieter parts of the river seem tailor-made for ducks and waders. Fishing is great for Bald Eagles and Great Blue Heron in the whitewater of the Potomac River.

BIRD LIFE

There may be no single reason for the extraordinary number of warblers found at this riverside park, but the one uncontested fact is that they are present in abundance. A total of 50 warblers are found in the continental United States: 34 of these have been seen at Great Falls Park in spring and fall. Hooded and Kentucky Warblers can be seen along the Ridge and Swamp Trails. Other common warblers include Wilson's, Yellow-rumped, Pine, Blackpoll, and Golden-winged Warblers, as well as American Redstarts and Northern Parula.

Although it may seem intimidating

BIRDS TO LOOK FOR

**Turkey Vulture • Mallard •
Bufflehead • Bald Eagle • Red-
shouldered Hawk • Pileated
Woodpecker • American Robin •
Blackpoll Warbler • Northern Parula •
American Redstart • Prothonotary
Warbler • Mourning Warbler • White-
throated Sparrow • Northern
Cardinal • Rose-breasted Grosbeak**

Thirty-four species of warblers, including the Northern Parula, have been observed here.

to distinguish one warbler from among the many species, each is associated with a collection of special traits (and haunting grounds) that help identify it. The Prothonotary Warbler's orange and yellow hues are most often flashed in pockets of swampland, for example. The same habitat also suits the yellow-breasted Mourning Warbler, a six-inch-long songster that hops rather than walks.

Warblers aren't the only reason to birdwatch at Great Falls Park, however. The park is home to 17 duck species, from Mallards to Buffleheads; ten species of raptors, including owls and hawks; and seven species of woodpeckers. Turkey Vultures are present year-round and Black Vultures may be seen spring through fall. Bald Eagles and Red-shouldered and Red-tailed Hawks may be observed hunting for prey along the edge of the river.

Great Falls Park has 15 miles of trails from which birdwatchers can see all of the above-mentioned bird life. The River Trail offers impressive views of the rock-walled Mather Gorge, but demands some maneuvering around boulders. The Swamp Trail provides opportunities to see a variety of birds, from waders to warblers. It also passes by Clay Pond, where Wood Duck often nest and Green and Great Blue Heron can be observed. To navigate the trails, pick up a map in the Visitor Center, which is near the main parking lot.

The White-throated Sparrow *can be distinguished from a host of other sparrows by the strongly outlined white throat patch.*

111

VISITING

The time to see the largest number of warblers and other birds, as well as a bounty of wildflowers, is the first two weeks of May. Look for Wood Duck sitting calmly in the trees, and enjoy the profusion of blooming Spring Beauty, Virginia Bluebells, and Wild Azalea. Songbirds active in the summer months include the Carolina Wren, Indigo Bunting, Scarlet Tanager, Rose-breasted Grosbeak, and Eastern Bluebird.

In fall and winter, ducks take over the river. An abundance of familiar backyard birds, including the American Robin, Northern Cardinal, and White-throated Sparrow can also be spotted during winter, scratching for seeds and waiting out the cold weather. Permanent residents at Great Falls Park include an assortment of woodpeckers – Pileated, Red-bellied, Downy, Hairy, and Red-headed Woodpeckers.

Visitors should stay on the park trails to reduce the risk of injury and protect the park's wildlife and natural resources. Use caution on all rocks, particularly near the river where sand and water make the rocks slippery.

HIGHLIGHTS

Visitors to Great Falls Park are asked to report any sightings of endangered species. These include the Peregrine Falcon, Swamp Sparrow, and Double-crested Cormorant. Other endangered species are included in the park's checklist, available at the Visitor Center.

Site Map and Information

GREAT FALLS PARK

🚗 From Washington, D.C., take I-495 north approximately 8 miles to Virginia Route 193 (the Georgetown Pike) and follow it west 4.2 miles to its intersection with Old Dominion Drive (where there is a park sign). Turn north and continue one mile to reach the park entrance.

🕐 Daily, 7 a.m. to sunset, year-round.

⬤ Christmas Day.

ℹ️ Great Falls Park, 9200 Old Dominion Drive, McLean, VA 22102. The Visitor Center is open daily; hours vary according to time of year, so call ahead.

📞 (703) 285-2965; www. nps.gov/gwmp/grfa

💲 $4 per vehicle; $2 per pedestrian.

♿ The Visitor Center is wheelchair accessible.

🅰 None on-site. Camping is available at Lake Fairfax in nearby Reston; call (703) 471-5415 for reservations.

🐦 An informal group of birdwatchers meets every Sunday at 8 a.m. in the Visitor Center's courtyard.

🛏 There are hotels, motels, and bed-and-breakfasts throughout the Washington, D.C., area; call the Fairfax County Tourism and Visitors Bureau at (703) 790-3329 for listings.

CRANESVILLE SWAMP PRESERVE

*An astonishing boreal bog in northeastern West Virginia harbors plants
and breeding birds that usually occur much farther north.*

No one knows what the Cherokees and Catawbas thought of this odd and even eerie place, featuring plants and animals found nowhere else in the region, but European settlers, starting in the 1790s, valued Cranesville Swamp for its abundant game and valuable lumber. This habitat was first protected in 1960, when The Nature Conservancy (TNC) established one of the first private natural areas in West Virginia. Today Cranesville Swamp Preserve consists of 1,650 acres under TNC protection, including nearly all of the swamp's wetlands and portions of some tributary streams.

Least Flycatchers *are attracted to this haven, where insects are abundant.*

except for here at Cranesville Swamp, the nearest natural stand to the north is 300 miles away in Pennsylvania.

In the bog areas, which the preserve's boardwalk trail explores, plants include sundew (an insectivorous plant), plus creeping snowberry, cranberry, and cotton grass. The preserve boasts not only a wide array of regionally common birds, but also several breeding birds that are rare nesters at this southern latitude.

HABITAT

Originally dominated by conifer trees, Cranesville Swamp was almost completely logged by 1893, which changed its nature forever. It is now a mosaic of conifer and hardwood swamps and bog peatlands. The area's relatively high elevation (2,650 feet), cool temperatures, and the poor drainage of the underlying clay and rock have contributed to form an unusual island of vegetation similar to that usually found much farther north, in places such as Maine or Canada. For example, tamarack is a tree common to Labrador and Alaska;

BIRD LIFE

About a mile from the preserve parking lot, the 1,500-foot boardwalk winds into bog vegetation, where breeding birds rare to this state are found. Among these are the Golden-crowned Kinglet, Alder Flycatcher, Nashville Warbler, and Northern Saw-whet Owl. A series of short trails from the preserve's parking lot and the

BIRDS TO LOOK FOR

Northern Saw-whet Owl • Yellow-bellied Sapsucker • Alder Flycatcher • Willow Flycatcher • Least Flycatcher • Great Crested Flycatcher • Eastern Phoebe • Carolina Wren • Golden-crowned Kinglet • Nashville Warbler • Black-throated Blue Warbler • Blackburnian Warbler • Northern Waterthrush • Swamp Sparrow

The Swamp Sparrow finds its food in the preserve's abundant swamps and bogs.

driveway into the preserve all lead through upland mixed conifer and hardwood forest to the boardwalk and can be combined for a two- to three-mile hike.

Those who associate swamps with insects are not alone – hungry flycatchers do, too. Cranesville Swamp Preserve is a great place to learn about empidonax flycatchers, considered the bane of birdwatchers because of their look-alike tendencies. All are drab olive, with slight eye rings and bold wing bars; they are distinguished by song and habitat preferences. Alder Flycatchers, Willow Flycatchers, and Least Flycatchers fall into the empid category and might be seen here.

Most birders are content to distinguish the empidonax flycatchers

The Carolina Wren's teakettle tea-kettle teakettle *song may be heard in every season.*

from other similar flycatching species. Here at Cranesville Swamp they can be compared to Eastern Wood-Pewees (no wing bars and a familiar, plaintive *pee-a-wee* song), Eastern Phoebes (a habit of pumping and spreading the tail), and Great Crested Flycatchers (a bright yellow belly). Other insect-loving birds include Red-eyed Vireos, along with an array of swallows (Cliff and Barn are common).

To get a panoramic view of the swamp, drive east and then south along West Virginia's Route 42 from the small village of Cranesville, West Virginia, into Maryland, and then head south on the White Rock Cranesville Road. The road flanks the eastern edge of the swamp. Frequent stops along the side of the road will yield more bog and wetland bird species, possibly including Yellow-bellied Sapsuckers, Northern Waterthrushes, Carolina Wrens, and Swamp Sparrows. Other common birds found throughout the swamp are Gray Catbirds, Veeries, Red-winged Blackbirds, and Black-capped Chickadees.

VISITING

Spring and summer bring the songs and calls of breeding birds to Cranesville Swamp Preserve. Although the birds quiet down by late August and early September, this is the time when the largest number of plants are blooming. Stay on the trails and boardwalk because plants are easily damaged by foot traffic. Ticks and biting insects are not as common

as might be expected, but prudence suggests long sleeves, long pants, and bug spray year-round. The area can be cool and wet, and sudden weather changes are common.

HIGHLIGHTS

Warbler-watching at Cranesville Swamp Preserve can be especially rewarding. The most striking birds are the Black-throated Blue Warblers, with a bold black, blue, and white pattern; Blackburnian Warblers, which sport fire at their throats; and Canada Warblers, which wear what looks like spectacles and a necklace. Mourning Warblers, Palm Warblers, and Common Yellowthroats also vie for attention.

Site Map and Information

CRANESVILLE SWAMP PRESERVE

🚐 Cranesville Swamp Preserve is in northeastern West Virginia, about 10 miles south of I-68 on the border with Maryland. Just east of the town of Cranesville on State Route 42, turn south onto the unpaved Burnside Camp Road (just across from a stone church). After 1 mile turn left onto a country road (no street sign) and follow Nature Conservancy signs to the parking area.

🗓 Daily, sunrise to sunset, year-round.

⬤ Never.

ℹ Cranesville Swamp Preserve, c/o The Nature Conservancy, Maryland/District of Columbia Chapter, 5410 Grosvenor Lane, Suite 100, Bethesda, MD 20814. There is visitor kiosk, but it is unstaffed.

📞 (301) 656-8673; www.tnc.org

💲 None.

♿ The trails and boardwalk should be wheelchair accessible by 2001; call the number above to confirm.

△ The nearest camping is at Swallow Falls State Park 10 miles away in Maryland; call (888) 432-CAMP for reservations.

👥 The Nature Conservancy offers occasional guided bird walks; call for a schedule.

🛏 Lodgings are available in nearby Oakland, MD, or Deep Creek Lake, MD. Call the Garret County Chamber of Commerce at (301) 245-4400 for listings.

CENTRAL
UNITED STATES

Felsenthal National Wildlife Refuge

*Abundant water resources and extensive hardwood forests make
this Arkansas refuge a haven for wintering waterfowl.*

The 65,000 acres of Felsenthal National Wildlife Refuge form the western boundary of the lower Mississippi River ecosystem. To make up for habitat loss caused by the dredging of the nearby Ouachita and Black Rivers, the Army Corps of Engineers created the refuge in 1975. Interestingly the refuge preserves many archaeological sites from the Caddo Indians. Although these fishing camps, villages, and temple mounds with ceremonial plazas are fragile and not open to the public, they are an indication of how important this complex ecosystem was to the original inhabitants.

Hooded Warblers *are
among the 26 species
of migrant warblers
attracted to this wet
habitat in spring.*

BIRDS TO LOOK FOR

Pied-billed Grebe • Wood Duck •
Gadwall • Ring-necked Duck • Bald
Eagle • American Coot • Barred
Owl • Chuck will's-widow • Red-
headed Woodpecker • Red-cockaded
Woodpecker • Tennessee Warbler •
Kentucky Warbler • Hooded Warbler

HABITAT

An intricate system of rivers, creeks, sloughs, and lakes crisscrosses the extensive bottomland hardwood forests of this wetlands complex. The higher ridges are occupied by pine trees and upland hardwoods. The diversity of habitats makes the refuge extremely attractive to a wide range of wildlife. This refuge is particularly well known for its huge flocks of wintering waterfowl – in recent years, the population has exceeded 300,000 ducks and geese.

From the start the refuge was managed to maintain an optimum habitat for wildlife. The main permanent body of water on the site is the 15,000-acre Felsenthal Pool, located at the center of the refuge, where the Ouachita and Saline Rivers converge. In the wintertime, managers carefully time flooding of the bottomland hardwood forest to duplicate the seasonal flooding that once occurred naturally in the area, more than doubling the overall water area.

BIRD LIFE

Flooded from approximately mid-November through the first week of June, the forests at Felsenthal National Wildlife Refuge are full of wetlands plants and an abundance of insects, crustaceans, and other waterfowl favorites. At least 20 species of duck winter at the refuge, including Mallard, Blue-winged Teal, Wood Duck, Gadwall, Bufflehead, American

The Barred Owl is found on the refuge's bottomland forests and pine woodlands.

Black Duck, and Ring-necked Duck. Other waterfowl, including Canada Goose, Pied-billed Grebe, and American Coot, are fairly common.

The refuge is also a strategically placed stopover point for birds migrating along the Mississippi flyway. The wet, insect-filled habitat is ideal for attracting warblers in the spring. At least 26 species have been spotted here on a regular basis, including Tennessee Warbler, Northern Parula, Hooded Warbler, and Kentucky Warbler. The dense bottomland forests of Felsenthal are also the perfect habitat in which to look for the Barred Owl. This chunky, dark-eyed owl breeds here and is common on the refuge year-round. In the fall, watch for Bald Eagles and Golden Eagles following migrating waterfowl down the flyway.

Look for Chuck will's-widow in the refuge's pine woodlands, located at the higher elevations. This large member of the nightjar family is a southern specialty, found only very rarely in the Northeast. Listen in the early evening for the loud, whistled song that gives the bird its name.

Pine woodlands are also highly attractive to woodpeckers. Felsenthal boasts eight species, including Red headed, Red-bellied, and Pileated Woodpeckers, along with breeding pairs of the endangered Red-cockaded Woodpecker. Look for the bird's black-and-white barred back, black cap, and large cheek patches.

The Chuck-will's-widow *sports the camoflaged plumage commonly found in the nightjar family of birds.*

VISITING

Felsenthal National Wildlife Refuge is a very big and very wet place. There are surprisingly few marked hiking trails, but a number of gravel roads and all-terrain-vehicle (ATV) trails provide good access to the refuge. Cars can follow the gravel roads, but birdwatchers should follow the ATV trails on foot only and be prepared for very wet, muddy terrain. Most of the trails and roads are open year-round, but visitors are advised to check with the refuge staff before setting out.

A good starting point is Pine Island, just south of the Visitor Center, along the eastern boundary of the refuge. A hiking trail loops through an upland area of pines and fields. The Crossett Harbor recreation site is a good place from which to view the vast Felsenthal Pool. Other bird-watching sites around the Felsenthal Pool are the Shallow Lake area and the region around the Felsenthal lock and dam at the southern end of the refuge.

HIGHLIGHTS

The endangered Red-cockaded Woodpecker nests in open stands of mature pine trees. At Felsenthal, artificial nest inserts have been placed in some trees to supplement the available natural cavities. Trees with nest cavities – natural or artificial – are marked with white bands. Stay at least 30 feet away from nest sites.

Site Map and Information

FELSENTHAL NATIONAL WILDLIFE REFUGE

🚗 From Crossett, take US Highway 82 west 5 miles to the Visitor Center.

⭕ Daily, sunrise to sunset, year-round.

◑ Some portions of the refuge are sanctuaries for wintering waterfowl and are closed from November 20 through January 31. However, birds on the Felsenthal Pool can still be observed easily from the southern part of the refuge.

ℹ️ Felsenthal National Wildlife Refuge, P.O. Box 1157, West Crossett, AR 71635. Visitor Center is open weekdays, 7:00 a.m.–3:30 p.m.; Sunday, 1:00–5:00 p.m.

📞 (870) 364-3167; http://southeast.fws.gov/felsenthal

Ⓢ None.

♿ Visitor Center, Woodland Wildlife Trail, and the fishing area are wheelchair accessible.

🅰 Eleven primitive campsites available on refuge; Crossett Harbor RV Park at (870) 364-6136 and the Grand Marais

Campground at (870) 943-2930 are nearby full-service campgrounds.

♟ None.

🛏 Motels available in nearby El Dorado and Crossett; call the El Dorado Chamber of Commerce at (870) 863-6113 or the Crossett Area Chamber of Commerce at (870) 364-6591 for listings.

LAKE CHICOT STATE PARK

A cypress swamp and the largest oxbow lake in the country attract a wide variety of birds to this lovely spot in southeastern Arkansas.

Some five centuries ago, the mighty Mississippi River ran where Lake Chicot is now. Over time, natural erosion shifted the river away to the east, but the bend the riverbed left behind became an oxbow lake – a crescent-shaped body of water some 20 miles long and nearly a mile wide. Fringed with stately cypress trees and majestic wild pecans, Lake Chicot today is the biggest oxbow lake in North America. Lake Chicot State Park, a 132-acre site at the northern end of the lake, is an excellent vantage point from which to enjoy the serene beauty of the lake and watch its abundant birdlife.

HABITAT

Lake Chicot is an excellent example of how human activity can destroy a habitat – and restore it. Starting in the early 1900s and continuing until the 1970s, Lake Chicot's pristine waters were damaged by the construction of levees and channels created for regional flood control. The natural flow of water into the lake was so altered that the lake began to fill up with silt very rapidly.

BIRDS TO LOOK FOR

Anhinga • Great Egret • Tricolored Heron • White Ibis • Wood Stork • Hooded Merganser • Mississippi Kite • Bald Eagle • Black-bellied Plover • American Golden-Plover • Bonaparte's Gull • Least Tern • Barred Owl • Horned Lark • Dickcissel

By 1970 it was clear that urgent steps were needed to save the lake and its surrounding habitat from disappearing altogether. The Army Corps of Engineers was called in to build two new dams and a diversion channel, augmented by a huge pumping station (which began operation in 1985) to send excess water on its way when flooding became a threat.

Least Terns, *which nest here, are found foraging on the lake at dawn and dusk.*

This reclamation effort worked so well that today Lake Chicot is classified as a clearwater lake. With its water quality and aquatic life restored, Lake Chicot once again attracts birds. The most rewarding way to watch them is from the lakeshore, woodlands, and cypress swamps of Lake Chicot State Park, which is nestled along the lake at its northern tip.

BIRD LIFE

Over 230 bird species have been recorded in Lake Chicot State Park and the surrounding area. The long, shallow shoreline and the abundance of fish make the lake particularly attractive to large wading birds, including the Great Blue Heron, Great

These White Ibis feed on the plentiful fish found in Lake Chicot's clear waters.

Egret, Tricolored Heron, White Ibis, and the occasional Wood Stork. Its location directly on the Mississippi flyway, a major migration route, makes it extremely attractive to all other birds, including migrating warblers.

The woodlands of the park are home to numerous owls, including Great Horned Owls, Eastern Screech-owls, and Barred Owls. The flat fields of the Mississippi delta region around the lake attract grassland birds such as Dickcissel and Horned Lark. Look for migrating shorebirds, including Black-bellied Plover and American Golden-Plover, which often pass through in the spring.

The Black-bellied Plover *can best be distinguished in the fall from the American-Golden Plover by its larger size and grayer plummage.*

In the summer, up to 3,000 herons, egrets, and Anhingas at a time can be seen in communal roosts in the trees fringing the lake. Various terns, including large numbers of breeding Least Terns, are also found foraging on the lake, especially at dawn and dusk. Mississippi Kites by the dozen spend the summer along Lake Chicot, where they can be observed swooping gracefully down to snatch dragonflies and other large insects from the air.

Birding at this park in the winter can be very rewarding – in terms of both species and numbers. The lake attracts large numbers of wintering ducks, geese, loons, and grebes, including Hooded

Mergansers, Pied-billed Grebes, and Wood Ducks. Where there are large numbers of ducks there are also often Bald Eagles to prey on them. In February, the 20 or more wintering Bald Eagles are the highlight of the park's annual Winter Wings Weekend. The most common wintering gull here by far is the Bonaparte's Gull.

VISITING

The birds of Lake Chicot State Park can be seen in two very enjoyable ways: on land or on the water. Both can be experienced within a single day. The one-mile Delta Woodlands Trail makes a loop through the woods by the Visitors Center, near the park entrance. This is a good route from which to see warblers in the spring and to look for owls. The roads that wind through the park are also ideal to use for spotting birds on foot or on bicycle. (From early spring through late fall, bikes can be rented at the park's marina.)

At sunset, take a ranger-led barge tour of Lake Chicot and the cypress swamps. These boat tours offer outstanding views of birds from the water, and visitors often see other wildlife, such as coyotes, opossums, and red and gray foxes. Call the Visitor Center for reservations. Boat rentals are also available at the marina.

HIGHLIGHTS

At dusk in the summertime, visitors to the park can enjoy the unforgettable sight of thousands of herons and egrets gliding in to roost for the night. Look for them in the many stands of cypress trees that line the lake.

Site Map and Information

LAKE CHICOT STATE PARK

🚗 From Pine Bluffs, take US 65 approximately 90 miles south to Highway 144. Follow Highway 144 northeast 8 miles to park entrance.

🕐 Daily, sunrise to sunset, year-round.

🌙 Never.

ℹ️ Lake Chicot State Park, 2542 Highway 257, Lake Village, AR 71653. Visitor Center is open daily, 8 a.m.–5 p.m.

📞 (870) 265-5480

💲 None.

♿ Fishing pier and some cabins are wheelchair accessible.

⛺ 14 cabins and 127 campsites on-site. Reservations required for cabins only; call (800) 264-2430.

👁 Call Visitor Center for information about ranger-led barge tours at sunset.

🏨 Motels available in nearby Lake Village; call the Chamber of Commerce at (870) 265-5997 for listings. Additional motels in nearby Greenville, Mississippi; call the Chamber of Commerce at (800) 467-3582.

Horseshoe Lake Conservation Area

Canada Geese, ducks, wading birds, and a wide range of forest species, including warblers and vireos, come together in this southern Illinois park.

Thousands of years ago, a bend formed in the Mississippi River as it flowed through what is now the southern tip of Illinois. The bend gradually turned into a basin and the river eventually changed its course, leaving behind a very large, shallow, horseshoe-shaped lake. Because the area was regularly flooded by spring rains, it was never heavily logged or extensively cleared for farming. To this day, the 2,400-acre lake and the 10,000 acres of surrounding woods and wetlands now known as the Horseshoe Lake Conservation Area are largely unspoiled, spectacularly beautiful terrain.

Habitat

The vegetation found around the main lake consists largely of trees such as bald cypress, water tupelo, and swamp cottonwood. This sort of swampland is common farther south, but it's rather unexpected for Illinois. In fact, this conservation area is southern-style swampland at its northernmost range.

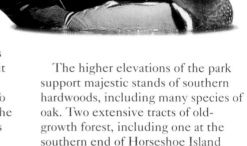

The Wood Duck *drake is easy to spot: its multicolored glossy plumage, sleek crest, and white facial stripes make it distinctive.*

The higher elevations of the park support majestic stands of southern hardwoods, including many species of oak. Two extensive tracts of old-growth forest, including one at the southern end of Horseshoe Island (which is really a peninsula that projects into the lake), are maintained as preserves within the park.

Bird Life

The first 49 acres of the park were purchased by the Illinois Department of Natural Resources in 1927 for development as a Canada Goose sanctuary. At that time, the lake was often flooded by spring rains but would go partially dry in the summer months. In the 1930s a spillway was built at the southern end of the lake to maintain the water depth at a more-or-less constant four feet.

The improved habitat made a big difference to the geese. Only about a thousand Canada Geese arrived for the winter of 1928; by 1944 the population had increased to 40,000. Today, thanks to even better management (grain crops are produced specifically for the

BIRDS TO LOOK FOR

Common Loon • Least Bittern • Little Blue Heron • Yellow-crowned Night-Heron • Canada Goose • Wood Duck • Bald Eagle • Bell's Vireo • Yellow-throated Warbler • Cerulean Warbler • Summer Tanager

This conservation area is now the winter home of more than 250,000 Canadian Geese.

geese to eat) and a vast expansion of protected acreage, the conservation area is the winter home of more than a quarter of a million Canada Geese. An active research program at Horseshoe Lake continues to provide important information about the migratory patterns of geese.

The shallow waters of Horseshoe Lake and the surrounding habitats attract numerous other birds as well. Wading birds, including Great Blue Herons, Green Herons, and rare Yellow-crowned Night-Herons, regularly nest in the trees fringing the lake, and Least Bitterns

Bald Eagles, *which prey on ducks, can often be found where large populations of waterfowl gather.*

skulk in the lush vegetation beneath the trees. The combination of a rich supply of acorns and abundant nesting cavities in ancient trees (cypress trees live for hundreds of years) makes the conservation area highly attractive to the colorful Wood Duck, which breeds in great numbers in the area. Migration brings other ducks, too, including the Ring-necked Duck, Blue-winged Teal, and Lesser Scaup.

The rich, moist woodlands around the lake, conveniently situated along the Mississippi Flyway, teem with many species of migrants. Warblers, including the Blue-winged, Prothonotary, and Kentucky, are abundant. The Yellow-throated Warbler forages in the upper branches of the cypress trees; the large white patch on the side of the head and the bold white eyestripe help identify it. Other songbirds, such as the White-eyed Vireo, Summer Tanager, and Vesper Sparrow, can also be found here often.

VISITING

The spectacular and unusual scenery of Horseshoe Lake makes it a popular recreation area, especially in the summer. Some hiking trails wind through the woods and wetlands, but for the best birdwatching, visit the 20-mile shoreline of the lake and the shores of Horseshoe Island. Four picnic areas and four campgrounds, all with parking areas, are spread around the lake, making it easy to get down to the shoreline. A good way to enjoy the birds here – and to reach the island, of course – is by boat. Bring your own or rent one at one of the nine boat-launching ramps located conveniently around the lake.

During the fall and winter, the lake is covered with large populations of waterfowl. In addition to the Canada Geese and some Snow Geese, this is a good time to see wintering Common Loons. The fall migration brings a range of ducks, including Ring-necked Ducks and Lesser Scaup. Look for wintering Bald Eagles at the southern end of the lake near the spillway. In the spring the park teems with many species, especially warblers and songbirds. Summer is a good time to enjoy the wading birds.

HIGHLIGHTS

Horseshoe Lake Conservation Area is managed in large part as a refuge for wintering Canada Geese. Every year some 250,000 of these distinctive birds – along with many ducks, loons, and other waterfowl – congregate on the shallow waters of the lake.

Site Map and Information

HORSESHOE LAKE CONSERVATION AREA

🚗 Illinois Route 3 skirts the eastern edge of the conservation area, about 7 miles north of Cairo. To enter the northern end of the park from Route 3, exit at Olive Branch Road; for the southern end, exit at East Side Drive.

◻ Daily, 24 hours, year-round.

⬤ Never.

🛈 Horseshoe Lake Conservation Area, P.O. Box 85, Miller City, IL 62962. Visitor Center open weekdays, 10:30 a.m.–4 p.m.

📞 (618) 776-5689

Ⓢ None.

♿ Campground and boat-launching ramps are wheelchair accessible.

🅰 Four on-site campgrounds ranging from full service to primitive.

🏨 None.

🛏 Horseshoe Lake Motel is adjacent to conservation area; call (618) 776-5201 for reservations.

ILLINOIS BEACH STATE PARK

*This park's rich diversity of habitats along Lake Michigan's coast form
a key migration stopover in northeastern Illinois.*

Stretching for six-and-a-half miles along the sandy western shore of Lake Michigan about 50 miles north of Chicago, Illinois Beach State Park is a popular place for both birds and people. Fortunately, this park combines so many interesting habitats in its 4,160 acres that there's plenty of room for all.

HABITAT
Some 15,000 years ago the Great Lakes region was entirely covered by a massive glacier. The glacier slowly melted, leaving behind a vast lake known to geologists as Lake Chicago. The lake gradually shrank, leaving behind the five smaller (but still very large) bodies of fresh water we call the Great Lakes. Over the millennia, Lake Michigan slowly continued to recede, and as it

Peregrine Falcons *often
fly low to the ground in
order to stalk their prey.*

receded it left behind high, sandy ridges, which represent the lake's earlier boundaries. In between the ridges and the current lake shore is a dramatic landscape of marshes, oak forests, and sand dunes that provide a wide array of habitats for plant and animal life.

It is this rich boundary habitat that made the 1964 formation of Illinois Beach State Park so critical. At one time beach ridges lined the shores of Lake Michigan, but over the past couple of centuries many of them have been destroyed by sand mining, industrial development, and other activities. Although preservation efforts began in 1888, it wasn't until 1948 that the state of Illinois purchased the first land parcels of what is now Illinois Beach State Park and almost 20 years later that it incorporated the 820-acre nature preserve. Today this park preserves nearly all the remaining beach-ridge shoreline habitat in the state.

Although the sandy beaches along Lake Michigan are the main attraction at Illinois Beach State Park, especially in the summer, the nature preserve also boasts some fine examples of dune and swale topography. (A swale is a marshy valley between ridges of sand dunes.) It also encompasses sand dune prairies, which are dunes and ridges covered with grasses.

BIRDS TO LOOK FOR

Red-throated Loon • Tundra Swan •
Oldsquaw • Broad-winged Hawk •
Merlin • Prairie Falcon • Peregrine
Falcon • Franklin's Gull • Little
Gull • Bonaparte's Gull • American
Pipit • Lark Sparrow • Nelson's
Sharp-tailed Sparrow • Snow Bunting

Bonaparte's Gulls can be spotted from Lake Michigan's coastline.

BIRD LIFE

The shores of Lake Michigan are an important migration route for birds in the Midwest. Rather than cross the open expanse of water, the birds follow the shoreline on their journeys north and south, often stopping over at Illinois Beach State Park.

The Lark Sparrow *can be identified by its distinctive head pattern and single dark breast spot.*

The dunes and grassy areas attract a range of sparrows year-round, including the occasional Lark Sparrow. Nelson's Sharp-tailed Sparrow, a fairly uncommon bird with a restricted range, turns up at Illinois Beach fairly often, especially in wet, grassy areas such as swales.

Look for Snow Buntings along the beaches and sand dunes in the winter. Horned Larks and Lapland Longspurs often are found alongside these fairly common sparrows. Small flocks of American Pipits are sometimes spotted on the beaches and in the fields in the winter.

Winter is also a good time to spot large flocks of waterfowl floating offshore in the icy lake waters. Look for Tundra Swans, Oldsquaws, and Common Goldeneyes, as well as Red-throated and Common Loons. Gull-watching is especially good on the shore in the fall and winter, when Bonaparte's, Franklin's, and Thayer's Gulls are all regularly seen. Rare gulls such as the Little Gull and Glaucous Gull often make winter appearances.

Illinois Beach State Park is a noted hawk-watching area. During the fall migration period, look for Prairie and Peregrine Falcons, Merlins, Northern Harriers, Broad-winged Hawks, and Bald Eagles on their way south.

VISITING

Enjoyable as this park is as a resort area during the warm summer months, the birdwatching is best when the weather is colder and the crowds of visitors smaller. The fall migration period is particularly rewarding. By September nighthawks and sparrows are moving through. Hawks are most visible in early to late October, followed by ducks and geese in mid-October to mid-November. Rare gulls start to turn up in mid October.

The birdwatching is good in the spring as well, especially in the marshy areas that warblers love. However, springtime birdwatchers may be distracted by the wonderful displays of blooming wildflowers. The nature preserve alone (in the South Unit of the park) contains more than 650 species of plants, including many colorful wildflowers and several native orchid species. A number of walking trails wind through the preserve. To avoid damaging the fragile dune habitat, please stay on them.

HIGHLIGHTS

The long shoreline of Illinois Beach State Park makes it a great spot for gull-watching. Rare visitors to the Great Lakes region, including Glaucous, Franklin's, Lesser Black-backed, Thayer's, and Little Gulls, may be seen here in the fall and winter months.

Site Map and Information

ILLINOIS BEACH STATE PARK

🚗 From Chicago, take I-94 north about 60 miles to Route 137 east and continue about 5 miles to Sheridan Road. To reach the nature preserve (the South Unit), go right on Sheridan Road, then left onto Wadsworth Road, and continue to the Visitor Center, just off the nature preserve parking lot.

⭘ Daily, sunrise to 8 p.m. (or sunset, whichever is sooner), year-round.

⭘ Never.

ℹ Illinois Beach State Park Nature Preserve, Lake Front, Zion, IL 60099. The Visitor Center is open daily, from approximately June through September, 9 a.m.-12 p.m. and 1 p.m.-3 p.m., and the rest of the year by appointment.

📞 (847) 662-4811; www.dnr.state.il.us/lands/landmgt/parks

⑤ None.

♿ Campsites, the fishing pier, and some trails are wheelchair accessible.

🅰 There are 244 full-service campsites on-site; call (847) 662-4811 for reservations.

🏕 None.

🏨 Illinois Beach Resort is on-site; call (847) 625-7300 for reservations. Numerous motels are also available in nearby Zion and Waukegan; call Lake County Illinois Convention and Visitors Bureau at (847) 662-2700 for listings.

INDIANA DUNES NATIONAL LAKESHORE

*Situated along the Indiana shore of Lake Michigan, this
preserve boasts an astonishing array of bird-attracting ecosystems.*

The Indiana dunes region stretches for some 45 miles along the southern shore of Lake Michigan, from Chicago's Illinois border through Gary, Indiana, to Michigan City, Indiana. Through strenuous volunteer efforts over more than 50 years, large portions of this beachfront area have been preserved, and the Indiana Dunes National Lakeshore is the largest of these protected areas. Stretching for nearly 25 miles along southern Lake Michigan (not all of it contiguous) and covering nearly 15,000 acres, the national lakeshore was authorized by Congress in 1966. Within the boundaries of the national lakeshore lies the 2,200-acre Indiana Dunes State Park, managed by the Indiana Department of Natural Resources.

HABITAT

What makes Indiana Dunes National Lakeshore so interesting is its diversity. Here, where northern and southern plant communities meet, it's not uncommon to see arctic bearberry and prickly pear cactus growing side by side. Compressed into this narrow strip of coast are habitats ranging from beaches and towering sand dunes (many over 100 feet high) to inland forests, extensive marshes, prairies, and bogs. This diversity of habitats is reflected in the great variety of bird life – more than 330 species! – that has been recorded visiting this site.

Lesser Scaup are found on the ponds and wetlands in spring and fall; Greater Scaup are common on Lake Michigan in winter.

BIRD LIFE

The location of Indiana Dunes National Lakeshore at the southern tip of Lake Michigan makes it an excellent spot for birdwatching during both spring and fall migrations. Birds heading in either direction skirt along the shores of the massive lake, which funnels them into the Indiana dunes region. Many spend a few days feeding and resting at this national park before moving on.

Two bird families are particularly conspicuous here. In March migrating raptors, including Red-Shouldered Hawks and Bald Eagles, pass overhead in substantial numbers. Later in the spring, warblers (many of

BIRDS TO LOOK FOR

Greater Scaup • Lesser Scaup • Red-breasted Merganser • Bald Eagle • Red-shouldered Hawk • Franklin's Gull • Caspian Tern • Forster's Tern • Blue-winged Warbler • Nashville Warbler • Cape May Warbler • Blackburnian Warbler• Bay-breasted Warbler • Connecticut Warbler •

Indiana Dunes is a stopover for many migrant birds, including Red-shouldered Hawks.

which breed farther north) abound in the lakeshore's extensive marshy areas. Look for Bay-breasted, Blackburnian, Blue-winged, Cape May, Connecticut, and Nashville Warblers. These same songbirds, in duller winter plumage, will pass through again in the fall.

A diverse group of gulls and terns are found along the shore of the park's Great Dunes. Bonaparte's Gulls and Ring-billed Gulls can be seen reliably year-round. Franklin's Gull, a relatively rare inland species, turns up with fair regularity in the summer and fall, when it's heading into winter plumage. Look for a smallish gull with a dark half-hood, red bill, and black-and-

The Blackburnian Warbler *male can be recognized by the fiery yellow throat, triangular ear patch, and the bold white patch on the wing.*

white markings on the tips of the wings. Caspian Terns, with their stocky bodies and thick orange bills, are common in the spring and fall. The elegant Forster's Tern, already in winter plumage by late August, passes through in the fall. Look for a dark eye patch, deeply forked tail, and white rump.

A number of ducks are also regularly seen at this national park during spring and fall migrations. Watch for Wood Duck, American Black Duck, Gadwall, American Wigeon, Redhead, Lesser Scaup, and Red-breasted Merganser on the lake or on ponds in the wetlands areas. Greater Scaup are commonly seen in the winter, rafting in large flocks on Lake Michigan.

VISITING

The challenge in visiting Indiana Dunes is deciding where to go first. The seven-mile Ly-co-ki-we Trail complex, which begins at the Dorothy Buell Visitor Center in the eastern part of the park, is a promising place for birders to start. These paths lead through open sandy areas and into woodland areas. Wetlands areas are interspersed; look here for warblers in the springtime. Look for park orientation signs, located in major parking areas, and for trail maps, located at major trailheads.

Several miles of trails in the Miller Woods section, in the western part of the park, wind through interdunal ponds, marshes, and black oak savanna (open grassy areas with widely spaced trees). Enjoy the wildflowers in the savanna and look for wading birds, such as Great Blue Herons, in the marshy areas. For a short but informative walk, follow the West Beach Succession Trail. In just a mile the trail transitions from beach to interdunal pond to oak forest, providing a peek into the amazing diversity found here.

HIGHLIGHTS

At least 337 bird species have been seen at Indiana Dunes National Lakeshore. Of these, some 113 are considered regular nesters in the park. Bald Eagles and Sandhill Cranes once bred here, but habitat destruction has kept these birds from nesting here. Park managers hope that restored habitat and improved water quality will once again attract them.

Site Map and Information

INDIANA DUNES NATIONAL LAKESHORE

🚘 From Michigan City, IN, take US Highway 12 west 15 miles to reach the Dorothy Buell Memorial Visitor Center.

🕐 Daily, sunrise to sunset, year-round.

⚫ Never.

ℹ Indiana Dunes National Lakeshore, 1100 North Mineral Springs Road, Porter, IN 46304. Visitor Center open daily, 8 a.m.–5 p.m. (until 6 p.m. in the summer); closed Thanksgiving, Christmas, and New Year's Day.

📞 (219) 926-7561; www.nps.gov/indu

💲 $4 parking fee at the West Beach lakeshore, from mid-May through Labor Day.

♿ Visitor Center, parking lots, campground, picnic areas, beaches, and some trails are wheelchair accessible. TTY number is same as park number, above.

🅰 Dunewood Campground has 79 campsites (no hookups); fees: $8-10 daily on a first-come, first-served basis. It is closed from November through March 31. Limited camping facilities are available in winter at Indiana Dunes State Park in nearby Chesterton; call (219) 926-4520 for reservations.

🍴 None.

🏨 Motels in nearby Michigan City, Pines, Chesterton, and Portage; call Lake County Convention and Visitors Bureau at (800) ALL-LAKE for listings.

JASPER-PULASKI FISH AND WILDLIFE AREA

Wetlands and open fields in northwestern Indiana attract a wide range of migrating birds, including Sandhill Cranes by the thousands.

Audible more than a mile away, the trumpeting *gar-oo-oo* call of the Sandhill Crane is unmistakable. At Jasper-Pulaski Fish and Wildlife Area every fall and spring, that remarkable sound heralds the arrival of tens of thousands of migrating Sandhill Cranes. It's a spectacle that had nearly vanished by the 1930s, when hunting, agricultural expansion, wetlands drainage, and other habitat changes led to the near-extinction of the Greater Sandhill Crane, the subspecies found in eastern North America. Stronger game laws and an increase in protected habitat have restored this subspecies to robust numbers – 65,000 to 75,000 birds.

HABITAT

Spanning just over 8,000 acres, Jasper-Pulaski Fish and Wildlife Area is one of Indiana's largest remaining wetland areas. At the core of the preserve is a 900-acre area that combines marsh, meadow, and open water in an ideal habitat for migratory birds, particularly Sandhill Cranes, as well as ducks and geese.

The area around the preserve, however, is just as important to the Sandhill Cranes. The nearby countryside is a mosaic of meadows, marshes, and rich farmland. The cranes roost in the marshes of the refuge at night but spread out into the surrounding countryside during the day to feed on insects, crayfish, frogs, small animals, root tubers, plant shoots, and grain.

Alder Flycatchers *are drawn to the large numbers of insects found in the wildlife area during warm weather.*

BIRD LIFE

Sandhill Cranes are the main birdwatching attraction in the wildlife area. These sleek, long-legged gray birds stand about four feet tall and have wingspans of seven feet. It's hard to mistake them for any other kind of bird.

In spring or fall, dawn and dusk are the ideal times to watch them. At sunrise the cranes fly out of the marshes and assemble in the nearby 300-acre grassy area known as Goose Pasture. There they mingle and call loudly before flying off to spend the day feeding in the neighborhood. Look for them in the harvested grain fields near the preserve. At the end of the day the birds reverse the process, gathering in Goose Pasture about half an hour before sundown. From there

BIRDS TO LOOK FOR

Least Bittern • Canada Goose • Redhead • Lesser Scaup • Bald Eagle • Golden Eagle • Wild Turkey • Northern Bobwhite • Virginia Rail • Common Moorhen • American Coot • Sandhill Crane • Alder Flycatcher • Kentucky Warbler • Hooded Warbler • Vesper Sparrow

Breeding Common Moorhens have a red forehead shield and a red bill with yellow tip.

they fly in large, noisy waves back into the marshes to roost for the night. For the best viewing of Sandhill Cranes, begin at the preserve's headquarters just before dawn or dusk. The observation tower at Goose Pasture, a short distance from headquarters, is one of the premier vantage points from which to watch the birds. They can also be seen from several ground-level viewing areas in Goose Pasture.

A second observation tower is located in the center of the 900-acre marsh area. Here the 1.3-mile Marsh Trail and the tower provide good views of all the birds to be seen at Jasper-Pulaski. Year-round, look for Common Moorhens, Least Bitterns, Virginia

Rails, and American Coots. During the fall and spring migration periods, spectacular numbers of Canada Geese and ducks such as Redheads and Lesser Scaup can be seen easily in the area. The large numbers of waterfowl attract Bald and Golden Eagles, which prey on injured and weak birds. (Note that from mid-October through December, during waterfowl-hunting season, the trail is open in the afternoon only.)

The high insect population of the marshes in warmer weather also makes them very attractive to flycatchers. In late May and June, listen for the distinctive wheezy, descending *weeb-ew* song of the Alder Flycatcher. An array of warblers,

Sandhill Cranes *are the main bird-watching attraction during their spring and fall migration.*

including Hooded and Kentucky Warblers, passes through during migratory periods.

VISITING

Sandhill Cranes migrate through Jasper-Pulaski Fish and Wildlife Area in two distinct seasons. In the fall the birds begin arriving in mid-September. Peak arrivals, often in the neighborhood of thousands of birds a day, don't occur until late October. In the spring fewer Sandhill Cranes come through and the migration pattern is somewhat more compressed. The peak arrival period at the preserve is late March. By the first of April most of the cranes are already gone, although a few pairs will remain to breed on the site.

Visitors to Jasper-Pulaski should remember that the site is managed largely as a hunting area for waterfowl (Sandhill Cranes cannot be hunted). The site does a good job of keeping hunters separated from crane watchers, but for personal safety, read and obey signs and stay out of restricted areas.

HIGHLIGHTS

Tefft Savanna Nature Preserve borders the western edge of Jasper-Pulaski Fish and Wildlife Area. Look within this outstanding example of oak barren or savanna (featuring sandy soil with open woodlands) for Wild Turkeys, Northern Bobwhites, and Vesper Sparrows. Call (219) 843-5012 for more information.

Site Map and Information

JASPER-PULASKI FISH AND WILDLIFE AREA

🚗 From US Highway 421 between San Pierre and Medaryville, turn west onto Indiana State Road 143. Go 1.5 miles to reach headquarters and parking area.

🕐 Daily, sunrise to sunset, year-round.

⬤ Never, although some portions are closed for part of the day during hunting season (mid-October through December) and during spring and summer waterfowl nesting.

ℹ️ Jasper-Pulaski Fish and Wildlife Area, 5822 North Fish and Wildlife Lane, Medaryville IN 47957. Headquarters, which serve as a Visitor Center, are open daily, 5 a.m.–8 p.m., October through December, and 8 a.m.–3 p.m. during the rest of the year.

📞 (219) 843-4841

💲 None.

♿ Headquarters, picnic area, and Sandhill Crane observation tower are all wheelchair accessible.

🏕️ 51 primitive camp sites are available on-site. For full-service campsites, call Tippecanoe River State Park at (219) 946-3213.

🍴 None.

🏨 Motels are available in nearby Rensselaer; call the chamber of commerce at (219) 866-8223 for information. Or call the Indiana Tourism Division at (800) 291-8844 for additional listings throughout Jasper, Pulaski, and nearby Stark Counties.

RIVERTON WILDLIFE AREA

*Watch waterfowl, shorebirds, woodland birds, and more at this large
and varied preserve in the southwestern corner of Iowa.*

Riverton Wildlife Area is one of birdwatching's better-kept secrets. This 2,747-acre (and growing!) preserve contains a range of habitats, plus its location along the Missouri River migration flyway attracts birds, sometimes in very large numbers. On a typical day in late April, anywhere from 5,000 to 15,000 shorebirds, can be seen here.

HABITAT

Riverton Wildlife Area was acquired in 1941 with the purchase of 721 acres. More acreage was added over the years, and all the land lies just north of the confluence of two rivers: the East and West Nishnabotna. Spring Creek also flows through the area year-round and is dammed to form a lake that is highly inviting to waterfowl wintering at the wildlife area when it is not frozen.

The water levels on the preserve are controlled by a series of dikes and a pumping station. In the spring the water level is lowered, creating large

mudflats – a habitat that is extremely attractive to migrating shorebirds, such as sandpipers. In mid-August flooding is begun to raise the water level in the lake and to create many wetland areas to attract migrating waterfowl. These wetlands areas are also ideal for rails, bitterns, and herons.

The wildlife area's upland areas and woodlands provide excellent food and cover for birds such as Ring-necked Pheasants, Indigo Buntings, American Redstarts, and Prothonotary Warblers.

Greater Scaup *are diving ducks and can usually be found on deep water.*

BIRD LIFE

Riverton Wildlife Area is notable for the large concentrations of shorebirds that can occur here, especially during the spring migration period. Look for the American Avocet, Hudsonian Godwit, White-rumped Sandpiper, Baird's Sandpiper, and Buff-breasted Sandpiper, which congregate on the mudflats, often in large numbers.

In the fall, the concentrations of shorebirds can be almost as large. In late August the birds start pouring in because the wildlife area is one of the few stopover points on the Missouri River flyway that isn't overgrown or dried out, even in dry years. The same

BIRDS TO LOOK FOR

American Bittern • Yellow-crowned Night-Heron • Snow Goose • Green-winged Teal • Greater Scaup • Bald Eagle • Hudsonian Godwit • White-rumped Sandpiper • Baird's Sandpiper • Buff-breasted Sandpiper • Franklin's Gull • Willow Flycatcher • American Redstart • Harris's Sparrow • Indigo Bunting

Shorebirds, including Baird's Sandpipers, are found on Riverton's mud flats.

mudflats and open water that attract shorebirds also attract terns and gulls. Least Terns and Franklin's Gulls are fairly common visitors.

As large as the concentrations of shorebirds can be, the concentrations of waterfowl on the preserve in the fall and winter are even larger. The fall duck numbers usually peak at over 20,000, while the number of wintering Snow Geese can top 200,000. Ducks include the American Black Duck, Green-winged Teal, and Greater Scaup. Check all the flocks of Snow Geese for the far less common Ross's Goose, also found here in winter. The Ross's Goose is smaller and has a shorter neck and rounder head; look also for the distinguishing stubby, triangular bill.

From mid-August into September, wading birds such as American Bitterns, Yellow-crowned Night-Herons, and Virginia Rails, concentrate on the mudflats for a final few weeks of feeding before they head south.

Although Riverton is most famous for shorebirds, it is also highly attractive to passerines, such as sparrows, flycatchers, and warblers. Check all brushy and grassy areas along the sides of the roads and dikes for such interesting birds as Harris's Sparrow and Willow Flycatcher.

VISITING

Visitors to Riverton Wildlife Area should begin by checking out the territory from the observation platform behind the headquarters area, along Country Road 330th Avenue. It gives a panoramic view of the preserve, making areas where shorebirds or waterfowl have concentrated easy to spot.

After pinpointing the hot spots, take the gravel road north past the observation platform, where it

The White-rumped Sandpiper's *call is a high-pitched* jeet.

137

soon intersects with the main east-west dike. This dike marks the entrance into the best birdwatching areas, but it can be accessed by foot only; park here by the side of the road. The dike passes through extensive marshy areas and mudflats. In April and May this trail is the best place the wildlife area to see shorebirds and waterfowl.

Return to the car and follow the gravel road around the western edge of the wildlife area, where it passes the pumping station. On foot, take the dike trail downhill through the woods, looking for warblers and other passerines in the spring. The dike follows the lake shore and then becomes a dam at the northern end of the lake. From here, the wintering geese, ducks, and grebes, plus

Double-crested Cormorants and American White Pelicans in April, May, and September, can be seen easily; shorebirds can be spotted on the mudflats to the north of the dam.

Riverton Wildlife Area is managed chiefly as a waterfowl hunting area. Parts of the area are closed between mid-September and the end of December. Obey all posted signs and do not enter restricted areas.

HIGHLIGHTS

Starting in December, Riverton Wildlife Area hosts anywhere from 30 to about 80 wintering Bald Eagles. The birds prey on the thousands of Snow Geese and other waterfowl that arrive between Thanksgiving and Christmas to take up winter residence here.

Site Map and Information

RIVERTON WILDLIFE AREA

From Shenandoah, take US 59 south 2 miles to Route 2. Follow Route 2 west for 9 miles to County Road 330th Avenue and go south for 2.5 miles to reach headquarters.

Daily, sunrise to sunset, year-round.

Never, although access to some areas is limited during hunting season, mid-September through December.

Visitor Information: Riverton Wildlife Area, c/o Iowa Department of Natural Resources Box 490, Sidney, IA 51652. Headquarters is open to the public daily, year-round, but no regular office hours are maintained.

(712) 374-3133

None.

The refuge headquarters and observation platform are wheelchair accessible.

None on-site. Campgrounds are available at nearby Waubonsie State

Park in Hamburg; call (712) 382-2786 for information.

None.

There are motels in nearby Glenwood, Hamburg, Nebraska City, Pacific Junction, and Shenandoah. Call the Shenandoah Chamber and Industry Association at (712) 246-3455 for listings.

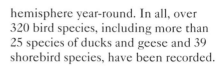

CHEYENNE BOTTOMS WILDLIFE AREA

Marshes, grasslands, and sandhills come together in south-central Kansas to create a vitally important habitat for birds and other creatures.

Every spring between March and May an estimated 45 percent of the North American shorebird population – up to 600,000 individuals – passes through Cheyenne Bottoms Wildlife Area during the northward migration period. It's no exaggeration to say that Cheyenne Bottoms, which was acquired by the state of Kansas in the 1950s, is one of the most important bird habitats in the entire western hemisphere year-round. In all, over 320 bird species, including more than 25 species of ducks and geese and 39 shorebird species, have been recorded.

HABITAT

What makes this complex of marshes, grasslands, and seasonal mudflats so special is a unique combination of geology and geography. Geologically, the 19,857-acre area is part of a 41,000-acre natural land sink that contains an extensive network of wetlands mixed with grasslands, low hills, and sand dunes. Site managers manipulate the water levels of large, shallow pools through a system of dikes, canals, and dams in order to provide optimal habitat for waterbirds.

Cheyenne Bottoms is located in south-central Kansas, an area that is a transition zone on the Great Plains. Here the lush vegetation of the eastern prairie blends with the more arid grasslands of the western prairie. The varied terrain and plant communities, along with its location squarely on the central flyway, make Cheyenne Bottoms a crucially important stopover point for birds on their seasonal journeys.

Baird's Sandpiper *may be distinguished from the other sandpipers by the solid buff color above and across its breast and its low* kreeep *call.*

BIRDS TO LOOK FOR

American White Pelican • White-faced Ibis • Greater White-fronted Goose • Canvasback • Redhead • Ruddy Duck • Mississippi Kite • Bald Eagle • Golden Eagle • Black Rail • Whooping Crane • Piping Plover • Black-necked Stilt • White-rumped Sandpiper • Baird's Sandpiper • Long-billed Dowitcher • Wilson's Phalarope

BIRD LIFE

The number and variety of waterfowl and shorebirds at Cheyenne Bottoms during spring and fall migration periods make visiting this wildlife area an unforgettable experience. The ducks and geese that stop at Cheyenne Bottoms include the Greater White-fronted Goose, Gadwall, Northern Pintail, Redhead,

Site managers manipulate the water levels to attract Black-necked Stilts and others.

Canvasback, and Ruddy Duck. Even Long-tailed Ducks (Oldsquaws), sea ducks that are rare in the interior regions of North America, have been spotted here.

The endangered Piping Plover is one of the many shorebird species found here – look for the orange legs and conspicuous white rump when the bird flies. Fortunate visitors might spot an American Golden-Plover passing through on the way to its nesting grounds near the arctic circle. Among the other shorebird species that stop here are Black-necked Stilt, White-rumped Sandpiper, Baird's Sandpiper, Pectoral

Sandpiper, Buff-breasted Sandpiper, Long-billed Dowitcher, Stilt Sandpiper, and Wilson's Phalarope.

Cheyenne Bottoms offers an astonishing range of other species as well. The raptors found on the site include Mississippi Kites, which breed nearby and are common here in summer, and Swainson's Hawks, regulars in spring, summer, and fall. In winter Bald and Golden Eagles are common, as are Prairie Falcons.

Look for the American White Pelican, abundant here during both migration periods. Although they are uncommon, White-faced Ibis have been nesting at Cheyenne Bottoms in recent years. In the spring and fall Sandhill Cranes are easily seen. In marshy areas, stay on the lookout for a number of rail species, including the King Rail, Virginia Rail, and Sora. The Black Rail, rare and hard to spot, breeds here between April and August.

The Canvasback *has a distinctive profile: a sloping forehead and long, slightly curved black bill.*

VISITING

For sheer number and variety, migration periods are the best times to visit here. Ducks and geese start arriving in February; that's also when the Sandhill and Whooping Cranes stop over. The American White Pelicans begin to arrive in March. The shorebird spectacle is concentrated in the few weeks between late April and mid-May.

The return journey south begins as early as July for some shorebird species, but the spectacular part of the fall migration at Cheyenne Bottoms really gets under way in October, when flights of thousands of Canada Geese, ducks, Sandhill Cranes, and shorebirds start to pass through. Whooping Cranes sometimes make a brief visit in late October or early November.

The pools at Cheyenne Bottoms are connected by a series of dikes that double as roads and walking trails. A few cautions apply. When walking, be sure to cross dikes only at foot crossings; the water depth in the ditches along the dikes can exceed four feet. And watch out for rattlesnakes, which are common here in the warm months.

HIGHLIGHTS

The birdwatching at Cheyenne Bottoms Wildlife Area is at its most spectacular in the spring, when the concentrations of shorebirds are huge. During this time nearly 90 percent of the continental population of Stilt Sandpipers and Wilson's Phalaropes pass through.

Site Map and Information

CHEYENNE BOTTOMS WILDLIFE AREA

🚗 From Great Bend, KS, drive 5 miles north on US Highway 281, then 2 miles east on Township Road 60.

⏱ Daily, 24 hours, year-round.

● Never.

ℹ Cheyenne Bottoms Wildlife Area, 56 NE 40 Road, Great Bend, KS 67530. There is no regularly staffed Visitor Center, but visitors are welcome at the office when staff is there. Call for reservations to use the photography blind, which functions as a hunters' blind in the winter.

📞 (316) 793-3066; (316) 793-7730 (for weather conditions)

Ⓢ None.

♿ The office and the photography blind (3 miles east of office) are wheelchair accessible.

🅰 There is a primitive campground (no water) on-site. Campgrounds are also

available in nearby Great Bend; call Great Bend Convention and Visitors Bureau at (316) 792-2750 for information.

🍴 None.

🏨 Motels available in nearby Great Bend; call the convention and visitors bureau at (316) 792-2750 for listings.

FLINT HILLS NATIONAL WILDLIFE REFUGE

*This haven for migrating waterfowl sits in a river valley
in eastern Kansas along the Central flyway.*

The name of this bird-rich site is actually somewhat misleading – Flint Hills National Wildlife Refuge is actually located just to the east of Kansas's gently rolling Flint Hills region. The slight geographic misnomer doesn't seem to confuse the birds, however. This large (slightly over 18,500 acres) and important migratory stopover point boasts a bird list of 294 species. The refuge, which was founded in 1966 and is managed by the U.S. Fish and Wildlife Service, is set along the upstream portion of the John Redmond Reservoir on land owned by the U.S. Army Corps of Engineers.

HABITAT

Located in the broad, flat Neosho River Valley, Flint Hills National Wildlife Refuge sprawls for nearly 10 miles along both sides of the river and includes an offshoot to the southwest, along Eagle Creek. Each year during fall and spring migration periods, thousands of ducks and geese are attracted to the refuge's extensive wetland areas, formed years ago when the Neosho River was dammed to create the John Redmond Reservoir.

The wetland areas include seasonally flooded marshes and hardwood river bottoms. Uplands woods and grasslands complete the mix, making the refuge enormously attractive not only to waterbirds but to other birds as well. In addition to the numerous species that stop over during migration, about 90 species breed here regularly.

Agricultural lands that border the refuge are shared with local farmers. The farmers harvest their portion, while the refuge plants grain crops, including corn and wheat, that are left standing to provide food for migrating waterfowl.

Tennessee Warblers, *among other warblers, abound in the refuge's marshes and wet woodland areas.*

BIRD LIFE

The main attraction for birdwatchers visiting Flint Hills National Wildlife Refuge is the spectacle of thousands upon thousands of migratory waterfowl. Four geese species are seen here in abundance in both the fall and spring – Greater White-fronted Goose, Snow Goose, Ross's Goose, and Canada Goose. Some 20 duck species also are regularly seen here. Look especially for Green-winged Teal,

BIRDS TO LOOK FOR

Clark's Grebe • Great Blue Heron • Greater White-fronted Goose • Ross's Goose • Green-winged Teal • Ruddy Duck • Bald Eagle • Virginia Rail • Upland Sandpiper • Wilson's Phalarope • Yellow-billed Cuckoo • Say's Phoebe • Tennessee Warbler • Orange-crowned Warbler • Nashville Warbler • Lapland Longspur

Clark's Grebes, usually found farther west, may be observed in wetland areas here.

American Wigeon, Redhead, Lesser Scaup, Red-breasted Merganser, and Ruddy Duck. The Tundra Swan is occasionally spotted during the spring and fall migration periods.

Clark's Grebe, a water bird that is generally found much farther west, is abundant at the refuge in the fall and spring. Look for the striking black-and-white plumage on the bird's long, graceful neck. The marshy areas are attractive to herons, including Great, Little Blue, and Green Herons, Virginia Rails, American Coots, and Wilson's Phalaropes, among others. A large population of overwintering Bald Eagles takes up residence in the refuge every autumn, attracted by the abundant duck population.

The grassy areas of the refuge are good places to see the Upland Sandpiper, particularly in the spring (when it breeds) and summer. This large sandpiper has a small head with large, dark eyes. Often the head is all that can be seen of the bird as it stalks insects in the fields. Other birds likely to be seen in the grassy areas include Lapland Longspur, in winter, and Say's Phoebe. The wooded areas are good places to watch both the Yellow-billed and Black-billed Cuckoos. The marshes and wet woodland areas abound with warblers – look for the Tennessee, Orange-crowned, and Nashville Warblers, among others.

VISITING

The best birdwatching is found along the refuge's gravel roads and from the contiguous parking areas, which lead visitors into marshy areas. For birdwatchers, the best strategy is to follow, on foot or by car, the gravel road that begins near the refuge headquarters building and runs along the east side of Burgess

The Wilson's Phalarope, which nests in the Flint Hills, is primarily an inland bird.

143

Marsh. The birdwatching is good along the Burgess Marsh Trail; there are two parking areas that also provide nice views out over the marsh. There are two other walking trails – Dove Roost and Headquarters – that are also worth exploring.

Migration periods – fall or spring – are ideal times to visit Flint Hills National Wildlife Refuge. Waterfowl numbers peak in November and March. The best time to watch perching birds is in April and May, when large numbers pass through the refuge on their way to breeding grounds farther north.

Although the refuge is managed as a habitat for migratory birds, with an emphasis on waterfowl, note that waterfowl hunting is allowed on the portion of the refuge south of the Neosho River. During peak waterfowl migration, the refuge north of the Neosho River is closed to all public entry, except for the Burgess Marsh area, which is open year-round to permitted, non-hunting activities.

HIGHLIGHTS

Flint Hills National Wildlife Refuge is an excellent spot to see the Greater White-fronted Goose, an eastern Great Plains specialty. As these beautiful birds travel back and forth from their breeding grounds above the arctic circle to their wintering grounds along the Gulf Coast of Texas, Louisiana, and Mexico, large flocks – numbering in the thousands – stop over at the refuge.

Site Map and Information

FLINT HILLS NATIONAL WILDLIFE REFUGE

🚗 From Emporia take I-35 south 15 miles to Highway 130. Follow Highway 130 east 8 miles to the town of Hartford. Turn west on Maple Avenue and continue 3 blocks to reach the refuge entrance.

🗀 Daily, sunrise to sunset, year-round.

⬤ The area north of the Neosho River is closed from November 1 to March 1. At times the refuge experiences flooding and roads must be closed; call ahead before visiting.

ℹ Flint Hills National Wildlife Refuge, P.O. Box 128, Hartford, KS 66854. Refuge headquarters, which serves as a Visitor Center, are open weekdays, 8 a.m.–4:30 p.m.

☎ 316) 392-5553; www.r6.fws.gov/refuges/FLINT

Ⓢ None.

♿ Refuge headquarters are wheelchair accessible.

🛆 Primitive camping is allowed throughout the refuge; all supplies and trash must be carried out afterward.

⚏ None.

🏨 There are many motels in nearby Emporia; call the Emporia Convention and Visitors Bureau at (800) 279-3730 for listings.

SABINE NATIONAL WILDLIFE REFUGE

Coastal marshes and bayous in the southwestern corner of Louisiana are a haven for waterfowl and wading birds.

The largest coastal marsh refuge on the Gulf of Mexico, Sabine National Wildlife Refuge consists of 124,511 acres of wetland habitat crucial for migrating and wintering birds. In the spring, Sabine's location directly on the coast makes it the first landfall for tired birds that have just crossed hundreds of miles of open water. In the fall, the refuge is a place for birds to rest and feed before taking off across the Gulf on the perilous journey south over open water. Not all the birds arriving at Sabine in the fall will go any farther. The warm climate, protected marshes, and rich food supply make the refuge an ideal wintering ground for thousands of ducks, geese, waders, and other waterbirds.

The Roseate Spoonbill's *pink and red body, not to mention the spatula-shaped bill, are unmistakeable.*

HABITAT

Sabine National Wildlife Refuge lies in a basin of wetlands and lakes found between the cherniers (oak ridges) that line the beaches of the Gulf of Mexico to the south and the coastal prairie found to the north. Fresh water from the Sabine and Calcasieu rivers flows into the basin and mixes with the salty water of the Gulf. The result is an extremely productive marsh, filled with fish, frogs, crabs, shrimp, and other food for the resident ducks and wading birds.

The refuge is also the perfect habitat for many other animals, including alligators, swamp rabbits, and the nutria. (A large, reddish brown, furry rodent introduced from South America, the nutria is now considered a destructive pest in southern wetlands.)

In the years since the refuge was established in 1937, 10 major water control structures; 61 miles of levees; and over 150 miles of canals, bayous, and waterways have been built to maintain the level and quality of the water.

BIRD LIFE

Large wading birds (herons, egrets, ibis, spoonbills, and storks), ducks, and geese are the specialties at Sabine National Wildlife Refuge. The marshes support an amazing variety of long-legged waders; look for the Tricolored Heron, the magnificent

BIRDS TO LOOK FOR

American White Pelican • Great Egret • Tricolored Heron • Reddish Egret • White Ibis • Roseate Spoonbill • Wood Stork • Snow Goose • Mottled Duck • Blue-winged Teal • Purple Gallinule • Common Moorhen • Tennessee Warbler • Hooded Warbler

The refuge's extensive marsh attracts the Purple Gallinule year-round.

Great Egret, and a Southern specialty, the Reddish Egret. The White Ibis and the White-faced Ibis both breed on the refuge, as does the beautiful Roseate Spoonbill. The threatened Wood Stork occasionally migrates through the refuge in late summer and early fall.

Two very common birds to watch for year-round in the refuge's marshy areas are the Common Moorhen and the closely related Purple Gallinule. Common Moorhens are readily seen

Common Moorhen *chicks may already sport the characteristic red bill with a yellow tip.*

swimming in open water or wading along the shore. These small, dark, chicken-sized birds have a red forehead shield, a red bill with a yellow tip, and a white rump. The Purple Gallinule is more brilliant, with a light blue forehead, yellow-and-red bill, and bright yellow legs.

Huge numbers of waterfowl pass through the refuge in the spring and fall, and some stay to spend the winter. Look for Gadwall, Green-winged Teal, American Wigeon, Northern Pintail, and Blue-winged Teal, all readily seen here. The Mottled Duck, a Gulf Coast specialty, breeds here and can be found at the refuge year-round. Wintering Snow Geese are seen in the early morning, north of refuge headquarters.

Waterfowl and waders may be the most visible birds at Sabine, but the site is also famous for the waves of colorful warblers and other songbirds that pass through in the spring. Watch for Tennessee,

Bay-breasted, and Hooded Warblers, among others, in the moist, brushy areas of the refuge. Cold fronts in March, April, and May sometimes keep these small birds from moving north out of the region for a while.

VISITING

With the protection of a powerful mosquito repellent in place, it's easy to enjoy the search for birds and other wildlife at Sabine National Wildlife Refuge. Highway 27, the only road through the refuge, has numerous pullouts in which to park and watch ducks, herons, egrets, and ibis, as well as other animals.

Year-round, the best way to see birds and other wildlife at Sabine National Wildlife Refuge is by walking Marsh Trail, located four miles south of the refuge headquarters, on the west side of

Highway 27. This 1.5-mile route offers an excellent opportunity to spot Common Moorhens and Purple Gallinules. Many duck species are generally visible in the surrounding marshes. Wading birds, including Roseate Spoonbills, are readily seen from the trail as well. Other marsh residents, including alligators and nutria, can be seen, too. Don't feed or approach the alligators; if they are blocking the trail, turn back or wait until they move out of the way.

HIGHLIGHTS

Sabine National Wildlife Refuge is famous for major concentrations of wintering ducks and geese. Some ducks begin arriving by August, and Snow Geese begin arriving in October, but December and January are peak season for waterfowl.

Site Map and Information

SABINE NATIONAL WILDLIFE REFUGE

- From Sulphur, LA, take Highway 27 south to Hackberry. Highway 27 passes through the refuge for 11 miles and offers the only access by vehicle. The Visitor Center and refuge headquarters are located 4 miles from the northern boundary of the refuge on Highway 27.

- Daily, sunrise to sunset, year-round.

- Never.

- Sabine National Wildlife Refuge, 3000 Holly Beach Highway, Hackberry, LA 70645. Visitor Center is open weekdays, 7 a.m.–4 p.m., and weekends, 12–4 p.m., except federal holidays.

- (337) 762-3816; http://southeast.fws.gov/sabine

- None.

- Marsh Trail and Visitor Center are wheelchair accessible.

- None on-site, but campgrounds are available in nearby Holly Beach; call the Southwestern Louisiana Convention and Visitor's Bureau at (800) 456-7952.

- None.

- Motels are available in nearby Sulphur; call the Convention and Visitor's Bureau at (800) 456-7952 for listings.

WHITEFISH POINT BIRD OBSERVATORY

This site at the northern tip of Michigan is situated along a natural corridor for birds migrating through the Great Lakes region.

Whitefish Point, located on the northeastern tip of Michigan's Upper Peninsula, is a spit of land jutting out into Lake Superior that is famous for shipwrecks as well as migratory birds. In the spring it is one of the premier sites in North America for observing the northward migration of birds, especially raptors and waterfowl. It is only slightly less outstanding for observing the fall migration southward.

The Whitefish Point Bird Observatory, founded in 1978, is a research center funded by memberships, donations, and grants from private and government institutions. It runs an extensive banding program that studies owls and passerines (an order of songbirds that includes more than half of all living birds) to learn more about their numbers and their migration patterns. The numbers of migrating waterbirds that stop by the site are also carefully tracked. In addition to its scientific programs, the observatory offers educational programs for visitors, including bird walks and banding demonstrations on big migration weekends.

Rough-legged Hawks, *usually seen one at a time, are found in large numbers at Whitefish during spring migration.*

HABITAT

The geography of Whitefish Point has turned it into a natural corridor that funnels in tens of thousands of birds as they travel through the Great Lakes region. Birds pass through the point on their way across the narrow strait that separates Whitefish Point from Ontario or on their way to the eastern or western ends of Lake Superior.

The approximately 30 acres of Whitefish Point are a mixture of dry coniferous forest (mostly jack pines), ponds and wetlands dotted with alders and willows, and sandy beach with dunes and beach grasses.

BIRDS TO LOOK FOR

Common Loon • Red-necked Grebe • Harlequin Duck • Oldsquaw • Northern Goshawk • Rough-legged Hawk • Merlin • American Golden-Plover • Pectoral Sandpiper • Great Gray Owl • Gray Jay • Boreal Chickadee • Pine Grosbeak

BIRD LIFE

Over 300 bird species have been recorded by researchers at Whitefish Point Bird Observatory. What's even more amazing than the quantity of species is the number of individual birds. In the course of a typical fall migration, for example, some 10,000 Common Loons will pass through the

Look for sea ducks, including the stubby-billed Harlequin Duck, during fall migration.

point. Flights of a thousand of these birds in one day have been recorded.

Waterbirds are the main draw during the fall migration period. Birders are virtually certain to see Common Loons, Red-throated Loons, Red-necked Grebes, and numerous duck species, including fish-eating mergansers and sea ducks such as scoters, Harlequin Duck, and Long-tailed Duck (Oldsquaw).

The Merlin *can be distinguished from the much larger Peregrine Falcon in flight; just look for its strongly barred tail.*

Shorebirds such as the American Golden-Plover, Pectoral Sandpiper, Solitary Sandpiper, and Baird's Sandpiper can be spotted passing through, as well as numerous gulls and terns, including Bonaparte's Gull, Ring-billed Gull, and Common and Black Terns. Rarities such as Little Gull, Black-legged Kittiwake, and Sabine's Gull turn up regularly at Whitefish Point.

In the spring over 20,000 raptors will migrate through. Hawks that are usually encountered only singly, such as Northern Goshawks and Rough-legged Hawks, are seen in large numbers here at this time. Boreal Owls and Great Gray Owls also show up reliably every spring.

Whitefish Point is also a good spot to watch songbirds, especially in the fall months. There are likely to be northern species such as Gray Jay, Pine Grosbeak, and Boreal Chickadee, and winter finches such as Hoary Redpoll. A range of migratory warblers, vireos, and sparrows all turn up at the point, as do longspurs, American Pipits, and Snow Buntings.

VISITING

The birds of Whitefish Point are abundant and concentrated into a small area, which makes them easy to spot. The fall migration period begins by mid-August, with waterbirds such as Red-necked Grebes, and continues into late November, when the last of the sea ducks have passed through. The spring migration is somewhat more concentrated, beginning in mid-March and ending by mid-May. The peak hawk migration period is mid- to late April.

The beach at the tip of the point is the best place to spot hawks and waterbirds; bring a scope to get good looks at the ducks and other waterbirds rafting in Whitefish Bay. Shorebirds often land on the beach; gulls and terns perch on the seawalls. Look for songbirds frequenting the feeding station near the visitor center

and foraging in the jack pines. Dabbling ducks, herons, rails, and warblers may be seen from the wooden walkways that take visitors to the ponds and wetlands.

The weather at Whitefish Point is highly unpredictable, but in general it tends to be cold and windy, even in the summer. Dress warmly no matter what the season.

HIGHLIGHTS

Visitors from around the world come to Whitefish Point in the spring and fall migration periods to watch spectacular numbers of waterbirds and raptors. Over 300 bird species have been recorded here; in a typical fall migration season more than 90,000 individual waterbirds will pass through the area.

Site Map and Information

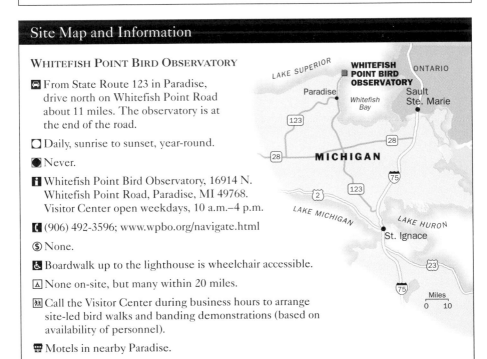

WHITEFISH POINT BIRD OBSERVATORY

🚗 From State Route 123 in Paradise, drive north on Whitefish Point Road about 11 miles. The observatory is at the end of the road.

🕐 Daily, sunrise to sunset, year-round.

⬤ Never.

ℹ Whitefish Point Bird Observatory, 16914 N. Whitefish Point Road, Paradise, MI 49768. Visitor Center open weekdays, 10 a.m.–4 p.m.

📞 (906) 492-3596; www.wpbo.org/navigate.html

💲 None.

♿ Boardwalk up to the lighthouse is wheelchair accessible.

🅰 None on-site, but many within 20 miles.

🔭 Call the Visitor Center during business hours to arrange site-led bird walks and banding demonstrations (based on availability of personnel).

🏨 Motels in nearby Paradise.

AGASSIZ NATIONAL WILDLIFE REFUGE

*Located at the juncture of three major ecosystems, this vast refuge
in northwestern Minnesota is famed for wetland birds.*

Eared Grebes *have blackish necks and
striking golden plumage
feathering out from the
eyes during breeding season.*

Ten thousand years ago, in what is now northern Minnesota, a vast lake some 700 miles long and 200 miles wide was formed by a melting glacier that once covered the land. Over the millennia the basin of that ancient lake turned into a paradise for wildlife – a broad, flat area covered with lakes and marshes.

In 1909 a major project to drain these wetlands and create agricultural land was begun; however, by 1933 the high cost and poor results of the project had become overwhelming to the developers. In 1937 all 61,500 acres of the land were sold to the federal government and became known as Mud Lake Migratory Waterfowl Refuge. In 1961 the name was changed to Agassiz National Wildlife Refuge in honor of Jean Louis Rodolphe Agassiz, a Swiss-American geologist who performed pioneering research on glacial movements during the 1830s.

HABITAT

Today the refuge is an oasis for wildlife and birds, surrounded by a sea of agriculture. Of the 61,500 acres in the refuge, nearly 41,000 are wetlands (composed of marshes, pools, and bogs); willow and aspen shrubland cover another 10,000 acres. A 4,000-acre area of black spruce and tamarack bog in the center of the refuge has been designated as a wilderness area and is off-limits to humans except on foot. Twenty large, shallow pools ranging in size from 100 to 100,000 acres dot the refuge; water levels are controlled by 125 miles of dikes.

BIRD LIFE

The refuge has an overall bird tally of 280 species, almost half of which nest on the site. Not surprisingly, the most abundant species are water-dependent birds. Five grebe species – Pied-billed, Horned, Red-necked, Eared, and Western – are seen here, and all five also stay to breed. The American Bittern, a stocky brown marsh bird, is a common breeding species. It is hard to spot, but in the spring and early summer it's easy to hear. Listen for the distinctive *oong-ka-choonk* song (often likened to the sound of a pump) coming from marshy areas with dense reeds. Peak spring warbler migration is from approximately May 15 to 25.

BIRDS TO LOOK FOR

Red-necked Grebe • Eared Grebe •
American Bittern • Gadwall • Blue-winged Teal • Ruddy Duck • Sandhill
Crane • Franklin's Gull • Forster's
Tern • Black Tern • Clay-colored
Sparrow • Le Conte's Sparrow •
Nelson's Sharp-tailed Sparrow

American Bitterns are just one of the many marsh birds that breed at Agassiz.

The same shallow, reedy habitat is a good place to look for another marsh bird, the Yellow Rail, and also for Le Conte's Sparrow and the much rarer Nelson's Sharp-tailed Sparrow. Look in the brushy areas for the Clay-colored Sparrow, the other sparrow specialty here during late spring and summer.

Many other water-dependent birds are attracted to the extensive pools and marshes of Agassiz. Seventeen duck species breed in this habitat every spring, including Blue-winged Teal, Mallard, Gadwall, Ruddy Duck, and Ring-necked Duck. A huge breeding

Franklin's Gulls *maintain a huge breeding colony here, consisting of as many as 20,000 pairs.*

colony of some 40,000 Franklin's Gulls is found here. Forster's Terns and Black Terns are also abundant and breed in the refuge. Numerous shorebirds, including Semipalmated Plover and Semipalmated and Least Sandpipers, are found on the mudflats, deliberately created every spring by lowering the water level of some of the pools.

In October, during peak fall migration, up to 100,000 ducks pass through the refuge, along with thousands of Canada Geese. Anywhere from 1,000 to 6,000 Sandhill Cranes pass through in late September.

VISITING
Winters in northern Minnesota are extremely cold. Visitors to Agassiz National Wildlife Refuge will definitely want to time their visits for the period between late April and the end of October. Even in summer, nights and early mornings can be chilly.

For the best birdwatching tour, start by visiting the 100-foot observation tower near refuge headquarters (a key can be checked out during office hours). The tower provides an excellent view of the 10,000 acres of Agassiz Pool. A lower observation deck looks out over Lansing Parker Pool; it is on the north side of Country Road 7 near the western edge of the refuge.

Although a number of gravel and dirt roads meander through the refuge, they're often not open to the public because of wet conditions. The best way to see the refuge's birds is to take the four-mile self-guided auto tour along Lost Bay Habitat Drive. Driving slowly along County Road 7 as it passes through the refuge provides good views and several birds. Moose can often be seen along the road, especially in June and in mid-September through October.

HIGHLIGHTS

Twenty-two duck species have been seen at this park. Of those species, 17 nest here. In an average year, nearly 7,500 pairs of ducks – 30 percent of them Blue-winged Teal – will breed on the refuge, producing upward of 25,000 ducklings, which may be seen from late May to mid-September.

Site Map and Information

AGASSIZ NATIONAL WILDLIFE REFUGE

🚍 From Thief River Falls, take State Highway 32 north 12 miles to Marshall County Road 7; turn east and follow for 11 miles to reach refuge headquarters on the left.

☐ Daily, sunrise to sunset, year-round. Lost Bay Habitat Drive is open during daylight hours May through October (depending on the weather).

⬤ Cold weather and bad road conditions can make visits difficult between November and March. Call ahead before planning a winter visit.

ℹ Agassiz National Wildlife Refuge, Route 1, Box 74, Middle River, MN 56737. Visitor Center is open weekdays, 7:30 a.m.–4:00 p.m. May through September it keeps weekend hours as well.

☎ (218) 449-4115; www.fws.gov/r3pao/agassiz

$ None.

♿ Refuge headquarters and Headquarters Trail are both wheelchair accessible.

△ Free primitive campgrounds are available at nearby state wildlife management areas. A city campground is available in nearby Thief River Falls; call (218) 681-2519 for information.

🚲 None.

🛏 Motels are available in nearby Thief River Falls and Grygla. Call the Thief River Falls Convention and Visitors Bureau at (800) 827-1629 for listings.

HAWK RIDGE NATURE RESERVE

*In the fall thousands upon thousands of hawks soar past this Minnesota
preserve near the western tip of Lake Superior.*

Every year, from early
August until early
December, Hawk
Ridge Nature
Reserve in
eastern Duluth provides
magnificent eye-level views of
tens of thousands of raptors
(birds of prey, including
hawks, eagles, falcons, and
owls) as they make their
annual migration southward.
Since 1950, when illegal
shooting of passing raptors was
stopped through the efforts of
local conservation groups, this
migration hot spot along Lake
Superior has attracted thousands of
visitors from every state and more
than 40 foreign countries.

In 1972, to preserve this perfect
viewing spot, the Duluth Audubon
Society raised funds for the city of
Duluth to purchase 115 acres on the
highest part of Hawk Ridge – bluffs
overlooking Lake Superior. Today the
reserve is managed by the Hawk
Ridge Management Committee,
under a trust agreement with the city.

The Northern Goshawk *has a
bold eyebrow that separates
its dark head from its
gray-blue back.*

HABITAT

The geography of the
Great Lakes is what
brings so many hawks to
this area. Every fall
migrating birds heading
south from breeding
grounds as far north as the
arctic circle reach the
shores of Lake Superior.
Preferring not to cross
such a large body of water, the
birds instead follow the
shoreline. Those that choose the
southwestern route eventually
funnel past the city of Duluth –
and thus the reserve.

The rocky cliffs that run parallel to
the lakeshore create updrafts that are
ideal for soaring birds such as hawks.
They can glide along for miles with
barely a flap of the wings.

BIRD LIFE

At least 20 species of raptors and
vultures have been seen at Hawk
Ridge Nature Preserve. Some, such as
the Peregrine Falcon and Gyrfalcon,
are rare visitors, while others, such as
the Broad-winged Hawk, pass over by
the tens of thousands each year during
their peak migration period in
September. Other buteos (high-soaring
hawks with long wings) commonly
seen at the reserve are the Red-tailed
Hawk and Rough-legged Hawk.
Accipiters (agile, woodland hawks with

BIRDS TO LOOK FOR

Turkey Vulture • Osprey • Bald
Eagle • Sharp-shinned Hawk •
Cooper's Hawk • Northern Goshawk •
Broad-winged Hawk • Red-tailed
Hawk • Rough-legged Hawk •
Golden Eagle • American Kestrel •
Merlin • Peregrine Falcon •
Gyrfalcon • Long-eared Owl •
Northern Saw-whet Owl

Osprey are just one of the many raptors that pass over this Great Lakes' reserve each fall.

long tails and short, rounded wings) such as the Sharp-shinned Hawk, Cooper's Hawk, and Northern Goshawk are also very common. Kites, such as Ospreys, and Turkey Vultures are also common.

In any given year several thousand Bald Eagles will pass by Hawk Ridge, most of them in late November and December. Golden Eagles are far rarer, but on average a hundred will pass over autumn's course. Among the falcons (powerful hunters with long wings), several hundred American Kestrel and Merlins regularly come through, mostly during October.

The preserve is also well-known for large flights of Long-eared Owls and tiny Northern Saw-whet Owls, which take place in October and November. Both of these species can be spotted here at dawn and dusk.

Serious research into raptor migration is a major activity at the reserve. A systematic count of migrating raptors has been conducted here every fall since 1951. The most valuable research at Hawk Ridge is conducted through the banding program. Staffed 24 hours a day from mid-August to late November, the banding station harmlessly captures, bands, and releases an average of 3,000 raptors every season. Information from recaptured birds and bands recovered from dead birds tell scientists a great deal about where the hawks go and how long they live.

Northern Saw-whet Owls *are small owls with reddish brown plumage above and white with reddish streaks below.*

VISITING

For sheer number and variety of raptors, the ideal time to visit Hawk Ridge is from the second week of September to the third week of October. If winds blow from the west or northwest, thousands of birds will pass through. On a day with precipitation or winds from the south or east, however, little or no migration may occur. The best time of day to see the birds is mid-morning to mid-afternoon.

On weekends from late August through mid-October, naturalists are available at the preserve to answer visitors' questions and arrange visits to the observation blind near the banding station. The famed Hawk Watch Weekend is scheduled to coincide with the peak Broad-winged Hawk migration in mid-September. Contributions support the reserve.

Visitors to the preserve should dress warmly (even in the summer) and wear hats, sunglasses, and sunscreen. Binoculars are a must, but spotting scopes aren't worth the bother – the hawks move too fast. The site has no visitor facilities except for portable toilets during the tourist season; bring a lawn chair or cushion to sit on.

HIGHLIGHTS

The migration of Broad-winged Hawks past Hawk Ridge peaks in mid- to late September. During this period, when conditions are favorable (a dry day with winds from the west or northwest), a river of thousands of Broad-wings streams past each hour.

Site Map and Information

HAWK RIDGE NATURE RESERVE

🚗 From downtown Duluth, take Superior Street east to 43rd Avenue. Turn left and follow for 1 mile to Glenwood Street. Turn left onto Glenwood Street and follow for 0.5 mile to Skyline Parkway at the top of the hill. Turn right onto Skyline Parkway and follow for 1 mile to the main overlook.

🕐 Daily, sunrise to sunset, year-round.

⬤ Never.

ℹ Hawk Ridge Nature Reserve, Duluth Audubon Society, c/o U.M.D. Biology Department, Duluth, MN 55804. The reserve does not have a Visitor Center; during Hawk Weekend, naturalists set up a display at the main overlook.

📞 No telephone; www.hawkridge.org

⑤ No fees, but donations are welcome.

♿ No special facilities.

⛺ None on-site.

🚶 Naturalist-led trips to the observation blind or raptor identification sessions are scheduled in person on the ridge.

🏨 Hotels, motels, and bed-and-breakfasts are available in Duluth; contact the Duluth Convention and Visitors Bureau at (218) 722-4011 for listings.

PRAIRIE STATE PARK

Bison, elk, Greater Prairie-Chickens, and over 500 wildflower species adorn this tallgrass prairie in west-central Missouri.

More than 13 million acres of tallgrass prairie once covered a large portion of the state of Missouri. Today only 65,000 acres of Missouri's tallgrass prairie remain, mostly as small, widely scattered parcels of land. The magnificent 3,700-acre Prairie State Park is one of the very few large prairie areas to have survived; in fact, it's the largest remaining tallgrass prairie in the state.

The park, acquired through the assistance of the Nature Conservancy and other nonprofit organizations, is administered by the Missouri Department of Natural Resources.

The Dickcissel *gets its name from its call,* dick dick dickcissel.

HABITAT

A tallgrass prairie is an enormously complex ecosystem, one that contains hundreds of different wildflower and grass species and a multitude of animal life, including many grassland birds and over 80 butterfly species, including the endangered Regal Fritillary. Central to the health of the prairie ecosystem are two things: bison and wildfire. Both prevent the invasion of trees and shrubs, remove accumulated grass mats, and recycle nutrients back into the soil.

To preserve Prairie State Park, the staff actually replicates wildfires with controlled burns as needed. Bison and

elk have also been reintroduced. Today the park's bison herd consists of more than 40 animals.

BIRD LIFE

More than 150 bird species, including such grassland specialties as the Upland Sandpiper, Northern Bobwhite, Dickcissel, Grasshopper Sparrow, and the rare Henslow's Sparrow, are found at Prairie State Park. Grassland birds tend to be well-camouflaged skulkers, and the prairie doesn't offer much in the way of perches. To maximize the chances of seeing – or at least hearing – them, visit in the spring, when the grass isn't as high and the birds are at their most vocal.

Of all the birds at Prairie State Park, the most sought-after is the Greater Prairie-Chicken. The park has one of the largest remaining populations in the state – about 75 birds, all that are left of a once-abundant population. In the spring the leks (courtship display areas) are easy to find. Just listen for the characteristic, very loud "booming" noises the male birds make about 10

BIRDS TO LOOK FOR

Mississippi Kite • Northern Harrier •
Greater Prairie-Chicken • Northern
Bobwhite • Upland Sandpiper •
Short-eared Owl • Scissor-tailed
Flycatcher • Grasshopper Sparrow •
Henslow's Sparrow • Dickcissel •
Yellow-headed Blackbird

The Yellow-headed Blackbird is at the eastern edge of its range here.

times a minute as part of their elaborate courtship ritual. The best time to see the courtship dancing is early in the morning or late in the afternoon. In the late autumn and winter, Greater Prairie-Chickens tend to form large flocks that are fairly easy to spot.

The gently rolling hills of Prairie State Park are also an excellent place to spot another grasslands specialty, the Scissor-tailed Flycatcher. Lucky birdwatchers visiting the park in the fall or spring migration seasons might spot a Yellow-headed Blackbird, which is at the eastern edge of its range here.

Several interesting raptors reside at Prairie State Park.

Mississippi Kites *capture insects in these rolling grasslands and eat them in flight.*

Year-round, look for the Northern Harrier flying fairly close to the ground as it searches for small rodents, frogs, and other prey. Even though the Mississippi Kite is a summer resident here, it's rarely spotted. Similarly, Short-eared Owls spend the winter at Prairie State Park but are seen only now and then. For both species, check with the Visitor Center to learn where they've been seen recently within the park.

VISITING

Prairie State Park offers 11 miles of well-marked hiking trails. The Drover's Trail begins near the Visitor Center and leads to some of the finest vistas in the park. The Gayfeather Trail goes through the 240-acre Regal Prairie Natural Area section of the park, a nearly undisturbed prairie community that offers a rich diversity of plant and animal life. A newer trail called the Path of the Sky People goes through the 240-acre Tzi-Sho Prairie Natural Area. Pronounced "tissue," *Tzi-Sho* is the Native American word for Sky People, a name for the Osage Indians who once lived in this region.

For magnificent displays of prairie wildflowers, visit Prairie State Park in the spring. This is also the best time to see the Greater Prairie-Chickens displaying on their leks. Visitors in the summer should plan to hike in the early morning or late evening to avoid the heat. Ticks and chiggers are common here in the summer, and lightning is a real danger on the open prairie. Avoid being outdoors during storms.

Bison roam freely in portions of Prairie State Park. For safety, always check at the Visitor Center for the location of the bison herd. Keep a safe distance from them and from the elk as well, which roam freely throughout the entire park.

HIGHLIGHTS

The lovely Dickcissel, a member of the cardinal family, has a black bib on a beautiful, bright yellow breast. Sadly, populations of this prairie bird have been in decline since the 1960s. Part of the problem is habitat loss in the midwestern United States, but pesticide poisoning in northern South America, where this species winters, is also to blame.

Site Map and Information

PRAIRIE STATE PARK

From Lamar, follow US 160 west 16 miles to State Highway NN and turn right onto Central Road (a gravel road).Follow for 3 miles to NW 150th Lane, turn right, and follow for 1½ miles to Township Road. Turn right on Township Road and continue to Visitor Center.

Daily, sunrise to sunset, year-round.

Never.

Prairie State Park, P.O. Box 97, Liberal, MO 64762. From January through March, the Visitor Center is open Wednesday through Saturday, 8:30 a.m.–5:00 p.m., and Sunday, 1 p.m.–5 p.m. From April through December, the Visitor Center is also open Tuesday, 8:30 a.m.–5:00 p.m.

(417) 843-6711

None.

The Visitor Center is wheelchair accessible. To reach the park's TDD, call (800) 379-2419.

Two campsites with water and pit latrines are available on-site, as well as a primitive campground reachable by foot only. Call the Visitor Center for reservations.

None.

Motels are available in nearby Fort Scott. Call the Fort Scott Area Chamber of Commerce at (800) 245-3678 for listings.

TABERVILLE PRAIRIE CONSERVATION AREA

*The mating calls of Greater Prairie-Chickens boom through the tallgrass
of this prairie preserve in west-central Missouri.*

One of the few surviving native tallgrass prairies in Missouri, and at 1,680 acres, one of the largest, Taberville Prairie Conservation Area has the distinction of being both a Missouri Natural Area and a National Natural Landmark. The land was acquired for the Missouri Department of Conservation by purchases in 1959 and 1961. The primary goal then and now is to preserve crucial habitat for the Greater Prairie-Chicken, an uncommon bird whose numbers are declining.

The Northern Bobwhite *female is a mottled reddish brown quail with striped flanks.*

HABITAT

Most of the land at Taberville Prairie Conservation Area is untouched tallgrass prairie. The mounds and rolling hills topped with sandstone outcroppings are covered with a sea of waist-high grasses. A beautiful, spring-fed stream runs through the western and central portions of the area and seven small ponds are scattered throughout the site.

BIRDS TO LOOK FOR

Northern Harrier • Greater Prairie-Chicken • Northern Bobwhite • Upland Sandpiper • Short-eared Owl • Scissor-tailed Flycatcher • Horned Lark • Grasshopper Sparrow • Henslow's Sparrow • Dickcissel

Unlike 99 percent of the prairie lands in Missouri, the Taberville prairie was never plowed for crops. It was used mostly for grazing; some of the grass was mowed for hay. Thus the site retains the astonishing variety of plant and animal life characteristic of the tallgrass prairie.

In all, more than 400 plant species are found on Taberville Prairie Conservation Area, including many hardy native grasses, such as Indian grass, big bluestem, and switchgrass, which grow to heights of several feet or more. The many flowering plants on the prairie attract large numbers of butterflies, including such midwestern specialities as Eyed Browns and Prairie Ringlets. The well-preserved prairie habitat is highly attractive to many grassland bird species.

To maintain the grasslands and keep shrubs and trees from taking over, conservation area managers use a combination of haying and deliberately set fires to simulate the effects of the grazing bison and natural prairie fires that occurred on the land before European settlement.

BIRD LIFE

When Taberville Prairie Conservation Area was purchased, the land held several hundred Greater Prairie-Chickens. Despite ongoing efforts by conservationists, the population of this

Taberville's tallgrass prairie is home to the now uncommon Greater Prairie-Chicken.

large, chicken-like bird has continued to decline. Today there are only about a hundred of these birds on the Taberville prairie – demonstrating a worrysome trend.

The Greater Prairie-Chickens may be fewer in numbers than decades ago, but they are still quite active. In March and April every year, the booming calls of the males – a deep *oo-loo-woo* sound that can be heard more than a mile away – resound from leks (courtship display areas) scattered around the area.

Visitors who follow the sound to the lek, or "booming" ground, will see the male birds

The Horned Lark *may be recognized by its distinctive facial pattern and black "horns," more prominent in the male than the female.*

performing an elaborate courtship display. In addition to ritual dancing displays, the male bird makes his neck feathers stand on end, shows off the fleshy yellow-orange combs above his eyes, and makes his booming call by inflating the golden air sacs on either side of his throat. Several males usually compete for the attention of the female birds at the lek, often through very aggressive behavior. When observing the spectacle, be sure to stay at least 30 yards away to avoid disturbing the birds.

The extensive grasslands of the conservation area are ideal habitat for many species of the plains, including Northern Bobwhite, Dickcissel, Grasshopper Sparrow, and Horned Lark. The uncommon and secretive Henslow's Sparrow is also found at Taberville. More often heard than

161

seen, this bird is best found by listening for its distinctive *se-lick* song, with the accent on the second syllable. The best field marks are the dark chestnut color of the wings and the large gray bill.

The Upland Sandpiper is spotted regularly here; often only its small head with large, prominent eyes can be seen among the tall grasses. In the summer look for Scissor-tailed Flycatchers snatching insects out of the air above the prairie. The Short-eared Owl, a fairly common bird of the open grasslands, is a winter resident. Year-round, Northern Harriers can be seen cruising low over the grass with upraised wings as they hunt small rodents, frogs, birds, and other prey.

VISITING

Aside from several parking areas, there are no facilities and no marked trails at Taberville Prairie Conservation Area

but birders can have a satisfying experience here without them. In general, the spring breeding season, from March to early June, is a favored time for birdwatchers to visit. In the spring the grass is short and the male birds are singing and calling loudly, making them easier to locate. Visitors to the conservation area in warm weather should be sure to use insect repellent, wear a brimmed hat, and bring plenty of water.

HIGHLIGHTS

In the spring Taberville Prairie Conservation Area is a good place to see the acrobatic courtship flight of the male Scissor-tailed Flycatcher. The bird's long, flowing tail feathers are dramatically displayed as it zooms up and down or in a zigzag pattern, sometimes ending with a reverse somersault.

Site Map and Information

TABERVILLE PRAIRIE CONSERVATION AREA

🚗 From El Dorado Springs, follow County Road H north 13 miles to the site's parking area. From Appleton City, take Highway 52 east 0.5 mile to County Road A and follow it south 2 miles to County Road H. Take County Road H south 7 miles to the parking area.

◻ Daily, 4 a.m.–10 p.m., year-round.

⬤ Never.

ℹ Taberville Prairie Conservation Area, c/o Missouri Department of Conservation, El Dorado Springs Office, 772 Highway 54, Box 106, El Dorado Springs, MO 64744. There is no Visitor Center.

☎ (417) 876-5226

⑤ None.

♿ No special facilities.

🅐 None on-site, but Countryside Campground is nearby; call (417) 876-9990 for information.

🚻 None.

🏨 Motels are available in nearby El Dorado Springs; call the chamber of commerce at (417) 876-4154 for listings.

CRANE MEADOWS NATURE CENTER

Visit this central Nebraska nature center along the Platte River to watch the largest springtime gathering of Sandhill Cranes in the world.

North America offers many spectacles for birdwatchers, but one of the grandest is the annual spring visitation of Sandhill Cranes to a 60-mile stretch along the Platte River in central Nebraska. These stately birds, with their distinctive bugling calls and remarkable courtship dancing, gather here by the hundreds of thousands to rest and feed for about six weeks before pushing north to breeding grounds in far away locations, such as Alaska and Siberia.

Crane staging area. The 625-mile long Platte River was once lined with wet meadows and grasslands, where the cranes could feed; numerous sandbars filled the broad, shallow river and offered roosting areas protected from predators.

Today, extensive water diversion for hydroelectric power and crop irrigation has destroyed vast areas of Sandhill Crane habitat along the Platte River. The only relatively undisturbed crane-friendly area is the 60 miles between Grand Island and Overton.

One of the best places to get information and sign up for a tour is Crane Meadows Nature Center, which is west of Grand Island. Established in 1989, the nature center consists of 250 acres of prime river habitat, a section of river woodlands, and a large stretch of native prairie. The nature center has viewing blinds from which to watch the reticent Sandhill Cranes up close. Crane Meadows is also an excellent place to see the huge numbers of migratory waterfowl and other birds that pass through the area during the spring migration period.

The Cinnamon Teal, *a dabbling duck, finds its food in small floating items on the water's surface.*

HABITAT

Early European settlers in Nebraska said that the Platte River was a mile wide and an inch deep. That was an accurate description not only of the river, but also of an ideal Sandhill

---

BIRDS TO LOOK FOR

Greater White-fronted Goose • Snow Goose • Gadwall • Cinnamon Teal • Bald Eagle • Greater Prairie-Chicken • Sandhill Crane • Piping Plover • Upland Sandpiper • Baird's Sandpiper • Least Tern • Orange-crowned Warbler

---

BIRD LIFE

The main attraction at Crane Meadows is the Sandhill Cranes. Among the oldest species of bird, Sandhill Cranes are large, grayish brown birds with long necks and long legs. They stand between three and four feet tall, weigh around seven to eight pounds, and have wing spans of five to six feet. Size aside, the large red patch on the head is a highly

Visit Crane Meadows for the annual Sandhill Crane migration.

visible field mark. Their distinctive bugling call can often be heard long before the birds are seen.

The average Sandhill Crane will spend approximately a month (between mid-February and mid-April) along the Platte River, flying in to roost on the river sandbars at dusk and flying out again to feed on waste corn in the nearby fields in the early morning. As the birds feed, they also "dance" as a way to strengthen the bonds between mates for the breeding season to come. Watch closely for their elaborate bowing displays, which feature outstretched wings and high leaps. As part of the dance, the birds often pick up

The Upland Sandpiper *is often seen alone perched on a tall post or fence.*

sticks or corncobs and toss them repeatedly into the air.

Sandhill Cranes aren't the only birds visitors watch at the Crane Meadows Nature Center. Spring is an excellent time to see Canada Geese, Snow Geese, and Greater White-fronted Geese; Snow Goose numbers alone can top two million. Ducks such as Green-winged Teal, Cinnamon Teal, Gadwall, and Canvasback abound.

Shorebirds such as the Upland Sandpiper, Baird's Sandpiper, and the rare Piping Plover are found along the river's mudflats in April and May. Look also for the Least Tern, which breeds along the river and generally can be spotted between April and October. In May six species of warbler are regularly seen at Crane Meadows in the woodlands along the river, including the Orange-crowned Warbler, usually found much farther west, and the Blackburnian Warbler, usually found much farther east and north. Other notable birds include Greater Prairie-Chickens and Bald Eagles.

VISITING

In general, Sandhill Cranes are very wary of humans. Despite their numbers along the Platte River during the crane season (mid-February to mid-April, peaking around March 17), it can be difficult to see them close up without disturbing them. The Crane Meadows Nature Center offers daily tours to viewing blinds at sunrise and sunset. A trained naturalist accompanies each group; weekend van tours to nearby crane-viewing areas are also offered. Crane Meadows also offers blinds and tours to watch the millions of migrating waterfowl in the region. Seven miles of hiking trails wind through the nature center's property and are a great place from which to see migrating warblers and other birds.

HIGHLIGHTS

Every spring in March and April nearly half a million migrating Sandhill Cranes gather on a 60-mile stretch of the Platte River in central Nebraska. This spectacular assemblage includes about 80 percent of the world's population of these magnificent birds and is the world's largest gathering of cranes of any sort.

Site Map and Information

CRANE MEADOWS NATURE CENTER

🚌 From Grand Island, take I-80 west 17 miles to exit 305. The Visitor Center is at the southeastern corner of the interchange.

◻ Monday through Saturday, 9 a.m.–5 p.m., year-round.

● Sundays.

🅷 Crane Meadows Nature Center, 9325 South Alda Road, Wood River, NE 68883. The Visitor Center keeps the same hours as the site: Monday through Saturday, 9 a.m.–5 p.m.

📞 (308) 382-1820; www.cranemeadows.org

Ⓢ Free to members of Crane Meadows Nature Center; $2 for nonmembers. Crane–viewing blind tours are $15 per person.

♿ The Visitor Center is wheelchair accessible.

🅐 None on-site. There are campgrounds at nearby Mormon Island State Park; call (308) 385-6211 for details.

🦩 The nature center offers daily crane-viewing tours during peak season. Waterfowl-viewing tours are also available. Call the Visitor Center for details.

🏨 Motels are available in nearby Grand Island; call the Grand Island Convention and Visitors Bureau at (800) 658-3178 for listings.

FORT NIOBRARA
NATIONAL WILDLIFE REFUGE

Buffalo, elk, and a wealth of grassland birds – from prairie chickens to a range of sparrows – inhabit this sandhill prairie refuge in north-central Nebraska.

Back in 1879 Fort Niobrara was built by the U.S. Army to keep the peace between arriving white settlers and Sioux Indians living on the nearby Rosebud Reservation. By the time it was officially closed in 1912, the buffalo that had once roamed the prairie in vast herds had been reduced to less than a thousand and the elk were almost extinct.

Sharp-tailed Grouse *males return to the same area each year to mate during breeding season.*

When Mr. J. W. Gilbert of Friend, Nebraska, offered six buffalo and 17 elk to the federal government that same year, the land around the former Fort Niobrara became their new home.

Today the 19,122 acres of Fort Niobrara National Wildlife Refuge trace back to this early refuge, and the buffalo and elk that graze on its prairies are descendants of the original animals. To help preserve the spectacular beauty of the wildlife refuge from development, the Nature Conservancy has purchased a 54,000-acre expanse of native prairie that abuts it.

HABITAT
The beautiful Niobrara River has cut a deep, wooded canyon through this region's dominant terrain – sandhill prairie, composed of rolling hills of sandy soil covered with tough prairie grasses and wildflowers. The result is a variety of habitats, ranging from lush river-bottom woodlands to upland pine forests to dry tallgrass prairie. These contain an amazing variety of plant and animal species, including 225 varieties of birds.

BIRD LIFE
The birds of Fort Niobrara National Wildlife Refuge are as varied as the terrain. Warblers such as the Yellow-breasted Chat, Black-headed and Blue Grosbeaks, and other songbirds are found in the wooded canyon. Grassland specialties such as Upland

BIRDS TO LOOK FOR

Rough-legged Hawk • Sharp-tailed Grouse • Greater Prairie-Chicken • Northern Bobwhite • Upland Sandpiper • Long-billed Curlew • Burrowing Owl • Horned Lark • Vesper Sparrow • Lark Sparrow • Grasshopper Sparrow • McCown's Longspur • Black-headed Grosbeak • Blue Grosbeak • Lazuli Bunting

The Lazuli Bunting provides a dash of color to this tawny prairie refuge.

Sandpipers and Western Meadowlarks perch on fence posts. Waterfowl, including Clark's Grebe, Lesser Scaup, Redhead, and geese, swim in the Exhibition Pasture Ponds, east of the Vistor Center. Bald Eagles, Golden Eagles, and Rough-legged Hawks soar overhead on the updrafts from the hills and river canyon.

Grassland birds are the primary reason for visiting Fort Niobrara, however, and the selection is outstanding. In addition to a small population of Greater Prairie-Chickens, an uncommon bird whose populations are declining elsewhere, the refuge also supports a fair number of Sharp-tailed Grouse. To distinguish this large bird from the closely related Greater Prairie-Chicken, look for the

The Blue Grosbeak
features a heavy bill and wide chestnut-colored bars on its wings.

mostly white and pointed tail. Like the Greater Prairie-Chicken, the Sharp-tailed Grouse performs ritual dances on leks (mating grounds). The male grouse makes a variety of noises, including a sharp, barklike *chilk* and a loud popping noise that sounds like a cork being pulled from a bottle.

Other partridges, grouse, and quail found on the refuge include Northern Bobwhite, Ruffed Grouse, Ring-necked Pheasant, and Gray Partridge.

Numerous members of the sparrow family are found at the refuge. Grassland specialists such as Savannah, Grasshopper, Vesper, and Lark Sparrows all breed on the refuge. The elusive Baird's Sparrow is a rare visitor here in spring and fall, while the Clay-colored Sparrow and Harris's Sparrow are seen fairly regularly.

McCown's Longspurs and Lapland Longspurs are regulars in the spring and fall – look for them mixed in with the flocks of Horned Larks that are common in the refuge year-round. During the spring and summer, the Long-billed Curlew is also common here; it breeds on the refuge in grassy meadows, usually near water.

VISITING

Fort Niobrara National Wildlife Refuge is a very large place. Fortunately, some of the refuge's most reliable birdwatching spots are easily accessible. The Bur Oak Picnic Area, just south of the river, is an excellent place to look for sparrows and warblers. The Fort Falls Trail takes visitors into the Niobrara River canyon, where warblers and grosbeaks can be found in the wooded areas. The best place to look for songbirds, including Lazuli Bunting, is the area just to the west of the refuge canoe launch site near the Cornell Dam. The prairie-dog town near the refuge

is practically guaranteed to produce at least one Burrowing Owl.

Note that the sandhills of Nebraska can be a harsh environment – very hot in the summer, and very cold in the winter. The best time to visit is in the spring, when Greater Prairie-Chickens and Sharp-tailed Grouse are dancing on their leks. Check with the staff to learn where the birds are displaying.

HIGHLIGHTS

The Sharp-tailed Grouse once had an ample range in the United States, but the conversion of prairie land to agriculture drastically reduced its habitat. Because the prairie habitat at this wildlife refuge is relatively undisturbed, the Sharp-tailed Grouse population, one of the country's southernmost, is thriving.

Site Map and Information

FORT NIOBRARA NATIONAL WILDLIFE REFUGE

🚗 From Valentine, follow State Highway 12 east 4 miles to reach the refuge entrance.

⏲ Daily, sunrise to sunset, year-round.

🌑 Never.

ℹ Fort Niobrara National Wildlife Refuge, HC 14, Box 67, Valentine, NE 69201. Visitor Center is open weekdays, 8 a.m.–4:30 p.m., and weekends from Memorial Day to Labor Day, 8 a.m.–4:30 p.m.

📞 (402) 376-3789; www.r6.fws.gov/refuges/niobrara/niobrara.htm

$ None.

♿ Visitor Center is wheelchair accessible.

🏕 None on-site. Alkali Fish Camp is 22 miles south of Valentine; call (402) 376-3479 for details.

🦌 None.

🏨 There are motels in nearby Valentine; contact the chamber of commerce at (800) 658-4024 for listings.

LOSTWOOD NATIONAL WILDLIFE REFUGE

*This western North Dakota refuge harbors countless prairie potholes,
creating a paradise for ducks and other waterbirds.*

Boasting as many as 100 breeding bird species and a checklist of 250 species in all, Lostwood National Wildlife Refuge is a fantastic place to watch birds. More than 4,000 wetlands, ranging from tiny ponds only a few feet across and a few inches deep to large basins covering many hundreds of acres and reaching depths of 10 feet, dot the rolling grasslands of the refuge. This pristine habitat especially attracts ducks and other waterfowl, water-dependent birds such as shorebirds, and grasslands species such as Sprague's Pipit, Sharp-tailed Grouse, and Baird's Sparrow.

Redheads *are heavy diving ducks, identified by their round heads and tricolored bills.*

HABITAT

Lostwood National Wildlife Refuge protects nearly 27,000 precious acres of prairie pothole terrain – a region of grassy hills and numerous marshes, shallow ponds, and small lakes. The refuge and the surrounding area produce more ducks every year than any other region in the lower 48 states; some 70 percent of the continent's waterfowl are hatched within this region.

What makes prairie potholes so productive, despite the region's harsh winters and hot, dry summers? The answer is water. When the last ice age ended some 12,000 years ago, the retreating glaciers left behind a vast terrain of lakes and wetlands interspersed with rolling hills covered by prairie grasses. Hundreds of bird species rely on the prairie pothole region for nesting habitat and as resting and feeding grounds during migration periods. What makes Lostwood National Wildlife Refuge so vital is that this sort of habitat is dwindling.

Prairie wildfires, which before the arrival of white settlers were just an integral part of the natural cycle, were suppressed in the region for many decades. The vast herds of bison were eliminated by the late 1880s. The result was that woody shrubs such as western snowberry, once kept out by fire and grazing bison, invaded the prairies, reducing the habitat for birds such as Baird's Sparrow and Swainson's Hawk. Today, the management plan for Lostwood (and for many other grassland nature preserves) uses prescribed burning to reduce woody plants and restore the natural prairie habitat.

BIRDS TO LOOK FOR

American Avocet • American Bittern •
Baird's Sparrow • Black Tern • Western
Grebe • Song Sparrow • Marbled
Godwit • Nelson's Sharp-tailed
Sparrow • Northern Bobwhite • Piping
Plover • Redhead • Sharp-tailed
Grouse • Sora • Sprague's Pipit •
Upland Sandpiper • Wilson's Phalarope

American Avocets are highly visible along the shores of the refuge's 4,000-plus wetlands.

BIRD LIFE

The grassland and wetland habitats in this national wildlife refuge support a remarkable variety of bird life. As many as twelve duck species reside here: five of the seven North American grebes, including Red-necked and Western Grebes.

Marbled Godwits *nest in the grasslands between lakes and ponds.*

The endangered Piping Plover nests in Lostwood, generally along the bare shorelines of alkaline wetlands. The American Avocet is a common breeding bird here, as are the Marbled Godwit, Willet, Upland Sandpiper, Spotted Sandpiper, Wilson's Phalarope, and Black Tern. The refuge has one of the highest known populations of Sharp-tailed Grouse in the United States. These birds perform their elaborate mating dance on some forty leks (dancing grounds) within the refuge. Look and listen for rails, including breeding Soras and Virginia Rails, and American Bitterns, among the dense aquatic growth around freshwater wetlands. Black-crowned Night Herons can be found as well.

Grasslands birds also are well-represented at Lostwood: Sprague's Pipit, Baird's Sparrow, Grasshopper Sparrow, Song Sparrow, Clay-colored Sparrow, and Chestnut-collared Longspur are among the species that nest here. In drought years, Lark Buntings may be found.

VISITING

Ducks such as Mallards and Pintails start arriving at Lostwood by the end of March. By late April they've been joined by some 18 other breeding and migrant duck species, geese, and an array of gulls, terns, sandpipers, and other shorebirds. Many of these species breed in the refuge throughout the spring and early summer months.

Late May and June are the best times to spot breeding grassland birds such as Sprague's Pipit and Baird's Sparrow. To see the Sharp-tailed Grouse assemble for courtship and display, visit very early in the morning in late April or early May. To minimize disturbance of the birds, watch them from behind the refuge's viewing blind, which looks onto a lek.

Autumn brings the spectacle of huge flocks of waterfowl taking off for points south. The only time not to visit is during the frigid winter, when temperatures are subzero.

The best way to get an overall feel for Lostwood is to follow the seven-mile auto tour through the refuge. The route, which has turnouts connecting to a hiking trail and the Lostwood Wilderness Area, runs through native prairies, a restored prairie area, a burned-over prairie, and a vast number of wetlands.

HIGHLIGHTS

Just how productive is the prairie pothole region? Here's the breakdown of breeding bird species on this refuge: 49 migratory songbirds, 21 waterbirds, 13 waterfowl, 9 raptors, and 3 upland game birds – for a grand total of 95 species.

Site Map and Information

LOSTWOOD NATIONAL WILDLIFE REFUGE

🚗 Located 18 miles west of Kenmare and 70 miles northwest of Minot. From Kenmare follow Ward County Road 2 12 miles west, then 4.5 miles south on Highway 8 to reach refuge headquarters. From Minot, take State Highway 52 north to State Highway 50 and follow it west to State Highway 8; take this 7 miles north to refuge headquarters.

☐ Wilderness area is open daily, sunrise to sunset, year-round. Self-guided auto tour and hiking trail are open from April (weather permitting) to early October.

◑ Christmas and New Year's Day.

🛈 Refuge Manager, Lostwood National Wildlife Refuge, 8315 Highway 8, Kenmare, ND 58746. Refuge headquarters are open weekdays, 7:30 a.m.–4:00 p.m.

📞 (701) 848-2722

⑤ None.

♿ Refuge headquarters are handicapped accessible.

🅰 None on-site, but campgrounds are available in nearby Kenmare, Stanley, and Powers Lake.

▦ None.

🏨 Motels are available in nearby Kenmare, Stanley, and Powers Lake; hotels, motels, and bed-and-breakfasts are available in Minot, 20 miles southeast of Kenmare.

THEODORE ROOSEVELT NATIONAL PARK

*Spectacular badlands scenery, grassland birds, and Golden Eagles soaring
overhead grace this western North Dakota park.*

Theodore Roosevelt first came to the colorful North Dakota badlands as a young man in 1883. Already an experienced naturalist, he was struck by the rugged beauty of the area and the variety of wildlife. Although he had originally come to hunt bison, he eventually formed a partnership to ranch in this region. The national park that bears his name was established in 1947 and encompasses 70,446 acres, or some 110 square miles in two parts, which are enfolded by the Little Missouri National Grasslands. At first glance, the rough terrain might seem dry, barren, and inhospitable,

The Mountain Bluebird *can be spotted easily: look in the park's meadows and rangeland and around the campgrounds.*

BIRDS TO LOOK FOR

Bald Eagle • Golden Eagle • Sharp-tailed Grouse • Loggerhead Shrike • Black-billed Magpie • Mountain Bluebird • Spotted Towhee • Clay-colored Sparrow • Lark Sparrow • Baird's Sparrow • Black-headed Grosbeak • Western Meadowlark

but a closer look shows that it teems with life, including bison, prairie dogs, wild horses, elk, and nearly 200 bird species.

HABITAT

Although the terrain of this national park is varied – from native mixed-grass prairie to undisturbed Little Missouri River bottomland forest – it is the fantastic sculpturing of the badlands that make it so special. The ghostly buttes, plateaus, and spires, rising out of the prairies of the Great Plains, were created by more than 60 million years of stream, wind, and rain erosion. Streaked with pink, red, black, gray-blue, and ocher mineral bands, these natural sculptures create dramatic silhouettes against a blue sky.

Badlands are by definition dry, receiving only about 15 inches of rain a year, however, they support tough grasses, sagebrush and other woody plants, and a profusion of wildflowers, which in turn support a profusion of birds. The Little Missouri River, which meanders on a more-or-less north-south course through the park, provides another rich habitat for wildlife and birds.

BIRD LIFE

Bald Eagles pass through Theodore Roosevelt National Park during the fall migration period, but Golden Eagles breed here – along the Little Missouri River floodplain. A good place to look for them soaring above is at the North Unit's River Bend Outlook. Warm brown in color and with a wingspan of six feet or more,

A Black-billed Magpie perches on the back of a resting elk.

adult Golden Eagles are hard to mistake for any other bird. Their large, dark-colored nests can be seen perched high up on steep cliff sides. Visitors to Theodore Roosevelt National Park also have the chance to see juvenile birds: look for the white tail with a distinct dark band and the white patches on the undersides of the wings.

This park is also an excellent place to watch sparrows, including the park's very rare prize bird – the Baird's Sparrow – a small, brown-streaked bird with an ocher slash down the back of its head. The best time to look for these skulking ground feeders is in the early spring and summer, when the males perch to sing; however, even experienced birders rarely see the bird even then. Most have to content themselves with hearing the distinctive – and not very loud – song, described as two to three high *zzipps* ending with a lower-pitched trill. Other sparrows at Theodore Roosevelt are less challenging to spot. Among the Western specialties here are Spotted Towhee, Clay-colored

The Clay-colored Sparrow *is one of the many grassland birds attracted to the badlands.*

Sparrow, Lark Sparrow, Lark Bunting, and Chestnut-collared Longspur.

Although grassland birds are a specialty at Theodore Roosevelt, the variety of other species is surprising. In the spring, migrating Sandhill Cranes are frequently found along the Little Missouri River. The grayish northern Great Plains subspecies of the Common Nighthawk can be seen in the park. The beautiful Mountain Bluebird is easily seen, especially in meadows and open rangeland, and the Black-billed Magpie is common in the rangeland too. Look for Sharp-tailed Grouse in the sagebrush and grasslands area and also along river and stream edges in the canyons.

VISITING

Not only is Theodore Roosevelt National Park a big place, the North and South units are separated by some 70 miles. To do justice to the birds and wildlife in each unit and enjoy the many well-marked nature trails, try to spend at least a day in each one.

Perhaps the best introduction to the South Unit is the overlook at the Painted Canyon Visitor Center, off route 10 in the southeastern corner of the park, where visitors get a magnificent panorama of the broken topography and vivid hues of the North Dakota badlands. The 36-mile scenic drive begins at the Medora Visitor's Center. A number of trails come off this road at turnouts, including the short Ridgeline Nature Trail.

In the North Unit, start by taking the 14-mile Scenic Drive that goes from the entrance station to the Oxbow Overlook. Trailheads for several trails are found at turnouts. The Little Mo trail is a good place to look for Golden Eagles. The Buckhorn Trail off the Caprock Coulee Trail leads to a prairie dog town – look for Burrowing Owls here.

HIGHLIGHTS

The mixed grassland areas of Theodore Roosevelt National Park are a good place to hunt for the uncommon but generally elusive Baird's Sparrow. This bird has lost large portions of its breeding range elsewhere on the northern Great Plains, where native prairie grass has been converted to cropland.

Site Map and Information

THEODORE ROOSEVELT NATIONAL PARK

🚗 The South Unit entrance is at Medora off I-94, 17 miles west of Belfield and 63 miles east of Glendive. The North Unit entrance is off Highway 85, 15 miles south of Watford City and 55 miles north of Belfield.

🚪 Daily, 24 hours, year-round.

⬤ Visitor centers closed Thanksgiving, Christmas, New Years Day.

ℹ️ Theodore Roosevelt National Park, Box 7, Medora, ND 58645. The visitor centers are open sunrise to sunset, year round.

📞 South Unit: (701) 623-4466; North Unit: (701) 842-2333

💲 Seven-day entrance pass $5 per person, with a maximum of $10 per carload.

♿ Visitor centers, campgrounds, and some trails are wheelchair accessible.

🏕 Cottonwood Campground (South Unit) and Juniper Campground (North Unit); fees;

no reservations required, but calling ahead is strongly encouraged.

🐎 Showdon Country Outfitters (701-623-4568) offers horseback rides along the South Unit's trails. Little Knive Outfitters (800-438-6905) offers horseback rides in and near the North Unit.

🏨 Motels are available in nearby Watford City (North Unit); and Medora, Dickinson, Belfield, and Beach (South Unit).

GREEN LAWN CEMETERY AND ARBORETUM

A tree-filled oasis in downtown Columbus is a magnet for
a surprising variety of migrating birds.

The average cemetery isn't a particularly inviting place to visit, much less to birdwatch, but Green Lawn Cemetery and Arboretum is not an average cemetery. Founded in 1848, Green Lawn is a 360-acre, beautifully landscaped park that incorporates a ravine, a large pond, open fields, and an estimated 3,000 trees – including seven state champions for size. It's a green, peaceful haven for both people and birds.

The Indigo Bunting *male sports a deep blue plumage during breeding season.*

magnificent flowering trees and shrubs were planted – wooden sign posts now identify many of the varieties.

Some 80 acres of the cemetery are undeveloped fields. In addition, the areas around the large pond near the center and the shallow, wooded ravine near the main entrance were allowed to grow up into a dense tangle of shrubs and woods. This sort of wild habitat is ideal for many birds, of course; more than 200 species have been spotted at Green Lawn.

HABITAT

In contrast to the manicured tidiness of most cemeteries, Green Lawn Cemetery and Arboretum has a much more natural appearance. The founders had the foresight to leave hundreds of large trees on the property. In later years thousands of

BIRD LIFE

This site is an excellent spot for passerines – perching birds such as warblers, thrushes, flycatchers, and finches – especially in spring. In all, 24 warbler species are seen here frequently during migration, with another dozen or so seen infrequently but regularly.

Warblers such as the Mourning, Connecticut, Wilson's, and Canada, as well as the Yellow-breasted Chat (also a species of warbler) can be spotted in brushy and shrubby areas of the cemetery and arboretum. This habitat also attracts Lincoln's Sparrow and Fox Sparrow. American Woodcock can almost always be found in the early spring in the ravine near the main entrance. Northern Saw-whet Owls have been found roosting during the day in dense yew plantings in March and April.

BIRDS TO LOOK FOR

Pied-Billed Grebe • Yellow-crowned Night-Heron • Blue-winged Teal • American Woodcock • Northern Saw-whet Owl • Veery • Swainson's Thrush • Connecticut Warbler • Mourning Warbler • Wilson's Warbler • Fox Sparrow • Mourning Warbler • Mourning Warbler • Lincoln's Sparrow • Rose-breasted Grosbeak • Indigo Bunting

---

This cemetery attracts many spring songbirds, included the Rose-breasted Grosbeak.

One of the best places to see birds at Green Lawn is the large pond near the center of the cemetery (within Sections 65 and 85, just south of the chapel). Formerly a small quarry, the pond, or "pit," as it is often called by local birdwatchers, is surrounded by tangled vegetation that attracts warblers and sparrows, as well as Rose-breasted Grosbeaks, Evening Grosbeaks, and Northern Cardinals. Waterbirds as varied as Pied-billed Grebes, Blue-winged Teal, Hooded Mergansers, Wood Ducks, and Solitary Sandpipers all turn up on and around the pond with regularity.

About a hundred yards west of the western end of the pond, an ornate iron bridge spans the shallow ravine. The bridge, completed in 1898, is an excellent vantage point from which to birdwatch. The brushy slopes of the ravine are especially attractive to thrushes, including the Hermit, Swainson's, Gray-cheeked, and Wood Thrushes, as well as the Veery, another thrush.

In addition to the spring migrants, Green Lawn has a fair number of species that nest on its grounds, including the Yellow-crowned Night-Heron, Yellow-billed Cuckoo, Eastern Wood-Pewee, Cedar Waxwing, and Indigo Bunting. Year-round residents including the Great Horned Owl, Carolina Chickadee, and Carolina Wren. Cooper's Hawks winter at Green Lawn.

The Yellow-crowned Night-Heron *has a white crown and cheek patches, and during breeding, white head plumes.*

VISITING

Green Lawn Cemetery and Arboretum is renowned as a spring migrant trap – a place that attracts large numbers of migrating birds. On a sunny morning in late April or early May, it's possible to tally at least 60 species. Spring migration peaks in the first two weeks of May, but migrants continue to pass through into June.

Numerous paved roads lead through the cemetery and arboretum. To reach the pond and bridge, follow the red stripe from the main entrance to the first road past Section 85, turn right, and park near the grave of Emil Ambos, whose tombstone is topped by a large statue of himself fishing. To reach the pond, walk past the shrubbery on the north side of the road. To get to the bridge, return to the road and continue west past the pond another 100 yards.

The Columbus Audubon Society (see telephone number below) is active in leading birding tours of Green Lawn in the spring and fall. This group also has created a butterfly garden near the administration building and offers butterfly tours in the summer.

HIGHLIGHTS

According to Tom Thomson, author of *Birding in Ohio* (Indiana University Press, 1994), the breakdown of bird species seen at Green Lawn is: 13 hawks; 5 owls; 6 woodpeckers; 10 flycatchers; 7 thrushes; 7 vireos; 38 warblers; 2 tanagers; 14 sparrows; 9 blackbirds and orioles; and 15 different buntings, finches, and grosbeaks.

Site Map and Information

GREEN LAWN CEMETERY AND ARBORETUM

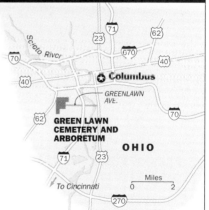

- From downtown Columbus, take I-71 south about 2.5 miles to the Greenlawn Avenue exit. Go west on Greenlawn Avenue for 0.75 mile to the main entrance.

- Daily, year-round; 7 a.m.–7 p.m. in spring and summer and 7 a.m.–5 p.m. in fall and winter.

- Never.

- Green Lawn Cemetery and Arboretum, 1000 Greenlawn Avenue, Columbus, OH 43223. The administration is open to the public, weekdays, 8:30 a.m.–4:30 p.m., and Saturdays 8:30 a.m.–noon.

- (614) 444-1123

- None; however, contributions to Friends of Green Lawn are appreciated.

- Numerous paved roads are vehicle- and wheelchair accessible.

- Two nearby campgrounds are Buckeye Lake at (800) 562-0792 and Tree Haven Campground at (740) 965-3469.

- Call the Columbus Audubon Society at (614) 451-4591 for tour information.

- Lodging available in Columbus; contact the Greater Columbus Convention and Visitors Bureau at (800) 354-2657 for listings.

MAGEE MARSH WILDLIFE AREA

*A vast freshwater marsh and sandy beach along Lake Erie's Ohio shore
boast an abundance of easy-to-view bird life.*

Centuries ago the Lake Erie coast in northern Ohio consisted mostly of large marshes that teemed with bird and animal life. Human settlement over the last couple of centuries has reduced the marshes to a fraction of their former extent. Fortunately, Magee Marsh Wildlife Area, among other area havens, preserves important expanses of lakeshore marsh, attracting a checklist of more than 300 birds.

American Bitterns, *among other large wading birds, nest in the park.*

HABITAT

Magee Marsh's 2,000 acres are positioned next to Ottawa National Wildlife Refuge's 4,601 acres and the smaller adjoining Crane Creek State Park 79 acres. Combined, the three sites preserve a very large and varied expanse of wet meadows,

shrubby vegetation, grassy marshes, shallow ponds and impoundments, and sandy lakeshore.

The wetlands along Lake Erie are a crucial stopover point for migratory birds – and Magee Marsh is one of the most accessible places to see them.

In the spring, the wildlife area is an outstanding place to see warblers heading north; in the spring and fall, dramatic numbers of waterfowl pass through.

BIRD LIFE

The spring waterfowl spectacle at Magee Marsh begins in March, when several hundred Tundra Swans pass through the region. Look for them in the shallow ponds and offshore on Lake Erie. An amazing number of duck species begin to appear from March to May. Among the surface-feeding ducks that are seen frequently in the marshy areas are Wood Ducks, American Black Ducks, Gadwall, Green-winged Teal, American Wigeon.

Look for diving ducks such as Canvasbacks, Lesser Scaup, Buffleheads, and Ruddy Ducks rafting offshore on the lake. The waterfowl that pass through the park in the spring come through again on their way back south, although the fall migration is more spread out, lasting from August through November.

The Lake Erie shoreline is one of the best places in Ohio to see nesting Bald Eagles. Several nesting pairs

---

BIRDS TO LOOK FOR

American Bittern • Black-crowned
Night Heron • Tundra Swan •
American Wigeon • Lesser Scaup •
Bald Eagle • White-rumped
Sandpiper • Dunlin • Short-eared
Owl • Blue Jay • Tree Swallow •
Mourning Warbler • Canada Warbler •
Yellow-headed Blackbird

Tree Swallows are easy to spot behind the Sportmen's Migratory Bird Center.

have been returning regularly to the Magee Marsh region. Although nest sites in the park and adjoining refuges are always closed to the public, look for the birds soaring in the sky above. Hawks migrate through the park from March to early May. This is a good time to watch Broad-winged Hawks and Red-shouldered Hawks. In late March and April Northern Saw-whet Owls can be found hiding in evergreens; at dusk look for Short-eared Owls hunting low over the marshes during the spring and fall.

Shorebirds such as Black-bellied Plovers, Dunlin, and White-rumped and Pectoral Sandpipers find the wet meadows, shallow ponds, and exposed mudflats of Crane Creek State Park highly attractive. Look for them in the spring and fall. Large

wading birds such as American Bitterns, Great Blue Herons, Great Egrets, and Black-crowned Night-Herons can be spotted stalking around in the marshes from spring through fall, and all these species nest within the wildlife area.

In the spring the massive numbers of waterfowl at the park can sometimes overshadow the large numbers and variety of songbirds found here. Be sure to take the popular Magee Marsh boardwalk bird trail, a 0.6-mile path that winds

Tundra Swans *featured black facial skin around the beak, generally tapering to a yellow spot positioned in front of the eye.*

through forested beach and marshland. In late April and May it is not uncommon to spot 20 to 30 warbler species in a single morning. Look especially for Prothonotary, Mourning, Canada, Wilson's, and Hooded Warblers, as well as Northern Waterthrushes.

VISITING

Magee Marsh Wildlife Area offers outstanding birdwatching with minimal effort. Just inside the park's entrance, the Sportsmen's Migratory Bird Center provides visitors with a quick introduction to the area. Get a site map and find the shallow ponds behind the center. They are a good place to look for shorebirds. Yellow-headed Blackbirds, Purple Martins, and Tree Swallows can be found

around here as well. The easily accessible boardwalk is a veritable songbird bonanza.

The optimal month for birding at Magee Marsh Wildlife Area is May, when spring migration is at its peak in terms of both numbers and variety. However, along the shores of Lake Erie this time of year can be surprisingly cold – so remember to dress warmly.

HIGHLIGHTS

In the spring, migratory songbirds can be seen at Magee Marsh in large numbers as they gather together before pushing north across Lake Erie. Large flocks of Blue Jays, sometimes totaling thousands of birds, can be seen from mid-April to mid-May.

Site Map and Information

MAGEE MARSH WILDLIFE AREA

- From Toledo, follow State Route 2 east 22 miles to reach the wildlife area entrance. From Port Clinton, follow State Route 2 west for 17 miles to the entrance.

- Daily, sunrise to sunset, year-round.

- Access is limited during waterfowl hunting season, from mid-October through December.

- Magee Marsh, 13229 West State Route 2, Oak Harbor, OH 43449. Sportsmen's Migratory Bird Center is open weekdays, 8 a.m.–5 p.m. From March through October, the center is also open on Saturday and Sunday (hours vary).

- (419) 898-0960

- None.

- The Sportsmen's Migratory Bird Center and the boardwalk trail are both wheelchair accessible.

- Campsites are available at nearby East Harbor State Park; call (419) 734-5857 for reservations.

- Tours are offered for organized groups. Call the migratory bird center for details.

- Motels, hotels, and bed-and-breakfasts in nearby Toledo; call the Greater Toledo Convention and Visitors Bureau at (800) 243-4667 for listings. For listings in Port Clinton, contact the Ottawa County Visitors Bureau at (800) 441-1271.

BLACK MESA NATURE PRESERVE

*The foothills of the Rocky Mountains meet the shortgrass prairie
at this bird-rich site in the Oklahoma panhandle.*

Rising abruptly from the plains of the Oklahoma panhandle, Black Mesa is a basalt-capped plateau formed eons ago by the lava flow from an ancient volcano. The basalt cap protected the underlying rock from erosion by the nearby Carrizo Creek and dry Cimarron River. Today the top of the steep-sided mesa is 600 feet above the surrounding plains. In fact, at 4,973 feet above sea level, it is the highest point in Oklahoma.

Black Mesa Nature Preserve protects 1,700 acres, or about 60 percent of the mesa top in Oklahoma, along with talus (rocky debris) slopes and an extensive area of prairie at the base of the mesa.

The Western Kingbird *is common in dry open country.*

HABITAT

The preserve contains both the shortgrass prairie of the Great Plains and the pinyon-juniper woodlands of the Rocky Mountain foothills. Wherever habitats meet, the plant and animal life is quite diverse, and Black Mesa is no exception. The top of the nearly flat mesa is covered with shortgrass prairie plants, such as little bluestem and grama grass. The steep talus slopes are covered with pinyon, juniper, and shrub oak. The nearby stream and river valleys are lined with willow and cottonwood trees.

In all, Black Mesa Nature Preserve is home to 31 plant and animal species that are rare in the state of Oklahoma. Black bears, bobcats, mountain lions, mule deer, and pronghorns are among the mammals seen here.

BIRD LIFE

The bird species found at the nature preserve include a number that are at the farthest edge of their usual range. The Black-throated Sparrow, for instance, is a bird that is quite common in the arid Southwest. Not only is this bird also found at Black Mesa, but it breeds in the talus slopes at the foot of the mesa. The Curve-billed Thrasher, another bird of the southwestern desert, is at the northernmost extreme of its range here.

The pinyon-juniper habitat of the talus slopes attracts a number of birds generally found in the mountains to the west, including Bushtits and

BIRDS TO LOOK FOR

Swainson's Hawk • Ferruginous Hawk • Golden Eagle • Scaled Quail • White-throated Swift • Say's Phoebe • Cassin's Kingbird • Western Kingbird • Steller's Jay • Western Scrub-Jay • Pinyon Jay • Chihuahuan Raven • Mountain Chickadee • Bushtit • Curve-billed Thrasher • Black-throated Sparrow

This preserve features Steller's Jays, plus Pinyon Jays and Western Scrub-Jays.

Mountain Chickadees. The prize bird of this habitat is the Pinyon Jay, a large, beautiful bird with overall blue plumage; it would be hard to mistake this bird for any other. Look – and listen – for large flocks feeding noisily in the scrubby woods; hundreds of birds may gather together. Other jay species also find the pinyon-juniper woodlands at Black Mesa to their liking. Western Scrub-Jays breed here, while Steller's Jay, a dark blue bird with a prominent black crest, is a seasonal visitor from the Rocky Mountains in late fall to early spring.

The Scaled Quail is another nature preserve specialty.

The Swainson's Hawk may be spotted soaring over the prairie with uptilted wings.

This bird is fairly common farther south in Texas, but here it is at the northeastern edge of its range. Look for a chunky, grayish bird with a crest of white-tipped feathers. In the fall these quail gather into flocks, or coveys, that can be seen foraging in the scrubby areas at the foot of the mesa.

The steep sides of the mesa rising from the grassland create powerful updrafts of warm air. Look overhead to see soaring birds such as the Ferruginous Hawk, Golden Eagle, and Swainson's Hawk. Look also for the Chihuahuan Raven, a large, crowlike bird with a wedge-shaped tail. White-throated Swifts and Say's Phoebes nest in the many crevices and cracks on the mesa slopes.

VISITING

A visit to Black Mesa Nature Preserve can be a little challenging. The terrain is rough, the temperatures can vary from -30 degrees in winter to 112 degrees in summer, there's no water (although there are violent thunderstorms in the summer), and rattlesnakes are not uncommon. The climb to the top of the mesa and back is made via a rugged trail and takes approximately four hours.

Even without climbing the mesa, however, visitors to the nature preserve can have an enjoyable birdwatching experience. The shortgrass prairie around the parking area and trailhead and the talus slopes at the base of the mesa are easily accessible and good bird habitat. The pinyon-juniper habitat that covers the talus slopes is particularly productive.

The best seasons for visiting Black Mesa Nature Preserve are spring and fall. Visitors can avoid extremes of heat and cold, and there is less likelihood of being caught without shelter in a dangerous thunderstorm. Even so, bring plenty of water, dress in layers, and wear sturdy footgear.

HIGHLIGHTS

Both the Western Kingbird and the less common (but similar-looking) Cassin's Kingbird are found at the preserve. To identify the Western Kingbird, look for the black tail with white edges on the outer feathers and listen for the one-syllable *whit* call. The Cassin's Kingbird has a dark brown tail with no white and gives a two-syllable *chi-bew* call.

Site Map and Information

BLACK MESA NATURE PRESERVE

🔲 From Boise City, take State Highway 325 west 27 miles to Kenton. Continue for 8 miles to a blacktop road marked Black Mesa Nature Preserve and turn north. Follow this road for 5 miles to reach the preserve parking area, which is on the north side of the mesa. (Look for the large gray and white trailhead sign.)

🔲 Daily, sunrise to sunset, year-round.

🔲 Never.

🔲 Black Mesa Nature Preserve, c/o Black Mesa State Park, HCR 1, Box 8, Kenton, OK 73946. The preserve has no formal Visitor Center, but visitors can drop by the state park's office/ranger station for information; open every day but Sunday, 8 a.m.–6 p.m.

🔲 (580) 426-2222

🔲 None, but donations are appreciated.

🔲 None.

🔲 Campgrounds are available at nearby Black Mesa State Park; call (580) 426-2222 for details.

🔲 None.

🔲 Motels are available in Boise City; call the Boise City/Cimarron County Chamber of Commerce at (580) 544-3344 for listings.

LITTLE RIVER NATIONAL WILDLIFE REFUGE

This large area of nearly untouched river bottomland and hardwood forest in southeastern Oklahoma is a boon to birds and other wildlife.

Naturalists consider Little River National Wildlife Refuge one of the finest remaining examples of rich bottomland forest in the United States. Once cleared of its many hardwood trees, this rich forestland makes fertile agricultural land – which was the fate of most of the rest of the bottomland forest habitat in Oklahoma and elsewhere in the United States. Little River National Wildlife Refuge was established in 1987 primarily as a haven for wintering and migrating waterfowl. At that time 7,500 acres were conveyed to the refuge by The Nature Conservancy. More land along the Little River has been acquired since then, and today the refuge consists of nearly 15,000 acres.

HABITAT

Little River National Wildlife Refuge straddles the floodplain of the Little River, so most of the refuge is low-lying bottomland forest. In addition to a portion of the river itself, the refuge contains numerous shallow oxbow

lakes and sloughs or marshy areas. The bottomlands are forested with species such as willow oak, water oak, white oak, sweetgum, bald cypress, and holly. In the higher, drier areas, loblolly pine, hickory, chestnut oak, pin oak, and walnut trees are more common.

Overall, Little River National Wildlife Refuge is a damp place with a lot of standing water. In the winter the bottomlands flood naturally (helped

Bell's Vireo *sings a series of scolding notes that help identify this secretive bird.*

along by some beaver dams), creating the ideal habitat for wintering waterfowl. In the spring and summer large numbers of insects and the lush growth of berries and other plant food make the refuge ideal for warblers and other woodland species. More than 225 bird species have been tallied here.

BIRDS TO LOOK FOR

Little Blue Heron • Great Egret • Wood Duck • Gadwall • American Wigeon • Blue-winged Teal • Red-shouldered Hawk • Pileated Woodpecker • White-eyed Vireo • Bell's Vireo • Brown-headed Nuthatch • Gray-cheeked Thrush • Yellow-throated Warbler • Swainson's Warbler • Painted Bunting

---

BIRD LIFE

Among the many woodland birds that find the damp forest at Little River highly attractive are a number of vireo species. White-eyed, Yellow-throated, Bell's, and Red-eyed Vireos are all seen regularly here. Thrushes, including Swainson's Thrush and the Gray-cheeked Thrush, can be seen in suitable habitat. This refuge is also a

The river's bottomlands are home to woodland birds such as this Painted Bunting.

good place to look for the gaudy Painted Bunting. Check in low brushy areas, especially along creeks. Listen for the loud, resonant drumming of the Pileated Woodpecker. This largest of North American woodpeckers prefers dense, mature forests and is easily found at Little River National Wildlife Refuge. Look also for the large, rectangular holes this bird excavates in tree trunks and stumps.

Thirteen warbler species, including Yellow-throated and Kentucky Warblers, nest on the refuge; in all, 29 warbler species are seen at the refuge. The big challenge for birdwatchers visiting this refuge is spotting – or even hearing – the elusive Swainson's Warbler. This drab little warbler prefers exactly the sort of damp, tangled hardwood forest that abounds at Little River. If it's seen at all, it's only a fleeting glimpse near or on the ground amid dense vegetation. The odds of hearing the bird are better, especially in April and May. Listen for the male's very loud, ringing *whee whee whee whip-poor-will* song. The call note, given by both males and females, is a long, loud *chip*.

The flooded forest at Little River is the winter home for a large numbers of ducks. Mallards and Wood Ducks are very common from November through February, as are Gadwall, American Wigeon, and Hooded Mergansers. Blue-winged Teal and Northern Shovelers are common during fall and spring migrations.

Little Blue Herons *feed methodically in the refuge's oxbow lakes and marshes.*

The numerous waterfowl at Little River in the winter attract several Bald Eagles to the area along the river each year. Look also for Red-shouldered Hawks near the water and in the moist woodlands. In the upland areas of the refuge, where pines are more common, look for the Brown-headed Nuthatch. Little River is just about the only place to find this bird in Oklahoma.

Several heron rookeries (nesting colonies), including those of Great Blue Herons, Great Egrets, and Little Blue Herons, are found on the refuge. Visitors may contact the refuge headquarters about locations of active heron rookeries.

VISITING

Little River National Wildlife Refuge is basically undeveloped wilderness, and access isn't particularly well defined. Although several gravel roads run through the refuge, there is currently no main entrance, visitor center, marked hiking trails, or other facilities. There aren't any parking areas or pull-outs, but refuge authorities allow visitors to park by the side of the roads for birdwatching – just be careful not to block traffic. Because the roads in the refuge are sometimes closed due to flooding or management needs, always check with the refuge headquarters in nearby Broken Bow and pick up current maps before visiting.

HIGHLIGHTS

The secretive Swainson's Warbler is rarely seen, but is it rare? Researchers aren't sure, but they do know that Little River National Wildlife Refuge is about the only place in Oklahoma where the bird can be found. In 1998, 46 of these birds were recorded here.

Site Map and Information

LITTLE RIVER NATIONAL WILDLIFE REFUGE

🚐 IFrom Broken Bow, follow US 70 south approximately 5 miles to the western end of the refuge.

⛺ Daily, sunrise to sunset, year-round.

⬤ Never; however, roads are sometimes closed by flooding. Pick up a current map from refuge headquarters.

ℹ️ Little River National Wildlife Refuge, 635 South Park Street, PO Box 340, Broken Bow, OK 74728. Refuge headquarters, open weekdays, 7:30 a.m.–4 p.m., function as a Visitor Center.

☎ (580) 584-6211; www.southwest@fws.gov

💲 None.

♿ No special accommodations, but the refuge roads serve as good observation points from which to view wildlife.

🅰 None on-site. Campgrounds are available at nearby Lake Pine Retreat; call (580) 494-6464 for details.

🍴 None.

🏨 There are motels in nearby Idabel and Broken Bow; call the Oklahoma Department of Tourism and Recreation at (800) 652-6552 for listings.

Badlands National Park

Rugged terrain, colorful rock formations, and broad grasslands are home to plenty of birds in this immense southwestern South Dakota park.

The Lakota Sioux who still make their home in this region call the sharply eroded pinnacles, buttes, and gullies of this part of southwestern South Dakota "mako sica" – literally, "bad lands." Despite the name and the apparent emptiness of the terrain, Badlands National Park supports a surprising amount of plant and animal life. The park sprawls over nearly 244,000 acres, including the 64,000-acre Sage Creek Wilderness Area. The largest protected area of mixed-grass prairie in the National Parks system is contained within the park.

The Mountain Bluebird *hovers above insects before dropping down to snatch them.*

Established in 1939 as Badlands National Monument and redesignated a national park in 1978, Badlands National Park is visited every year by more than a million people. The park is so large, remote, and undeveloped that it provides a genuine wilderness experience even at the peak of the summer tourist season.

Habitat

The Badlands are a vast wilderness of rugged cliffs and gullies, interspersed with broad areas of mixed-grass prairie. This is a land of extremes. In the summer the Badlands climate is very hot and dry, although it is often punctuated by violent thunderstorms. In the winter, winds that roar in from the arctic make the Badlands very cold – but still dry, with little snow.

Despite the climate extremes, the Badlands are full of life. At least 56 different grass species and hundreds of wildflower species are found on the Badlands prairies, where they thrive in the harsh, dry conditions. The plant community supports an abundance of wildlife, including black-tailed prairie dogs, pronghorns, bison, and the most endangered mammal in North America, the black-footed ferret.

Bird Life

Some 215 bird species have been recorded in Badlands National Park. As might be expected, grasslands sparrow species are a major attraction for birdwatchers. Birds such as the Clay-colored Sparrow, Lark Sparrow, Lark Bunting, Savannah Sparrow, and

BIRDS TO LOOK FOR

Bald Eagle • Rough-legged Hawk • Ferruginous Hawk • Golden Eagle • Sharp-tailed Grouse • Sandhill Crane • Baird's Sandpiper • Wilson's Phalarope • Burrowing Owl • White-throated Swift • Rock Wren • Mountain Bluebird • Clay-colored Sparrow • Brewer's Sparrow • Lark Bunting • Lapland Longspur

The Lapland Longspur creeps along open grasslands in search of seeds and other food.

Lapland Longspur are common here. Much rarer but still likely to be seen or heard are Brewer's Sparrow, Vesper Sparrow, Lincoln's Sparrow, and Harris's Sparrow.

In general, sparrows of the grasslands are elusive, lurking in the grass, popping up to give birdwatchers a tantalizing glimpse, and then disappearing. Because the prairie grasses at Badlands National Park can be several feet tall, the sparrows will more likely be heard than seen. This is also true of the other sought-after grassland bird here, the Sharp-tailed Grouse. Listen for a three-note clucking that sounds like *whucker-whucker-whucker.*

The raptors that soar elegantly over the grasslands are much easier to spot. Look up to see Bald Eagles, Ferruginous Hawks, Golden Eagles, Rough-legged Hawks, and Swainson's Hawks. These birds are hunting rodents and rabbits, which form the bulk of their prey.

Look for birds in the arid canyons and buttes of Badlands National Park as well. The Rock Wren, a small, active bird with a cinnamon-colored rump, can be seen and heard easily as it probes for food among the rocky debris at the foot of cliffs. White-throated Swifts nest in crevices in the park's cliffs and can be seen flying after insects in the canyons. Mountain Bluebirds can be found in brushy areas, especially near water. The Baird's Sandpiper, a bird that winters in Mexico and breeds in the high arctic, is commonly seen here taking advantage of intermittent pools and puddles in the spring and fall as it

The Rough-legged Hawk *lets out a loud screech when it senses danger.*

188

migrates through. Other migratory visitors include Sandhill Cranes, soaring overhead and sharing the rare water sources with numerous duck species. Wilson's Phalarope, which feeds as often on land as on water breeds at the park. Look for it on the grassy borders of shallow lakes and marshes in summer.

VISITING

To see the most birds here, allow a full day. Most visitors to the park spend their time in the Cedar Pass area of the park's North Unit – the best-known and easiest to explore of three units. A good starting point is the Ben Reifel Visitor Center. Several trailheads, including the half-mile Cliff Shelf Nature Trail and the short (quarter-mile) but fascinating Fossil Exhibit Trail, begin within five miles of the Visitor Center.

This is also a good starting point for following the scenic, 27-mile Badlands Loop Road. This steep, winding road is paved and has numerous pull-outs and scenic overlooks. From the Loop Road, the 10-mile roundtrip drive to the Roberts Prairie Dog Town is worth it; in addition to the prairie dogs, this area is home to Burrowing Owls. Be aware that the weather can be severe and shift from one extreme to another in a short time. Dress appropriately, drive cautiously, and carry extra water.

HIGHLIGHTS

The buffalo, bighorn sheep, and black-footed ferrets found in Badlands National Park are all native to the region, yet at one time all were extinct within the park. Those found in the park today are all descendants of reintroduced animals.

Site Map and Information

BADLANDS NATIONAL PARK

From I-90 take exit 110 near the town of Wall or exit 131 at Cactus Flat to SD 240 south. Follow SD 240 to the park's northern boundary (8.5 miles), where the road name changes to Badlands Loop Road. Follow Loop Road to reach the Ben Reifel Visitor Center in the North Unit.

Daily, 24 hours, year-round.

Never.

Badlands National Park, PO Box 6, Interior, SD 57750. Ben Reifel Visitor Center is open daily, 8 a.m.–4:30 p.m., with extended hours in spring, summer, and fall; call ahead for exact times.

(605) 433-5361; www.nps.gov/badl

$10 for a 7-day pass.

Ben Reifel Visitor Center and Fossil Exhibit Trail are wheelchair accessible.

Cedar Pass Campground offers full facilities for $10 per night. Sage Creek, a primitive campground, is free. Both campsites operate on a first-come, first-served basis.

None.

Cedar Pass Lodge is in the North Unit; call (605) 433-5460 for reservations. Motels are available in nearby Wall and Kadoka; call South Dakota Tourism at (800) 732-5682 for listings.

SAND LAKE NATIONAL WILDLIFE REFUGE

This protected habitat in the rolling grasslands of northeast South Dakota attracts migratory birds by the thousands.

Only a bit more than a century ago, the land around Sand Lake National Wildlife Refuge was a vast, rolling prairie, interrupted only by the slow-moving James River. When settlers brought farming and cattle-grazing to this part of northeast South Dakota in 1887, they caused serious degradation of the natural wildlife habitat. By the 1930s the migrating waterfowl and other birds that depended on the grasslands and the extensive marshes had dwindled alarmingly in number. In 1935 the 21,498-acre Sand Lake National Wildlife Refuge was established to preserve critical wildlife habitat.

Franklin's Gulls *maintain their largest breeding colony here.*

HABITAT

Visitors to this refuge are never far from water. The James River meanders southward through the refuge, opening out into Mud Lake and Sand Lake (the two are separated by a dam). These two large, shallow lakes form the heart of the refuge, covering over half the territory; wetlands cover much of the rest. Cottonwoods and willows line the lakeshores, and green ash and Russian olive trees were planted as windbreaks in the early days of the refuge.

The open, grassy areas of the refuge were once croplands. Today most have been replanted with native grasses such as big bluestem, little bluestem, and switchgrass. The grassy cover provides habitat for animals such as red foxes and striped skunks, along with grassland birds such as the Horned Lark and the Chestnut-collared Longspur. Hawks such as the Swainson's Hawk soar above, looking for small grassland rodents.

Extensive stands of reeds mix with open water throughout the refuge, providing an abundance of year-round wildlife and bird habitat.

BIRD LIFE

Since 1935, 266 species of birds have been recorded on the refuge. Given the refuge's watery habitat and location along the Central flyway, it is not a surprise that many of these are wading birds, waterfowl, and shorebirds. From March to May and September through November, birds such as the Western Grebe, American White Pelican, Black-crowned Night-Heron, White-faced Ibis (rare in this

---

BIRDS TO LOOK FOR

Western Grebe • American White Pelican • White-faced Ibis • Snow Goose • Gadwall • Redhead • Lesser Scaup • Ruddy Duck • Bald Eagle • Swainson's Hawk • Golden Eagle • American Coot • Marbled Godwit • Franklin's Gull • Horned Lark • Chestnut-collared Longspur

---

The refuge's lakes and wetlands draw migratory waterfowl, including these Redheads.

part of the country), and American Coot are found at the refuge.

Thousands of Snow Geese and Canada Geese pass through during spring and fall migration periods. The refuge was once home to a captive flock of some 200 Giant Canada Geese. This subspecies was near extinction in 1962, when the Fish and Wildlife Service and the State of South Dakota began a joint effort to restore the birds to their former range. Since then, several thousand of these extremely large geese have been released into the wild, where they have established successful breeding populations.

Vast numbers of ducks float on the lakes, ponds, and marshes at Sand Lake. Many stay to breed, including Gadwall, Blue-winged Teal, Redhead, Lesser Scaup, and Ruddy Duck. The muddy shores and shallow waters of the refuge are also attractive to shorebirds, both in migration and during the breeding season. This is a good place to see Willets, Marbled Godwits, American Avocets, and Wilson's Phalaropes, among at least 25 other species.

Sand Lake is also home to the world's largest breeding colony of Franklin's Gulls. This attractive little gull of the prairie, identified by its black hood and a faint pinkish color, was once seriously threatened by habitat loss; the extensive wetlands of Sand Lake and similar refuges have been crucial to its survival.

The White-faced Ibis, *although rare, is worth looking for wading in the refuge's marshes.*

191

Check the willows and cottonwoods on the east side of Sand Lake for roosting Bald Eagles and Golden Eagles in spring. So many Bald Eagles pass through the area in early spring that the refuge sponsors an annual Eagle Day Open House.

VISITING

Visitors to Sand Lake should start at the refuge headquarters, near the Columbia Recreation Area at the southwestern end of the site. A 100-foot tower near the headquarters offers a good bird's-eye view of the refuge. A nearby pond is a great spot for seeing ducks and geese.

Although there is a three-quarter-mile hiking trail beginning at the recreation area, most visitors to Sand Lake take the 15-mile driving loop that begins near headquarters. The

well-marked loop follows the shore of Sand Lake, with a dozen pull-outs for parking. The route also crosses the dam between Sand Lake and Mud Lake, an excellent spot for watching waterfowl. Further on, an observation deck overlooking Sand Lake from the southeast is another excellent spot to see a variety of water-dependent birds. In all, 40 miles of roads wind through the refuge.

HIGHLIGHTS

The world's largest colony of Franklin's Gulls – more than 100,000 pairs – nests at Sand Lake National Wildlife Refuge. These small, black-hooded gulls spend the winter along the Pacific coast of South America from Peru to Chile and return every year to the prairie marshes to breed.

Site Map and Information

SAND LAKE NATIONAL WILDLIFE REFUGE

🚗 From Aberdeen, take Highway 281 north 15 miles to Highway 10 east. Continue for approximately 12 miles then turn south onto County Road 16 and follow it for 3 miles to refuge headquarters.

◻ Daily, sunrise to sunset, year-round.

⬤ Never.

🅷 Sand Lake National Wildlife Refuge, 39650 Sand Lake Drive, Columbia, SD 57433. Refuge headquarters functions as a Visitor Center. It is open weekdays, 8 a.m.–4:30 p.m. year-round, weather permitting.

📞 (605) 885-6320; www.r6.fws.gov/sandlake

⑤ None.

♿ Refuge headquarters are wheelchair accessible.

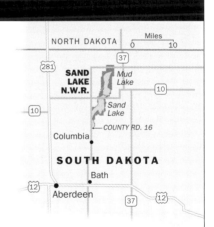

🅰 None. Public campgrounds are available in nearby Richmond Lake State Park; call (800) 710-2267 for details.

🅝 None.

🏨 There are motels in nearby Aberdeen; contact the Aberdeen Chamber of Commerce at (605) 225-2860 for listings.

ARANSAS NATIONAL WILDLIFE REFUGE

This world-famous refuge on the Gulf Coast of Texas is the winter home of the only wild migrating population of the endangered Whooping Crane.

When the original 47,261 acres of Aransas National Wildlife Refuge were purchased in 1937, one of the main goals was to preserve critical winter habitat for the 29 or so Whooping Cranes left in the world. Today the migratory population of Whooping Cranes is up to a record 188 – still a tiny, endangered population, but one that has been saved by the presence of this safe haven. Over the years additional land acquisitions have brought the total acreage protected by Aransas National Wildlife Refuge up to 59,000.

Bay-breasted Warblers *are just one of many migrants that stop here on the way to or from Central America.*

HABITAT

The Whooping Cranes – and an impressive 398 other bird species – are drawn to Aransas National Wildlife Refuge, which provides its favorable habitat along the Gulf Coast of Texas. The refuge is bordered on the east by San Antonio Bay, ringed by tidal marshes, and criss-crossed by tidal slough areas. Most of its acreage (about 80 percent) consists of the Blackjack Peninsula, which is fringed by mud flats and saltwater and brackish marshes. The interior of the peninsula is grasslands and mottes (thick clumps of trees such as live oak and redbay), interspersed with numerous freshwater ponds and marshes.

BIRD LIFE

The variety of habitats at Aransas, combined with its mild climate, make the refuge a veritable banquet table to a huge range of birds, especially water-loving birds. Six of the seven North American grebes can be seen here. Both the American White and Brown Pelican can be seen at Aransas; the Brown Pelican breeds here. Storms may bring large seabirds like the Magnificent Frigatebird inland. Large wading birds are spectacular and abundant; the Reddish Egret, Roseate Spoonbill, White Ibis, and White-faced Ibis are readily seen in the marshes year-round. Numerous ducks and geese float on the various bodies of water, from the bay to the inland ponds. Two of the more unusual ones to look for in the freshwater marshes are the Fulvous Whistling-Duck and the

BIRDS TO LOOK FOR

Brown Pelican • Magnificent Frigatebird • Reddish Egret • White Ibis • Roseate Spoonbill • Whooping Crane • Piping Plover • Bonaparte's Gull • Gull-billed Tern • Inca Dove • Groove-billed Ani • Common Pauraque • Ladder-backed Woodpecker • Chestnut-sided Warbler • Blackburnian Warbler • Bay-breasted Warbler • Blue Grosbeak

The Brown Pelican dives to catch fish in its pouch.

Black-bellied Whistling-Duck, both of which breed on the refuge. Shorebirds feed by the thousands on the tidal mud flats and in the coastal marshes, especially in August. Look here for birds such as the Black-bellied Plover, the Piping Plover, the Black-necked Stilt, and the Long-billed Curlew. Gulls such as Bonaparte's and Franklin's Gull turn up regularly, as do Caspian, Gull-billed, Forster's, and Least Terns.

Magnificent Frigatebirds *may be seen along the coast, or inland, after storms.*

Because Aransas National Wildlife Refuge is strategically located on the migration flyway to and from Central America, numerous songbirds pass through. Spring migration at Aransas is famed throughout the birding world. In April and May dozens of songbird species can be spotted easily in the wooded and scrubby areas of the refuge. Among the more colorful are Bay-breasted, Blackburnian, Chestnut-sided, and Hooded Warblers, as well as Summer Tanagers and Indigo and Painted Buntings. The woodlands are also a good place to look for the Inca Dove, Groove-billed Ani, Common Pauraque, and Ladder-backed Woodpecker.

Whooping Cranes are the main attraction, however. The birds begin arriving at the refuge in late October, four to six weeks after leaving Canada, and start departing again in March. The tallest bird in North America, the Whooping Crane stands five feet tall and has a wingspan of seven feet. White all over with black wing tips, red facial skin, and long black legs, it is easy to identify.

Whooping Cranes mate for life. The elaborate dancing displays they perform and their loud *kerloo ker-lee-loo* calls are believed to help keep the bond between mates strong. From the refuge, small groups of two to seven of the birds usually can be seen feeding in distant salt marshes, but the best way to get a close-up view is to take one of the boat tours offered by several operators from mid-December through March.

VISITING

A visit to Aransas National Wildlife Refuge is unforgettable, so allow at least a full day to see the site properly. Most visitors follow the 16-mile auto tour loop; it begins at the Visitor Center and has numerous pull-off

areas for birdwatching. The first five miles of the route follow the shoreline; a number of short walking trails, some ending in observation platforms, lead off this part of the road. At the 40-foot observation tower overlooking Mustang Lake and San Antonio Bay (a good place to see Whooping Cranes), the route turns inland and passes through the refuge's bird-rich grasslands and woodlands for 11 miles.

HIGHLIGHTS

Whooping Cranes arrive in Port Aransas by late October and are gone by late March. Port Aransas hosts an annual Whooping Crane Festival the last weekend of February. For details call (800) 45-COAST.

Site Map and Information

ARANSAS NATIONAL WILDLIFE REFUGE

🚗 From Rockport, follow Highway 35 north 25 miles. Turn right onto FM 774 and follow for 9 miles to FM 2040. Turn right onto FM 2040 and follow for 6 miles to reach refuge entrance.

◻ Daily, sunrise to sunset, year-round.

⬤ Never.

ℹ Aransas National Wildlife Refuge, PO Box 100, Austwell, TX 77950. Visitor Center is open daily, 8:30 a.m.–4:30 p.m.

☎ (361) 286-3559; http://southwest.fws.gov

💲 $3 per person or $5 per carload.

♿ Visitor Center and the Butterfly Walk trail are wheelchair accessible. To reach TDD, call (361) 286-3409.

⛺ Not allowed on-site. Campgrounds, including RV campsites, available in nearby Port Lavaca and Port Aransas.

🚶 Reservations are needed for boat tours to see Whooping Cranes. For those starting from Fisherman's Wharf (Rockport

Harbor), call (800) 782-BIRD; from Fisherman's' Wharf (Port Aransas), call (800) 605-5448; from Port Lavaca, call (800) 556-7678.

🛏 Numerous motels are available in nearby Rockport, Fulton, and Port Lavaca. Call the Rockport-Fulton Area Chamber of Commerce at (800) 242-0071 for listings.

BENTSEN-RIO GRANDE VALLEY STATE PARK

This birdwatchers' mecca, situated in the Rio Grande Valley on the Texas-Mexico border, is home to numerous birds seen nowhere else in the United States.

Whenever birdwatchers draw up top-10 lists of birdwatching spots in the United States, Bentsen-Rio Grande Valley State Park is sure to be somewhere near the top. The reason is simple: more than 290 bird species have been spotted in the park, including about 34, such as the Plain Chachalaca and Green Jay, that are more commonly found farther south in Mexico. By visiting Bentsen, birders can add these species to their life lists for the United States. The 588 acres that compose this park were donated by private owners in 1944 and opened as a park the same year.

The Common Pauraque *sings a low* pur *or two followed by a high* wheeer.

HABITAT
Two habitat types – both very attractive to birds – predominate at Bentsen-Rio Grande Valley State Park. Much of the park is chaparral –

areas of thick brush made up of thorny shrubs and small trees such as prickly pear and mesquite. Two large resacas – low-lying former river channels or oxbow lakes – border the park, as does a portion of the Rio Grande river. The banks of the resacas and the river are covered with luxuriant growth of cedar elm, hackberry, ebony, Mexican ash, and other trees that represent the northernmost extension of the Mexican subtropics. The water that fills one of the resacas provides habitat for a number of waterbirds, such as the Least Grebe and Black-bellied Whistling Duck.

BIRD LIFE
The bird life at Bentsen-Rio Grande Valley State Park is amazingly diverse, especially during the spring migration period from March to May, but the park also has a large number of resident birds.

The dry chaparral areas are the ideal place to look for the birds typical of the arid American Southwest and northern Mexico. Birds easily found here include the Greater Roadrunner and the pheasantlike Plain Chachalaca. (The latter, reclusive bird is hard to spot but easy to hear. Listen for the frequent, ringing *cha-cha-lac* call.)

BIRDS TO LOOK FOR

Black-bellied Whistling Duck • Hook-billed Kite • Plain Chachalaca • White-tipped Dove • Groove-billed Ani • Elf Owl • Lesser Nighthawk • Common Pauraque • Golden-fronted Wood-pecker • Ladder-backed Woodpecker • Great Kiskadee • Rose-throated Becard • Green Jay • Clay-colored Robin • Long-billed Thrasher • Tropical Parula • Altamira Oriole

---

Watch birds such as this Green Jay not generally seen elsewhere in the United States.

Long-billed Thrashers and Olive Sparrows are also found in the chaparral. Check the scrubby trees for Golden-fronted and Ladder-backed Woodpeckers. Two members of the nighthawk family, the Lesser Nighthawk and the Common Pauraque, are Bentsen specialties. At night these birds can be seen throughout the chaparral, often standing on the shoulders of the roads.

The woodland areas around the resacas and along the banks of the Rio Grande attract species more typical of tropical regions, such as the White-tipped Dove. The Groove-billed Ani, a large black bird that wags its long tail, can be seen perched in the trees. The hard-to-spot Green Kingfisher perches on branches near water and lives in the park year-round.

Tyrant flycatchers such as the Brown-crested Flycatcher (very common), Great Kiskadee, and Rose-throated Becard are Bentsen trademarks. The Rose-throated Becard is rare but regular at Bentsen year-round. This park is famous for a variety of other woodlands birds, especially the Green Jay (very common), Clay-colored Robin, Tropical Parula, Altamira Oriole, and Audubon's Oriole.

Raptors that seen soaring overhead include the White-tailed Kite and the rare Hook-billed Kite; Gray Hawks are occasionally seen. In April and May thousands of Broad-winged Hawks stream past on their return trip north.

The White-tipped Dove *makes a call that sounds like a person blowing across the top of a bottle.*

VISITING

The optimal season for visiting Bentsen-Rio Grande Valley State Park is December through the end of March. The weather then is cool in the evening and early morning, and comfortably warm and sunny the rest of the time. During the winter/spring season, the park offers special birdwatching tours and a daily birding information center.

The birdwatching tours are an excellent way to see the birds and other wildlife here. A handicapped-accessible bus picks up participants at 7 a.m. at the Group Pavilion, located next to the boat ramp; the tours last six to eight hours. Reservations are required and a modest fee is charged; the income benefits the park.

For visitors who prefer to see the park on their own, there are two excellent hiking trails. The Singing Chaparral Nature Trail, a one-mile loop through the chaparral to a dry water hole and back, begins near the park entrance. The longer Rio Grande Hiking Trail is a 1.9-mile loop that goes down to the river and back; it begins in the eastern end of the park.

HIGHLIGHTS

Bentsen-Rio Grande Valley State Park is home to five breeding owl species: the Barn Owl, Eastern Screech-Owl, Great Horned Owl, Ferruginous Pygmy-Owl, and the smallest owl in the world, the Elf Owl. Look for the Elf Owl roosting in the cavities of trees.

Site Map and Information

BENTSEN-RIO GRANDE VALLEY STATE PARK

🚗 From Mission, take US 374 west 1 mile to Inspiration Road exit. Take a right onto Business Route 83 (Loop 374) and continue west for 2.5 miles to FM 2062 south. Follow FM 2062 for 2.6 miles to Park Road 43, which leads into the park.

🕐 Daily, 7 a.m.–10 p.m., year-round.

◉ Only for extremely bad weather, such as hurricane warnings.

ℹ️ Bentsen-Rio Grande Valley State Park, PO Box 988, Mission, TX 78573. Headquarters, which functions as a Visitor Center, are open daily, 8 a.m.–5 p.m.

📞 (965) 585-1107; www.tpwd.state.tx.us

💲 $2 per person; children under 12 are free.

♿ The Visitor Center, Singing Chaparral Nature Trail, and tour bus are all wheelchair accessible.

⛺ Both primitive campsites (water only) and trailer campsites are available; call (512) 389-8900 for information and reservations.

Numerous commercial campsites and RV parks are also available in nearby Mission.

🔭 For details about park-run birdwatching tours, call (956) 519-6448.

🏨 Numerous motels are available in nearby Mission and McAllen. Call the Mission Chamber of Commerce at (800) 580-2700 or the McAllen Chamber of Commerce at (956) 682-2871 for listings.

HORICON NATIONAL WILDLIFE REFUGE

The largest freshwater cattail marsh in the United States makes this refuge in southeastern Wisconsin a favored rest stop for migrating waterfowl.

In 1846 Rock River, which ran through the huge Horicon Marsh in southeastern Wisconsin, was dammed. The dam changed the marsh into the largest artificial lake in the world at the time, but it also caused serious flooding of neighboring farmland. In 1869 the dam was removed, and the lake gradually reverted to marsh. Following a long struggle by local conservationists, the Horicon National Wildlife Refuge was established in 1941.

The 21,000-acre refuge, which encompasses the northern two-thirds of the marsh, is managed by the U.S. Fish and Wildlife Service. The 11,000-acre southern third of the marsh is administered by the Wisconsin Department of Natural Resources as the Horicon Marsh State Wildlife Area. The two agencies work together to manage the marsh as one huge wetland ecosystem.

Greater Scaup *females sport a gray-brown plumage with white coloring around the bill.*

HABITAT

Millennia ago, Horicon Marsh was a shallow glacial lake. The lake bed gradually filled with silt and decayed vegetation and turned into a massive marsh. Today cattails cover thousands of acres of Horicon Marsh – so many, in fact, that it is the largest cattail marsh in the United States.

Water levels in the national wildlife refuge (and the state-owned one as well) are manipulated seasonally to attract the maximum number of birds and other wildlife, including red foxes, river otters, and muskrats.

BIRD LIFE

Horicon Marsh is a stopover point for migrating birds in both spring and fall. During these seasons it's not uncommon to find more than a hundred species on the refuge in a single day; more than 219 species have been recorded in all.

In the fall, almost a million Canada Geese pass through; between 200,000 and 300,000 can be seen in one day during peak migration periods. Other waterfowl to watch for at the refuge include Trumpeter and Tundra Swans, Redheads, Green-winged Teal, Greater Scaup, Northern Shovelers, and Hooded Mergansers. The number of American White Pelican (from 300 to 500 each fall) is increasing steadily. Bald Eagles are present in fall, although not always easy to spot, and Peregrine Falcons fly through

BIRDS TO LOOK FOR

American White Pelican • Great Blue Heron • Canada Goose • Trumpeter Swan • Tundra Swan • Redhead • Greater Scaup • Hooded Merganser • Baird's Sandpiper • Forster's Tern • Nashville Warbler • Chestnut-sided Warbler • BlackburnianWarbler

Almost a million Canada Geese use Horicon Marsh as a migratory rest stop.

regularly then. The mudflats at Horicon National Wildlife Refuge attract numerous migrating shorebirds, including some – such as Baird's and Buff-breasted Sandpipers and Red-necked Phalarope – that winter in Central or South America and breed much farther north. A visit to Horicon offers a rare chance to see these birds during their stopovers in the United States.

In the spring warblers pass through in substantial numbers. About 28 species are spotted regularly in the refuge in a variety of habitats. Look for Nashville, Chestnut-sided, Black-throated Green, and Blackburnian Warblers.

Not all the birds that come to

The Trumpeter Swan *emits a loud honking call, often compared to the sound of a car horn.*

Horicon Marsh are just passing through, however. The refuge has the largest nesting population of Redheads east of the Mississippi River. Great Blue Herons, Great Egrets, Green Herons, and Black-crowned Night-Herons all breed here as well. In fact, the marsh supports the largest rookery of Great Blue Herons in the state.

VISITING

Although a good deal of Horicon National Wildlife Refuge is too environmentally sensitive to be open to the public, there are many public-use areas where visitors can easily see the varied bird life from a variety of different vantage points.

The Visitor Center offers a viewing platform looking out onto the marsh. Another good viewing area is found just off Highway 49 on the northeastern edge of the refuge. The Bud Cook Hiking Area, a few miles to the north of the Visitor Center, includes a 1.66-mile loop trail through an area of upland prairie habitat. In the northwestern corner of the refuge, another hiking trail complex offers three foot trails and the Horicon Ternpike, a seasonal (mid-April to mid-September) 3.2-mile auto tour route from which to see Forster's Terns. The short (0.4 mile) Egret Trail, accessible from the auto route, includes a stretch of floating boardwalk that goes past a heron rookery. Excellent views out into the marsh can also be had from Main Dike Road, in the southern portion of the refuge.

The numbers of Canada Geese peak in November, but most visitors prefer to come in October, when the temperatures are warmer and the fall colors on the marsh are most spectacular. The duck population peaks in April, and the warblers are most abundant in May. The Horicon Marsh Bird Festival is held the second weekend in May, an excellent time for birdwatching in the refuge.

HIGHLIGHTS

Most of the million Canada Geese that visit Horicon Marsh every autumn spend the breeding season 850 miles to the north on the shores of Hudson Bay; from the refuge they will fly another 450 miles to winter in the more mild climate of southern Illinois.

Site Map and Information

HORICON NATIONAL WILDLIFE REFUGE

From Milwaukee, take State Highway 45/41 north to State Highway 49 at Brownsville. Turn west and continue about 8 miles to Horicon Marsh. Turn south onto County Highway Z (the first road to intersect Highway 49 at the northeastern corner of the marsh) and follow it 3.5 miles to the Visitor Center.

Daily, sunrise to sunset, year-round.

Never.

Horicon National Wildlife Refuge Complex, W4279 Headquarters Road, Mayville, WI 53050. Visitor Center is open Monday through Friday, 7:30 a.m.–4:00 p.m., and fall weekends, 9:00 a.m.–6:00 p.m.

(920) 387-2658, extension 24; www.fws.gov/r3pao/horicon

None.

Visitor Center, Marsh Haven Nature Center, and some trails are wheelchair accessible.

Campsites are available at nearby state recreation areas; call the Horicon

Chamber of Commerce at (920) 485-3200 for listings.

Free guided tours are available; call the general information number listed above. Canoes are not allowed in the national-wildlife-refuge portion of the marsh.

Motels are available in nearby Fond du Lac; call the Fond du Lac Convention and Visitor's Bureau at (800) 937-9123 for listings.

DENALI NATIONAL PARK AND PRESERVE

Wandering Tattlers and Arctic Warblers populate the rugged wilderness of national park in Central Alaska.

Native Athabascans named the 20,320-foot mountain at the center of this national park and preserve Denali meaning "the high one." Including this majestic mountain, generally known as Mount McKinley, Denali National Park covers six million acres – more area than the state of Massachusetts – offering even big animals such as grizzly bears and moose plenty of room to roam.

Most of Denali's birds arrive from more southerly climes to enjoy spring and early summer in Alaska. Blackpoll Warblers return from the western Caribbean, while Arctic Warblers travel all the way from the Philippines. These elaborate, out-of-the-way migratory routes fascinate researchers, who are just beginning to uncover their secrets.

American Golden-Plovers *slowly acquire their breeding plumage during the northward migration.*

HABITAT

The public park road and shuttle bus route provide access to a good representation of many of the park's habitat types. The noble mountainous backdrop of the Alaska mountain range is underscored by the glaciers and resultant wide, flat river valleys beneath, where the park's few trees lie. Tundra, found at higher elevations, by definition has no trees – only dwarf shrubs and wildflowers. Each of these habitats is home to a group of bird species specifically suited to the conditions they find there. Compared to the bird lists of more southerly locations, the park's may seem to be lacking in diversity. However, an alluring number of birds common here are seen only rarely in the lower 48 United States.

BIRD LIFE

Begin by exploring the park headquarters and hotel area. Check out the spruce trees for two of the classic north country species – Boreal Chickadee and Bohemian Waxwing. Look also for Northern Hawk Owls, which will be far more abundant some years than others, depending on the quantity of snowshoe hares.

Only the first 13 miles of park road are open to private vehicles, but the rich habitat along the banks of the Savage River is found at the end of the public road. Look for Harlequin Ducks and Mew Gulls along the river waters and for Willow Ptarmigan on the vegetated river bars.

BIRDS TO LOOK FOR

Harlequin Duck • Oldsquaw • Barrow's Goldeneye • Gyrfalcon • Willow Ptarmigan • Rock Ptarmigan • American Golden-Plover • Wandering Tattler • Long-tailed Jaeger • Mew Gull • Boreal Chickadee • Arctic Warbler • Northern Wheatear • Bohemian Waxwing •

In winter the Willow Ptarmigan's white plumage blends with the snowy tundra.

From here on travel is by shuttle or tour bus; many find it a relief not to have to negotiate the steep turns through this increasingly wild country. It takes a few days to explore the entire route.

A favored first stop is at Igloo Creek to look for more Harlequin Ducks and for two sought-after boreal (northern) nesters: Wandering Tattler and Arctic Warbler. Another place to check for these species is the adjacent Tattler Creek. Arctic Warblers don't usually show up until mid-June, but once they arrive their buzzy, toneless songs are heard incessantly.

Continuing on the park road, watch the area between Polychrome Rest Area and Eielson Visitor Center for

Barrow's Goldeneye *is one of many birds that breeds at Denali.*

Northern Wheatears and Gyrfalcons. Also in this section, the road traverses both Highway Pass and Thorofare Pass, where tundra flats harbor nesting habitat for Long-tailed Jaegers as well as American Golden-Plovers. The same dry alpine tundra flats are also a good place to watch Rock Ptarmigans (found primarily on alpine tundra slopes) and Willow Ptarmigans (which generally prefer willows on river bars).

Be sure to stop at Stony Hill to look for American Golden-Plovers, Rock Ptarmigans, and Northern Wheatears, and check the ridges above Eielson Visitor Center for Surfbirds. Past Eielson Visitor Center toward Wonder Lake the landscape is dotted with ponds that boast waterfowl including Red-throated Loons, Greater White-fronted Geese, and Oldsquaws. At Wonder Lake itself look for Barrow's Goldeneyes, as well as Arctic Terns, which fly up to 22,000 miles a year on their journey from here to Antarctic waters and back.

VISITING

From early June through July Denali National Park and Preserve's year-round residents, such as Willow Ptarmigans and Boreal Chickadees, are joined by migrants from such exotic climes as the South Pacific (Long-tailed Jaegers) and Africa (Northern Wheatears).

Many birders dislike the idea of being dependent on the park shuttle bus system. However, flexibility and a well-researched grasp of the bus

system will allow even first-time visitors to fully experience the incredible birds of the far north in this wilderness. Birders with several days will probably want to camp in one of the campgrounds along the bus route. Those with more limited time often choose the eight-hour trip to Eielson Visitor Center and back instead.

HIGHLIGHTS

Don't pass up the opportunity for a multi-day adventure into the backcountry. Along the Toklat River hikers are serenaded by the Semipalmated Plovers as they keep an eye out for predators, including the grizzly bear. Many other areas are worth backpacking in as well; call the Visitor Center for advice, maps, and permit information.

Site Map and Information

DENALI NATIONAL PARK AND PRESERVE

🚗 237 miles north of Anchorage and 120 miles south of Fairbanks, the park is accessible via Alaska Highway 3, Alaska Railroad, and scheduled air service. Private vehicle use is limited, but a shuttle bus service operates along the wilderness road from the park entrance.

◻ Daily, 24 hours, year-round. Shuttle buses operate from late May to mid-September.

◑ Never, although bad weather makes portions of the park impassable.

ℹ Denali National Park and Preserve, P.O. Box 9, Denali Park, Alaska 99755. Visitor Access Center and Eielson Visitor Center open daily, 7:00 a.m.–8:00 p.m., from late May to mid-September.

☎ (907) 683-2294; www.nps.gov/dena

💲 $10.00 per family or $5.00 per person, good for 7 consecutive days. For shuttle bus reservations call (800) 622-7275.

♿ The visitor centers, ARA Denali Park Hotels, and many park shuttle buses are wheelchair accessible.

🅰 Call (800) 622-7275 for reservations at park campgrounds. Pick up a permit at the Visitor Center for backcountry camping.

🎫 Call for schedule of ranger-led tours.

🏨 Denali Wilderness Center operates two lodges on-site that cater to birders; call (907) 683-2290 for reservations.

CAVE CREEK CANYON

This southeastern Arizona hot spot offers birders a golden opportunity to see an avian ambassador from Mexico – the Elegant Trogon.

The Spanish explorer Francisco Vásquez de Coronado was in search of gold when his expedition surveyed southern Arizona in 1540. Instead of the mythical Seven Cities of Cibola, the explorers found a vast country of rugged mountain ranges. Above Cave Creek Canyon the Chiricahua Mountains rise like islands from a desert sea into the clouds, where they capture moisture, more precious than gold to these parts. The resulting habitat seems miraculous compared to the arid deserts below.

HABITAT

In nearby Mexico the single largest habitat type is the Sierra Madrean pine-and-oak woodland: its northernmost outpost is found here in southern Arizona. Representative species from this typical Mexican habitat include birds such as Strickland's Woodpeckers and Mexican Jays and trees like alligator juniper and Apache pines.

Cave Creek flows from the Chiricahua mountain range, which

*This **Montezuma Quail** chick already sports the plump, short-tailed body that will distinguish it as an adult.*

has more land at a higher elevation than any of the other nearby ranges. This makes the area resemble the Rocky Mountains, complete with high meadows and subalpine flora.

Cave Creek Canyon itself is a long avenue of trees. Although sycamores are the most conspicuous trees, evergreen oaks are abundant – as are junipers, bigtooth maples, madrones, walnuts, and ash. In shady areas at higher elevations, Douglas firs stand serene. Pink, rounded rock formations define the canyon walls.

BIRD LIFE

Beginning at the information station, the birders' yellow-brick road winds up into a shade-dappled forest of Arizona sycamore and enters the best habitat in the United States in which to spot Elegant Trogons. In addition to these colorful tropical birds, birders who walk stretches along this paved road may come across Montezuma Quail, Band-tailed Pigeons, Acorn and Strickland's Woodpeckers, Sulphur-bellied Flycatchers, Mexican Jays, and Bridled Titmice.

South Fork Road, a dirt track about a mile beyond the entrance to Stewart Campground, is prime Trogon land. Elegant Trogons may be patrolling the picnic area at the end of this road, or

BIRDS TO LOOK FOR

Zone-tailed Hawk • Peregrine Falcon • Montezuma Quail • Flammulated Owl • Whiskered Screech-Owl • Elf Owl • White-throated Swift • Elegant Trogon • Strickland's Woodpecker • Greater Pewee • Black Phoebe • Mexican Jay • Hepatic Tanager

Look in Cave Creek Canyon's sycamore forests for the colorful, tropical Elegant Trogon.

they may be found along the lovely South Fork Trail beyond where up to 10 pairs of Trogons nest in the stately sycamores. At the picnic area and along the trail, look also for Blue-throated Hummingbirds, Hepatic Tanagers, Hutton's Vireos, and Black-throated Gray and Grace's Warblers. Don't forget to gaze up at the towering cliffs for a possible sighting of Peregrine Falcons and White-throated Swifts.

The Zone-tailed Hawk *soars on uptilted wings and drops from a low glide to capture its prey.*

Back along the main road, the canyon is pocked with the volcanic-remnant caves for which it is named. A left turn onto Herb Martyr Road leads to the Southwestern Research Station, where visitors should look in the cottonwood grove for Zone-tailed Hawks, Black Phoebes, Cassin's Kingbirds, and Acorn Woodpeckers. Further on, at Herb Martyr Campground, the habitat around the Main Fork of Cave Creek harbors Bushtits, Spotted Towhees, Greater and Western Wood-Pewees, Grace's Warblers, and Painted Redstarts.

In this narrow canyon habitat, birders may hear more birds than they see. Listen for the Sulphur-bellied Flycatcher's unmusical squeak. The strange, low-pitched, unmusical call of the Elegant Trogon sounds like a frog or a hen turkey – a deep, monotonous *cowmp*. Many first-time visitors hear a resident turkey and believe they've found their trogon.

The Greater Pewee is easily identified by its melodious call, *Jose Maria (Ho-SAY Mah-REE-ah)*.

VISITING

Summer offers the best chance to see the area's avian specialties. Be sure to save some time for night birding; Cave Creek Canyon is famous for owls. Listen along the South Fork of Cave Creek for Western and Whiskered Screech-Owls, Northern Pygmy-Owls, Flammulated Owls, and Elf Owls.

A visit to the Chiricahua Mountains is not complete without a drive to the higher elevations. Those who brave the narrow, steep gravel road will be rewarded by a magnificent view of 7,974-foot Silver Peak on the left and 8,544-foot Portal Peak on the right, with Cave Creek cutting a chasm below. To get there, drive past the Southwestern Research Station; the road turns to gravel but is accessible to the average passenger car. (Drive with care; follow the custom of sounding your horn before each curve.)

Drive on to explore the high-elevation evergreen forest of Rustler Park and Campground, looking there for White-throated Swifts; Red-faced, Grace's, and Olive Warblers; and Cordilleran Flycatchers.

HIGHLIGHTS

Each July volunteers conduct the annual Elegant Trogon Census. Participants sometimes record over 20 trogons in the census area, and more than 70 other bird species also are observed and recorded. Call the ranger district (listed below) for dates, times, and locations.

Site Map and Information

CAVE CREEK CANYON

🚗 From Portal, Arizona, head west up Cave Creek Canyon Road.

🔲 Daily, 24 hours, year-round.

⬤ Never.

ℹ️ Douglas Ranger District, 3081 North Leslie Canyon Road, Douglas, AZ 85607. Visitor information booth open weekdays, 9 a.m.–4:30 p.m., April through September; no phone on premises.

📞 (520) 364-3468 (ranger district)

⑤ None.

♿ No special facilities.

🅰 Several U.S. Forest Service campgrounds on-site. Call ranger district for information.

👥 Most U.S. birding tour companies offer service in southeastern Arizona. One regional company is High Lonesome

Ecotours, Sierra Vista, AZ; call (800) 743-2668. To arrange for custom guide service, contact Southeastern Arizona Bird Observatory at (520) 432-1388 or sabo@SABO.org.

🛏 Cave Creek Ranch (cottages); call (520) 558-2334 for information.

RAMSEY CANYON PRESERVE

Ten species of hummingbirds have been spotted in a single summer day at this small Nature Conservancy Preserve in southeastern Arizona, near the Mexican border.

Renowned for its scenic beauty and rich array of plant and animal life, Ramsey Canyon is located at an ecological crossroads, where habitats and species from the Sierra Madre of Mexico, the Rocky Mountains, and the Sonoran and Chihuahuan deserts commingle. Here rare species found in few other places on earth, such as the Ramsey Canyon leopard frog and the lemon lily, dwell in a safe haven.

Although almost 30,000 people visit the preserve each year, Nature Conservancy managers believe the impact of visitors is lighter than that of past influences, including road building, stream channelization, introduction of exotic species, timber cutting, and fire suppression efforts. Ecological restoration is an ongoing priority at the preserve, and in recent years projects have included stream renewal and the removal of exotic vegetation. Plans also are underway to conduct controlled burns for the health of the ecosystem.

Wild Turkey *toms have large wattles that change color, depending on their emotional state.*

HABITAT

The abrupt rise of the Huachuca Mountains from the surrounding arid grasslands creates what could best be described as sky islands. In Ramsey Canyon, this "island" habitat blends a spring-fed stream, a northeast orientation, and a deep canyon to create a moist, cool wonderland. In addition to Sierra Madrean pine-and-oak woodlands, stands of Arizona sycamore flourish here on this 380-acre site. Southwestern rarities such as the ridge-nosed rattlesnake and the lesser long-nosed bat call the canyon home.

BIRD LIFE

The approach to Ramsey Canyon Preserve will yield birds typical of the mesquite savanna, a grassland with scattered trees and drought-resistant undergrowth. These include Red-tailed Hawks, Scaled Quail, and Greater Roadrunners. A stop at the Brown Canyon trailhead, 2.1 miles from the highway, puts birders right on the border between the grasslands and a green wall of oak woodlands.

BIRDS TO LOOK FOR

Wild Turkey • White-throated Swift • Magnificent Hummingbird • Broad-tailed Hummingbird • Elegant Trogon • Strickland's Woodpecker • Mexican Jay • Bridled Titmouse • Eastern Bluebird • Black-throated Gray Warbler • Grace's Warbler • Painted Redstart • Yellow-eyed Junco

A Magnificent Hummingbird extracts nectar from a flowering cactus.

Here a number of birds can be spotted – Canyon Towhee, Curve-billed Thrasher, Verdin, and Pyrrhuloxia – that won't be found even a hundred yards into the canyon.

Visitors arriving at the parking area often head directly to the hummingbird viewing area and pollinator garden. The greatest variety of hummers can be seen during fall migration, which takes place from July to September. Other birds found around the visitor center include Wild Turkey, Mexican Jays, Bridled Titmice, and in the summer, Plumbeous Vireos, Black-throated Gray Warblers, Black-headed Grosbeaks, and Scott's Orioles. Look also in the vicinity of the visitor center for Acorn and Strickland's Woodpeckers, Zone-tailed Hawks, Greater Pewees, Sulphur-bellied

The Mexican Jay *is common in the pine-and-oak canyons of the Southwest.*

Flycatchers, Grace's Warblers, and Painted Redstarts. Elegant Trogons are always a distinct possibility.

To add to the avian diversity, take a detour on the Hamburg Trail, a switchback up to the Hamburg Mine area. It is a strenuous hike, especially for visitors from low elevations, so allow at least four hours to complete the five-mile round trip. In the first mile there's a good place to rest – an overlook that provides good birding as well. Check here for White-throated Swifts, Violet-green Swallows, and Rock Wrens. After this, the trail crosses Ramsey Creek and continues on to an intersection with Brown Canyon Trail. Past this intersection, and for the next mile to the Hamburg Mine area, Red-faced Warblers are a common sight. Look for Yellow-eyed Juncos, Hairy Woodpeckers, Common Ravens, both White-breasted and Red-breasted Nuthatches, Cordilleran Flycatchers, Warbling Vireos, and Western Tanagers, too.

VISITING

The best months for birding at the preserve are April through September. Spring weather is usually cool and dry; early summer is dry and hot, although temperatures average 15°F cooler than those in Tucson. July and August bring regular afternoon rainstorms. Fall and winter have plenty to offer, avian and otherwise; of course, the most obvious draw is the reprieve from northern winters. Beginning in late October and peaking in November, the fall colors can be

fabulous with the sycamores and cottonwoods bursting into flaming oranges and yellows. A few hummers winter on the preserve and can be found at the feeders.

HIGHLIGHTS

Spend a lazy late-spring afternoon watching the hummingbird feeders for such rewards as Blue-throated, Magnificent, Black-chinned, Anna's, and Broad-tailed Hummingbirds. With luck, they might be joined by Calliope and Rufous Hummers. In late summer, sought after jewels such as Berylline, Violet-Crowned and White-eared Hummingbirds may surprise the attentive watcher.

Site Map and Information

RAMSEY CANYON PRESERVE

🚌 Take Highway 92 south from Sierra Vista for 6 miles and turn right on Ramsey Canyon Road. The 21 parking spaces at the preserve are available on a "first come" basis; these cannot accommodate vehicles that are longer than 18 feet.

🕐 Daily, March through October, 8 a.m.–5 p.m.; November through February, 9 a.m.–5 p.m.

⬤ Thanksgiving, Christmas, and New Year's Day.

ℹ The Nature Conservancy, Ramsey Canyon Preserve, 27 Ramsey Canyon Road, Hereford, AZ 85615. Visitor Center hours same as site hours.

📞 (520) 378-2785; www.tnc.org/infield/map.html/

⑤ None.

♿ Vistor Center, parking area, hummingbird viewing area, and pollinator garden are wheelchair accessible.

🔺 None on-site.

🔭 Call the preserve for details about their guided nature walks, which take place several times a week April through September, and more extensive adventures available throughout the year.

🏨 Ramsey Canyon Inn Bed & Breakfast is adjacent to preserve; call (520) 378-3010 for reservations.

POINT REYES NATIONAL SEASHORE

An extraordinary 470 bird species have been recorded in this northern California seaside park.

Point Reyes is the stage for a dramatic meeting between land and sea. Pounding surf, treacherous currents, shifting fog, and windswept cypress trees set the scene, while thousands of birds – from resident landbirds to ocean vagrants – play leading roles.

Snowy Plovers
and other varieties of plovers are attracted to the lagoons of Point Reyes in the fall.

Three types of terrain form the backdrop: the pasture lands of Pierce Point and Drake's Estero, the shrubby ridges and California laurel valleys east and west of Limantour Road, and the forests and meadowlands in the southeastern end of the park.

BIRDS TO LOOK FOR

Pacific Loon • Brown Pelican •
Brant • Wood Duck • Surf Scoter •
Snowy Plover • Common Murre •
Pigeon Guillemot • Tufted Puffin •
Band-tailed Pigeon • Allen's
Hummingbird • Acorn Woodpecker •
Wrentit • Tricolored Blackbird

HABITAT

Point Reyes's 111 square miles offer an amazing variety of habitats, and numerous hiking trails and many miles of driving tours encourage access to every one of them. Grassland, thickets of dwarf trees and shrubby plants, and willow-lined streams and ponds draw woodpeckers, sparrows, hummingbirds, and nuthatches. A wide array of grebes, herons, egrets, ducks, geese, shorebirds, and raptors frequent the large estuaries and marshlands. Outer Point Reyes projects into the Pacific Ocean, where, in the fall or winter, birders with good scopes may spot Pacific and Common Loons, Pigeon Guillemots, Surf Scoters, Common Murres, and Black Oystercatchers.

BIRD LIFE

Of all the national parks in the United States, Point Reyes National Seashore easily wins top honors for avian diversity. Four areas provide access to representative habitats and are known as hot spots among birders.

Only five miles south of the Bear Valley Visitor Center, the Five Brooks Pond area is home to Band-tailed Pigeons, Acorn Woodpeckers, Allen's Hummingbirds, and Olive-Sided Flycatchers. Scan the grasslands for Tricolored Blackbirds. On the water's edge, look for Green Herons and Wood Ducks. North of the pond on Stewart Trail, look for Red-shouldered Hawks, Pygmy Nuthatches, and Winter Wrens.

Watch for Tufted Puffins among the rocks near the Point Reyes Lighthouse.

An autumn drive along Limantour Road to Muddy Hollow and Limantour Beach will yield scores of shorebirds in the wetlands and along the beach: look for Western, Semipalmated, and Least Sandpipers. The pond at the end of the road harbors American Bitterns, Virginia Rails, and Soras. At the beach check for Pacific, Common, and Red-throated Loons. Look also for Red-necked Grebes, Brant, and Surf Scoters.

At the Abbotts Lagoon area, take a three-mile walk through coastal scrub (look for Wrentits and the endemic Nuttall's White-crowned Sparrows), across an isthmus between two lagoons, and over sand dunes to the ocean beach. In the fall, the lagoons attract Pacific and Lesser Golden-Plovers, as well as Snowy Plovers and ducks such as Northern Shoveler and Ring-necked.

The Pigeon Guillemot *may be seen off the Pacific Coast using a spotting scope.*

A trip to Point Reyes would be "pointless" without a visit to the tip, where the Point Reyes Lighthouse offers a spectacular view of bird life. The 20-mile drive is mostly through pastureland; in the fall check among the Horned Lark flocks for Lapland Longspurs. A colony of approximately 12,000 Common Murres nests on the rocky cliffs near the lighthouse. A few Tufted Puffins usually can be seen close to the colony as well.

VISITING

Bird-watching is exceptional here throughout the year, but during fall migration it's especially rewarding. Diving ducks, such as Lesser Scaup and Ring-necked Ducks, begin to arrive in late September and become abundant by late October. Common Goldeneyes arrive in late October, usually with a few Barrow's Goldeneyes and Hooded Mergansers. October also brings a flurry of Palm Warblers and American Tree Sparrows.

The other seasons have their charms, too. Spring brings migrating warblers, such as Townsend's, Hermits, and Black-throated Grays, plus a replay of the fall's shorebirds and waterfowl, especially Brant. In the summer, gawk at the huge Common Murre colony near the lighthouse.

Winter brings waterfowl such as Red-breasted Mergansers, American Wigeon, and Redheads to the bays. Look in forested areas for Red-breasted Sapsuckers.

HIGHLIGHTS

The Point Reyes Bird Observatory offers the opportunity to observe an active banding station. Biologists frequently check the mist nets, which are set up at sunrise and kept open for six hours. Captured birds are gently extracted, then banded, measured, and released unharmed. Call (415) 868-0655 for seasonal schedules.

Site Map and Information

POINT REYES NATIONAL SEASHORE

🚌 From San Francisco, take Highway 1 north 35 miles to reach Bear Valley Visitor Center.

🕐 Daily, sunrise to sunset, year-round.

⬤ Christmas.

ℹ Point Reyes National Seashore, Point Reyes Station, CA 94956. Bear Valley Visitor Center is open weekdays, 9 a.m.–5 p.m.; weekends and holidays, 8 a.m.–5 p.m.

📞 (415) 663-1092; www.nps.gov/pore

💲 None.

♿ All 3 Visitor Centers are wheelchair accessible. Limantour Beach has a paved bird-watching trail; Abbotts Lagoon has a hardtop trail leading to an overlook.

🏕 Four hike-in campgrounds on-site (no car camping). Permits are available at Bear Valley Visitor Center. Call weekdays, 9 a.m.–2 p.m, for reservations.

🔭 For schedules of seasonal guided bird walks, call Point Reyes Bird Observatory at (415) 868-1221, ext. 33, or Audubon Canyon Ranch at (415) 868-9244.

🏨 Many motels, hotels, and bed-and-breakfasts are available along the Marin Coast and Highway 1.

SONNY BONO SALTON SEA NATIONAL WILDLIFE REFUGE

Yellow-footed Gulls in the summer and waterfowl in the winter make this southern California hot spot a year-round attraction.

This birding hot spot, on the southern end of an inland sea, is considered a globally significant bird habitat; however, believe it or not, it's also been described as a Chernobyl for birds. It all began about a hundred years ago, when canals were dug to divert the Colorado River and irrigate the surrounding Imperial Valley. A series of misfortunes caused the canal system to fail, and in 1905 and 1906 the Colorado River emptied into a low-lying, forbidding region of southern California, creating the Salton Sea.

A variety of geological conditions had combined to create similar seas here over the ages, and this one was expected to evaporate as the others had. But almost a century later it still exists, growing more salty and polluted with agricultural runoff each year. Although this man-made body of water attracts more birds than any single resource in the nation (some say up to four million birds in the winter), these huge concentrations and the polluted conditions also make the sea a perfect breeding ground for avian botulism and avian cholera, ongoing problems facing wildlife managers.

The Snow Goose *is one of many winter visitors to the Salton Sea's coastal wetlands.*

HABITAT

Located in the Sonoran Desert just north of El Centro, California, the 35-mile-long Salton Sea and surrounding habitat include 35,815 acres of open water and salt marsh, plus 1,785 acres of pasture and freshwater marsh. The refuge boasts one of the most diverse arrays of bird species of any national wildlife refuge in the West. Birdwatchers flock here in ever increasing numbers to search for the more than 380 species that have been recorded. Although the national wildlife refuge was founded in 1930, it was not called the Sonny Bono Salton Sea until 1998, after the death of California congressman Sonny Bono, who was instrumental in recent cleanup efforts.

BIRD LIFE

The Salton Sea, where 15 species of gull are known to occur, is a good

---

BIRDS TO LOOK FOR

Brown Pelican • Wood Stork • Snow Goose • Ross's Goose • Cinnamon Teal • Northern Pintail • Yuma Clapper Rail• Sora • Wilson's Phalarope • Red-necked Pharlarope • Laughing Gull • California Gull • Yellow-footed Gull • Verdin • Cactus Wren • Abert's Towhee

Although rare inland the Laughing Gull is a common visitor at the Salton Sea.

place to learn the challenging art of gull identification. Gulls come in a black-and-gray rainbow of species, and their plumages also vary according to age. Most birders find it easiest to start their identification practice with adult plumage.

A visit to the refuge during the blistering height of summer will often yield a gull seldom seen elsewhere in the United States: the Yellow-footed Gull. Adult Yellow-footed Gulls have dark slate-gray wings, yellow eyes, and yellow legs and feet. They visit the Salton Sea after nesting in Mexico's Gulf of California and are most numerous between July and September. Check near the ponds in the Hazard Tract portion of the refuge, off of Garst Road. Other gulls common during this season are the Laughing

The Sora *is found in the refuge's fresh and saltwater marshes; listen for its whinny followed by a high-pitched* keek.

Gull (black legs and feet) and the California Gull (dark eyes and light gray wings).

Another rare challenge to search for in the marshes is the seldom seen but often heard Yuma Clapper Rail, an uncommon subspecies of the Clapper Rail. These cattail-lurkers breed in the freshwater marsh and are found by listening for their dry *kek, kek, kek* notes, given in a series of 10 or more. Sora, another rail, give a descending whinnylike call and a sharp, high-pitched *keek*. Both birds are most easily found near the southern tip of the sea, around the edges of ponds along the Hardenberger Trail. They are easiest to spot in June and July, when they take their young out in the open to explore.

For more straightforward birding, take a short hike along the Rock Hill Trail, where the rows of trees teem with birds such as Abert's Towhees and

Verdins year-round. The trail also follows the western dike, a promising place to look for Ospreys and some of the sea's hordes of wintering waterfowl, including Snow, Ross's, and Greater White-fronted Geese. Look on the open water for Wilson's and Red-necked Phalaropes.

The best place to view thousands of wintering ducks is at the nearby Wister Marshes (administered by the California Department of Fish and Game). To reach them, drive through the small town of Niland on State Highway 111. Look for Northern Pintail, Cinnamon Teal, and Gadwall.

Finally, stroll through Brawley's residential areas (a few miles south of the refuge) looking for Gila and Ladder-backed Woodpeckers, Greater Roadrunners, and Cactus Wrens. The town's Riverview Cemetery is another famous birding spot.

VISITING

For the most species diversity, not to mention the best weather, visit from November through the end of May. Summer, although very hot, is the best season to see Yellow-footed Gulls.

HIGHLIGHTS

Each February birders from around the world converge at the Salton Sea International Bird Festival. They come to participate in educational seminars, field trips, and the birding trade show, but the big draw is the possibility of seeing more than 100 species in a single day. For more information call (760) 344-5FLY.

Site Map and Information

SONNY BONO SALTON SEA NATIONAL WILDLIFE REFUGE

🚗 From I-8 at El Centro, take State Route 111 to Sinclair Road and head west to Visitor Center at the corner of Sinclair and Gentry Roads.

▢ Daily, sunrise to sunset, year-round.

⬤ Never.

ℹ Sonny Bono Salton Sea National Wildlife Refuge, 906 West Sinclair Road, Calipatria, CA 92233. Visitor Center, which includes a wildlife exhibit and bookstore, is open weekdays, 7:30 a.m.–3:30 p.m., and some weekends. Call ahead.

☏ (760) 348-5278

Ⓢ None.

♿ Visitor Center is wheelchair accessible, as is Rock Hill Trail (a flat, dirt path), unless the weather is wet.

🅰 Several campgrounds nearby; call Visitor Center for suggestions.

👥 Trail guides are available for groups of 5 or more. Reservations must be made 2 weeks in advance.

🚌 The Imperial County area has a wide array of accommodations; call El Centro Chamber of Commerce at (760) 352-3681 for a map and listings.

UPPER NEWPORT BAY ECOLOGICAL RESERVE

*White-tailed Kites and Blue-winged Teals flock to the waters
of this lovely California preserve.*

One of the truly amazing things about Upper Newport Bay Ecological Reserve is its location, smack in the middle of Orange County, California, which is fast becoming one of the most urbanized areas in the country. A 752-acre ecological reserve – with a stunning array of easy-to-view wildlife – is the last thing visitors expect to find here.

In the 1960s the Upper Newport Bay area was slated to become a huge marina, complete with opulent waterfront homes. Visitors to this unique reserve are all indebted to the concerned citizens and local environmental groups who lobbied against and eventually blocked the development.

broad expanse of water to be found at high tide becomes a tiny trickle, barely a foot wide, at low tide. Small inland California streams feed the bay fresh water, while the daily tides bring in Pacific seawater. The result is that six distinct habitat types exist within the reserve: marine, intertidal, brackish water, freshwater marsh, riparian, and upland. All of them host a remarkable selection of bird life.

The Black Skimmer *uses its lower mandible, which is longer than its upper one, to skim the shallows for fish.*

HABITAT

Called "Back Bay" by local residents, Upper Newport Bay Ecological Reserve is a constantly changing landscape of marshes, mudflats, and open water. The Back Bay is a true estuary: its water level rises and falls with the tides. The

BIRDS TO LOOK FOR

Western Grebe • Blue-winged Teal • Cinnamon Teal • Northern Pintail • Green-winged Teal • Canvasback • White-tailed Kite • Merlin • Clapper Rail • American Avocet • Elegant Tern • Least Tern • Black Skimmer • Marsh Wren • California Gnatcatcher • Savannah Sparrow

BIRD LIFE

Back Bay is a major wintering site for numerous species. As early as mid-August, southbound migrants begin to show up at the reserve's bay – particularly shorebirds. Black-bellied Plovers, still in their breeding plumage, come from their arctic nesting areas. Dowitchers, Red Knots, and sandpipers all retain some of the red-brown plumage tones typical of the breeding season. In early fall waterfowl such as Green-winged, Cinnamon, and Blue-winged Teal, Northern Pintail, Canvasbacks, American Wigeon, Mallards, and more begin to dominate the reserve.

The male Green-winged Teal has a chestnut-colored head with a dark green ear patch.

The mild southern California winter brings many other overwintering species, such as Elegant Terns, Black Skimmers, and Peregrine Falcons. Lincoln's Sparrows are frequent winter visitors. Several species of grebe are winter residents: Western, Horned, Eared, and Pied-billed.

Other marsh species seen readily around the reed beds are Sora, Marsh Wren, Common Yellowthroat, and Red-winged Blackbird. An endangered subspecies of the Savannah Sparrow, the Belding's Savannah Sparrow, nests in the reserve's marshes.

Numerous birds typical of the chaparral are resident in the arid scrub bordering the reserve's wetlands. To locate California Gnatcatchers, listen for the birds' kittenlike mew in the upland brush behind the freshwater impoundment about halfway along Back Bay Drive.

Several kinds of raptors can also be seen at Back Bay year-round. Watch for Cooper's Hawks and Red-shouldered Hawks in the wooded area near the freshwater pond. Red-tailed Hawks commonly soar over the bay or perch on trees along the hillsides. Ospreys hunt for fish in the open water. A lucky birdwatcher might spot the beautiful White-tailed Kite. Merlins occasionally cruise through, and Northern Harriers commonly course the fields, searching for small animals. Snowy Egrets, Great Egrets, and Great Blue Herons forage for small fish at the estuary's edges. The Upper Bay is home to the world's largest

The California Gnatcatcher *is found in the sage scrub of southwest California.*

nesting population of the light-footed subspecies of the Clapper Rail. The bay is the best site for observing this bird, especially during high tides, when the birds are flushed from cover. Look for them in cordgrass areas, especially near Back Bay Drive at Shellmaker Island just where the reserve starts.

VISITING

The best times for birdwatching in the area are from late August through early April, when migrants and winter residents are usually present in good numbers. Plan to spend a least a couple of days hiking the site and another day exploring the waterways. For those who don't have boats, rentals and charters are available.

Winter is an ideal time for a visit. Temperatures are moderate, bird migrations are plentiful, and Common Yellowthroats, blackbirds, and sparrows are nesting.

The entire refuge is open for hiking year-round. Back Bay offers two miles of hiking trails and many scenic photography sites.

HIGHLIGHTS

Earth Day is a big day at Upper Newport Bay. Celebrate with the Newport Bay Naturalists and Friends at Shellmaker Island. Festivities include naturalist-led tours along the Clapper Rail trail and canoe and kayak trips, plus much more. Call (949) 640-6746 for dates and details.

Site Map and Information

UPPER NEWPORT BAY ECOLOGICAL RESERVE

▣ From Long Beach, take I-405 east to Highway 73 and follow it southeast to the Jamboree Blvd. exit. Turn west and continue to the southern terminus of Back Bay Drive (the last right turn before the Pacific Coast Highway) to reach refuge entrance.

◻ Daily, 7 a.m. to sunset, year-round.

◉ Never.

ℹ Newport Bay Naturalists and Friends, 600 Shellmaker, Newport Beach, CA 92660. Information Center open Wednesday through Saturday, 10 a.m.–5 p.m.

☏ (949) 640-6746; www.newportbay.org

⑤ None.

♿ A wheelchair-accessible, paved pedestrian trail stretches along the entire Back Bay Drive.

⛺ None on-site. Nearby Newport Dunes has RV and tent camping; call (800) 765-7661 for reservations.

⚅ For information about naturalist-led activities contact Newport Bay Naturalists and Friends at (949) 640-6746.

🏨 The Hyatt Newporter hotel is right next door; call (949) 729-1234 for reservations. Or contact the Newport Beach Chamber of Commerce at (949) 729-4400 for additional listings.

MONTE VISTA NATIONAL WILDLIFE REFUGE

*Majestic Sandhill Cranes reign at this high-altitude refuge
in the heart of south-central Colorado.*

This National Wildlife Refuge may be most famous for its Sandhill Cranes, but they certainly aren't the only bird in town. The 14,189-acre wetlands complex is also designed as a haven for migrating and nesting waterfowl, migrating shorebirds, wintering Bald and Golden Eagles, and Peregrine Falcons, as well as an elk herd and a variety of other wildlife.

It wasn't too long ago that the Blue Sky People (Ute Indians) lived and hunted in this valley. Then, during Spanish and American tenures, settlers began farming the land and wildlife habitat started to dwindle. But, ironically, the advancement of agriculture made the existence of this refuge possible. Irrigation canals and ditches were developed, turning Monte Vista into an artificially created wetland within a region that receives only seven inches of precipitation a year.

Black-necked Stilts
*and other waders
are attracted to
the refuge's vast
wetlands.*

HABITAT

As Sandhill Cranes fly to and from their wintering grounds of Bosque del Apache, New Mexico, they come upon a remarkably flat valley, 50 miles wide and 100 miles long, cupped between two snowcapped mountain ranges: the San Juan range to the west and the Sangre de Cristo mountains to the east. Within this refuge, the birds find nearly 100 small wetland basins and nearby barley fields where they can rest, feed, and engage in bonding and courtship rituals. Upland areas here consist of mostly low vegetation, but a few clumps of cottonwoods provide some shelter for songbirds and owls.

BIRD LIFE

When migrating Sandhill Cranes are residing at Monte Vista, huge concentrations of them roost in the wetlands at night. For an unforgettable sight, arrive just at dawn on a frosty spring morning, when they begin to disperse. Crane numbers peak in mid-March, when waterfowl numbers are also vast.

When the sun rises enough to help identify the ducks, Cinnamon Teal, Northern Pintails, Ruddy Ducks, Redheads, and American Wigeon will

BIRDS TO LOOK FOR

White-faced Ibis • American Wigeon • Cinnamon Teal • Ruddy Duck • Swainson's Hawk • Prairie Falcon • Sandhill Crane • Black-necked Stilt • American Avocet • Wilson's Phalarope • Great Horned Owl • Short-eared Owl • Sage Thrasher • Brewer's Sparrow

Both spring and fall bring abundant waterfowl such as this Ruddy Duck.

be revealed. It's always a treat to view large numbers of waders, and Monte Vista is a great site for American Avocets, White-faced Ibis, Wilson's Phalaropes, and Black-necked Stilts. Away from the water, Great Horned Owls are incubating eggs in their cottonwood nests in early spring.

The Great Horned Owl, *the fiercest of the owls, hunts its prey by night.*

By May the cranes are gone, but breeding season is in full swing, featuring nesting Virginia Rails, Soras, and resident waterfowl. Colonial nesters such as herons, egrets, and ibis are starting to build their nests. Drive the three-mile auto tour to find migrating shorebirds, including Western Sandpipers and, less commonly, Pectoral, Baird's, and Least Sandpipers. Listen for chatter in the cattails to locate an abundance of Marsh Wrens, too.

Throughout the summer the edge habitat, between ponds and uplands, yields Savannah Sparrows and Short-eared Owls. Nesting Sage Thrashers and Brewer's Sparrows may be seen in upland habitats. Brewer's Blackbirds and Western Meadowlarks will be singing here as well. This season is the best time to observe Swainson's Hawks, plus Red-tails, Kestrels, and Prairie Falcons. Summer ponds and wetlands harbor Common Snipe, as well as Yellow-headed and Red-winged Blackbirds.

In the fall the cranes pass through again, but they do not arrive in the concentrated numbers seen in the spring. Observe each flock carefully to spot the few (but much taller) Whooping Cranes attached to this population of Sandhills. Cooler weather means waterfowl populations are rising again and will peak in October with over 35,000 birds.

In the wintertime, area residents enjoy the large number of Bald Eagles residing at the site. Birders seek

Golden Eagles and wintering hawks, such as Ferruginous Hawks, Rough-legged Hawks, and Northern Harriers.

VISITING

Visit Monte Vista twice in the spring to experience the full range of birding opportunities. Mid-March is a must-visit time for peak numbers of cranes and waterfowl, but it is not until May that breeding birds and migrant songbirds are here and winter is good for raptors. Fall once again sees ample numbers of cranes and waterfowl. In addition to the car tour route along the dikes, irrigation ditches, and artificial ponds, several county roads bisect the refuge. County Road 3 East offers views of shorebird habitats, waterfowl,

and colonial herons and egrets. County Road 6 East affords access to more wetlands. State Highway 15 is good for viewing a long row of cottonwoods – among the scarce trees within this refuge. A small gravel road parallel to the highway is the place to look for nesting Great Horned Owls.

HIGHLIGHTS

In mid-March each year the small town of Monte Vista throws a party to welcome both the Sandhill Cranes and the nature-lovers that flock to see them. The Monte Vista Crane Festival includes bus tours, workshops, and educational exhibits. Call (719) 852-3552 for details.

Site Map and Information

MONTE VISTA NATIONAL WILDLIFE REFUGE

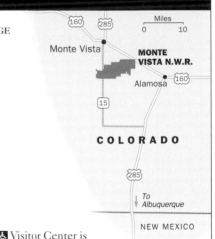

From Fort Myers, a 3-mile causeway leads directly onto Periwinkle Way, which deadends onto Tarpon Bay Road. Take a right, then a left onto Sanibel Captiva Road; the Visitor Center is 2 miles away, on the right.

☐ Auto tour route open daily, sunrise to sunset, year-round.

● Never.

◪ Monte Vista shares a common Visitor Center with Alamosa National Wildlife Refuge: Alamosa/Monte Vista National Wildlife Refuge Complex, U.S. Fish and Wildlife Service, 9383 El Rancho Lane, Alamosa, CO 81101. It is open weekdays, 7:30 a.m.–4 p.m.; closed holidays and weekends. (To get there, go east from the town of Alamosa on Route 160 for 4 miles, turn right onto El Rancho Lane at the refuge sign, and continue for 2.5 miles to the Visitor Center.)

◪ (719) 589-4021

⑤ None.

♿ Visitor Center is wheelchair accessible.

🄰 None on-site. Campgrounds available at nearby Great Sand Dunes National Monument; call (719) 378-2312.

🚻 None.

♨ Lodging available in nearby Monte Vista or Alamosa. For listings, call Monte Vista Chamber of Commerce at (800) 852-2731 or Alamosa Chamber of Commerce at (800) 258-7597.

ROCKY MOUNTAIN NATIONAL PARK

*From the grand high peaks to their residents – including ptarmigans and
Rosy-finches – the Colorado perspective dazzles birders!*

Birdwatchers who explore the West will find themselves returning again and again to high ground – the Rocky Mountains. And Rocky Mountain National Park, all 415.2 square miles of it, is preeminent among high-elevation birding sites. Even its lowest point (7,522 feet, near Estes Park) is higher than any east of the Mississippi. This land of alpine birds has 98 peaks that each reach over 11,000 feet in elevation.

HABITAT

Although there are 13 different types of habitat found in the park, some are more common than others. Riparian habitat, along the bottoms of river valleys, is home to birds such as the American Dipper, Lincoln's Sparrow, and an array of wood warblers including Yellow, Wilson's, and MacGillivray's. Over one-third of the park is tundra, patrolled by raptors such as Golden Eagles and Northern Harriers. Blue Grouse and Red-naped Sapsuckers are abundant in the aspen groves. Coniferous forests provide

BIRDS TO LOOK FOR

Golden Eagle • Prairie Falcon •
White-tailed Ptarmigan • Blue Grouse •
Red-naped Sapsucker • Clark's
Nutcracker • Pygmy Nuthatch •
American Dipper • Mountain Bluebird •
Hermit Thrush • MacGillivray's
Warbler • Lincoln's Sparrow •
Brown-capped Rosy-Finch • Cassin's
Finch • Evening Grosbeak

food and shelter for Pine Grosbeaks and Golden-crowned Kinglets.

One of the most unique habitats in the park is the krummholz (also known as wind timber) – groups of stunted and gnarled conifers that have been exposed to the harshest winter conditions imaginable. Birdwatchers often find the much-sought-after White-tailed Ptarmigan here.

BIRD LIFE

Although higher-elevation birds residing in this national park are the

The Lincoln's Sparrow *can be found in the park's meadows; listen for its rich, lively trill.*

most coveted because they often can't be found in other habitats, the bulk of the bird population is concentrated among the ponderosa pines in the lower elevations. To start, pick up maps at Beaver Meadows Visitor Center (which also serves as the park's headquarters, on the east side of the park) off Highway 36, or at the Fall River Visitor Center off Highway 34 (also on the east side of the park), and ask rangers about which birds are likely to be spotted. Check the lower-elevation open meadow and scattered

Molting three times a year, the White-tailed Ptarmigan always blends with its habitat.

ponderosa pines for Mountain Bluebirds and Green-tailed Towhees. From there, visit the mixed groves of ponderosa pine, Douglas fir, and quaking aspen near either Moraine Park or Endovalley. Look for Evening Grosbeaks, Cassin's Finches, and an assortment of woodpeckers. Of the six woodpeckers that frequent this habitat, the Northern Flicker is the most common.

Bear Lake provides great access to the birds of the dense coniferous forests found in the backcountry. Hikers will find Olive-sided Flycatchers and, if they are lucky, Hermit Thrushes.

The Evening Grosbeak, *primarily a mountain dweller, can be most readily identified by its noisy clee-ip or peeer calls.*

To explore the tundra, drive from the Beaver Meadows or Fall River Visitor Centers up the winding Trail Ridge Road. This is the park's main east-west road and one of the world's most spectacular drives. Clark's Nutcrackers are common at any pull-out. Just beyond Rainbow Curve, visitors will encounter wind timber forests. Stop and look for White-crowned Sparrows.

At approximately 11,500 feet the tundra begins and the clear, sparkling air will intoxicate birdwatchers – or is it the lack of oxygen? From late June, a beautiful sash of wildflowers accent the most common birds of the tundra, Horned Larks and American Pipits. Another common tundra dweller, the White-tailed Ptarmigan, is harder to spot due to its protective camouflage. Don't be surprised to spot a Prairie Falcon; ptarmigans are their favorite food. Hike the Tundra Communities Trail for Brown-capped Rosy-Finches, a species found exclusively in Colorado and New Mexico. Just above treeline is best.

Continuing on the Trail Ridge Road past the

Alpine Visitor Center, the road drops into the river drainage watershed of the Cache la Poudre River. Look along the riverbank for Spotted Sandpipers. When you arrive at the Lake Irene picnic area, stop for Gray Jays, Evening Grosbeaks, and other forest birds.

Nearby Timber Creek Campground in the Kawuneeche Valley makes a great overnight stop. Wake up to the sounds of winnowing Common Snipes, honking Pygmy Nuthatches, and the song of Hermit Thrushes.

VISITING

Although the breeding birds arrive in early June, the wildflowers don't bloom until later in the month. To get the best of both worlds, visit in late June and July. Birdwatching is fruitful through September, and the roads are usually kept open until mid-October. Plan to spend at least three days exploring the park. Be aware of the high altitude and take things slowly.

HIGHLIGHTS

The most unique aspect of Rocky Mountain National Park is the grand expanse of tundra on which birdwatching is accessible by car. Both Trail Ridge Road and Old Fall River Road offer easy summer access to this windswept ecosystem, where the views seem to span forever, and the birds have few places to hide.

Site Map and Information

ROCKY MOUNTAIN NATIONAL PARK

🚗 From Denver, take US Route 34, 36, or 7 approximately 70 miles to the east entrance and Bear Meadow's Visitor Center. From Granby, follow Highway 40/34 north 12 miles to the west entrance and Kawuneeche Visitor Center.

◻ Daily, 24 hours, year-round.

⬤ Trail Ridge Road is closed from approximately mid-October through Memorial Day due to severe weather.

ℹ Rocky Mountain National Park, Estes Park, CO 80517. Beaver Meadows Visitor Center and Kawuneeche Visitor Center are open daily except December 25. Fall River Visitor Center is open daily, approximately April through October. The Alpine Visitor Center is open daily, approximately Memorial Day through mid-October.

📞 (970) 586-1206; www.nps.gov/romo

💲 $10 per vehicle for a 7-day pass.

♿ All Visitor Centers are wheelchair accessible, as are trails at Bear Lake,

Beaver Boardwalk, Sprague Lake, and Coyote Valley.

⛺ There are 5 campsites on-site; call (800) 365-2267 for information.

🚶 The National Park Service can arrange tours with park naturalists for groups; call (970) 586-1310 for information.

🛏 There is lodging in nearby Grand Lake and Estes Park; call (800) 443-7837 or (800) 531-1019 for listings.

HALEAKALĀ NATIONAL PARK

Explore Maui as it once was, and witness the last remaining habitat for the greatest concentration of endangered birds in the United States.

Haleakalā, on the island of Maui, is a patchwork of volcanic landscape, fragile rainforest ecosystems, and rare, undeveloped coastline. Of its 30,183 acres, 19,270 are wilderness. Originally a unit of Hawaii National Park that included what is now Hawaii Volcanoes National Park on the neighboring Island of Hawaii, Haleakalā became a separate entity in 1960.

The Nēnē, *or Hawaiian Goose, may be spotted in this island park.*

HABITAT

Haleakalā consists of two districts. The summit area ranges from cloud forests to alpine cinder-desert. The second district, Kīpahulu, includes coastal rainforest and cloud forest habitat. The species of plants and animals unique to

---

BIRDS TO LOOK FOR

ʻUaʻu (Dark-rumped Petrel) • Koa ʻE ʻUla (Red-tailed Tropicbird) • ʻIwa (Great Frigatebird) • Nēnē (Hawaiian Goose) • Pacific Golden-Plover • Pueo (Hawaiian Short-eared Owl) • ʻAmakihi (Yellow-Green Honeycreeper) • ʻAlauahio (Maui Creeper) • ʻIʻiwi and ʻApapane (Red Honeycreepers)

---

the park, and to the Hawaii Islands generally, evolved from colonizers that traveled a minimum of 2,500 miles (the nearest continent is North America). Endemic species include specialized insects that pollinate fragile plants and several species of Hawaiian Honeycreeper, birds with curved bills designed to feed on the nectar of native tubular flowers. The native birds here are not ones birders will find in most field guides to North American birds, but they are part of a densely woven ecological fabric like no other on the planet.

BIRD LIFE

This park is one of a few places visitors can see rare Hawaiian forest birds. Usually the first stop for birders is in the summit area: the Hosmer Grove Nature Trail, a short (half-mile) hiking trail off Highway 378 just inside the park boundaries. Four forest birds are commonly seen here, including two Red Honeycreepers – the ʻApapane and the ʻIʻiwi – and two species of Yellow-Green Honeycreepers – the ʻAmakihi and the ʻAlauahio. Of these, the ʻAlauahio, or Maui Creeper, can be seen only at Haleakalā, and only at sites above 4,500 feet.

Also found in Hosmer Grove and along the Halemauʻu Trail is the Pueo, or Hawaiian Short-eared Owl. Halemauʻu Trail begins at the 8,000-square-foot parking lot, 3.5 miles

At Haleakalā, observe birds not found in the continental U.S., like this colorful ʻIʻiwi.

above headquarters. The first mile gradually descends through native shrubland to the valley rim. The owl, which is brown and buffy white, is most active at dawn and dusk, and can often be seen soaring overhead on cloudy days. Unfortunately nonnative species such as chukars, pheasants, doves, pigeons, sparrows, mynas, meijiro, and house finches also inhabit the summit area. These alien birds are a threat to native birds, because they serve as disease vectors.

The Nēnē, or Hawaiian Goose, can sometimes be spotted near headquarters or at a variety of roadside overlooks along the park road, at elevations of 7,000 to 8,000 feet. This goose has a black head and nape and a gray-brown body. Its bill and partially

webbed feet are black. Only about 200 Nēnē reside in the park, since predation by introduced rats and mongoose has taken a heavy toll.

In Kīpahulu, which is the coastal area of the park, several trails from the ranger station lead to great views of the coastline or to waterfalls. Common native birds seen from these well-marked trails include the ʻIwa (Great Frigatebird), Koa ʻE ʻUla (Red-Tailed Tropicbird), Pueo, and Pacific Golden-Plover. Nonnative species include an assortment of mynas, sparrows, cardinals, and chickadees. The ʻUaʻu (Dark-rumped Petrel) found in this area during summer months is now endangered and, for

The ʻAmakihi, or Yellow-Green Honeycreeper, *is found in the upper forested and shrubland areas of the park.*

nesting, restricted to rocky cliffs above 8,000 feet in elevation. They cannot be seen because their nesting areas are off-trail, but their haunting cries may be heard from the summit area's Kalahaku Overlook at night.

VISITING

The weather in Haleakalā National Park, and especially the summit area, is unpredictable. Although the temperature may be warm, always be prepared for wind and heavy rain. The weather changes rapidly at high elevations. Those with heart or respiratory problems, or pregnant birdwatchers, should check with their doctors before visiting the high-elevation summit area.

In the Kīpahulu area the weather is warm and heavy rain is common. Always check with the park rangers before entering the pools and never swim if flood warnings are posted. Mosquitos can be pesky in this area.

HIGHLIGHTS

On the third Saturday of every month, visitors can join a host of volunteers at the Nature Conservancy's Pukalami office to help efforts to eliminate alien weed species at the Waikamoi Preserve adjacent to Haleakala. For more information and reservations, call (808) 572-7849.

Site Map and Information

HALEAKALĀ NATIONAL PARK

- The summit district is a 1.5-hour drive from Kahului via roads 37, 377, and 378. The Kīpahulu district (between Hana and Kaupo in eastern Maui) can be reached via Highway 36. Driving time is 3 to 4 hours each way.

- Daily, 24 hours, year-round.

- Never.

- Haleakalā National Park, PO 369, Makawao, HI 96768. Summit area headquarters are open daily, 7:30 a.m.–4 p.m. Visitor Center is open daily, sunrise to 3 p.m. The Kīpahulu district ranger station is open daily, 9 a.m.– 5 p.m.

- (808) 572-4400; www.nsp.gov/hale

- $10.00 per vehicle per week.

- Summit area headquarters, Visitor Center, and Hosmer Grove picnic area are wheelchair accessible. The ranger station in the Kipahulu area is accessible.

- The Hosmer Grove Campground in the summit area area and the primitive campground in the Kīpahulu district are

both available on a first-come, first-served basis.

- The Nature Conservancy leads an interpretive hike through Waikamoi Preserve on the second Saturday of every month. Call the Maui Field Office at (808) 572-7849 for reservations.

- There are no hotels or concessions within Haleakalā National Park. For lodging information call the Hawaii Convention and Visitors Bureau at (808) 244-3530.

Deer Flat National Wildlife Refuge

In early fall shorebirds on the mudflats bring birdwatchers flocking to this refuge near Nampa, Idaho.

Deer Flat was one of the first national wildlife refuges, established in 1909 by executive order of President Theodore Roosevelt. Lake Lowell, the centerpiece of the refuge, was created not for wildlife but as an irrigation reservoir to support and promote local agriculture. The lake's attractiveness to birds is a serendipitous by-product. A variety of aquatic and upland habitats draw an array of birds to this 11,350-acre refuge.

The Northern Goshawk *feeds on the refuge's songbirds, ducks, and small mammals.*

Habitat

This lowland region is arid, with sunny summers and comparatively mild winters. The borders of the refuge support sagebrush, rabbit brush, and bunch grass. In the riparian areas, along the bottom of the river valley, trees such as cottonwood, willow, and Russian olive provide cover and food for birds, deer, and other wildlife. The reservoir itself is a very significant waterfowl wintering area along the Pacific flyway; waterfowl populations can reach as high as 100,000 ducks.

Also included within the refuge boundaries is a 113-mile stretch along the Snake River that contains 107 islands (many seen only by boat), providing an important corridor for migrating birds and nesting areas for Canada Geese.

Bird Life

It is possible to drive all the way around Lake Lowell, and stops at strategic locations will yield an interesting variety of both water- and land birds. If the lake's water level is low during the early fall (this doesn't happen every year), the refuge offers excellent opportunities to spot shorebirds, including Western and Least Sandpipers, and occasionally Sanderlings, which are attracted to the exposed shorelines.

Gotts Point, accessed from Greenhurst Avenue, is one of the more productive birding areas on the lake. Park at the gate and walk along the refuge patrol road. Look along the shore for American Avocets and a variety of other shorebirds in early fall. The woodlands bordering the patrol road accommodate Great Horned Owls and Western Screech-Owls, and occasionally a Northern

BIRDS TO LOOK FOR

Western Grebe • Clark's Grebe • American White Pelican • Canada Goose • Wood Duck • American Wigeon • Northern Goshawk • Sanderling • Western Sandpiper • Caspian Tern • Great Horned Owl • Lewis's Woodpecker • Western Kingbird • Lincoln's Sparrow

Clark's Grebe can be identified by its orange bill and the shape of its cap.

Saw-whet Owl. During spring and fall migration look for a variety of warblers, including Yellow-rumped, Black-and-white, and Wilson's Warblers, and watch for Wood Ducks in the wetter wooded areas.

Schaffer's Access, a second stop along the lake off of Tio Lane, offers marshland and woodland birds. This is a prime location during spring migration for sparrows, including White-throated, Vesper, and Lincoln's Sparrows. The habitat on the western side of the patrol road at Schaffer's Access is favored by the hard-to-find Northern Goshawk.

At the lake's Upper and Lower Dam recreation areas, birdwatching can yield prolific results, especially during spring and early fall migrations. Look for

Lewis's Woodpecker *feeds on insects, fruit, and nuts, which it shells, then stores in tree crevices.*

Lewis's Woodpeckers, Western Kingbird, and Hermit Thrushes. From both of these vantage points, scan the open water of the lake during late fall for large flocks of ducks. Up to 500 Ruddy Ducks have been spotted at once.

Summer on the lake brings Clark's and Western Grebes. Although the two species seem very much alike to the human eye (and were considered a single species for more than a hundred years), recent studies have shown that they seldom interbreed. Slightly distinctive breeding displays and breeding calls help them tell each other apart. Outside of breeding season, both Clark's and Western Grebes frequent the same bays and estuaries, often side by side, but observers can distinguish between the two by taking note of their different facial patterns.

No visit to the refuge is complete without exploring the island habitats along the Snake River. Although the best way to visit the islands is by boat (no rentals or tours are available), birdwatching is also good from River Road, which runs along the northern bank of the river beginning near Walter's Ferry, about 20 miles from the Visitor Center. From March to May, Canada Geese will be seen sitting on eggs on the nesting platforms. Caspian Terns and American White Pelicans will be plying the air overhead. Common Goldeneyes, American Wigeon, and Pied-billed Grebes also thrive in the river habitat.

VISITING

The best time to visit the refuge depends on what a birder wants to see. To see the grebes' dancelike breeding display, visit in spring. Mid-April is a great time to spot fuzzy, just-hatched goslings. In early fall, if there is a drought, big drawdowns on Lake Lowell result in several thousand acres of exposed shoreline, attracting shorebirds by the thousands. For large concentrations of waterfowl, visit in mid-October though December.

HIGHLIGHTS

Clark's Grebes, not easy to find in their nesting habitat elsewhere, are common at Deer Flat National Wildlife Refuge. Watch their courtship "dance" in early summer, or come to see the fuzzy white babies hitchhiking on their parents' backs in August. These waterbirds mingle but do not breed with Western Grebes, also found at the refuge.

Site Map and Information

DEER FLAT NATIONAL WILDLIFE REFUGE

🚗 From downtown Nampa, (just south of I-84), take 12th Avenue south to Lake Lowell Avenue. Turn right and head west for 4 miles to reach the Visitor Center.

◻ Daily, sunrise to sunset, year-round.

⬤ The Gotts Point area is closed October through January. Most of the lake's waters are closed October through April 15.

ℹ Deer Flat National Wildlife Refuge, 13751 Upper Embankment Road, Nampa, ID 83686. Refuge headquarters, which also serve as a Visitor Center, are open weekdays, 7:30 a.m.–4 p.m., year-round, except federal holidays.

📞 (208) 467-9278; www.pacific.fws.gov/deer

$ None.

♿ Visitor Center and boat launches are wheelchair accessible. A dirt road provides access to Gotts Point.

⛺ None on-site or nearby.

🚻 None.

🏨 Hotels, motels, and bed-and-breakfasts are available in nearby Nampa; call the Chamber of Commerce at (208) 466-4641 for listings.

SNAKE RIVER BIRDS OF PREY NATIONAL CONSERVATION AREA

This conservation area set along the Snake River in southern Idaho boasts North America's largest concentration of nesting birds of prey.

The staff at Celebration Park – Idaho's only archaeological park, located within this national conservation area – can point hikers to an ancient etching of a falconlike bird that demonstrates how long this area has been valued for its raptors. Archaeologists add that early inhabitants of these lands also imbued eagle feathers and other raptor-related symbols with great significance.

Today, bird- and wildlife watchers cherish this area as the North American epicenter of bird of prey breeding.

HABITAT

Along the Snake River, cliffs of basalt tower hundreds of feet above the water, creating several crevices, cracks, and ledges where birds of prey build their nests. The birds launch from these cliffside aeries to soar and hunt on the warm air currents rising from the canyon floor. The 756 square miles of finely textured upland soil that comprise the Snake River National Conservation Area are a perfect home for large populations of ground squirrels and jackrabbits, which serve as sustenance for the 15 species of raptors that breed here and the nine species that pass through during their annual migrations.

The Long-billed Curlew *may be spotted by its musical call – cur-lee – and, of course, its extremely long thin bill.*

This national conservation area is Prairie Falcon heaven. The approximately 200 pairs that nest here, a significant percentage of the total U.S. population of these birds, rely on the abundance of Piute ground squirrels found at the site. The nesting success of other raptors, especially Golden Eagles, is tied to the population cycles of black-tailed jackrabbits at the site.

BIRDS TO LOOK FOR

Turkey Vulture • Osprey • Northern Harrier • Swainson's Hawk • Red-tailed Hawk • Ferruginous Hawk • Golden Eagle • American Kestrel • Prairie Falcon • Long-billed Curlew • Barn Owl • Great Horned Owl • Burrowing Owl • Cliff Swallow • Western Tanager • Bullock's Oriole

BIRD LIFE

The 56-mile auto tour route, beginning at the Kuna Vistor Center and following Swan Falls Road, offers

The Burrowing Owl is just one of many raptors that nests at the conservation area.

many opportunities to see raptors, beginning with the Northern Harriers and American Kestrels that patrol the nearby agricultural lands. Soon the tour reaches wilder terrain, featuring open shrub and grasslands and one of the largest Burrowing Owl colonies in the United States. Check the power lines here for Swainson's Hawks. Surprisingly, a shorebird, the Long-billed Curlew, nests in these same short grasslands; most other shorebirds breed much farther north.

Dedication Point, at mile 15.5 on the tour, provides breathtaking views of the Snake River Canyon. Look for Prairie Falcons, Red-tailed Hawks, and Golden Eagles in flight. The Common Raven's

The Turkey Vulture *rocks from side to side when it flies, flapping its wings only occasionally.*

raptorlike, acrobatic flight often tricks birdwatchers into thinking they've spotted a new bird of prey.

From the overlook at Dedication Point, watch also for Canyon and Rock Wrens, Say's Phoebes, and White-throated Swifts. In the shrubs along the short nature trail, listen for Sage and Brewer's Sparrows and Western Meadowlarks.

Birdwatchers should make a stop at Swan Falls Dam, where cottonwoods provide a roost in the spring and summer for Turkey Vultures. Bullock's Orioles nest in the trees.

At mile 39 is Celebration Park, which is especially promising in the spring, when both migrating raptors and songbirds, including Osprey and Western Tanagers, use the forest along the river as a travel corridor. A Golden Eagle pair nests just across the river. During late evening, owl-watchers should survey the cliffs behind the park for Great Horned Owls and Barn Owls. Downstream, Cliff Swallows nest beneath the Guffy Bridge.

Two other notable birding spots are off the auto tour route. There are three "duck" ponds at the Ted Trueblood Wildlife Area, accessed from Highway 67 just north of Grand View. In the summer White-faced Ibis, Black-necked Stilts, Caspian Terns, and American Avocets are found here. Winter visitors observe Trumpeter Swans and Rough-legged Hawks. Spring brings the return of Ospreys, migrant shorebirds, such as Long-billed Dowitchers and Dunlins, and a variety of swallows. A visit to C.J. Strike Wildlife Management Area will offer more opportunities to watch wetland and lake birds. The best birding site is the Jack's Creek Sportsman's Access off of State Highway 78, past Grandview.

VISITING

The best raptor-viewing season is spring – mid-March through June. During April, viewing opportunities decline as birds tend to stay close to their nests. By July, fiery hot canyon temperatures drive raptors away.

HIGHLIGHTS

Be sure to take a side trip to the World Center for Birds of Prey, just south of Boise. Visit the state-of-the-art museum and educational facility, where live Bald, Golden, and Harpy Eagles, California Condors, and Peregrine Falcons are on display. Call (208) 362-8687 for tour details.

Site Map and Information

SNAKE RIVER BIRDS OF PREY NATIONAL CONSERVATION AREA

🚗 From Boise or Nampa, take I-84 to Exit 44 at Meridian. Take Highway 69 south 7.5 miles to the town of Kuna. Turn south on Swan Falls Road and proceed to the conservation area.

⬜ Daily, 24 hours, year-round.

⬤ Never.

ℹ Snake River Birds of Prey National Conservation Area, c/o Bureau of Land Management, 3948 Development Ave., Boise, ID, 83705. Visitor Center, in the town of Kuna, is open weekdays, mid-April to September 1, 8 a.m.–3 p.m.

📞 (208) 384-3300; www.id.blm.gov/bopnca

⑨ None.

♿ No special facilities.

🅰 Backcountry camping permitted.

Campgrounds available at nearby Bruneau Dunes State Park; call (208) 366-7919.

📷 Call Birds of Prey Expeditions at (208) 327-8903.

🛏 Accommodations are available in Meridian, Boise, and Mountain Home; visit www.visitid.org for listings.

Bowdoin National Wildlife Refuge

Measure quality by the quantity of intriguing birds per mile, and the 15-mile auto tour route through this remote northeastern Montana refuge garners five stars.

Bowdoin National Wildlife Refuge lies in the Central flyway – a great waterfowl migration corridor extending from Canada to Mexico. The 15,550-acre refuge also serves as a major nesting area for gulls, pelicans, and avocets. Before European settlers came here, nomadic plains people – Cree, Gros Ventures, and Assiniboine – hunted and trapped the birds drawn to the marshes and lakes of this site and the surrounding lands. Ancient stone circles, probably used as bases for tepees, testify to those seasonal visits to these lands.

Snowy Owls *can be spotted here in winter; their thick plumage protects them from the elements.*

Habitat

The Milk River drains the eastern slopes of the Montana and Alberta Rockies, replenishing 5,000-acre Lake Bowdoin. The river's contribution is vital, since the region receives only 12 inches of precipitation per year. Manmade dikes hold the spring runoff, creating a welcome year-round supply of fresh water that was previously unavailable.

During fall migration up to 30,000 ducks, including Gadwall, Northern Shoveler, and American Wigeon, plus Tundra Swans and Canada and Snow Geese find safe resting and feeding conditions on the waters and marshes of the wildlife refuge.

Spring is the best season for birds, however, with several thousand ducks, including Redheads and Lesser Scaup, nesting on the refuge. American White Pelicans, Caspian Terns, California Gulls, and Ring-billed Gulls nest on islands in the main lake. Colonies of Franklin's Gulls, White-faced Ibis, and Black-crowned Night Herons are found in the marshes.

Wetlands may be the primary habitat here, but the refuge also protects over 6,000 acres of native prairie, home to birds such as pipits, longspurs, Western Meadowlarks, Baird's Sparrows, Horned Larks, and Swainson's Hawks, and mammals including white-tailed jackrabbits, Nuttall's cottontails, coyotes, and striped skunks. Whitetail deer and pronghorn are also common residents, and mule deer are seen occasionally.

BIRDS TO LOOK FOR

Eared Grebe • American White Pelican • White-faced Ibis • Tundra Swan • American Wigeon • Swainson's Hawk • Sharp-tailed Grouse • Franklin's Gull • California Gull • Snowy Owl • Sprague's Pipit • Bohemian Waxwing • Baird's Sparrow • Chestnut-collared Longspur •

American White Pelicans are especially visible from Pelican Point.

BIRD LIFE

Visit Bowdoin in the spring if possible, and plan on exploring the auto tour route, with frequent stops for short walks to good vantage points. Near refuge headquarters, visit the boat landing at the western edge of Lake Bowdoin to see nesting Eared Grebes and Franklin's Gulls. With the help of a scope, a lucky birder might also spot nesting White-faced Ibis.

By mid-May the Sprague's Pipits and Baird's Sparrows will have arrived and can usually be spotted at the beginning of the tour route in the grasslands between headquarters and Long Island. At Long Island there are about a thousand Ring-billed and California Gull nests. The islands at Pelican Point (Site 5 on the auto tour) teem with American White Pelicans and other colonial nesters, including Great Blue Herons and Double-Crested Cormorants. A scope is useful to bridge the distance here too.

After passing Tour Site 6, park near the locked gate on the east side of Big Island, before the first railroad crossing. A half-mile walk past the gate onto Big Island leads to a weedy grassland where Baird's Sparrows, Sprague's Pipits, Chestnut-collared Longspurs, and nesting Marbled Godwits can be found. Farther along the tour route at Goose Island Pond, look for Northern Harriers, Virginia Rails, Spotted Sandpipers, and Common Yellowthroats. In the

American Wigeon *and many other ducks are attracted to this site along a major waterfowl migration corridor.*

summer, Yellow-headed Blackbirds croak and cavort.

The threatened Piping Plover is an important refuge bird; however, it is unlikely to be seen, since this tiny bird is rare in its range. Fewer than 2,800 breeding pairs of Piping Plovers were reported in the United States and Canada in 1995. Records show the plover has bred at the Bowdoin refuge.

VISITING

The best birding is in mid-May through June, but don't overlook the summer and fall. In summer the wildlife refuge's marshes are crowded with American Coots and Eared Grebes. Secretive Soras and American Bitterns often can be heard, and even seen, throughout the wetlands on summer evenings.

Fall migration is quite showy, with as many as 8,000 Sandhill Cranes sometimes gathering at the refuge every October. Goose Islands Pond is

an excellent spot to spy shorebirds during migration – Long-billed Dowitchers are abundant.

Those willing to brave severe winter conditions will be rewarded with Snowy Owls, Lapland Longspurs, Northern Goshawks, and large flocks of Bohemian Waxwings. Late winter and early spring are the best times to see Sharp-tailed Grouse, which gather to feed in the Russian olive trees along the auto tour route. Early spring provides the best chance to see McCown's Longspurs, too; ask at refuge headquarters for specifics.

HIGHLIGHTS

The butterfly-like display of the easy-to-find Sprague's Pipit makes the trip to Bowdoin National Wildlife Refuge worth it. Visitors can lie on their backs in the grasslands to watch the tiny bird's high, fluttery flight and let its flutelike song rain down on them.

Site Map and Information

BOWDOIN NATIONAL WILDLIFE REFUGE

🚗 Located 7 miles east of Malta, on old Highway 2.

◖ Daily, sunrise to sunset, year-round.

◕ Roads may be closed after heavy rain- or snowfall.

ℹ Bowdoin National Wildlife Refuge, HC 65 Box 5700, Malta, MT 59538. Headquarters open weekdays, 8 a.m.–4:30 p.m.

☎ (406) 654-2863

Ⓢ None.

♿ Headquarters and observation blind on the Pearce Waterfowl Production Area, adjacent to the refuge, are wheelchair accessible.

🏕 None on-site. Campgrounds available 12 miles to the northeast of the refuge at Trafton Park in Malta, Nelson Reservoir.

🍴 None.

🏨 Several motels and bed-and-breakfasts in nearby Malta; call the Chamber of Commerce at (406) 654-1776 for listings.

GLACIER NATIONAL PARK

Spanning more than a million acres of priceless habitat, this protected land in northwestern Montana is a treasure chest for bird lovers.

In 1901 naturalist George Bird Grinnell described Glacier and environs as the "Crown of the Continent." Ice-age glaciers more than half a mile deep carved this jagged crown and left behind some of the most spectacular scenery in the world. For jewels, the park flashes 1,000 species of flowering plants early each June, plus miles of forest – spruce, subalpine fir, and whitebark pines, to name a few varieties. Of course, the many birds adorning the flora are gems as well, but sightings of grizzly bears and mountain goats sometimes distract even the most dedicated birder.

The Barrow's Goldeneye *drake has a white crescent on each side of its face, plus a white breast and sides.*

HABITAT

Glacier possesses a natural landmark that divides west from east – the Continental Divide. The west side of the park has a generally lower elevation and is warmer and more moist. In the spring birds have been known to return here as much as two to three weeks earlier than to the eastern half of the park. Lodgepole pine, Engelmann spruce, western white pine, western larch, and western redcedar fill the forests.

The colder, higher east side has twice as many glaciers and more alpine habitat, where subalpine fir and whitebark pine grow. The latter, an important higher-elevation species that has been declining precipitously in recent years because of disease and fire suppression, relies on Clark's Nutcrackers, which spreads its seeds, as its sole means of propagation.

BIRD LIFE

Apgar Village, on the west side of the park, is a good starting point for a summer birding tour. From the Apgar ranger station, a stroll to the McDonald Creek Bridge and then along Camas Creek Road might yield Red-naped Sapsuckers, Swainson's Thrushes, MacGillivray's Warblers, Black-headed Grosbeaks, and Red Crossbills. About 300 yards north of the bridge, the road to Fish Creek Campground is a good place to spot Chestnut-backed Chickadees, Pileated Woodpeckers, and more.

Back at Apgar, Lake McDonald beckons. Ten miles long and a mile wide, with craggy summits towering in the background, the lake is one of the focal points of the park. Check the lake from the picnic area for Common Loons, Common Mergansers, and

BIRDS TO LOOK FOR

Harlequin Duck • Barrow's Goldeneye • Golden Eagle • White-tailed Ptarmigan • Blue Grouse • Calliope Hummingbird • Steller's Jay • Clark's Nutcracker • Common Raven • American Dipper • Black-headed Grosbeak

Common Ravens roost in a mountainside nest.

other waterfowl. A drive along the lake on Going-to-the-Sun Road requires several birding stops, including Sprague Creek Campground, home to Violet-green Swallows, Varied Thrushes, and Chipping Sparrows. About five miles north of Lake McDonald Lodge, Avalanche Creek picnic area on McDonald Creek is a good place to look for Harlequin Ducks, Calliope Hummingbirds, and Common Ravens; Vaux's and Black Swifts have also been sighted here. Harlequin Ducks are known to nest along upper McDonald Creek during May and June. Only about 40 pair breed in this ecosystem and, although observation is not discouraged, rangers caution birders to be careful not to disturb these senstive birds.

Just down the road across Avalanche Creek, the handicapped-accessible Trail of the Cedars provides admittance to good habitat for American Dippers, Varied Thrushes, Winter Wrens, Golden-crowned Kinglets, and Townsend's Warblers.

Going to the Sun Road then winds its precipitous way to the top of Logan Pass, which sits at timberline on the Continental Divide. In the steep miles before the summit, look for Blue Grouse, Golden Eagles, and Steller's Jays. At the summit the path to Hidden Lake Overlook (southwest from the Visitor Center) is one of the best places in

Blue Grouse *males have inflatable sacks on each side of the neck covered by white feathers.*

the West to see American Pipits, Gray-crowned Rosy-Finches, and White-tailed Ptarmigan.

The east side of the park offers several excellent birding locations, too. Sunrift Gorge, not to be missed even if it were birdless, is an excellent spot for American Dippers and Gray Jays. Check Rising Sun Campground for Clark's Nutcrackers and the grassland along Two Dog Flats for Ruffed Grouse and Lazuli Buntings. The lakes around Many Glacier area offer a variety of waterfowl, including Barrow's Goldeneyes. In wooded areas here, look for Red-naped Sapsuckers and Western Wood-Pewees. Farther south, at East Glacier Hotel, Rufous and Calliope Hummingbirds are attracted to the many feeders.

VISITING

Summer may be busy in the park, but birders should not let that discourage them – July is emphatically prime time for birdwatching. Brave the crowds and stay at least 3 days. Also consider building in time to visit perimeters of Glacier, like the Polbridge and Two Medicine regions.

HIGHLIGHTS

Birders instinctively know they could never adequately cover this destination in only a day or two, so most totally immerse themselves in a three- to five-day adventure that includes camping, hiking, canoeing on Lake McDonald, a drive over Going-to-the-Sun Road, and at least one of the famous ranger-led walks.

Site Map and Information

GLACIER NATIONAL PARK

- Located in northwestern Montana on the US/Canadian border. Access from the east or west is via US Highway 2.

- Daily, 24 hours, year-round.

- Because of heavy snow, most of Going-to-the-Sun Road is closed to motor vehicles from mid-October through late May or mid-June.

- Glacier National Park, PO Box 128, West Glacier, MT 59936. Most park services and facilities are available from late May through September.

- (406) 888-7800; www/nps.gov.glac

- $10 for single vehicle entry pass, valid for 7 days.

- Many trails and services have special access. A full listing of accessible facilities and programs is available by mail or at entrance stations. Call (406) 888-7806 to reach TDD.

- Thirteen campgrounds on-site. Most campgrounds are first come, first served, but for reservations call (800) 365-CAMP.

- Glacier Institute offers a variety of 1- to 2-day birding courses; call (406) 755-1211 for details.

- Lodges and hotels are located throughout the park. Several of them are managed by Glacier Park Incorporated; call (602) 207-6000 for reservations.

RED ROCK CANYON NATIONAL CONSERVATION AREA

Desert birds and other southwest specialities entice birdwatchers to this starkly beautiful Mohave Desert conservation area near Las Vegas.

The striking Keystone Thrust Fault, the result of a 65-million-year-old collision between gray limestone and red sandstone plates, dominates the landscape throughout Red Rock Canyon National Conservation Area. Gray limestone rocks from an ancient ocean have been shoved over red sandstone, forming one of the most dramatic thrust faults found anywhere.

Golden Eagles *can be seen soaring, with wings uplifted slightly, or pouncing on snakes, birds, and other prey.*

This 197,000-acre park was set aside as a recreation area in 1967 and received additional protection in 1990, when it was designated a National Conservation Area. A 13-mile, looping, scenic drive showcases not only its special geological features, but the plants, birds, and other creatures that dwell in this desert habitat.

HABITAT

The Mojave Desert, which covers 54,000 square miles of southeastern California and Nevada, forms a transition between the hot Sonoran Desert and the cooler, higher terrain of the Great Basin region. The climate is characterized by extreme variation in daily temperature and an average annual precipitation of less than 10 inches. Prominent plants here are Mohave yucca and, at higher elevations, Spanish Bayonet. The area boasts deep sandstone canyons that provide a perennial water supply, cool temperatures, and a wide variety of vegetation. This variable habitat creates a haven for over 190 species of birds – some desert specialists and some generalists making use of the available habitat.

BIRD LIFE

The joke is that it's so hot in the Mojave Desert birds have to use pot holders to pull worms out of the ground. And it's true that one cannot hike in Red Rock Canyon without wondering how the birds thrive in such a seemingly inhospitable environment.

Golden Eagles, Red-tailed Hawks, and other raptors often seen soaring above the canyon walls conserve water by drifting in high-altitude air

BIRDS TO LOOK FOR

Red-tailed Hawk • Golden Eagle • Gamble's Quail • Mourning Dove • Greater Roadrunner • Western Scrub-Jay • Verdin • Cactus Wren • Rock Wren •Phainopepla • Sage Sparrow • Black-headed Grosbeak • Scott's Oriole • Lesser Goldfinch •

Cactus Wrens find shelter in the canyon's cactuses and thorny bushes.

currents, where strong winds allow them to stay aloft with little exertion and temperatures can be 20°F cooler than at ground level. They replenish their water supplies by feeding on the moisture-rich flesh of small animals.

The Black-headed Grosbeak *is one of the many migrant birds seen here in spring and fall.*

The Greater Roadrunner, the poster bird of the desert, also consumes prey with a high moisture content (lizards, snakes, and ground squirrels). This bird, occasionally sighted along the Scenic Loop Drive, also pants to keep cool and excretes excess salt through nasal glands.

The Cactus Wren is another desert bird commonly seen along the scenic drive. Although best suited for life in a cholla cactus, these birds sometimes explore the interiors of cars for picnic leftovers. (Their natural diet includes spiders and insects.) A pair of Cactus

Wrens will often build several nests in a cholla but use only one to raise their young. The nests, which resemble footballs, are made from desert plant stems and flower stalks.

Some southwestern birds, including Phainopepla, Gambel's Quail, and Verdin, are common in arid parts of the conservation area as long as water is available nearby. Check along the hiking trails off the scenic drive that lead to springs, such as the Willow Springs Loop Trail.

The Mourning Dove is especially prolific in the Red Rock area, even though it needs daily drinking water in order to survive. During the spring months, it nests in shrubs or cactus within a mile of a spring or deep-canyon stream.

In the higher-elevation, pinyon pine areas, look for Ladder-backed Woodpeckers and Western Scrub-Jays. In desert shrublands, look for typical desert species such as Lesser Goldfinch, Black-throated Sparrow, Sage Sparrow, Scott's Oriole, and Black-chinned Hummingbird. Rock Wrens are among the most common birds in this habitat.

VISITING

The one-way Scenic Loop Drive leads into a variety of habitats, and the hiking trails along the route lead walkers who wish to explore them more thoroughly deeper into dry desert, deep canyons, and oasis habitats. Spring and fall provide the most excitement for birdwatchers here. Summer is for the hearty: carry a minimum of four liters of water on a hike and watch out for rattlesnakes. Although trails may be snowy, winter days can also be pleasant for birding.

HIGHLIGHTS

Migration generates an odd scene: forest birds in the desert. Almost every species of bird that breeds in the western United States migrates through Red Rock Canyon National Conservation Area. During peak migration, Western Tanagers, Black-headed Grosbeaks, and many other species can be seen. Fall migration begins in mid-August; spring migration runs from March until mid-May.

Site Map and Information

RED ROCK CANYON NATIONAL CONSERVATION AREA

🗺 From downtown Las Vegas, follow I-15 to Charleston Blvd/Nevada Highway 159 Take this 16.5 miles west to reach the Visitor Center and the beginning of Scenic Loop Drive.

☐ The 13-mile Scenic Loop Drive is open daily, 7 a.m.–sunset, year-round.

⬤ Never.

🛈 Red Rock Canyon National Conservation Area, HCR 33, Box 5500, Las Vegas, NV 89124. Visitor Center is open daily, 8 a.m.–4:30 p.m. except Christmas and New Year's Day.

📞 (702) 363-1921; www.redrockcanyon.blm.gov

💲 $5 per vehicle.

♿ Visitor Center and short trails at Willow Springs Picnic Area and the Scenic Drive and Dedication Point Overlooks are wheelchair accessible.

🏕 Nearby 3-Mile Campground provides tent and some RV sites, but no hookups.

👣 Call for schedules of naturalist-guided walks and programs.

🏨 Bonnie Springs Motel is an Old West–themed motel on-site; call (702) 875-4400 for reservations.

RUBY LAKE NATIONAL WILDLIFE REFUGE

*The ringing calls of Trumpeter Swans echo off the snow-capped Ruby Mountains
on this remote eastern Nevada refuge.*

Explorer John C. Fremont was the first to call the 200,000-square-mile desert covering most of Nevada the Great Basin. Early trapper and mountain man Jediah Strong Smith was less polite, describing the region as "completely barren."

Although most of the area is very arid, the Great Basin's few spring-fed marshes sustain a vibrant life zone. Over 160 springs flow into Ruby Lake National Wildlife Refuge, defying the surrounding desert. Birds and other wildlife flock to the 17,000 acres of verdant marsh that lie along the eastern flank of the rugged and scenic Ruby Mountains.

large cottonwoods and willows in the riparian zones provide homes for many songbirds. On adjacent national forest lands, rocky slopes rise to 11,000 feet and provide a haven for an introduced game bird much sought after by birdwatchers – the Himalayan Snowcock. In all, 225 species of birds have used this refuge as home or stopover point.

The Redhead *is just one of the ducks that nests at the refuge in spring and summer.*

HABITAT

The refuge is located at an elevation of 6,000 feet and encompasses not only marsh but meadow, sagebrush, and riparian areas that cover 37,632 acres total. In the wetlands, islands scattered throughout pockets of open water and bulrush marshes provide nesting habitat for ducks, herons, and ibis.

Native sagebrush harbors species endemic to the Great Basin, and the

BIRDS TO LOOK FOR

White-faced Ibis • Trumpeter Swan • Canvasback • Redhead • Northern Harrier • Himalayan Snowcock • Sage Grouse • Sandhill Crane • Western Kingbird • Yellow-breasted Chat • Green-tailed Towhee • Black-throated Sparrow • Sage Sparrow

BIRD LIFE

The bulrush marsh along the 6.5-mile auto tour route, which starts two miles north of refuge headquarters at Bressman Cabin, is the setting of an odd rite between two duck species. These are the Canvasback, one of the largest and fastest-flying ducks in North America, and the Redhead, which resembles the Canvasback, except for its rounder head and shorter, tricolored bill. Redheads frequently lay their eggs in Canvasback nests; the eggs are then incubated and the chicks raised by the Canvasbacks. This type of behavior, called nest parasitism, occurs in as many as 70 percent of the Canvasback that nest at Ruby Lake National Wildlife Refuge.

The Trumpeter Swan – a favorite here – breeds on the refuge's wetlands.

Also on the auto tour route it is possible to spot a colony of 200 pairs of White-faced Ibis, about 2.5 miles along on the right. Other birds that occur along the route include Yellow-headed Blackbirds, Marsh Wrens, and Yellow-breasted Chats.

To experience the other habitats of the refuge, follow County Road 767, which bisects the western side of the refuge. Starting from the south, at Narciss Boat Landing Road, look for nesting Sandhill Cranes in the meadows. White-faced Ibis feed in the meadows, and throughout the area Northern Harriers and Mountain Bluebirds will be hunting their prey – rodents and insects.

The Yellow-breasted Chat *spends much of its time in the sagebrush; start by listening for its jumbled song, a combination of clucks, rattles, and more.*

Still along the county road, in the lower elevations, sagebrush benches hold the sparrows endemic to that habitat – Sage and Black-throated – plus several others, including Vesper and Lark Sparrows. At higher elevations, juniper and pinyon pine areas are home to Green-tailed Towhees, Juniper Titmice, and Blue-gray Gnatcatchers.

The riparian areas along Cave Creek (near headquarters) and near the fish hatchery (one mile south of headquarters) support the greatest concentration of songbirds. Listen in the willow clumps and among the cottonwood trees for the *I'm-so-sweet-sweet-sweet* songs of Yellow Warblers, the scolding calls of Western Kingbirds, and the chattering of Northern Orioles.

Although not found on the refuge, the Himalayan Snowcocks are the primary reason many birders come to this area. This grouselike bird is an introduced species found nowhere else in North America. The search for snowcocks requires a strenuous hike. The area of highest concentration for this very rare species is along the cliffs at the top of Liberty Pass on Ruby Crest Trail, 76 miles from the refuge. It's best to search for them from mid-July through August when the snow has melted.

VISITING

The best season for birdwatching at this refuge is late May and early June, when the many species of breeding birds are establishing their territories. Later in June, after the territories are set up, the birds are more secretive.

Fall is a pleasant time for birdwatching at the refuge too, with migrating birds and large concentrations of waterfowl providing the attraction. Despite the harsh winters, some 60 bird species are tallied in the Christmas bird counts, including Bald Eagles, Rough-legged Hawks, and Trumpeter Swans.

HIGHLIGHTS

During the first two hours after dark, the ringing calls of Trumpeter Swans returning to their roosts can be heard echoing off the mountains. Just take a post near open water. The trumpetlike tones are most intense during a winter full moon, because the increased light makes the swans more active and the cold air conducts sound better.

Site Map and Information

RUBY LAKE NATIONAL WILDLIFE REFUGE

🚗 The refuge is about 65 miles south and east of Elko, or 90 miles north and west of Ely. From the town of Wells, where I-80 and State Highway 93 intersect, take State Highway 93 south to Route 229. Turn south on County Road 767 to reach the refuge entrance.

◻ Daily, 1 hour before sunrise until 2 hours after sunset, year-round.

⬤ Never.

🛈 Ruby Lake National Wildlife Refuge, HC 60, Box 860, Ruby Valley, Nevada 89833. Refuge headquarters are open weekdays, 7 a.m.–4 p.m., excluding holidays.

📞 (775) 779-2237.

💲 None.

♿ Several viewing platforms and parking areas are wheelchair accessible.

🅰 South Ruby Campground, 2 miles south

of headquarters, is open Memorial Day through Labor Day; call (800) 280-2267 for reservations.

🔭 To see Himalayan Snowcocks, contact Elko Guide Service at (775) 744-2277.

🏨 The closest accommodations are in Elko; call the Chamber of Commerce at (775) 738-7135 for listings.

Bosque del Apache National Wildlife Refuge

Join thousands of Snow Geese and Sandhill Cranes in a raucous celebration of life at this central New Mexico river valley refuge.

The Rio Grande – the river that is the heart of New Mexico – pulses strong at Bosque del Apache National Wildlife Refuge. This desert oasis lies along 12 miles of the Rio Grande in river valley that has long been prized by humans for its fertile soil and abundant animal life. From the days of its earliest pueblo-dwelling inhabitants and the area's annexation by the United States in 1846, the yearly drama of the arrival of wintering Sandhill Cranes has animated the cottonwoods, willows, and marshlands of the Rio Grande river's floodplain.

the floodplain to today's productive state. Shallow marshes, manmade impoundments, and cultivated fields supply a winter home to nearly 12,000 cranes; 25,000 geese; and 40,000 ducks – more than ever before. Year-round the refuge is also home to songbirds, deer, elk, bobcats, and mountain lions.

Bird Life

One of the wintering Sandhill Cranes' favorite roosts is just inside the north entrance to the refuge along Old Highway 1; those who arrive early can watch the sunrise and listen to the raucous cranes prepare to spread out to the nearby feeding grounds.

The area around the Visitor Center, about four miles farther down the road, is a good place to see smaller birds and to gather information before setting out on the auto tour. A sign at the Visitor Center lists the numbers of ducks, cranes, eagles, and more that have been sited on the wildlife refuge.

Hooded Merganser *winter at Bosque del Apache, along with hordes of other waterfowl.*

Habitat

By the time this 86-square-mile refuge was established in 1939, the river had been diminished by irrigation and the wintering crane flocks had been decimated by uncontrolled hunting. Only 17 Sandhill Cranes wintered along the cottonwood-lined Rio Grande, an area referred to as Bosque del Apache, or woods of the Apaches.

It has taken over 50 years of creative and patient management to bring

BIRDS TO LOOK FOR

Snow Goose • Ross's Goose • Gadwell • Northern Pintail • Hooded Merganser • Bald Eagle • Cooper's Hawk • Golden Eagle • Wild Turkey • Gambel's Quail • Sandhill Crane • Greater Roadrunner • Vermilion Flycatcher • Pyrrhuloxia • Blue Grosbeak • Song Sparrow

Migrating flights of Sandhill Cranes often fly so high they cannot be seen from the ground.

During winter, the birds attracted to the Visitor Center by the ever-full birdfeeders include hordes of White-crowned Sparrows, and often Pyrrhuloxias, Gambel's Quails, and Spotted Towhees. A Cooper's Hawk, drawn by the hundreds of birds, can often be seen in the cottonwoods around the buildings.

The 12-mile, one-way auto tour (with a two-way cutoff for those who want to end the tour early) offers looks at some of the highest concentrations of waterfowl, cranes, and eagles in the Southwest. Look for Gadwalls, Hooded Mergansers, Northern Pintails, and Ruddy Ducks in the ponds and diked lakes next to the gravel road. Consider bringing a camera with a telephoto lens – a 300-millimeter lens and a car-window mount will create great close-ups. Any winter gathering of waterfowl draws Bald Eagles; a few are always seen on the tour route, along with the occasional Golden Eagle.

The auto tour offers plenty of opportunity to see the Snow Goose and the less common Ross's Goose. Although the two species are the same color and have the same general shape, the smaller Ross's Goose has a shorter neck and a much smaller bill.

The Song Sparrow's *plumage is variable, but its call – a nasal* **chimp** *– distinguishes it.*

Wintering sparrows along the southern end of the auto tour's marsh loop include Brewer's, Lincoln's, Song, Sage, Vesper, and Savannah Sparrows. A short walk along the Lagoon Trail and the Marsh Overlook Trail will increase your chances of spotting the Greater Roadrunner.

Although winter is prime time for visiting Bosque del Apache, other seasons have their appeal as well. In

April and May neotropical songbird migration is a key attraction, along with breeding ducks (including Cinnamon Teal and Redheads). Summer is hot and mosquitoes abound but nesting species including Vermilion Flycatchers, Say's Phoebes, Blue Grosbeaks, and Wild Turkeys make the discomforts worthwhile.

VISITING

Bosque del Apache National Wildlife Refuge is probably the most popular birdwatching site in New Mexico. In this sparsely populated state, it is one of the only places where birdwatchers are likely to run into each other. In fact, the Visitor Center and tour loop can be downright crowded on winter weekends. Winter weather can be quite lovely with sun and warm temperatures, but it can also be as cold as 10°F. During the spring, summer, and fall, mosquito repellent is a must, unless you wish to drive the tour route with your windows closed.

HIGHLIGHTS

Many consider the yearly Festival of the Cranes, held in mid-November, to be the nation's premier birding event. This annual series of workshops, lectures, demonstrations, and guided tours has enchanted thousands of adults and children for over a decade. Contact the Socorro Chamber of Commerce at (505) 835-0424.

Site Map and Information

BOSQUE DEL APACHE NATIONAL WILDLIFE REFUGE

◨ The refuge is 90 miles south of Albuquerque off I-25. Take exit 139 at the tiny town of San Antonio, and continue east a quarter of a mile on US 380 to San Antonito. Following the refuge signs, turn right onto Old Highway 1 at the flashing signal. Proceed 9 miles to the Visitor Center.

◻ The auto-tour route and hiking trails are open from one hour before sunrise to one hour after sunset, year-round.

⬤ Never.

🅷 Bosque del Apache National Wildlife Refuge, P.O. Box 1246, Socorro, NM, 87801. The Visitor Center is open weekdays, 7:30 a.m.–4 p.m., and weekends, 8 a.m.–4:30 p.m.

🄲 (505) 835-1828; http://southwest.fws.gov/refuges/newmex/bosque

⑤ $3 per vehicle, per day.

🅱 Visitor Center, picnic area, and viewing platforms are wheelchair accessible.

🅰 Nearby Birdwatchers RV Park offers RV and tent sites; call (505) 835-1366.

🈳 During the winter the refuge often schedules free weekend tours; stop by the Visitor Center for a schedule.

🛏 Casa Blanca Bed & Breakfast is 8 miles from the refuge; call (505) 835-3027 for reservations. Or call the Socorro Chamber of Commerce at (505) 835-0424 for listings.

SAUVIE ISLAND WILDLIFE AREA

This island preserve at the confluence of two major rivers in northern Oregon is a prime meeting site for migrating birds.

When the explorers Meriwether Lewis and William Clark visited Sauvie Island in April of 1806, they reported that it was teeming with waterfowl. A visit to this historic location allows birdwatchers to imagine what it would have been like to go birdwatching with Captain Lewis, who was not only an adventurer but also a ground-breaking naturalist.

The Great Egret, *a large heron, can be easily distinguished from the Great Blue Heron by its black legs and feet.*

For centuries before European occupation, the island was a summer and fall home to Multnomah Indians, who used the rich area to hunt, fish, and gather food.

HABITAT

Interconnected sloughs, streams, and ponds make this 12,000-acre wildlife area an ideal wetland habitat for birds. Farming operations provide 1,000 acres of grains for foraging ducks and geese. The island, the southern half of which is privately owned, once flooded regularly with the seasonal rush of high water from the Willamette and Columbia Rivers. Now a dike system on the southern half of the site controls the water levels of some of the wetlands, but in most of the wildlife area the water levels vary daily with the tidal fluctuation of the Columbia River.

The northern half of Sauvie Island serves as a rest stop for two to three million migratory wildfowl and as the winter home for more than 200,000 ducks and geese.

BIRD LIFE

Each spring and fall over 2,500 Sandhill Cranes stop on Sauvie Island on their way to and from California. They are most easily seen in the fields along Oak Island Road. At road's end, on the shore of Sturgeon Lake, visit the Oak Island portion of the wildlife area to see some of the two dozen other species of waterfowl that rest on the island, including Northern Pintail, American Wigeon, and Snow Goose.

Sauvie Island is known for its sparrows. The blackberry tangles at the entrance to Oak Island provide a fine opportunity to spot many species, especially during the winter. The large wintering flocks often include White-crowned, Golden-crowned, Fox, Lincoln's, and Song Sparrows.

BIRDS TO LOOK FOR

Great Blue Heron • Great Egret • Snow Goose • Tundra Swan • American Wigeon • Northern Pintail • Bald Eagle • Merlin • Sandhill Crane • Long-billed Dowitcher • Caspian Tern • Western Scrub-Jay • Fox Sparrow • Golden-crowned Sparrow

The Great Blue Heron is at home in this island habitat.

During the summer, after the hordes of waterfowl fly north to breed, Oak Island is a hot spot for resident and breeding birds, including Black-headed Grosbeaks, Bullock's Orioles, and White-breasted Nuthatches. The two-mile Oak Island Trail (closed in the winter), offers great summer birding; look for Bewick's Wrens, Western Scrub-Jays, and Bushtits.

Oak Island is not the only good birding spot on Sauvie. In late summer and fall when water levels are low, check the mudflats at Coon Point Lookout (off Reeder Road) for thousands of migrating shorebirds, including Long-billed Dowitchers, Dunlins, Western and Least Sandpipers, plus Greater and Lesser Yellowlegs.

The Merlin *uses its powerful hooked beak to sever the spinal column of its prey.*

As you travel driveable roads in the wildlife area during winter, look for some of the 40 to 50 Bald Eagles that winter on the island. (Numbers peak in February.) Other raptors, including Red-tailed and Rough-legged Hawks, can be spotted on power poles or soaring overhead. Peregrine Falcons hunt waterfowl and Merlins chase small birds. Thousands of Tundra Swans provide another winter birding treat; look for them in the fields along Reeder Road.

Rentenaar Road, a left turn off of Reeder Road past Coon Point, is a year-round hot spot for sparrows, including Swamp, Harris's, and Clay-colored Sparrows. Wetlands along this road also harbor up to 14 species of ducks in the winter, including Northern Shoveler and Northern Pintail. During March and April, bring a spotting scope and walk from the parking lot at the end of the road to the

253

top of the dike to see up to 20 Bald Eagles feeding on spawning carp. At the end of Reeder Road, hike the 2.5-mile trail to the Warrior Rock Lighthouse site. This trail is adjacent to the Columbia River, where Buffleheads and Common Goldeneyes dive for fish and, in the summer, Caspian Terns fly overhead.

VISITING

Many of the 250 bird species on the Sauvie Island checklist can be found here during the spring and fall. Although access to the interior of the refuge is not allowed during winter, sheer numbers of waterfowl provide the attraction. Most species can be seen from the wildlife area's two main

access roads – Oak Island Road and Reeder Road. Waterfowl hunting is permitted seasonally every other day, and it is very popular here. To plan a visit on a no-hunting day, call ahead for information.

HIGHLIGHTS

Spend the sunset hour on Coon Point watching Great Blue Herons hunt for minnows. This wetland bird, common throughout North America, deserves special notice here, where populations are extraordinarily high. At times, as many as 100 herons, plus large numbers of Great Egrets, can be observed on Sturgeon Lake, in the center of the refuge.

Site Map and Information

SAUVIE ISLAND WILDLIFE AREA

🚗 Sauvie Island is 10 miles northwest of downtown Portland, at the confluence of the Willamette and Columbia Rivers. Take US Route 30 to the Sauvie Island Bridge. The wildlife area is concentrated on the northern end, and can be reached via Reeder Road, Oak Island Road, and the Sauvie Island Road.

🔲 Day use only, 4 a.m.–10 p.m., year-round.

◉ There is no access to the interior of the refuge from October 1 through April 15, but most bird species can be watched from the main access roads.

ℹ Sauvie Island Wildlife Area, 18330 NW Sauvie Island Road, Portland, OR 97231. Visitor Center is open weekdays, 8 a.m.–12 p.m. and 1 p.m.–5 p.m.

📞 (503) 621-3488.

💲 Parking permit is $3.50 per day or $11 per year.

♿ A wheelchair-accessible wildlife-viewing platform is available on Reeder Road, just north of the Columbia/ Multnomah County Line.

🏕 Nearby Reeder Beach RV Park allows limited tent camping; call (503) 621-3098.

🏨 None.

🛏 There are 2 bed-and-breakfasts on the island: Westlund's River's Edge B&B at (503) 621-9856 and Sauvie Island B&B at (503) 621-3216. (There are no gas stations or restaurants on the island.)

BEAR RIVER MIGRATORY BIRD REFUGE

*Waterfowl thrive here on the wetlands between the fresh water of the Bear River
and the alkaline waters of Utah's Great Salt Lake.*

In 1983 the Great Salt Lake, which lies just east of the Bear River Migratory Refuge, rose to historic levels and inundated the area. Wildlife habitat and visitor facilities alike were destroyed in the flood. Tenacious volunteers began working to restore the refuge as soon as the waters receded, and today it boasts huge numbers of swans, ducks, and shorebirds. A new Visitor Center is being planned; it is scheduled to open in 2002.

The Loggerhead Shrike *features a banditlike mask and a small hooked beak.*

HABITAT

The Bear River is a small, snow-fed stream that originates in the Uinta Mountains of Utah, travels north to Wyoming through Idaho, and then back again into Utah, where it meets the Great Salt Lake at the refuge. The wetlands created by the meeting of the river and the lake offer a waterfowl haven.

During the summer, much of the river's water is pumped away for agricultural use. Historically, low water levels in the marshes at the delta contributed to huge waterfowl die-offs due to avian botulism. Since the inception of the refuge in 1928, wildlife managers had struggled to understand what caused these die-offs and to improve conditions. The recent flooding, although very destructive, provided an opportunity for managers

to reduce botulism by creating smaller, deeper lakes and wetlands (called impoundments), which they can use to manipulate water levels during botulism outbreaks. This management technique has made the Bear River refuge one of the premier autumn swan-watching sites in the United States.

BIRD LIFE

Along Forest Street, which leads into the refuge from the freeway, open fields, desert scrub, and the winding river provide great habitat for Short-eared Owls, Loggerhead Shrikes, and Northern Harriers. In the fall Horned Larks and Brewer's, Vesper, and Savannah Sparrows are common. On the refuge itself, a 12 mile auto tour provides access to large wetlands and lakes that harbor a grand variety of ducks, swans, geese, and shorebirds. American White Pelicans reside at the refuge much of the year, using the fish-filled pools as a

---

BIRDS TO LOOK FOR

Eared Grebe • Western Grebe • American White Pelican • Tundra Swan • Trumpeter Swan • Green-wing Teal • Redhead • Bufflehead • Northern Harrier • American Avocet • Marbled Godwit • Red-necked Phalarope • Short-eared Owl • Loggerhead Shrike • Brewer's Sparrow

Look for Western Grebes swimming on the Great Salt Lake.

food source. During breeding season the pelicans nest on an island in the Great Salt Lake, but they gather fish for their young at the Bear River refuge.

Another sight not to be missed during nesting season in June and July is that of young Western Grebes riding atop their parents' backs. Other nesters include American Avocets, Black-necked Stilts, Willets, Common Snipes, and Snowy Plovers. Look also for the young of Pied-billed and Eared Grebes, Northern Shovelers, and Redheads.

The advent of fall brings up to half a million ducks and geese to miles of wetlands along the auto tour. Birders who augment their binoculars with a higher-powered spotting scope will find it easier to identify the many Green-winged Teal, American

Wigeon, Common Goldeneye, Red-breasted Merganser, and Bufflehead. Fall (and spring) migrating shorebirds include Marbled Godwits, Red-necked Phalaropes, Snowy Plovers, and more.

The swans are the central fall attraction at Bear River. For a challenge, look among the thousands of Tundra Swans for the uncommon Trumpeter Swan (North America's other indigenous swan) or Mute Swan (an introduced Eurasian species). Although Mute Swans are the least likely swans to be spotted on the refuge, their S-shaped neck-stance and the adults' bright orange bills and forehead knobs make them the easiest to identify.

The Short-eared Owl *roosts on low perches or on the ground during daylight hours.*

Distinguishing Trumpeter from Tundra Swans is not easy. The most obvious difference is the Trumpeter's much larger size. Look also at their bills: the adult Tundra Swan has a black bill with a bit of a dip along the top and a yellow spot near the eye; the Trumpeter's bill is black with a straight-angle profile and no yellow.

VISITING

Although Bear River Migratory Bird Refuge covers 74,000 acres, most of the interior is closed to visitors to allow the waterfowl to feed and rest without being disturbed. Fortunately, the auto tour loop along the refuge's main lakes provides fine opportunities to view most of the 221 species on the refuge's bird list. (Don't be shocked

that the refuge is a swan-hunting site; hunters are given special access to certain areas during hunting season.)

The auto tour route is open year-round, but from January to mid-March road conditions are often trying and there are not many birds to see.

HIGHLIGHTS

Starting in mid-October, up to 35,000 Tundra Swans migrating from their Canadian nesting grounds gather on the refuge's lakes and wetlands. Their call, a quavering, high-pitched *oo-oo-oo!* is synonymous with autumn at Bear River. Usually the water freezes over by late November and the swans continue south, most of them to California.

Site Map and Information

BEAR RIVER MIGRATORY BIRD REFUGE

🚗 From Salt Lake City, take I-15 north 56 miles, past Brigham City to Exit 366. Take Forest Street east approximately 15 miles to the refuge entrance.

🗓 Daily, sunrise to sunset, year-round.

⬤ From January through mid-March, the auto tour is sometimes closed due to bad road conditions. Call ahead.

ℹ Bear River Migratory Bird Refuge, 58 South 950 West, Brigham City, UT 84302. There is a self-serve brochure kiosk at the refuge entrance, at the beginning of the tour route. A Visitor Center is scheduled to open in early 2002.

📞 (435) 723-5887; www.rg.fws.gov/refuges/BEAR/bear

Ⓢ None.

♿ The wildlife viewing platform is wheelchair accessible.

⛺ None on-site. There is camping in nearby Brigham City, Willard, and Mantura;

call the Brigham City Chamber of Commerce at (435) 723-3931 for listings.

🚶 None.

🏨 There are hotels, motels, and bed-and-breakfasts in nearby Brigham City; call the Chamber of Commerce at (see above) for listings.

OLYMPIC NATIONAL PARK

*Birds throng to the wilderness beaches, old-growth forests, and high peaks
of this coastal Washington national park.*

The lumberman's ax had already begun to fall in the Olympic Peninsula of northwestern Washington in the late 1800s when several forward-looking conservationists began to lobby for protection of this matchless wilderness. It was not until 1938 that the area was afforded the full protection of national park status.

Unlike many other national parks, there are no roads through the heart of this huge territory. (The park encompasses close to a million acres, 95 percent of which is wilderness). Instead, visitors may explore the perimeter of the park, approaching its interior via a number of different natural entrances to sample the stunning landscape within.

The Spotted Owl *takes refuge in the park's old-growth forest.*

HABITAT

Olympic National Park is one of North America's most diverse parks, the only one to combine high-elevation snowcapped peaks, temperate rain forest, and a 63-mile-long strip of windswept coastline, much of it accessible only to hikers. Before the Spotted Owl controversy of the 1980s and 1990s (when environmentalists and loggers went head to head over the fate of this species), the most famous features of Olympic National Park were the spectacular Olympic Mountains, which form a circular range in its center.

Temperate rain forest occurs only in New Zealand, southern Chile, southern Australia, and here on the northwest coast of the United States and Canada. Drenched by more than 12 feet of precipitation each year, this climate is the wettest in all of the lower 48 states. Majestic Sitka spruce and western hemlock grow to world-record heights – some nearly 250 feet tall and up to 58 feet in circumference.

BIRD LIFE

Hurricane Ridge, 17 miles south of the park's portal town of Port Angeles, provides a good starting point from which to enjoy the park's celebrated views and watch the alpine birds that dwell in the mountain hemlock, subalpine fir, and Alaska yellow cedar forests. Look at any time of year for Common Ravens and Gray Jays and, in summer, for Varied Thrushes among the trees.

BIRDS TO LOOK FOR

Harlequin Duck • Surf Scoter • Black Oystercatcher • Black Turnstone • Common Murre • Pigeon Guillemot • Marbled Murrelet • Spotted Owl • Vaux's Swift • Pileated Woodpecker • Gray Jay • Common Raven • Winter Wren • Varied Thrush

The Winter Wren can be identified by its stubby, often upturned tail, and the dark belly.

For rain forest exploration, two of the most productive sites accessible by car are the Hoh Rain Forest (91 miles southwest on Highway 101 out of Port Angeles) and the Quinault Rain Forest (farther south along 101, then east via North Shore Road). Along the short nature trails found in both of these forests, look for American Dippers, Vaux's Swifts (during breeding season), Winter Wrens, Varied Thrushes, and Pileated Woodpeckers.

Everyone wants to see the famous Spotted Owls and another endangered species, the Marbled Murrelet, but they are elusive, even for the pros. To increase the odds of spotting a Spotted Owl, look in dense,

The Common Raven *is numerous in the mountains and along the coastline.*

large stands of big trees, usually on a slope and near water. In addition to the Hoh Rain Forest, check the upper Quinault Valley in the southwestern part of the park and the Elwha Valley in the northern section. Marbled Murrelets nest in these forests, too, but they are extremely secretive nesters. To greatly increase your chances of seeing them, bring a spotting scope and check the salt water along the Strait of Juan De Fuca, and the harbor at Port Angeles. Finally, head toward the ocean to experience the park's wild coastline. Although much of Olympic National Park's beach is wilderness, several sites can be accessed by car. Rialto Beach is reached via a paved road just north of the town of Forks. Look for flocks of seabirds just off the southern end of the beach. Surf Scoters are common and Harlequin Ducks are also seen regularly. In early summer use a scope to view the nesting sites of Common Murres, Pigeon Guillemots, and Pelagic Cormorants.

Another fine coastal birding area is Ruby Beach, where the sand is pink because it contains tiny garnet crystals. Look here for Surfbirds, Black Turnstones, and a less common rock shorebird, the Rock Sandpiper.

VISITING

Birders may feel overwhelmed by this huge park, but a long weekend affords plenty of time to sample the habitats. Fall often brings clear weather and

migrating shorebirds and waterfowl. The rest of the year the weather can be cool and wet. Spring and summer are good for spotting nesting seabirds offshore. Winter is the time to look for birds in the forests and wintering ducks in the bays and estuaries.

HIGHLIGHTS

Bald Eagles and Black Oystercatchers accompany intrepid overnight hikers on the park's spectacular wilderness beaches. Beach backpacking requires special safety precautions (read the visitor publications for details), but close contact with the birds of tidal pools and surf is worth it.

Site Map and Information

OLYMPIC NATIONAL PARK

🚗 From Seattle, take a ferry 90 miles to Port Angeles, on the northern edge of the park. Call (206) 464-6400 for ferry schedules and fares. From Olympia, take US Highway 101 northwest about 50 miles to reach the southeastern edge of the park.

🗓 Daily, 24 hours, year-round.

⬤ Bad weather conditions may cause some roads and other areas to close temporarily. Call (360) 452-0329 for 24-hour recorded road and weather information.

ℹ️ Olympic National Park, 600 East Park Avenue, Port Angeles, WA 98362. Visitor Center, at 3002 Mount Angeles Road, Port Angeles, is open daily, year-round; call ahead for hours.

📞 (360) 452-0330; www.nps.gov/olym

💲 $10 per vehicle for a 7-day pass.

♿ The Visitor Center, several campgrounds, lodges, and nature trails are wheelchair accessible. Contact the Visitor Center for a brochure containing specifics. To reach TDD, call (360) 452-0306.

🏕 The 17 campgrounds on-site are available on a first-come, first-served basis.

🎫 The Olympic Park Institute offers tours (for groups of 12 or more) and educational seminars, including some about birdwatching. Call (360) 928-3720.

🏨 Several motels, cabins, and lodges are available within the park and nearby; call the Port Angeles Chamber of Commerce at (360) 452-2363 for listings.

Skagit Wildlife Area

*It may not snow often in the coastal areas of western Washington, but the winter
fields look white anyway – covered with Snow Geese and Tundra Swans.*

The Skagit is the
third-largest river
on the west coast of the
contiguous United
States. Nearly 3,000
streams contribute fresh water to this
majestic river, which in turn enriches
the great Puget Sound.

The delta surrounding the Skagit
Wildlife Area is rich agricultural land
that produces brilliant tulips and
daffodils in the spring, and
endless acres of vegetables
throughout the summer and
fall. Of the delta's extensive
fields and marshes, 15,000
acres have been set aside by
the state of Washington; here,
waterfowl and raptors
dominate the landscape during
migrations and in winter.

Habitat

These tidelands and intertidal
marshes provide one of the most
important and productive waterfowl
wintering areas in the Pacific flyway
and certainly one of the best estuaries
for birds in Washington. The shallow
bays and adjacent farmlands of the
Skagit Flats (as the area is known
locally) support large numbers of
swans, geese, ducks, and raptors.

Bird Life

Although the Skagit region is world
famous for its cultivated fields of
tulips, to the birdwatcher's eye it is
the dreary, windy dead of winter that
brings the most vibrant life to the area.
In November the party is just getting
started with the arrival of Trumpeter

and Tundra Swans migrating from
their summer homes in Alaska. Other
waterfowl begin to arrive at this time,
too, including the first of 27,000 Snow
Geese, many of which have migrated
from Wrangel Island in Siberia. Other
goose species include Greater White-
fronted Geese, Brant, and, of course,
Canada Geese.

The Dunlin
*seems
hunchbacked
when bent over
because of
its very short neck.*

More than 125,000 ducks, including
Mallards, American Wigeon, Northern
Pintail, and Green-winged Teal winter
here, too. The waterfowl numbers
peak in November but stay high
through February. Observe the winter
festivities of the waterfowl – which
include loafing in muddy grain fields
and dabbling in marshy waters – along
Fir Island Road, starting about a mile
west of the town of Conway (exit 221
off I-5) and continuing for six miles to
the road's end.

BIRDS TO LOOK FOR

**Greater White-Fronted Goose •
Snow Goose • Brant • Trumpeter
Swan • Tundra Swan • American
Wigeon • Green-winged Teal •
Gyrfalcon • Peregrine Falcon • Sora •
Greater Yellowlegs • Dunlin • Snowy
Owl • Short-eared Owl**

Skagit is known for its wintering waterfowl, including Brant, a species of goose.

The Jensen Access, which is the nucleus of the wildlife area, is located near the west end of Fir Island Road (about 2.5 miles west of Wiley Road), at the end of Maupin Road. After parking, approach the dike quietly and look over cautiously – this area is known for its large flocks of Dunlin, and also for thousands of Snow Geese.

Wherever waterfowl gather in numbers like this, predators will be lurking about – or, more likely, soaring about. Skagit Flats is famous for its wintering raptors, including Gyrfalcons, a species seldom found farther south. Look also for Peregrine Falcons, Bald Eagles, Northern Harriers, and Snowy and Short-eared Owls.

The Snowy Owl, *if immature or female, may possess dark bands and spots on its otherwise snowy plumage.*

One of the best places to look for all these species is on the two-mile loop trail beginning at the Skagit Wildlife Area headquarters. In the summer this is a good place to look for nesting species, including Tree Swallows, Marsh Wrens, Virginia Rails and Sora, and Cinnamon Teal. The Jensen Access, headquarters, and the nearby North Fork Access (near the Jensen Access) areas are best visited after hunting season, which lasts from mid-September through January. February turns out to be a great time to birdwatch here; the hunters are gone and the waterfowl seem to know it.

For birding in Skagit Wildlife Area during hunting season, visit the two new reserves that will remain closed to hunting year-around. One is the Johnson-

DeBay Slough Swan Reserve, northeast of the town of Mount Vernon, about 15 miles from headquarters. Contact headquarters for a map to the site.

The Hayton-Fir Island Farm Reserve, three miles west of headquarters off of Fir Island Road, is great for spotting lots of Snow Geese. Plans for this area include a short walking trail along the dike. Visitors are likely to spot more shorebirds here, including Lesser and Greater Yellowlegs and Western Sandpipers.

VISITING

The best time to visit Skagit Wildlife Area is November through late February. Go early in the day, before the wind picks up, but stay for sunset to hear the geese and swans as they head to their shallow-water roosts –

honking and flying low on rustling wings. Management requests that birdwatchers be considerate of local landowners and their property.

If birders must enter areas open to hunting, they should wear camouflage clothing and avoid disturbing the hunters. Avoid the headquarters area altogether during pheasant-hunting season, which runs from late September through late November.

HIGHLIGHTS

More than 3,400 swans winter in the Skagit Valley. Spend some time listening to the trumpetlike call of the Trumpeter Swan and compare it to the higher-pitched honk of the smaller, more abundant Tundra Swan. The two species often mingle in the same flock.

Site Map and Information

SKAGIT WILDLIFE AREA

Headquarters are 60 miles north of Seattle, about 8 miles south of Mount Vernon, and approximately 2 miles west and 1 mile south of Conway. Take Exit 221 off I-5 at Conway, head west on Fir Island Road to Wylie Road, then turn south to reach wildlife area.

Daily, sunrise to sunset, year-round.

Never.

Skagit Wildlife Area, 21961 Wylie Road, Mount Vernon, WA. The site has no Visitor Center.

(360) 445-4441

$10 per vehicle, per year; decals are available where hunting and fishing licenses are sold.

The Hayton-Fir Island Farm Reserve and Johnson-DeBay Slough Swan Reserve are wheelchair accessible.

The nearest campsites are at Bayview State Park, 7 miles west of nearby Burlington. Call (800) 452-5687 for reservations.

None.

Motels and bed-and-breakfasts are available in nearby Mount Vernon; contact the Chamber of Commerce at (360) 428-8507 for listings.

SEEDSKADEE NATIONAL WILDLIFE REFUGE

Join the birds of sage and river in celebrating Wyoming's historic wild west at this riparian refuge.

Early Native Americans called this portion of the Green River the "Seeds-ke-dee-agie," meaning "River of the Prairie Hen," but it was simply the Green River to the mountain men who used it as a crossroads from 1825 until 1840.

Although the area was popular with Indians and fur trappers, and the river was used as a passageway by Oregon Trail emigrants, Seeds-ke-dee-agie offered very little attraction for white settlers. The location was remote, the soil poor, and the climate cold and arid. It was not until the 1880s that settlement in the area around the refuge began in earnest.

The Cinnamon Teal may be identified by the male's strikingly cinnamon-colored head, neck, and belly.

BIRDS TO LOOK FOR

Trumpeter Swan • Cinnamon Teal • Northern Pintail • Bald Eagle • Golden Eagle • Prairie Falcon • Sage Grouse • Sandhill Crane • Mountain Plover • Burrowing Owl • Mountain Bluebird • Sage Thrasher • Sage Sparrow • Gray-crowned Rosy-Finch

HABITAT

Seedskadee National Wildlife Refuge was established in 1965 to mitigate the habitat loss when Flaming Gorge and Fontenelle reservoirs were constructed in the Green River area. The 26,382-acre refuge lies in the heart of the Great Basin country, where the summers are short and the winters long and severe. The refuge forms a very narrow riparian corridor that stretches along 36 miles of the Green River in southwest Wyoming.

Before the advent of modern management, the refuge's marshlands were seasonally disturbed by either floods or droughts. The flow of water is now managed and river water is directed into natural basins as needed. Dense stands of native grasses and shrubs are maintained to provide cover for nesting ducks. In the cottonwoods and willow thickets of the bottomlands, the vegetation is managed to produce a mix of older and younger trees, which provides food and shelter to songbirds, hawks, and owls, and other wildlife.

In the sagebrush and on the lower riparian terraces, years of heavy livestock grazing decimated the native plants, but fences and prescribed fires are being used to bring back the vitality of this refuge habitat.

BIRD LIFE

Although dam construction and other changes have altered the habitat in and around Seedskadee, many of the

The refuge's sagebrush areas are home to arid-land birds, such as this Sage Grouse.

birds that the Indians and early settlers knew are the same birds seen today. Canada geese and a variety of ducks have nested along the river for centuries; Sage Grouse, Mountain Bluebirds, and other arid-land birds still call from the sage shrubs. The refuge list, compiled since the early 1900s, now includes over 225 birds.

Though the Native Americans named this area after the Sage Grouse, they certainly were familiar with the other, less conspicuous sage-dwellers, too. In any sagebrush areas along the refuge's auto tour, listen on spring and summer mornings for Sage Thrashers (they have a robin-like song) and Sage Sparrow (these sing a series of chords).

The Burrowing Owl *can be differentiated from other small owls by its longer legs.*

Also along the tour route, a handful of Sandhill Cranes nest in the wet meadows. In the wetlands, look for nesting Trumpeter Swans, Northern Pintails, and Cinnamon Teal.

Just south of headquarters, walk the dike tops in mid-June and into July to see the Sage Grouse hens bring their new broods to the lower river terraces to drink.

West of the refuge headquarters, across Highway 372, several pairs of Burrowing Owls can often be spotted during nesting season. This area, called the Dry Creek unit, is fenced, but birders are welcome to walk inside the fence looking for the owls and the other species common in this area, including

Ferruginous Hawks, Golden Eagles, and Prairie Falcons. These many raptors prey on the scattered white-tailed prairie dog towns found here. Another less commonly observed bird, the Mountain Plover, also nests on Dry Creek Unit. Check barren-looking areas for the plovers.

In the early fall at Seedskadee, shorebirds stop in migration; look for Baird's Sandpipers along the river and Least Sandpipers in the wetlands. Trumpeter Swans arrive in the fall, too.

Winter is a good time to spot the Trumpeter Swans that stay over in the refuge all winter; look also for Golden and Bald Eagles and Rough-Legged Hawks. During normal to severe winters, Gray-crowned Rosy-Finches are regular visitors to the feeders at headquarters.

VISITING

Summer and fall are the best seasons to visit the refuge. In the fall the moose are in rut and Sandhill Cranes are staging for migration along the river and in the wetlands. The best variety of waterfowl is seen in October. In the spring, nesting and calling birds are the attraction, but the mosquitos often hold visitors hostage.

HIGHLIGHTS

To experience the best the refuge has to offer, float the river on a summer day. Look for Golden Eagle nests, Great Blue Heron rookeries, and Red-tailed and Swainson's Hawks' nests. Boat rentals and commercially outfitted trips are available; contact the refuge for details.

Site Map and Information

SEEDSKADEE NATIONAL WILDLIFE REFUGE

🚗 From the city of Green River, take I-80 west to State Highway 372. Exit at La Barge Road and continue northwest to refuge headquarters, a 39-mile drive in all.

🕐 Daily, sunrise to sunset, year-round.

⬤ Although the refuge lands are open daily, some roads may be closed seasonally.

ℹ️ Seedskadee National Wildlife Refuge, P.O. Box 700, Green River, Wyoming 82935. A small Visitor Center is located in refuge headquarters.

☎ (307) 875-2187; www.r6fws.gov/refuges/seedskad

$ None.

♿ Visitor Center is wheelchair accessible.

⛺ None on-site, but 4 campgrounds available upstream of the refuge. The nearest is at Slate Creek, which offers primitive camping for free along County Road 8; call (800) FL-GORGE for details.

🎣 Contact refuge headquarters for a complete list of permitted outfitters.

🏨 Hotels and motels are available in Green River, about 40 miles northwest of the refuge. There are no restaurants or other services near the refuge. Contact the Green River Chamber of Commerce at (307) 875-5711 for details.

YELLOWSTONE NATIONAL PARK

*The world's first national park provides a fabulously beautiful
backdrop to the West's best birds.*

Yellowstone was the first national park ever founded. It is also incredibly popular. In fact, with 3.1 million guests visiting the park's 2.2 million acres each year, park management continually looks for ways to spread out the impact on this treasure that sometimes seems to be too well loved.

The powerful features that first led to the preservation of Yellowstone as a

The Osprey *is now fairly common at the park due to conservationists' efforts.*

national park were geological: there are more geysers and hot springs here than found in the rest of the world altogether. Areas of concentrated geothermal activity – geyser basins, as they are called – create openings in the forests and attract a wide variety of wildlife.

HABITAT

Because most of the park is protected as wilderness, this rich tapestry of mountains, rivers, and meadows is stressed by its many admirers only on the edges. The interior ecosystem provides a wide range of virtually

undisturbed habitat types that some have compared to Africa's Serengeti, and it is home to the largest and most varied wildlife populations found in North America. Large mammals, such as bison, elk, and grizzly and black bears are a prime feature, and wolves have been reintroduced recently. Birds (over 300 documented species) provide dashing color to Yellowstone's ravishing wildlife backdrop.

BIRD LIFE

The popular Fishing Bridge, on the north shores of Yellowstone Lake, is one of the best birding spots in the park. Even children can easily spot and identify their fellow fishermen: Belted Kingfishers, Ospreys, and American White Pelicans. Look farther offshore, both here and at the Lake Hotel waterfront, to spot ducks, gulls, and terns such as Barrow's Goldeneyes, California Gulls, and Caspian Terns. Smaller birds found around the Fishing Bridge Museum include Chipping Sparrows, Red Crossbills, and Mountain Chickadees.

From Fishing Bridge, birders driving north along the Yellowstone

BIRDS TO LOOK FOR

American White Pelican • Harlequin Duck • Barrow's Goldeneye • Osprey • Swainson's Hawk • Golden Eagle • California Gull • Caspian Tern • Great Gray Owl • Red-naped Sapsucker • Violet-green Swallow • American Dipper • Mountain Bluebird • Western Tanager • Western Meadowlark • Red Crossbill •

The Western Tanager breeds in the park's coniferous forests.

River may spot American Dippers, Harlequin Ducks, and Swainson's Hawks. A hike into Yellowstone's own Grand Canyon, north of Fishing Bridge near Canyon Junction, offers an opportunity to birdwatch in some of the most spectacular scenery anywhere. The waterfalls, cliffs, and subalpine forest are so inspiring that birdwatchers may forget to look at the abundant Violet-green Swallows and Clark's Nutcrackers.

While still in the canyon area, consider going on a Great Gray

The Great Gray Owl *is the largest owl in North America; listen for its call, a series of whoos.*

Owl hunt. Although chances of seeing one of these enigmatic Yellowstone birds are slim, up to 100 pair nest in the park and are seen sometimes around Canyon Junction. Dawn and dusk are the times to try.

Even farther north, the road up Dunraven Pass will bring birdwatchers within easy striking distance of the alpine zone – the habitat above 10,000 feet. The three-mile, high-altitude hike along Chittenden Road Trail provides a rare panoramic view of the park. Allow several hours and bring lots of drinking water. Along the way look for Blue Grouse, Hairy Woodpeckers, American Pipits, Golden Eagles, and Steller's Jays.

Head north again and take a side-trip into some of Yellowstone's lower, open sagebrush country, found by heading east from Tower Junction. The grasslands of the foothills yield Sage Thrashers, Golden Eagles, Western Meadowlarks, Red-tailed Hawks, Vesper Sparrows, and more.

Forty miles west of this area, in the northwestern corner of the park, is one of the best birding areas in all of

Yellowstone – the Mammoth Hot Springs vicinity. Near Mammoth Campground, look in the conifers for the common Williamson's Sapsucker and in the aspens for the rarer Red-naped Sapsucker. At the hot springs themselves birdwatchers might spot a Mountain Bluebird or a Townsend's Solitaire. Killdeers are often seen on the ground near the thermal features.

VISITING

To observe a diversity of birds, visit during early breeding season (from the beginning of June to early July) and again after the young have fledged (mid-August to mid-September). Because visitors sometimes appear in overwhelming numbers, birdwatchers should be on their best behavior, making make every effort to not disturb the birds of Yellowstone, especially those that are nesting.

HIGHLIGHTS

The geysers – and hot springs, fumaroles, solfataras, and mudpots – are a prime Yellowstone attraction for humans and birds alike. Find a comfortable observation post at one and study the individual birds that are drawn there. In particular, watch a Mountain Bluebird fly up from a snag to catch insects. Look closely – what kind of insect is on the menu today?

Site Map and Information

YELLOWSTONE NATIONAL PARK

▣ There are numerous approaches and entrance stations to this 3,400-square-mile park. One of the most popular routes is to take State Highway 191 south from Bozeman, Montana, about 80 miles to enter on the west side of the park.

◘ Daily, 24 hours, year-round.

◕ The only closures are caused by road construction and weather-related restrictions.

🛈 Yellowstone National Park, P.O. Box 168, WY 82190-0168. The park has many Visitor Centers, including Fishing Bridge, Albright, Old Faithful, Canyon, and Grant Village. From mid-April through late October they are generally open daily 8 a.m.–7 p.m.

☎ (307) 344-7381; www.nps.gov/yell

Ⓢ $20 per car for a 7-day pass that includes access to Grand Teton National Park (just south of Yellowstone).

♿ The pamphlet "Visitor Guide to Accessible Features in Yellowstone National Park" is available online and at all Visitor Centers. To reach TDD, call (307) 344-2386.

Ⓐ Five of Yellowstone's campgrounds are

operated by AmFac Parks & Resorts; call (307) 344-7311 for reservations. Seven campgrounds are operated by the National Park Service on a first-come, first-served basis.

🔭 The Yellowstone Association Institute offers several birdwatching courses each summer; call (307) 344-2294 for information.

🛏 Lodging in Yellowstone is operated by AmFac Parks & Resorts; call (307) 344-7311 for information.

CANADA

ALBERTA

BRITISH COLUMBIA

MANITOBA

NEW BRUNSWICK

NEW FOUNDLAND

NORTHWEST TERRITORIES

NOVA SCOTIA

ONTARIO

PRINCE EDWARD ISLAND

QUEBEC

SASKATCHEWAN

YUKON

ELK ISLAND NATIONAL PARK

*Just east of Edmonton, this Alberta park is a remarkable remnant of an earlier,
wilder North America – home to bison, moose, elk, and, above all, birds.*

Visitors to Elk Island National Park are often surprised to find that it is not an island at all – at least not in the usual sense. The park is surrounded not by water but by a sea of civilization, including heavily cultivated farmland, ranches, and houses. In fact, it lies less than 25 miles (35 kilometers) east of Edmonton, a major urban center and the capital of the province. Despite the surrounding hubbub, wildlife – including an astounding array of birds, plus bison, moose, elk, and deer – roam freely here. Beavers, which were once threatened by over-trapping, now build dams and swim in the park's lakes and ponds.

The Black-crowned Night-Heron *hunts by night and roosts by day and can be found in the park's wetlands.*

HABITAT
It's amazing how much Elk Island's hilly, uncultivated land differs from the developed flatlands of the nearby countryside. A patchwork of varying habitats such as spruce forest, aspen parkland, and wetlands, the park features "knob and kettle" topography: small, rounded hills with depressions nestled among them. These depressions trap water, creating small wetlands, bogs, and beaver ponds that provide food and habitat not only for beavers but for abundant wading birds and waterfowl as well.

Elk Island National Park was created in 1906, when five men from nearby Fort Saskatchewan petitioned the government to set aside 16 square miles (26 square kilometers) as an elk preserve. In 1913 the preserve became a national park, and since that time it has expanded to 75 square miles (120 square kilometers), including Lake Astotin. Animals roam freely within the park, but fences enclose the park to keep them safe from hunters and avoid damage to nearby farms.

BIRDS TO LOOK FOR

Common Loon • Horned Grebe • Red-necked Grebe • Double-crested Cormorant • Black-crowned Night-Heron • Barrow's Goldeneye • Northern Goshawk • Common Tern • Forster's Tern • Black Tern • Boreal Owl • Northern Saw-whet Owl • Yellow-bellied Sapsucker • Three-toed Woodpecker • Black-backed Woodpecker

BIRD LIFE
A total of 250 species of birds have been recorded at Elk Island, including numerous kinds of warblers, flycatchers, wading birds, and birds of prey. Transition zones, such as forest edges and lake shores, are especially good areas for birding in the park because the greatest diversity of species occurs there.

Common Terns are a frequent sight above, especially during breeding season.

Visitors will enjoy viewing the living symbol of the Friends of Elk Island Society – the Red-necked Grebe. The raucous calls of these breeding waterbirds echo across the park's lakes as they perform their courting rituals each spring and later rear their young. Red-necked, Horned, Eared, Pied-billed, and Western grebes are all found in the park.

Three species of tern – Forster's, Common, and Black – forage at Lake Astotin, the largest and deepest lake in the park, although only the Black Tern nests there. Unlike Forster's and Common Terns, which live primarily on small fish they catch by plunge-diving into the lake, Black Terns eat mostly insects. These

The Double-crested Cormorant *features a large pouch at its throat that is yellow-orange year-round.*

fascinating relatives of gulls seem to be on the wing constantly, trying to pick off insects flying over the marshes and meadows, as well as the lake.

A number of wading birds, including Great Blue Herons and Black-crowned Night-Herons, can be found in the park's wetlands, including small ponds formed by beaver dams. A relative newcomer to the park, the night-heron was first sighted here in 1958 and is now increasing in numbers. The Double-crested Cormorant is another water bird that was rarely seen in Elk Island until recently; now it nests at the park, where it can be spotted from April to October.

Birdwatching is wonderful from the Living Waters Boardwalk, which extends over a marsh near the eastern shore of Lake Astotin. In the warmer months a wide range of interesting birds can be watched up close, including Canada Geese with their broods of goslings; Red-necked Grebes; and magnificent Common Loons, whose distinctive tremolo calls echo across the lake.

VISITING

The information center at the main entrance is a good place to begin any exploration of the park. Brochures, maps, and books are available here and staff members bestow helpful advice about where to find birds of particular interest. Astotin Theatre, an interpretive center on the eastern shore of Lake Astotin, offers environmental education programs by reservation. A spotting scope permanently mounted behind the center allows visitors to watch

waterfowl – and, if they're lucky, beavers – swimming in the distance.

The park offers 11 hiking trails, ranging in length and difficulty. The Living Waters Boardwalk is an easy 150-yard-long stroll with great views of Lake Astotin and its surrounding marshes. The Wood Bison Trail, an 11-mile (18 kilometer) trek through woodland habitat rich in birds, bison, moose, elk, and deer, takes approximately six hours to complete.

HIGHLIGHTS

In the spring several pairs of Elk Island's beloved Red-necked Grebes nest on Lake Astotin. Their nest structures, which float, are easy to spot while walking along the shoreline trail. In early summer, the spectacle of young grebes riding on their parents' backs is sometimes seen.

Site Map and Information

ELK ISLAND NATIONAL PARK

🚗 From Edmonton follow Highway 16 (the Yellowhead Highway) east toward Fort Saskatchewan. After approximately 23 miles, Highway 16 will bisect Elk Island; the main entrance is on the left.

🕐 Daily, 24 hours, year-round.

⏱ During the summer months, the Lake Astotin area closes at approximately 11 p.m.

🏠 Elk Island National Park, Site 4, RR 1, Fort Saskatchewan, Alberta, Canada T8L 2N7.

☎ (780) 992-2950

💲 Adults $4 (CAN); Seniors (over 65) $3; youths (6 to 16 years old) $2; Children (under 6) free; adult groups $8; senior groups $6; Commercial Groups $2 per person.

♿ The information center, the Shoreline Trail, and camping and picnic sites are all

wheelchair accessible.

⛺ 80 sites are available at Sandy Beach Campground. The group camping at Oster Lake takes reservations; call (780) 992-2950.

🍴 None.

🏨 Hotels and motels are available in nearby Lamont and Fort Saskatchewan.

JASPER NATIONAL PARK

*For breathtaking views from high in the Canadian Rockies, and more than
250 species of birds, this vast national park in Alberta is unsurpassed.*

Perched on the eastern side of the Great Divide in the rugged Canadian Rockies, Jasper National Park provides a rich visual spectacle to the many hikers, campers, and sightseers who visit each year. Within the park's boundaries – more than 4,200 square miles (10,878 square kilometers) of rugged wilderness – you can see huge mountain peaks, glaciers, and picturesque valleys and an incredible variety of wildlife, including mule deer, bighorn sheep, grizzly and black bears, and mountain goats, not to mention many birds. The park has more than 660 miles (1,062 kilometers) of hiking trails.

Jasper National Park was established in 1907; a few years later, the Canadian transcontinental railroad was built through the Rockies, providing access to anyone who wanted to visit this amazing area. Jasper is certainly one of the world's premier parks and has been designated part of the Canadian Rockies' World Heritage Site. Each year, more than 2 million people pass through its gates to view its scenic splendor.

HABITAT

A variety of habitats exist in Jasper National Park, ranging from tundra and alpine meadows in the higher elevations to lakes, sloughs, and riverine habitats in the broad, forested valleys. The wide variation in altitudes and habitat types within the boundaries of the park makes for a large number of bird species, and the fact that the park lies along the Continental Divide means that visitors may find species from both the western side of the Rockies (birds more typical of the wet forests of British Columbia) and the eastern side (birds from the open prairies and park lands of Alberta).

Oldsquaws *and other waterfowl may be observed at the north end of Talbot Lake.*

BIRD LIFE

More than 250 species of birds have been recorded at Jasper National Park. For good numbers and variety of

BIRDS TO LOOK FOR

Horned Grebe • Red-necked Grebe • Surf Scoter • White-winged Scoter • Oldsquaw • Barrow's Goldeneye • Hooded Merganser • Osprey • Bald Eagle • White-tailed Ptarmigan • Northern Pygmy-Owl • Boreal Owl • Boreal Chickadee • American Dipper • Bohemian Waxwing • Fox Sparrow

Fox Sparrows, and a host of other sparrows, may be found foraging in the undergrowth.

waterfowl from spring through early fall, visit Talbot Lake. The northern end of the lake hosts nesting Common Loons and numerous Canada Geese. There's also usually a nesting pair of Ospreys. These amazing raptors, nicknamed "fish hawks," make high speed dives after fish, plucking them from just below the water's surface. When they carry off the fish, which can be a foot or more long, they invariably point the fish's head forward to make it more streamlined and easier to carry. Lucky birders might even see a Bald Eagle chase an Osprey and steal its fish – a favorite trick of these much larger raptors.

Watch for Red-necked Grebes and Horned Grebes foraging in the shallow water at the lake's edge or carrying their tiny chicks on their backs. Beautiful Hooded Mergansers, as well as Oldsquaws, Common and Barrow's Goldeneyes,

White-winged and Surf Scoters, and other interesting waterfowl are also found at the northern end of Talbot Lake. Look for Harlequin Ducks – one of this continent's prettiest ducks – along the Athabasca River near the town of Jasper, in the middle of the park. Here birders might also spot an American Dipper.

For those who like moonlight owl walks, try Cottonwood Slough, less than two miles (3.5 kilometers) from Jasper. There, on early spring nights, Great Horned Owls, Barred Owls, Northern Saw-whet Owls, and Boreal Owls can be heard. During the day a birdwatcher might spot a Northern

Surf Scoters *nest near water on the park's tundra.*

Pygmy-Owl – a day-hunting species – in the town of Jasper. These tiny owls sometimes can be found sitting in the open on trees or telephone wires or attacking House Sparrows or other small birds at feeders.

VISITING

The best time to watch birds at Jasper National Park is from late March through September, a temperate period that covers both spring and fall migrations as well as the breeding season. (Of course, always be prepared for cold weather when in the high mountains.) Even in winter this immense park is home to interesting birds such as Willow and White-tailed Ptarmigans, Mountain and Boreal Chickadees, Bohemian Waxwings, and Red-breasted Nuthatches. Please adhere to park regulations; call or stop by the Visitor Center before exploring.

HIGHLIGHTS

Take the Sky Tram to the Whistlers to get a spectacular view of the area. Tramway staff provide an interpretive talk on the way up in the tram and along the trail. The alpine meadows and boulder piles are good places to look for Fox Sparrows, American Pipits, and White-tailed Ptarmigans.

Site Map and Information

JASPER NATIONAL PARK

🚗 From Edmonton, Alberta, take Highway 16 northwest approximately 190 miles (360 kilometers). The town of Jasper – which contains a park information center and other services – is in the middle of the park. The park can also be reached from the south, traveling west from Calgary, Alberta, on Highway 1, then north on Highway 93 (the picturesque "Icefields Parkway") to the park entrance.

🕐 Daily, 24 hours, year-round.

⬤ Some facilities are closed during the winter due to bad weather; call ahead.

ℹ️ Jasper National Park, PO Box 10, Jasper, Alberta T0E 1E0, Canada. Visitor Center (at 500 Connaught Drive in Jasper) is open daily, 8 a.m.–7 p.m., May 1 through October 15, and 9 a.m.–5 p.m. the rest of the year. (Hours subject to change; call ahead.)

📞 (780) 852-6176; www.parkscanada.gc.ca/jasper

💲 $5 (CAN) per adult; $4 (CAN) per senior (over 65); $2.50 (CAN) per youth (6 to 16); free for children under 6.

♿ The park is equipped for the disabled.

🏕️ More than 1,700 campsites are available, ranging from primitive to deluxe with electricity, showers, and hookups. Of the 11 campgrounds in the park, Whistlers and Wapiti are the most popular. Campsites cannot be reserved in advance, so be sure to get one early in the day at the height of the tourist season in July and August.

👥 Contact Jasper Tourism and Commerce at (780) 852-3858 for listings of licensed guides. The Friends of Jasper Park also give tours; call (780) 852-4767.

🏨 Hotels are available in the town of Jasper in the middle of the park; call the general information number for listings.

MOUNT REVELSTOKE NATIONAL PARK

*Breathtaking beauty and a wide range of bird-rich habitats abound in this
undervisited park in the rugged mountains of southeastern British Columbia.*

It is difficult to think of an adequate superlative to describe the scenic beauty of Mount Revelstoke National Park. Perched high in the Selkirk Mountains of southeastern British Columbia, near the confluence of the Illecillewaet and Columbia Rivers, this 100-square-mile (260-square-kilometer) park encompasses a varied landscape of rugged snow-capped peaks and alpine meadows, as well as lush rainforests on the valley floor.

The Nashville Warbler *is distinguished from other warblers with white eye rings by its gray head, olive back, and yellow throat.*

The citizens of the nearby city of Revelstoke recognized the area's beauty long ago. The city completed a trail to the summit of the mountain in 1908 and later built trails to several alpine lakes. After a great deal of lobbying by local residents, the national park was established in 1914. Numerous hiking trails can be accessed through the park, leading to alpine meadows and other scenic attractions. The summit area is 16 miles (25.7 kilometers) from the park's entrance and is the head of several trails, which vary in level of difficulty. The Meadows-in-the-Sky Parkway is open from early to late June through mid-October, depending on the amount of snow.

HABITAT

Mount Revelstoke National Park lies in the "interior wet belt" of British Columbia – an area that receives large amounts of precipitation each year. The Columbia Mountains (of which the Selkirk Mountains are a part) form a lofty obstacle to the warm, damp weather systems that pass over them, often discharging precipitation in the form of rain and snow. These unique conditions have created a temperate inland rainforest in the valley bottoms. Consisting mostly of dense old-growth woodlands, with western redcedar and western hemlock the dominant plant species, these forests are very similar in appearance and vegetation to coastal rainforests. The valleys host a full range of wildlife such as grizzly bears and moose, as well as Steller's Jays, Winter Wrens, and more.

The park has more than 40 miles (64 kilometers) of hiking trails. The Giant Cedars Trail is a particularly beautiful and easy walk through an old-growth forest of hemlock and cedar, with some 600- to 800-year-old trees.

BIRDS TO LOOK FOR

White-tailed Ptarmigan • Calliope
Hummingbird • Gray Jay • Steller's
Jay • Clark's Nutcracker • Black-
capped Chickadee • Chestnut-backed
Chickadee • Boreal Chickadee •
Nashville Warbler • MacGillvray's
Warbler • Pine Grosbeak • Red
Crossbill

This park is home to four species of chickadees, including the Black-capped Chickadee.

Midway up the mountain is a subalpine region, with forests of spruce, fir, and mountain hemlock, which give way higher up to lush mountain meadows studded with a colorful array of wildflowers. This is a land of mountain caribou and grizzly bear, and birds such as Pine Siskins, Clark's Nutcrackers, and Gray Jays.

Finally, visitors will pass out of the treeline into alpine tundra habitat, with meadows of heather and sedge, as well as lichen-covered rocks – home to mountain goats, marmots, and White-tailed Ptarmigan.

BIRD LIFE
The 16-mile (25.7-kilometer) drive up the mountain provides a fascinating and relatively easy opportunity for birdwatchers to visit several vastly different habitat. At the base of the mountain, look for Calliope Hummingbirds in June, and Western Tanagers. When leaving the valley bottom, say goodbye to the American Redstarts, Nashville Warblers, and Black-capped Chickadees and hello to Chestnut-backed Chickadees, MacGillivray's Warblers, and Townsend's Warblers. The habitat changes drastically when driving into the subalpine forest. There, watch for Red Crossbills working diligently to extract the seeds from pine cones with their oddly crisscrossed bills. Also look for Pine Grosbeaks in the conifers. Both Mountain and Boreal Chickadees can also be seen here.

Red Crossbill
females display grayish olive rather than brick red plumage, but their crisscrossed bills are unmistakable.

Continuing on to the parking area at Balsam Lake, about a mile below the summit, either take a Parks Canada shuttle bus to the top, or hike one of the many trails. Watch for Fox Sparrows and Gray Jays. Hiking east on the Eva Lake Trail leads through an area where Northern Hawk Owls sometimes nest. In the alpine tundra areas, look for White-tailed Ptarmigan and rosy-finches.

VISITING

Late June is a great time to visit to see the highest number of species, although interesting birdwatching opportunities abound all summer.

But if high-country hiking is the goal, it's better to go in August, when temperatures are warmer and the wildflowers are in bloom. The park is not as accessible once the snowfall starts, usually in mid-October.

HIGHLIGHTS

Revelstoke is one of the few places where birdwatchers can see four species of chickadee – Black-capped, Boreal, Chestnut-backed, and Mountain – in one day. Just drive slowly up the Meadows-in-the-Sky Parkway, stopping frequently to look for chickadees as the altitude changes.

Site Map and Information

MOUNT REVELSTOKE NATIONAL PARK

▣ From Kelowna, take Highway 97 north 120 miles (193 kilometers) to Trans Canada Highway, which runs through the southeastern section of the park. Most visitors take the Meadows-in-the-Sky Parkway 16 miles (26 kilometers) to the summit area.

◻ The Meadows-in-the-Sky Parkway is open daily, 7 a.m.–10 p.m.

◉ The Meadows-in-the-Sky Parkway is generally not passable from mid-October (or first snowfall) through late June.

🅷 Mount Revelstoke National Park, P.O. Box 350, Revelstoke, British Columbia V0E 2S0, Canada. The Parks Canada Administration Building next to the post office in West Revelstoke serves as a Visitor Center. It's open daily, 9 a.m.– 5 p.m., April 1 through June 15, and 8 a.m.–8:30 p.m., June 16 through September 1.

🅒 (250) 837-7500; www.parkscanada.pch.gc.ca/revelstoke

⑤ Daily, annual, group, and senior rates available.

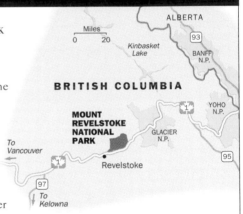

🔥 The Meadows-in-the-Sky Parkway, Skunk Cabbage Nature Trail, and summit area facilities are wheelchair accessible.

🅰 None on-site. Campsites are available in nearby Albert Canyon Hotsprings Primitive and the city of Revelstoke.

🏃 Contact Revelstoke Alpine Adventure Company at (888) 837-5417 or Summit Cycle Tours at (888) 700-3444.

🛏 There are hotels and motels in nearby Revelstoke; call the chamber of commerce at (250) 837-5345 for listings.

PACIFIC RIM NATIONAL PARK RESERVE

This picturesque Vancouver Island park features wild offshore islands, majestic old-growth forests, and isolated beaches.

Probably the best word to describe the scenery in this national marine park is dramatic. Exposed to the power of the Pacific Ocean, this is a land where massive rolling waves pound the shore, where the bellow of sea lions echoes above the roar of the surf, and where huge gray whales feed offshore.

Since 1803 more than 240 ships have foundered on the west coast of Vancouver Island, earning this rugged coast the title "Graveyard of the Pacific." Today, birdwatchers and other park visitors enjoy hiking on the West Coast Trail – a path originally cut along the coast to help rescuers reach stricken vessels.

HABITAT

Pacific Rim National Park Reserve, which was dedicated in 1970, includes 123,000 acres (50,000 hectares) of forest, offshore islands, beaches, and ocean. It consists of three units – Long Beach, the Broken Group Islands, and the West Coast Trail.

The Long Beach unit boasts beautiful ocean beaches and rugged,

The Rufous Hummingbird, *which features a primarily reddish-brown tail and back, can be found on the Broken Group Islands.*

rocky headlands. The Wickaninnish Center, an excellent interpretive center located near the water's edge, provides information about local habitats and wildlife, including northern sea lions, birds, and the more than 20,000 gray whales that migrate through these waters. Telescopes are set up in several areas for watching whales and sea lions, as well as birds.

The Broken Group Islands are a separate unit of the park, consisting of an archipelago of more than 100 small islands and rocks in Barkley Sound. Reachable only by boat, these islands provide a challenging experience for the kayakers and canoeists who visit.

The third unit in the park is the West Coast Trail, a 48-mile (77-kilometer) path taking visitors through dense, old-growth coastal rainforest. The terrain is quite varied, and the hiking is strenuous. To protect the area's natural habitat from overuse, the park requests that visitors make reservations before hiking on the trail,

BIRDS TO LOOK FOR

Red-throated Loon • Common Loon • Black-footed Albatross • Leach's Storm-Petrel • Surf Scoter • Bald Eagle • Black Turnstone • Pigeon Guillemot • Rhinocerous Auklet • Tufted Puffin • Band-tailed Pigeon • Rufous Hummingbird • Pileated Woodpecker • Steller's Jay • Orange-crowned Warbler

BIRD LIFE

An impressive number of bird species, nearly 260 in all, have been recorded in this sprawling park and vicinity.

281

The plaintive wail of Common Loons can be heard over Grice Bay.

The park's 57 breeding residents include the strikingly marked Red-throated Loon, the majestic Bald Eagle, the clown-like Tufted Puffin, and the tiny Rufous Hummingbird.

Long Beach is a good vantage point from which to scan offshore with a spotting scope for seabirds such as Black-footed Albatrosses and Northern Fulmars, as well as the three species of scoters and Harlequin Ducks, all of which can be seen year-round. During spring and fall migrations a variety of shorebirds visit this beach, including Sanderlings, Dunlins, Black Turnstones, and Surfbirds.

Grice Bay, at the northern end of the

The Tufted Puffin *is named for the pale yellow tufts on the top of its head.*

Long Beach unit is an excellent place to observe Common Loons and an occasional Red-throated Loon diving for small fish. In spring there are usually numerous Buffleheads.

The Broken Group Islands in Barkley Sound host an amazing array of breeding seabirds in spring and summer. There are tiny but agile Leach's Storm-Petrels, which have colonies on Cleland Island and Seabird Rocks, and Brandt's Cormorants, which nest on Sea Lion Rocks. Most of these plant-covered islands are home to Rufous Hummingbirds as well. Bald Eagles are present in the area year-round. Ospreys dive for fish and frequently have to skirmish with the eagles for their catch. Some of the other birds breeding on the islands in Barkley Sound are Pigeon Guillemots,

Rhinoceros Auklets, Tufted Puffins, and Pelagic Cormorants.

While walking in summer on the West Coast Trail, or on one of the park's forest trails, birders should listen for the loud *wuck-a-wuck-a-wuck* call of the Pileated Woodpecker. Visitors are also likely to hear the loud *coo* of band-tailed pigeons and perhaps the more subtle *trill* of the Western Screech-Owl at that time of year. Other forest birds to look for are Swainson's Thrushes, Brown Creepers, Townsend's Warblers, Hermit Thrushes, and Steller's Jays.

VISITING

Any time of year can be productive for birdwatching at this reserve, though

spring and fall migrations are best for finding large numbers of species. Spring migration peaks in April and May. Migrant shorebird numbers peak in August, but many fall migrants can be seen through October.

HIGHLIGHTS

You must own or rent a boat, canoe, or kayak to get to the Broken Group Islands. Small colonies of Rhinoceros Auklets and Tufted Puffins are found on Seabird Rocks. Pigeon Guillemots nest on Seabird Rocks and Florencia Islands. Ospreys nest on Varga Island. For information about boat tours or rentals, call Lady Rose Marine Services at (800) 663-7192.

Site Map and Information

PACIFIC RIM NATIONAL
PARK RESERVE

🚗 Take a ferry from Horseshoe Bay (northern Vancouver) or Tsawawwen (southern Vancouver) to one of the two ferry terminals in Nanaimo. The park is on the west coast of Vancouver Island and can be reached on Highway 4 via Port Alberni. Bus service is available. Call (604) 444-2890 for details.

🚪 Daily, 24 hours, year-round.

⬤ Some beaches are closed 11 p.m.–6 a.m.

ℹ Pacific Rim National Park Reserve, Box 280, 2185 Ocean Terrace Road, Ucluelet, British Columbia, Canada V0R 3A0. Wickaninnish Center is open daily, 10:30 a.m.–6 p.m., mid-March through mid-October.

📞 (250) 726-7721; www.harbour.com/parkscan/pacrim

💲 $3 (CAN) per vehicle, per 2 hours; $8 per vehicle, per day; $3 per person by bus.

♿ Shorepine Bog Trail and Wickaninnish Center are wheelchair accessible.

🅰 The Long Beach unit has fully equipped camping facilities; call Discover Camping at (800) 689-9025 for reservations. The Broken Group Islands also have 8 campgrounds, accessible only by boat.

🏕 Sea to Sky Expeditions offers a guide service, kayak rentals, and bed-and-breakfast accommodations; call (800) 990-8735 for details.

🛏 Hotels, motels, and bed-and-breakfasts are available in the nearby towns of Ucluelet and Tofino, both on Vancouver Island.

CHURCHILL AND VICINITY

Chill winds blowing across Hudson Bay have created a piece of the arctic in Manitoba – complete with plant and bird life typical north of the arctic circle.

The town of Churchill, Manitoba, named after the river that runs past it, lies hundreds of miles south of the arctic circle, but you'd never know it. Churchill and the surrounding region boast many of the same kinds of fascinating habitats and wildlife that are found in areas far to the north. That's because the town lies on the western shore of a chilly inlet of the Atlantic Ocean, Hudson Bay, producing a climate much harsher than is usually found at this latitude.

Ross's Gull, *first discovered at the site in 1980, is one of Churchill's main birding attractions.*

This arctic climate creates an amazing spectacle for wildlife watchers, who may enjoy the area's celebrated polar bears in the fall and an intriguing array of birds, plus migrating beluga whales, in the late spring and summer.

BIRDS TO LOOK FOR

Pacific Loon • Merlin • American Golden-Plover • Whimbrel • Hudsonian Godwit • Dunlin • Stilt Sandpiper • Short-billed Dowitcher • Ross's Gull • Arctic Tern •Northern Hawk Owl • Short-eared Owl • Blackpoll Warbler • Harris's Sparrow • Smith's Longspur

However, few birds are around during the area's miserably cold winter, which begins in October and ends in May.

HABITAT

The town of Churchill is surrounded by a massive wilderness with a rich variety of habitats: both wet and dry tundra, coniferous forest, mossy bogs, and chilly lakes. Near Hudson Bay is classic tundra habitat – flat, spongy, low-lying vegetation – but a short distance inland lies a transition zone that features sparsely forested coniferous woodland.

In this land of extremes the period of warmer weather is all too brief. However, numerous migratory birds, many from thousands of miles away, make their way here each breeding season to take advantage of the abundant insect life. They do not stay long: they nest in early June through early July, raise their young, and leave. By early August many are already headed southward to more temperate wintering grounds.

BIRD LIFE

During the warmer months the Churchill area is one of the most preferred (if not easily accessible) places in North America to view the stunning breeding plumages of a wide variety of shorebirds. An unassuming bird such as the Short-billed Dowitcher blossoms into a rich cinnamon-colored beauty on its breeding grounds. Other noteworthy shorebirds to see are American Golden-Plovers, Hudsonian Godwits, Stilt Sandpipers, Whimbrels, and Common

Arctic Terns perch on icebergs in the frigid Hudson Bay.

Snipes, all of which breed within easy driving – and sometimes walking – distance of the town of Churchill.

One of the better birding spots in the area is the Granary Ponds, which consist of several shallow pools behind grain elevators less than a mile by road from the Churchill Hotel. In addition to most of the above-mentioned shorebirds, which forage here, watch the nesting colony of Arctic Terns and numerous ducks, including Greater Scaup, American Wigeon, and Northern Shovelers. A lucky birder might even spot a Ross's Gull, Churchill's most sought-after species.

Go a couple of miles farther northwest by road to reach Cape Merry, where the Churchill River flows into Hudson Bay. Here are American Pipits

The Whimbrel *can be spotted in its breeding plumage during Churchill's warmer months.*

hopping about in the rocks, a variety of gulls, and numerous Common Eiders floating offshore or drifting on the icebergs that pass by even in midsummer.

Goose Creek Road, another great place to birdwatch, runs about 10 miles (16 kilometers) through several different habitats. In its marshy areas and ponds, watch many dabbling ducks, including Northern Pintails and Green-winged Teals. Its spruce forests provide a good chance of spotting interesting woodland nesters: Harris's Sparrows, Three-toed Woodpeckers, Northern Shrikes, Boreal Chickadees, and even Northern Hawk Owls.

To see Pacific Loons, drive to Farnworth Lake, about six miles outside of Churchill, where a number of pairs of these elegant birds nest along its edges in late spring and summer. With their ruby-red eyes and the bold black-and-white lines running diagonally down their necks, they are one of the north country's most unforgettable birds. Also look for Harris's Sparrows and Blackpoll Warblers, plus Bonaparte's Gulls nesting in the small trees beside the lake.

VISITING

Because Churchill is inaccessible by automobile, visitors must travel from Winnipeg by either air or train; the latter takes about 38 hours. Cars and vans can be rented in Churchill and they are a necessity unless you plan to birdwatch only at the Granary Ponds and other areas within easy walking distance of the center of town. The weather is unpredictable in Churchill, so a warm car is nice to have. Birders come to the area as early as May to see migrants, but June through early July is generally the peak time to view a wide variety of bird life.

HIGHLIGHTS

Although Ross's Gull is primarily an Old World species that breeds in arctic Siberia, a nest was found in Churchill in 1980. This beautiful gull has become one of the main reasons birdwatchers visit the area. Birders visiting in June through early July have an excellent chance of seeing Ross's Gulls, especially around the Granary Ponds.

Site Map and Information

CHURCHILL AND VICINITY

🚗 Canadian Airlines International offers 3 flights a week from Winnipeg to Churchill; call (800) 426-7000 from the US or (800) 592-7303 from Canada, or contact a travel agent. VIA-Rail runs 3 train trips a week from Winnipeg to Churchill; call (800) 561-3949 (US) or (800) 561-8630 (Canada).

☐ The Churchill area is not a park or refuge; travelers can move about the area freely 24 hours a day. Optimal birding times are from the last week of May through the second week in July.

◑ Birders should avoid the area's coldest period, from December well into May.

🛈 Churchill Chamber of Commerce, P.O. Box 176, Churchill, Manitoba R0B 0E0, Canada. Offices located at 211 Kelsey Boulevard in Churchill.

📞 (204) 675-2022 (for Chamber of Commerce)

Ⓢ None.

♿ Limited. Some hotels and restaurants are wheelchair accessible, and wheelchair-accessible vehicles are available. Call Chamber of Commerce for details.

🅰 No formal camping areas.

🏕 Churchill Wilderness Encounter, P.O. Box 9, Churchill, Manitoba R0B 0E0, Canada; telephone (800) 265-9458.

🛏 There are several motels and bed-and-breakfasts in Churchill. Call Chamber of Commerce for listings.

RIDING MOUNTAIN NATIONAL PARK

This picturesque national park in southwestern Manitoba provides habitat for a spectacular array of wildlife, including more than 250 species of birds.

Riding Mountain National Park is home to some of the richest variety of bird life in North America during the nesting season. Located in southwestern Manitoba, this massive park is an "island" preserve set on the edge of the Manitoba Escarpment. It includes 1,145 square miles (2,966 square kilometers) of picturesque rolling hills and valleys, which provide habitat for a wide range of wildlife such as wolves, moose, lynx, elk, and abundant birdlife, including many nesting birds.

The Merlin flies over the park looking for birds, small rodents, or large insects.

HABITAT

Riding Mountain incorporates three distinct vegetation zones: eastern deciduous forest, northern boreal forest, and western grasslands. Evergreen forests of white and black spruce, jack pine, balsam fir, and tamarack, as well as quaking aspen and white birch, make up the boreal forest that covers the high areas of the park. Along the base of the escarpment, the park's lowest and warmest region, thrives the eastern deciduous forest of hardwoods, shrubs, vines, and ferns. To the west, extensive sections of the park are covered with meadows and grasslands. This beautiful windswept environment supports a variety of grasses and wildflowers, which are at the height of their beauty in June and July, coinciding with the nesting of numerous local birds.

The climate in the park is characterized by warm summers and frequent storms. January is the coldest month and most of the snowfall takes place from December through March.

BIRD LIFE

Over 250 species of birds have been recorded at the park, and more than 160 of them are regular nesters. The lakes and contiguous boreal forests that lie along the foot of the escarpment in the eastern part of the park are home to the Common Loon, all six species of grebe found in Canada, American White Pelicans, Double-crested Cormorants, Great Blue Herons, many species of ducks, and Forster's Terns.

BIRDS TO LOOK FOR

Bald Eagle • Merlin • Spruce Grouse • Sharp-tailed Grouse • Northern Saw-whet Owl • Three-toed Woodpecker • Great Crested Flycatcher • Yellow-throated Vireo • Gray Jay • Boreal Chickadee • Sprague's Pipit • Connecticut Warbler • Mourning Warbler • Le Conte's Sparrow • Indigo Bunting

Look for the Gray Jay in the park's northern boreal forests.

Bald Eagles can be seen at several park lakes including Whirlpool, Audy, and Moon Lakes. Ospreys, Turkey Vultures, Northern Goshawks, Cooper's Hawks, Merlins, and Spruce Grouse are frequently seen. Northern Saw-whet Owls are common around Clear Lake, as are Barred Owls.

Boreal Chickadees, Gray Jays, and both Three-toed and Black-backed Woodpeckers are frequently found in the boreal forest. The village of Wasagaming is also a good place to look for a variety of warblers and various other boreal species, which can be seen in the tall spruces. The deciduous forests are noted for Great Crested Flycatchers, Eastern Wood-Pewees, and Yellow-throated Vireos.

The grasslands in the western part of the park, especially at Lake Audy Prairie, are good places to spot Sprague's Pipits. Sharp-tailed

Grouse and Western Meadowlarks are generally easy to find in the agricultural fields to the south and southwest of the park.

VISITING

Many of the park's trails – including Arrowhead, Brulé, Boreal Island, Burls and Bittersweet, Ominnik Marsh, Fire Trail, and Beach Ridge – are self-guided; hikers follow signs or take along informative booklets. The Evergreen Trail, which begins at the north shore of Lake Katherine, is the place to go to spot Connecticut and Mourning Warblers, as well as Le

The Eared Grebe *is one of five grebes found in the park's lakes.*

Conte's Sparrows. Ma-ee-gun Trail leads to many boreal species. Burls and Bittersweet Trail is a good place to look for most migrating species, and hikers may spot several eastern deciduous-nesting species. Highway 361 – where it runs west from Highway 5 at McCreary to the park's Mount Agassiz Ski Hill – is a good place to look for eastern birds, such as Indigo Buntings, Golden-winged Warblers, and Eastern Towhees.

During winter look for Northern Goshawks, Three-toed Woodpeckers, winter finches, and crossbills. In spring and early summer check out the waterways around Minnedosa to see a wide variety of waterfowl.

HIGHLIGHTS

During breeding season, the male Sprague's Pipits perform their courtship displays at Riding Mountain in the early morning. These birds fly into air, then spiral down, singing all the way. Spot them in the grasslands at the western section of the park.

Site Map and Information

RIDING MOUNTAIN NATIONAL PARK

🚌 From the south, Highway 10 connects Brandon, which is 59 miles (95 kilometers) away, to the townsite of Wasagaming. Highway 19 enters the park through the escarpment region to the east.

🔾 Daily, 24 hours, year-round.

⬤ Never, although many of the facilities at the townsite of Wasagaming close when the summer season ends.

ℹ️ Riding Mountain National Park, Wasagaming, Manitoba R0J 2H0, Canada.

📞 (800) 707-8480; www.parkscanada.pch.gc.ca/riding

💲 $3.25 (CAN) per day for adults, with reduced rates for seniors, children, and groups; $7.50 (CAN) for a 4-day pass for adults.

♿ The park offers services and facilities to visitors with mobility, hearing, and visual disabilities. The Visitor Center, Administration Building, Theater, and Community Center are all handicapped accessible. Wishing Well Trail, Lakeshore Walk, and Ominnik Marsh Trail are wheelchair accessible. To reach the TTY, call (204) 848-2001.

🏕 Many camping opportunities – from primitive to full-facility – exist at Wasagaming and throughout the rest of the park. Call the number above for reservations and information.

🚐 The park offers backcountry tours, step-on guided bus tours, personal guides, and group tours. For a detailed listing of licensed outfitters, call (800) 707-8480. Self-guided opportunities and interpretive programs are also available throughout the park.

🏨 Hotels and motels are available within the townsite of Wasagaming, except in winter. The nearby village of Onanole offers year-round accommodations.

Grand Manan Archipelago

*For an amazing collection of breeding and migrant landbirds and seabirds,
this tiny island group off eastern New Brunswick is unbeatable.*

One of the top birdwatching areas in eastern Canada, the Grand Manan Archipelago consists of a large, 55-square-mile (142-square-kilometer) main island and 20 smaller ones, which boast a combined bird list of 365 species. This site is also well known for its breeding birds, which include some fascinating seabird colonies on the rocky offshore islands.

Specimens of many of the birds found on the archipelago can be viewed at the Grand Manan Museum, located along the main road, in the middle of Grand Manan Island. The museum is open each summer from June through September and includes a Visitor Center.

The Golden-crowned Kinglet has plumage similar to the Ruby-crowned, but it features an orange or yellow crown patch bordered by black and white stripes.

HABITAT

The archipelago is a varied landscape that includes massive cliffs and rocky intertidal areas, mudflats and sandflats, estuaries, headlands, brushy fields, coniferous and mixed woods, as well as various ponds, bogs, and marshes. The deep marine waters of the Bay of Fundy to the north and east of the islands are attractive to foraging pelagic (ocean-going) birds and whales. In a single day birdwatchers can explore alder thickets and spruce woods for forest songbirds; walk the beaches in search of shorebirds and look for eiders offshore; check ponds for dabbling ducks, Pied-billed Grebes, and various marsh birds; listen for sparrows in the beach grass; and scan the seas from a rocky headland to spot Atlantic Puffins, Wilson's Storm-Petrels, and Razorbills.

BIRD LIFE

The Grand Manan birdwatching experience starts with the 90-minute ferry ride to the island. The rich sea life in the Bay of Fundy provides an abundant feast for pelagic birds as well as for whales – particularly in late summer and early fall. Birdwatchers can spot Greater and Sooty Shearwaters, Razorbills, Northern Gannets, Common Eiders, Black Guillemots, Wilson's Storm-Petrels, Atlantic Puffins, and more.

From Long Eddy Lighthouse, at the northernmost end of Grand Manan Island, birders can scan seaward with

BIRDS TO LOOK FOR

Greater Shearwater • Sooty Shearwater • Wilson's Storm-Petrel • Leach's Storm-Petrel • Northern Gannet • Common Eider • Black Guillemot • Atlantic Puffin • Red-breasted Nuthatch • Golden-crowned Kinglet • Ruby-crowned Kinglet • Black-throated Green Warbler • Blackpoll Warbler • Black-and-white Warbler

During the ferry ride look for Northern Gannets and other seabirds in the Bay of Fundy.

binoculars or a spotting scope. The waters offshore, below the lofty cliff, usually host Herring, Great Black-backed, and Bonaparte's Gulls; Double-crested Cormorants, and Parasitic or Pomarine Jaegers.

Swallow Tail, a short rocky point extending from the northeastern part of the island, is an excellent area to look for migrating songbirds. A short walk from the village of North Head and the ferry landing, this picturesque spot hosts scores of warblers (including Magnolia, Black-and-white, Cape May, and Yellow Warblers), as well as Lincoln's and White-throated Sparrows and other passerines (perching songbirds) in April and May, during spring migration, and in August through October, during fall migration. It's

Black-and-white Warblers *and a host of other migrant songbirds are easy to see at Rocky Point in both spring and fall.*

also a good spot to see Black-legged Kittiwakes in the fall and winter.

Dock Road is a good place in summer to see nesting species. Look for Red-breasted Nuthatch, Purple Finch, Golden-crowned and Ruby-crowned Kinglets, Black-throated Green Warbler, and Cedar Waxwing.

The tidal marshes at Castalia, about one-third of the way along the eastern side of the island, provide excellent habitat for a variety of birds. Look for waterfowl in the marshes and offshore. The nearby sand- and mudflats are well known for the diversity of shorebird species seen in spring and fall, such as Black-bellied Plover, Whimbrel, Least Sandpiper, Semipalmated Sandpiper, Semipalmated Plover, and Sanderling.

The Anchorage Provincial Park, about two-thirds of the way along the eastern side of the island, offers campsites and interpretive programs, as well as some great birdwatching opportunities in its woods and bog. Right beside it is the Grand Manan Migratory Bird Sanctuary. Herons, a variety of ducks, Pied-billed Grebes, and gulls are often found here. Birdwatchers should look for shorebirds such as Sanderlings at the beach, scan offshore for Common Eiders and Double-Crested Cormorants, and search the spruce and fir woods for nesting songbirds, such as Yellow-bellied Flycatchers and Blackpoll Warblers.

VISITING

To see migrating passerines, April and May and August through October are the best times to visit. Seabirds nest locally from mid-May through July, as do land birds. To view the highest number of pelagic species (and whales too), birdwatchers should visit from August through October.

HIGHLIGHTS

A trip here wouldn't be complete without a boat tour around the islands. Several local boat-tour operators (see Guide Services below) offer day trips from late spring through early fall, giving birders a chance to see several species of pelagic birds, such as Leach's Storm-Petrels, Black Guillemots, Northern Gannets, Atlantic Puffins, and more.

Site Map and Information

GRAND MANAN ARCHIPELAGO

📠 From Bangor, Maine, drive north on Highway 9 to St. Stephen, New Brunswick. Take Route 1 east about 4 miles (6.4 kilometers) past the town of St. George to a well-marked right turn that leads to Black's Harbour and the Grand Manan Ferry Terminal. The ferry operates year-round. For information on the rates and schedule call (506) 662-3724.

☐ Grand Manan Archipelago is not a park or refuge; travelers can move about the main island freely 24 hours a day.

● Never.

🅷 Grand Manan Museum, 1141 Route 776, Grand Manan, New Brunswick E5G 4E9, Canada. The museum and its Visitor Center are open from June through September, Monday through Saturday, 9 a.m.–4 p.m., and Sunday, 1 p.m.–5 p.m.

📞 (506) 662-3524; http://personal.nbnet.nb.ca/gmtains

⑤ None.

🅺 The Grand Manan Museum, including

its Visitor Center and reading room, are wheelchair accessible.

🅰 The Anchorage Provincial Park has campsites and an RV service station; call (506) 662-7022 for details.

🏚 For boat tours, contact Sea Watch Tours at (506) 662-8552; SeaView Adventures, (506) 662-3211; or Island Coast Boat Tours, (506) 662-8181.

🏨 The east coast of Grand Manan Island has numerous hotels, motels, and bed-and-breakfasts. Contact the Grand Manan Tourism Association at (506) 662-3442 for listings.

KOUCHIBOUGUAC NATIONAL PARK

Rich estuaries, bogs, forests, and salt marshes make this New Brunswick park an
irresistible sanctuary for birds, seals, moose, and other fascinating wildlife.

Established as a national park in 1979, Kouchibouguac derives its unusual name from an early Micmac Indian description of the area – *Pijeboogwek* or "river of the long tideway." It is indeed a place that's heavily influenced by tides, which each day fill the park's estuaries with saltwater, mixing with the freshwater flowing seaward from the rivers, and creating rich shallows of brackish water where numerous shorebirds feed.

Red-breasted Mergansers *are among the birds that nest around the park's barrier islands.*

Located on the north shore of the Northumberland Strait, Kouchibouguac National Park is protected from the rough ocean waves

and currents by a 15.5-mile (25-kilometer) stretch of barrier islands and sand dunes.

HABITAT

The estuaries are only one type of habitat within this 92-square-mile (238-square-kilometer) park. The blend of coastal and inland habitats, including lagoons, sand dunes, beaches, rivers, forests, and fields, provide habitat for a remarkable variety of birdlife – and the park makes the preservation of these ecosystems its first priority.

Acadian forest – with black and red spruce, balsam fir, white cedar, aspen, and birch – is the dominant habitat, filling just over half of the park's area. Inland from the marshes lie spectacular 8,000-year-old peat bogs. The barrier islands and sand dunes are relatively flat and low. Storms periodically sweep across the barrier islands and wash away the beach grass and strand, but it soon grows back, providing nesting habitat for terns and plovers.

BIRD LIFE

More than 230 species of birds have been recorded at Kouchibouguac, approximately 90 of which are regular nesters. One of the barrier islands, Tern Island, is home to the largest nesting colony of Common Terns in the entire Maritime Provinces (and also one of the largest in Canada).

Even more interesting to birdwatchers are the endangered Piping Plovers that nest at

---

BIRDS TO LOOK FOR

Northern Gannet • Red-breasted Merganser • Common Eider • Osprey • Piping Plover • Semipalmated Sandpiper • Lesser Yellowlegs • Herring Gull • Great Black-backed Gull • Common Tern • Gray Jay • Brown Thrasher • Black-throated Green Warbler • Blackburnian Warbler • Saltmarsh Sharp-tailed Sparrow

A huge nesting colony of Common Terns is found on a nearby barrier island.

Kouchibouguac from May into July. On average, 12 pairs of these rare birds raise young on the barrier islands and sandspits of the park. Other species nesting in and around the barrier islands are Great Black-backed Gull, Herring Gull, Ring-billed Gull, and Red-breasted Merganser.

Both Kelly's Beach and Callander's Beach provide good vantage points from which to scan the park's system of lagoons and estuaries, but a spotting scope is definitely an asset. During spring and fall migrations, 25,000 birds – mostly waterfowl – have been counted in the lagoons.

From Kelly's Beach, hike on a boardwalk across the dunes to the edge of the Northumberland Strait. From here Northern Gannets and Ospreys (which are the park's emblem) are commonly seen diving dramatically

into the sea. Waterfowl, such as Surf Scoters and Common Eiders may also be present, during spring migration. Piping Plovers are also sometimes spotted foraging along the beach. Birdwatchers may also see Saltmarsh Sharp-tailed Sparrows.

The wooded areas are year-round home to the Gray Jay – a long-tailed, pale gray bird, which lacks the crest of the Blue Jay but not the cheeky jay personality. From late May to early June, these woods also host scores of migrating warblers, including Blackburnian, Black-throated Green, Black-and-white, Black-throated Blue, and more.

During the same period, on the beaches, watch for shorebirds such as Semipalmated Sandpipers,

The Brown Thrasher *has a curved bill, long tail, and yellow eye.*

Greater and Lesser Yellowlegs, and others. Earlier in spring, from mid-April to mid-May, is the best time to look for northward-migrating raptors, such as Sharp-shinned Hawks, Merlins, and Peregrine Falcons. Massive numbers of Canada Geese also pass through Kouchibouguac in October and November.

Visiting

Kouchibouguac National Park has an excellent Visitor Center, an extensive interpretive program, numerous hiking and bicycling trails, and approximately 30 miles (50 kilometers) of road, which make all areas of the park readily accessible to birdwatchers.

The largest number of species are present in late May and again in mid-September, but birdwatchers can enjoy the park virtually anytime between the beginning of May and the end of September when the weather is most cooperative.

HIGHLIGHTS

Sign up for the park's Voyageur Marine Adventure, a three-hour journey in a large Voyageur canoe, which runs daily from June through September. Paddle past the tern colony at Tern Island or near rare Piping Plovers. Call the general information number below for details.

Site Map and Information

Kouchibouguac National Park

▣ The park is located in Kent County, about 60 miles (100 kilometers) north of Moncton, New Brunswick. Take Highway 15 to Shediac and then go north on either Highway 11 or take the more scenic Route 134 to reach the park entrance.

◻ Daily, 24 hours, year round, with full services from mid-May through mid-October.

◓ Never.

🄷 Kouchibouguac National Park, c/o Parks Canada, 186 Route 117, New Brunswick E4X 2PI, Canada. Visitor Center is open daily, 8 a.m.–8 p.m., from mid-May to mid-September.

🄲 (506) 876-2443;
www.parkscanada.pch.gc.ca/
kouchibouguac

Ⓢ $3.50 (CAN) per adult; $2.75 per senior (over 65); $1.75 per youth (6–16); free for children (under 6); $7 per family.

🄳 Visitor Center and the following nature trails – Kelly's Beach, Salt Marsh, Beaver, and White Cedar – are all wheelchair accessible. To reach TTY, call (506) 876-4205.

🄰 South Kouchibouguac Campground is on-site; call (506) 876-1277 for reservations.

🄺 Kayakouch Inc. offers multi-day, guided kayak tours and also rents kayaks; call (506) 876-1199 for details.

🏨 Motels, bed-and-breakfasts, and rental cottages available in nearby St.-Louis-de-Kent, Kouchibouguac, and Richibucto.

Gros Morne National Park

*Awe-inspiring scenery and a prodigious variety of bird life await visitors
to this fascinating park on the rugged west coast of Newfoundland.*

Established in 1973,
Gros Morne
National Park preserves
a spectacular
697-square-mile
(1,805-square-kilometer) piece
of Newfoundland's west coast
that is world-renowned for its
geological features. It includes a
large section of the Long Range
Mountains, which rise abruptly up to
2,624 feet (800 meters) above flat
coastal lowlands. These mountains
face the Gulf of Saint Lawrence and
create the highland backbone of the
park – a massive plateau formed from
blocks of granite bedrock that were
uplifted thousands of years ago by the
violent movement of tectonic plates
and then carved by glaciers. Visitors
can hike to the top of the mountains
to see the glacier-carved gorges from
above and watch wildlife such as arctic
hare and Rock Ptarmigan foraging on
the alpine plateau.

The Surf Scoter *male
features a multicolored,
bulging bill that bears
a large black spot.*

Habitat

Two distinct landscapes exist within
Gros Morne: a coastal lowland running
along the Gulf of Saint Lawrence and
an alpine plateau in the Long Range

BIRDS TO LOOK FOR

Surf Scoter • Rock Ptarmigan •
Whimbrel • Red Knot • Semipalmated
Sandpiper • White-rumped Sandpiper •
Dunlin • Glaucous Gull • Arctic Tern •
Three-toed Woodpecker • Olive-sided
Flycatcher • Yellow Warbler •
Blackpoll Warbler • Snow Bunting •
Common Redpoll

Mountains. But within these
landscapes lie a variety of habitats:
coastal plain, piedmont moraines,
slopes and upland areas, hills, beaches,
intertidal zones and estuaries, cliffs,
and sand dunes. The park also
includes bird-rich bogs, meandering
brooks, and some deep ponds
surrounded by vertical cliffs hundreds
of feet high.

Bird Life

At Saint Paul's Inlet, in the northern
part of the park, numerous shorebirds
gather for low-tide feeding in the
mudflats, from late July through
September. (Ask for tide information
at the Visitor Center.) Least and
Pectoral Sandpipers, Ruddy
Turnstones, Common Snipes, and
Hudsonian Godwits are found foraging
on the newly exposed mudflats by late
July. A couple of weeks later, White-
rumped and Semipalmated
Sandpipers, Red Knots, Short-billed
Dowitchers, and Whimbrels show up.
Dunlins and Baird's Sandpipers arrive
in September – although the latter are
difficult to spot.

Earlier in the summer (in June and
July) both Common Terns and Arctic

Semipalmated Sandpipers, among other shorebirds, gather on the mudflats.

Terns nest near Saint Paul's Inlet. Horned Larks also nest in the grassy areas above the mudflats. In winter, Saint Paul's Bay hosts numerous waterfowl, such as Surf Scoters, and gulls. Look for Iceland, Glaucous, and even Ivory Gulls.

South from Saint Paul's Inlet, near the entrance to the next inlet (Bonne Bay), is Lobster Cove Head. In summer, listen for male Bobolinks performing their bubbling *bob-o-link* song in the meadow near the lighthouse run by Gros Morne staff. Visitors may also hear the distinctive trills of Lincoln's Sparrows and Fox Sparrows and the pretty *o sweet Canada Canada Canada* song of the White-throated Sparrow.

Rock Ptarmigan *may be found in the park's alpine tundra; look especially near the top of Gros Morne Mountain.*

The woods in the lowland part along the James Callaghan Trail hold an assortment of interesting songbirds, including Common Redpolls, Swamp Sparrows, Olive-sided Flycatchers, and more. It takes about two hours to walk from the parking lot to the base of Gros Morne Mountain and back. Ambitious hikers can take this trail all the way to the summit (see Highlights for details).

The roads leading around the two arms of Bonne Bay (Highway 430 and Highway 431) provide good places to watch birds. Ospreys often fly over the bay, Northern Harriers course the open fields, and American Kestrels hover there, looking for mice and insects. Sometimes a Merlin will flash past – not much bigger than the American Kestrel but worlds apart in terms of speed and flying ability. At Rocky Harbour, a community adjacent to the park, whales, seals, and porpoises often swim within

easy binocular-viewing distance.
A walk through the area in spring
and summer can yield colorful
warblers, such as the Blackpoll,
Yellow, and Mourning.

VISITING

Although birdwatchers can find
interesting winter species – such as the
aforementioned scoters, gulls,
longspurs, and Snow Buntings – at
Gros Morne National Park, it can be
uncomfortably cold at that time of year.
Late spring through early fall is a far
more enjoyable and productive time to
look for birds here. Near Rocky

Harbour there is a great interpretive
center, where visitors can pick up a
map of all the local hiking trails.

HIGHLIGHTS

The James Callaghan Trail to the top
of Gros Morne Mountain is well worth
the six-hour round-trip hike. Look for
Three-toed Woodpeckers and Olive-
sided Flycatchers in the woods, and
Swamp Sparrows and Spotted
Sandpipers at the base. At the top of
the mountain, in the alpine meadows,
Rock Ptarmigan, Horned Larks, and
Water Pipits are routinely spotted.

Site Map and Information

GROS MORNE NATIONAL PARK

🚗 From North Sydney (in Nova Scotia)
take a ferry to Port aux Basques,
Newfoundland. Then take Route 1 (the
Trans Canada Highway) north 160 miles
(257.4-kilometers) to Deer Lake. From
Deer Lake, take Route 430 (the Viking
Trail) north toward Saint Anthony 19
miles (30.6 kilometers) to the park
entrance kiosk at Wiltondale. Another
option is to take a regular commercial
flight to Deer Lake and rent a car there.

⬜ Daily, 24 hours, year-round.

⬤ Never.

ℹ️ Gros Morne National Park, P.O. Box 130,
Rocky Harbour, Newfoundland A0K
4N0, Canada. The park headquarters at
Rocky Harbour are open weekdays year-
round, 8:00 a.m.–4:30 p.m. (except
holidays). Visitor Center hours vary by
season; call (709) 458-2066 before visiting.

📞 (709) 458-2417; www.grosmorne.pch.gc.ca

⑤ $5 (CAN) per adult; $4 per senior (over
65); $2.50 per youth (6 to 18 years old);
free for children under 6; $10 per family.

♿ The Visitor Center and the boardwalk at
Berry Head Pond, 3.5 miles (5.6

kilometers) north of Rocky Harbour off
Highway 430, are wheelchair accessible.
To reach TDD, call (709) 772-4564.

⛺ On-site campgrounds include Shallow
Bay, Berry Hill, Lomond, and Trout
River; call (800) 563-6353 for
reservations.

👥 Call Gros Morne Adventure Guides at
(709) 458-2722 or Discovery Outtripping
Company at (709) 634-6335.

🏨 Several motels and small inns are
available in the villages of Norris Point,
Rocky Harbour, Trout River, and
Wiltondale, all within or near the park.

NAHANNI NATIONAL PARK RESERVE

*A place of awesome beauty, this park in the heart of Canada's
Northwest Territories offers unrivaled scenic splendor for adventurous birders.*

Birders who like to visit out-of-the-way places will absolutely love Nahanni National Park Reserve. Not only is it unreachable by highway, the closest road is almost 40 miles (64 kilometers) away and downriver, making it virtually a necessity to fly into the park in a hired bush plane or helicopter. The heart of the park is the South Nahanni River, which flows for 300 miles (483 kilometers) through the park, cutting through four canyons and plunging over Virginia Falls, which is twice the height of Niagara Falls.

Nahanni is a long, narrow park, encompassing much of the South Nahanni River, the Flat River, several creeks and streams, and the surrounding mountains. Established in 1974, Nahanni National Park Reserve was put on the United Nations Educational, Scientific, and Cultural Organization (UNESCO) World Heritage list in 1978. People who visit Nahanni to canoe down its rivers, hike through its forests, canyons, and alpine tundra areas, or view its abundant wildlife will not be disappointed.

HABITAT

Nahanni National Park Reserve is a remarkable landscape with high, rugged mountains, deep canyon walls, lush alpine tundra, luxuriant virgin forests of spruce and aspen, steaming hot springs, and intriguing limestone cave complexes. Here, visitors will not find gas stations, department stores, telephones, or any communities. It is a true wilderness, virtually unchanged for centuries. The park has wonderful natural hot springs and several other places, with beautiful tufa (porous rock) deposits, a couple of which form great mounds, rising nearly 100 feet (30 meters) in the air. The wildlife sightings are spectacular. Bears, both grizzly and black, moose, dall sheep, and mountain goats are often seen in the valleys and wooded areas.

Yellow-rumped Warblers *winter farther north than any other warbler species.*

BIRD LIFE

More than 180 species of birds have been seen in Nahanni National Park Reserve. The area contains a mix of species – some more commonly seen in areas far to the south, such as Blue

BIRDS TO LOOK FOR

Pacific Loon • Lesser Scaup • Bufflehead • Common Goldeneye • Bald Eagle • Sharp-shinned Hawk • Spruce Grouse • Blue Grouse • Three-toed Woodpecker • Boreal Chickadee • Gray-cheeked Thrush • Bohemian Waxwing • White-winged Crossbill

The Bufflehead's large, almost puffy head makes it easy to identify.

Grouse, and others more typical of the far north, such as Arctic Terns. Many species of birds can be spotted while canoeing, at least in the calmer stretches of the river. The valleys are broad in places, with rich deltas and wide alluvial fans, where the rivers have deposited silt and soil for millennia. Taking time to hike in the forests and tributary canyons along the way can yield sightings of a host of northern species. Birders should look for Northern Hawk-Owl, Three-toed Woodpecker, Boreal Chickadee, Gray-cheeked Thrush, Bohemian Waxwing, and White-winged Crossbill in the wooded areas. Three species of grouse (Spruce, Blue, and Ruffed) can also be spotted there. In the deep gorges, Sharp-shinned Hawks and Peregrine Falcons are seen perched on ledges or flying over, searching for prey.

The river and Yohin Lake and Rabbitkettle Lake should be checked closely for waterfowl, which could include Pacific and Red-throated Loons, Northern Shovelers, Common Goldeneye, Bufflehead, Lesser Scaup, Green-winged Teal, and more. Bald Eagles can also be seen there.

White-tailed Ptarmigan usually stay high above, in their typical alpine tundra habitat, where they are sometimes pursued by Gyrfalcons or Golden Eagles. The massive alluvial fan at Prairie Creek is a good spot to see nesting Chipping

The Sharp-shinned Hawk *may be spotted soaring over this remote national park.*

Sparrows and Savannah Sparrows, as well as Upland Sandpipers and Common Nighthawks.

VISITING

The best time to visit Nahanni is from June through August. During other times of year, the weather can be dangerously cold, and there are far fewer birds. Birders should stop at the park's visitors center at Fort Simpson to view the extensive displays on the history, culture, and geography of the area, and obtain the necessary permits and pay the day-use fee. To reach the

park itself, visitors must hire a helicopter or float plane or take a guided tour with an outfitter. Wolverine Air (403) 695-2263 offers air service to the park.

HIGHLIGHTS

Yohin Lake is an important nesting area for waterfowl, including the rare Trumpeter Swan. Although no public access is allowed here, these stately birds may be watched as they forage along the South Nahanni River, from Yohin Bridge to Nahanni Butte.

Site Map and Information

NAHANNI NATIONAL PARK RESERVE

🚗 Fort Simpson, Northwest Territories, is the jumping off point for most trips to the park and can be reached by commercial airlines or road. From Edmonton, Alberta, take Highway 16 west about 18 miles to its junction with Highway 43, and continue north all the way to the city of Peace River. From there, take the Mackenzie Highway (Highway 35) north into the Northwest Territories, where it becomes Highway 1 and continue west to the park offices at Fort Simpson.

🅾 Daily, 24 hours, year-round.

⬤ Very few people attempt a visit outside the June through September period.

ℹ Nahanni National Park Reserve, PO Box 348, Fort Simpson, Northwest Territories X0E 0N0, Canada. The offices, which function as a Visitor Center, are open daily 8:30 a.m.–5:00 p.m. from mid-June to mid-September and on weekdays only throughout the rest of the year.

☎ (867) 695-3151

⑤ $10 (CAN) per person.

♿ No special facilities.

🅰 Primitive campsites are available at

Rabbitkettle Lake, the Rabbitkettle Portage, Virginia Falls, and Kraus Hotsprings.

🎫 There are three licensed companies: Nahanni River Adventures at (867) 668-3180; Nahanni Wilderness Adventures at (403) 637-3845; and Wilderness Adventure Company/Blackfeather at (705) 746-1372.

🛏 Motels and bed-and-breakfasts are available in Fort Simpson; call the Chamber of Commerce at (867) 695-3555 for listings.

WOOD BUFFALO NATIONAL PARK

Straddling the Northwest Territories and Alberta, Canada's most imposing national park boasts nesting Whooping Cranes and free-roaming bison.

Wood Buffalo National Park is not just the largest park in Canada; it is one of the largest parks in the entire world. Encompassing approximately 17,000 square miles (44,807 square kilometers) of wilderness, this amazing site hosts a staggering array of wildlife, including millions of migratory waterfowl, plus numerous wolves, lynxes, beavers, and of course the bison for which the park was named.

The Bufflehead *is one of many waterfowl found at the Peace-Athabasca Delta during spring and fall migration periods.*

Established in 1922 to protect a small herd of wood bison, the park is home to one of the largest free-roaming, unregulated populations of bison in the world. It is also distinguished by having the only wild breeding population of the endangered Whooping Crane. (Visitors are not allowed in or near the birds' nesting area during their breeding period, from spring to fall.)

HABITAT

Wood Buffalo National Park is composed of a varied patchwork of habitats, including shallow lakes, muskeg bogs, vast salt plains, and boreal forest of spruce, balsam fir, jack pine, aspen, and poplar. Slow-moving streams, as well as larger waterways such as the Athabasca, Peace, and Slave rivers, also wind through this massive wilderness. The Peace-Athabasca Delta area, one of the largest inland freshwater deltas on the entire planet, hosts millions of waterfowl each year.

BIRD LIFE

More than 225 species of birds have been recorded at Wood Buffalo National Park; 142 of them nest here. The best birdwatching site in the park is the Peace-Athabasca Delta. Here the waters of the large, slow-moving Peace, Athabasca, and Birch Rivers converge to form a massive wetland area that attracts birds from all four of the North American flyways during spring and fall migrations. The variety of species and the number of birds are staggering – Trumpeter Swan, White-winged Scoter, Common Goldeneye, Bufflehead, Northern Pintail, American Wigeon, and Green-winged Teal, as well as Osprey, Peregrine Falcon, Short-eared Owl, and both Golden and Bald Eagles – to name only waterfowl and raptors.

BIRDS TO LOOK FOR

Red-necked Grebe • American White Pelican • Trumpeter Swan • Northern Pintail • Green-winged Teal • Greater Scaup • Lesser Scaup • Bufflehead • Osprey • Bald Eagle • Golden Eagle • Peregrine Falcon • Whooping Crane • Short-eared Owl • Pine Grosbeak • White-winged Crossbill

The park protects the only breeding population of Whooping Cranes found in the wild.

The delta also provides excellent opportunities to mix backcountry wilderness canoeing and camping with birdwatching – although it is highly recommended that visitors hire a licensed park guide to help them explore the backcountry safely.

A prime delta destination is Sweetgrass Station, which lies south of the Peace River in the middle of huge delta meadows. The marshlands here attract a myriad of bird species. It's a 10-hour paddle from Peace Point (where cars are left) to Sweetgrass Landing. Only experienced canoeists should attempt this trip. (Another option is to hire a guide.) The seven-mile trail to Sweetgrass Station, which begins at Sweetgrass Landing, cuts

The Peregrine Falcon, *found in the park's wetlands and salt plains, is a local nester.*

through a boreal forest habitat.

Less adventuresome park visitors can experience the unique habitats and birdlife of the park without having to venture deep into the wilderness. Pine Lake Campground, about 37 miles (60 kilometers) south of Fort Smith, is an excellent place for family camping or day visits. The birding here is great: Common Loons, White-winged Scoters, Red-necked and Horned Grebes, and Buffleheads are often present on the water and White-winged Crossbills, Pine Grosbeaks, and other songbirds can be spotted in the woods. The Lakeside Trail, which leads from the Pine Lake Campground to the Kettle Point Group Camp, is a four-mile hike (6.4 kilometers) through aspen and spruce forest.

Another interesting and easily accessible place to birdwatch is the Salt Plains Overview. From Fort Smith, take Highway 5 west for 18.6 miles (30 kilometers), then turn south at the sign and drive for an additional 6.2 miles (10 kilometers). From this lookout birders sometimes spot Peregrine Falcons and Bald Eagles – both of which are local nesters – and get an excellent view of the park's salt plains. For a closer look, take the switchback trail down to the plains.

VISITING

Although the park itself can be visited year-round, the peak season for tourists runs from Memorial Day weekend in late May through Labor Day in September. The best times to visit are in late May or in September,

when there are fewer mosquitoes and other insects and more birds (because of the migrants present at those times). For much of the rest of the year the park is unpleasantly cold and fewer birds are present.

HIGHLIGHTS

The rocky islands in the Slave River hosts the northernmost nesting colony of American White Pelicans in the continent. These birds are fascinating to watch as they fish in the swift-moving river, often in large groups.

Site Map and Information

WOOD BUFFALO NATIONAL PARK

🚗 The MacKenzie Highway (Highway 35) intersects Highway 5 just south of the town of Hay River. From there, take Highway 5 east to Fort Smith, about 163 miles (262 km), where park headquarters and the main Visitor Center are located. Fort Smith can also be reached via regular commercial flights from Edmonton, Alberta.

🕐 Daily, 24 hours, year-round.

⬤ Never. An all-weather access road leading to Fort Smith is maintained year-round; however, parts of the park may be closed when snowfall is heavy.

ℹ️ Wood Buffalo National Park, Box 750, Fort Smith, Northwest Territories, Canada X0E 0P0. The Fort Smith Visitor Center and Fort Chipewyan Visitor Center are open daily, 9 a.m.–6 p.m., mid-June through August, and weekdays, 9 a.m.–5 p.m., the rest of the year.

📞 (867) 872-7960; www.parkscanada.pch.gc.ca/buffalo

Ⓢ None.

♿ Visitor Centers are wheelchair accessible, as are the Pine Lake Campground, and day-use areas. All-terrain wheelchairs are

loaned by request. To reach the Fort Smith TDD, call (867) 872-3727.

🅰️ Pine Lake Campground and Kettle Point Group Camp are on-site. Backcountry camping is permitted; register at one of the Visitor Centers and obtain fire and use permits.

👥 Contact park headquarters for an up-to-date list of licensed guides.

🏨 Hotels, motels, and bed-and-breakfasts are available in the towns of Fort Smith and Fort Chipewyan; call the Fort Smith Chamber of Commerce at (867) 872-2014 for listings.

CAPE BRETON HIGHLANDS NATIONAL PARK

This spectacular park, straddling the northern end of Nova Scotia's famed Cape Breton Island, is a place of awesome scenic splendor and diverse wildlife.

Established in 1936, Cape Breton Highlands National Park is a magnificent landscape of barren highlands, verdant forests, and rugged coastline. Three hundred and sixty-six square miles (950 square kilometers) in size, it protects some of the last remaining wilderness in Nova Scotia.

The Cabot Trail – one of the most scenic drives in the world – follows the park's western, northern, and eastern boundaries. Named for explorer John Cabot, who first set foot on the island in 1497, this 186-mile-long (300-kilometer) highway provides a breathtaking view of the park's rugged slopes and forests as well as of the beautiful Margaree Valley. The Cabot Trail also provides access to all of the park's other hiking trails, which take visitors through a wide range of bird-rich habitats and to numerous panoramic vistas.

The Pine Grosbeak *male features a distinctive rose-colored plumage.*

The geological diversity of Cape Breton Island is remarkable. The park contains the highest point in Nova Scotia – White Hill, rising 1,745 feet (532 meters) above sea level – and the west coast of the park has sea cliffs more than 984 feet (300 meters) high.

HABITAT

A great diversity of habitats exists within the park. The western shore rises above the Gulf of St. Lawrence to a broad plateau, covering a large area of the park. The interior high plateau is similar in many ways to subarctic regions far to the north. It has dry, rocky barrens, sphagnum bogs, and stunted spruce forest. Some large areas of the central plateau have no trees at all. Most of the rest of the park consists of mixed woodlands of conifers and hardwoods, typical of Acadian forest. The eastern shore of Cape Breton Highlands National Park, which borders the Atlantic Ocean, is also rocky but has many picturesque coves and sandy beaches at the mouths of valleys.

BIRD LIFE

The staff at one of the park's information centers at Cheticamp or Ingonish Beach offer tips on the most productive areas for specific birds. They can also recommend trails based

BIRDS TO LOOK FOR

Double-crested Cormorant • Northern Goshawk • Ruffed Grouse • Black-bellied Plover • Whimbrel • Ruddy Turnstone • White-rumped Sandpiper • Herring Gull • Great Black-backed Gull • Common Murre • Black Guillemot • Boreal Chickadee • Bay-breasted Warbler • Blackpoll Warbler • Mourning Warbler • Pine Grosbeak • White-winged Crossbill

Great Black-backed Gulls are one of the large seabirds seen along this rough coastline.

on their levels of difficulty and scenic beauty. In all the park has 26 trails, ranging in difficulty from a 20-minute stroll to mountainous climbs. Some of the trails that will take visitors through a variety of habitats and afford stunning views are the Skyline Trail, Jack Pine/Coastal Trail, and L'Acadien Trail. The Lone Shieling Trail winds through a virgin hardwood forest.

Common Murre *nest in colonies on the Bird Islands, just off Cape Breton's coast.*

From coastal viewpoints, birdwatchers should look for Northern Gannets making dramatic dives offshore. The coastal cliffs at the park host nesting Great Black-backed Gulls, Herring Gulls, Double-crested Cormorants, Great Cormorants, and Black Guillemots. Arctic Terns and Common Terns also nest near the park and can be seen over the water diving for tiny fish.

In summer many interesting northern forest songbirds nest in the park's vast woodlands, including the Blackpoll, Bay-breasted, Mourning, Blackburnian Warblers; the Boreal Chickadee; Pine Grosbeak; Pine Siskin; and the Red and White-winged Crossbills, some of which reach the southern limit of their breeding range here. Spruce Grouse and Ruffed Grouse, as well as their main predator, the Northern Goshawk, are commonly seen in the park's wooded areas. On inland ponds birdwatchers should be on the lookout for Red-breasted Mergansers, Common Mergansers, Common Goldeneyes, Ring-necked Ducks, and American Black Ducks.

Visitors who come from August through October should search the park's coastline for several migrating shorebirds, which could include Whimbrels, Ruddy Turnstones, Black-bellied Plover, and White-rumped Sandpipers.

VISITING

One of the best ways to explore Cape Breton Highlands National Park is to start at the Cheticamp Information Center on the western entrance to the park, taking full advantage of its extensive tourist services, and then drive around the perimeter of the park counterclockwise, exiting at Ingonish Beach. The Cheticamp Information Center offers a 10-minute slide show about the park, as well as a children's corner. Park staff present interpretive displays during July and August. Visitors who want to see the park in the full glory of its autumn foliage should go there in late September or early October. Visitors should plan on spending at least four days at the park.

HIGHLIGHTS

South of the national park, just off the east coast of Cape Breton Island, are some tiny islands called the Bird Islands. Boat tour operators in Big Bras d'Or take passengers on cruises around the island, where they can see nesting colonies of Leach's Storm-Petrels, Razorbills, Great Cormorants, Double-crested Cormorants, Black Guillemots, and Common Murre, as well as gulls. Call (902) 674-2384 or (902) 929-2563 to make reservations.

Site Map and Information

CAPE BRETON HIGHLANDS NATIONAL PARK

🚗 From Sydney, take Route 125 west to the Trans-Canada Highway (105). Turn north on the Cabot Trail at St. Ann's Bay or just north of Baddeck and follow it to the park entrances at Cheticamp (western) or Ingonish Beach (eastern).

🕐 Daily, 24 hours, year-round.

⬤ Never, although some facilities are closed during winter.

🅷 Cape Breton Highlands National Park, Ingonish Beach, Nova Scotia B0C 1L0, Canada. Cheticamp and Ingonish Information Centers are open daily, 8 a.m.–8 p.m., late June to September 1.

📞 (902) 224-2306 (Cheticamp Information Center); www.parks.canada.pch.gc.ca

💲 $3.50(CAN) per adult; $2.50(CAN) per senior (65 and older); $1.50(CAN) per youth (6 to 16); free for children under 6; $8(CAN) per family.

♿ Both information centers and some park campsites, trails, and picnic areas are wheelchair accessible.

🅰 The park has 6 campgrounds. No reservations are accepted except for at group campgrounds and for wheelchair-accessible sites. Call the number above for details.

🎒 Call Outside Expeditions at (902) 963-3366 for information.

🛏 Motels are available in nearby Ingonish Beach, Cheticamp, Dingwall, Cape North, and Pleasant Bay.

AMHERST ISLAND

In good years, this tiny island just off the southeastern shore of Lake Ontario is
unsurpassed for viewing wintering owls and other fascinating raptors up close.

Although Amherst Island is barely 10 miles long and three miles (16 by 5 kilometers) wide at its broadest point, it is becoming a world-famous winter birdwatching locale. The reason? Owls. During some winters Amherst Island, together with adjacent Wolfe Island boast more individuals and more species of owls than any other birding area in North America. It is also a great place to watch other raptors, such as Rough-legged and Red-tailed Hawks and Northern Harriers.

Located in the northeastern corner of Lake Ontario, just a couple of miles offshore, the island is easily accessible by ferry year-round. (The ferry company keeps a channel open all winter, even when the surrounding water is frozen.)

Eastern Screech-Owls *have gray or brown plumage and feature tufted ears and yellow eyes.*

shoreline, and a scattering of small woodlots. There are numerous small farms with pastures, and also a vast cranberry bog. What makes the island, in good years, such a great place to find raptors is not its habitats so much as its prey base. Incredible numbers of meadow voles (small, mouselike rodents) provide a bountiful feast for any predator that makes its way to the island.

BIRD LIFE

The eastern tip of the island is the Kingston Field Naturalists' Amherst Island Reserve. This area is open to members and their accompanied guests only, so contact the organization in advance to obtain a member's assistance (number listed below). Except for this and a small public beach, the rest of the island is private property, but it has a network of paved and gravel roads that allow birdwatchers in cars to view most areas.

Winter owl viewing is normally done in the daylight hours. Birdwatchers should drive slowly, stopping frequently to check fence posts, trees, ground, rooftops, TV antennae, and hydro poles for owls. Short-eared Owls, Snowy Owls, and Eastern Screech-Owls are often seen perched on the ground or on ice floes just offshore. These, as well as Great Gray Owls and Northern Hawk Owls, often hunt during daylight, providing

HABITAT

Amherst Island is largely flat and open, with fields, marshes, limestone

BIRDS TO LOOK FOR

Northern Harrier • Red-tailed Hawk •
Rough-legged Hawk • American
Kestrel • Eastern Screech-Owl •
Great Horned Owl • Snowy Owl •
Northern Hawk Owl • Great Gray
Owl • Long-eared Owl • Short-eared
Owl • Boreal Owl • Northern Saw-
whet Owl • Northern Shrike •
Snow Bunting

Visit Owl Woods near the east end of the island to see Northern Saw-whet Owls.

spectacular views of these birds in flight. Birdwatchers should also look for Northern Shrikes perched on low trees and flocks of Snow Buntings and Lapland Longspurs on the roads and in the open fields.

The woodlot near the eastern end of the island – appropriately nicknamed "Owl Woods" – is the best place to look for Northern Saw-whet Owls, Boreal Owls, and Long-eared Owls, which roost there during the day. These woods are on private land, but the Kingston Field Naturalists have obtained permission from the owners to bird in this area; contact the organization to make arrangements to visit. Then follow the path leading to the clumps of small trees. Look on the ground for white droppings as well as small pellets of undigested fur and bone. Right above these telltale

Northern Hawk Owls *can often be seen hunting in the daytime.*

clues there may be a Northern Saw-whet or Boreal Owl staring down sleepily. Long-eared and Great Horned Owls are much more wary and tend to flush if approached.

Although winter is the most popular birding season at Amherst Island, spring and fall migrations are productive times, too. Numerous songbirds species, such as Swainson's Thrushes, Golden-winged Warblers, and Fox Sparrows, use the island as a stopover during migration periods. Shorebirds such as Whimbrels can be seen on the beaches, and waterfowl such as Brant and Greater Scaup may be spotted offshore. Upland Sandpipers, Short-eared Owls, Northern Harriers, and American Kestrels, as well as Clay-colored Sparrows, Bobolinks, and Horned Larks nest on the island in summer.

VISITING

Despite its year-round attractions, winter, in a good year, is the best time to experience Amherst Island. Unlike most birdwatching areas in Canada, which basically shut down when the snow starts to fall, it is just coming into its own in late January. Owls may continue to arrive all winter long, so birdwatchers visiting in February and early March tend to see the most owl species. Winter visitors should be sure to wear warm clothing. The weather can be extremely cold.

Before visiting Amherst Island, contact the Kingston Field Naturalists for an update. During some winters nearby Wolfe Island has more owls than Amherst Island – largely because its vole population peaks in different years. In addition to confirming the best island to visit, the organization will share which raptors and other birds have been seen so far that year.

HIGHLIGHTS

The Snowy Owls that show up on the island are a big attraction. Drive slowly along the gravel roads on both sides of Highway 95, watching for them sitting on fence posts or on the ground, or flying overhead. South Shore Road is another good place to look for Snowy Owls, and visitors should also scope ice floes offshore.

Site Map and Information

AMHERST ISLAND

🗺 From Syracuse, New York, take Route 81 into Canada. Turn west (toward Toronto) onto the MacDonald-Cartier Freeway (Highway 401) and follow it to Kingston. From there, take the scenic Loyalist Parkway (Highway 33) west 13 miles (21 kilometers) to Millhaven, which has year-round ferry service to the island. The ferry runs hourly from 6:20 a.m. to 1:20 a.m. and charges $3.50 (CAN) round-trip per passenger car.

🚻 Amherst Island is accessible by ferry year-round. Paved and gravel roads and a small beach are open to the public, but visitors should contact the Kingston Field Naturalists to arrange access to the reserve and other privately owned areas.

⬤ Never.

ℹ For general information, contact the Kingston Field Naturalists, P.O. Box 831, Kingston, Ontario K7L 4X6, Canada. There is no Visitor Center.

📞 (613) 549-8023
(Kingston Field Naturalists);
http://psyc.queensu.ca/~davids/kfn.html

$ None.

♿ No special facilities.

⛺ None on-site. Call the Tourist Center at (613) 548-4445 for listings of campgrounds on the mainland.

👥 Contact the Kingston Field Naturalists (see above) for details about group birdwatching trips on the island.

🏨 Three bed-and-breakfasts are available on the island: Stella Bay Bed and Breakfast at (613) 389-6725; Poplar Dell Farm Vacation Home at (613) 389-2012 (telephone/fax); and Anniversary House at (613) 389-8190.

LONG POINT

For spectacular warbler migrations and great hawk flights,
visit this amazing birdwatching oasis on Lake Erie's northern shore.

When it comes to birdwatching in Canada, few areas are as promising as southern Ontario's Long Point. More than 360 species of birds have been recorded on this sandspit, which thrusts eastward 19 miles (30 kilometers) into Lake Erie. For many birds migrating north in spring, Long Point is the first landfall after their arduous crossing of Lake Erie. In fall it's a jumping-off point for southbound migrants. And in summer birders can find an interesting array of local breeding birds, some of which are rare. It's no wonder that the site has been designated a World Biosphere Site by the United Nations.

Sharp-shinned Hawks, *abundant in the fall, prey primarily on small birds.*

precious habitats, a group of forward-thinking businessmen bought almost 15,000 acres (6,000 hectares) on this sandspit in 1866. Soon after, they formed the Long Point Company, with the goal of preserving the habitats and wildlife of this unique place.

The company ultimately donated much of their holdings to Canada's federal government, which now operates the land as a national wildlife area. Although much of this area is inaccessible to the general public, there are dozens of birding sites that are open to all.

HABITAT
Long Point offers a mix of habitats ranging from dry uplands to wet lowlands. Meadows, marshes, ponds, and sand dunes – and, consequently, a rich variety of bird life – are found on these lands. In summer birds of the northern boreal forests nest practically side by side with species that are more typically southern.

In the mid-19th century the ducks, geese, and swans of Long Point were being decimated by commercial hunters. To protect this area and its

BIRD LIFE
During spring migration Long Point is an excellent spot for warbler-watching. At the peak of migration in mid-May, Black-throated Green, Blackburnian, Cape May, Chestnut-sided, Orange-crowned, Tennessee, and Yellow-rumped warblers, along with many other warbler species, visit the

---

BIRDS TO LOOK FOR

Common Loon • Tundra Swan •
Canvasback • Hooded Merganser •
Bald Eagle • Sharp-shinned Hawk •
Broad-winged Hawk • Sandhill
Crane • Little Gull • Forster's Tern •
Black Tern • Short-eared Owl •
Pileated Woodpecker • Prothonotary
Warbler • Hooded Warbler

Thousands of Canvasbacks can be seen at Long Point during the spring.

sandspit en route from their wintering areas to their northern breeding grounds. Long Point Provincial Park, located at the end of Highway 59, is a great place to look for these warblers and other migrants. Visitors will enjoy the colorful breeding plumages of these songbirds and others, including Scarlet Tanagers, Baltimore Orioles, and Rose-breasted Grosbeaks.

Spring is also a spectacular season to view waterfowl. Thousands of Tundra Swans, Canvasbacks, Hooded Mergansers, and numerous other ducks and geese move through the area at this time of year.

Long Point's fall migration period also has its charms. The songbirds are not as brightly colored as in spring and summer, and they're relatively quiet; however, the cold-weather plumage of these migrating birds can provide interesting identification

challenges for birdwatchers. Autumn is also an especially good time for hawk-watching. Sometimes hundreds of Sharp-shinned Hawks can be seen on a single day in September. The provincial park is an excellent place to see them; look there for Northern Harriers as well.

Summer is a bonanza for Long Point birdwatchers. With luck they can find Prothonotary and Hooded Warblers breeding here, as well as Bald Eagles, Red-breasted Mergansers, Northern Pintail, Blue-winged Teal, King Rails, Short-eared Owls, and many, many others. At least 173 varieties of birds

Hooded Mergansers, *both male and female, feature fluffy rounded crests and thin bills.*

are known to have nested at Long Point. From June through mid-July it's not difficult for an avid birder to find more than 100 species of birds in a day.

VISITING

The Long Point Bird Observatory (LPBO) is an excellent place to begin any visit to this area. Stop by the Visitor Center for information about Long Point and LPBO's programs. Pick up an annotated checklist of Long Point's birds and a detailed regional bird-finding guide as well.

LPBO is a working research center operated by Bird Studies Canada. It uses professional ornithologists as well as numerous amateur birdwatchers to study both the migrant and breeding birds of Long Point. The nonprofit organization provides bird-banding demonstrations, which offer visitors the opportunity to view birds up close while they're being banded and released. To date, staff and volunteers have banded more than 600,000 birds of about 275 different species.

HIGHLIGHTS

Thousands of waterfowl migrate through the Long Point area each spring, including Tundra Swans. One place to look for these magnificent birds is near the dock at Port Rowan, from late March through mid-April.

Site Map and Information

LONG POINT

From Simcoe, take Highway 3 west to Highway 59 (or from Woodstock, take Highway 59 south). Continue south on Highway 59 to the north shore of Lake Erie. Long Point Bird Observatory is on Old Cut Boulevard, two streets before Highway 59 ends at Long Point Provincial Park. Parking is available on the other side of the boulevard.

Daily, during spring and fall migrations (April through mid-June and August through mid-November).

Winter (mid-November through March).

Long Point Bird Observatory, P.O. Box 160, Port Rowan, Ontario, Canada N0E 1M0. The observatory, including the Visitor Center, is open to the public during spring and fall migrations. One of three migration monitoring stations is open to the public daily, 6 a.m.– 12 p.m., during these periods.

(519) 586-2885 (during migration periods) or (519) 586-3531 (winter); www.bsc-eoc.org

None, but donations are welcome.

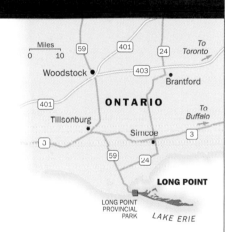

Services are available; call for details.

Campsites available at Long Point Provincial Park, Backus Conservation Area, and Turkey Point Provincial Park.

Organized tours can be arranged through the observatory; call ahead for reservations.

Hotels, motels, and bed-and-breakfasts are available in nearby Port Dover and Simcoe; call the Port-Rowan/Long Point Chamber of Commerce at (519) 586-7048 for listings.

PRINCE EDWARD ISLAND NATIONAL PARK

Picturesque beaches, red sandstone cliffs, and a rich mix of habitats make this popular park on Prince Edward Island a must-see for birdwatchers.

When French explorer Jacques Cartier first set foot on Prince Edward Island in 1534, he found a pristine island with forests of maple, larch, beech, oak, and hemlock, and friendly residents – the Mi'kwaq. But it didn't take the later European settlers long to cut down most of the trees to provide open land for farming and wood for building. Fortunately, the story didn't end there. Twenty-six miles (forty-two kilometers) of scenic coastline on the north shore of the island was set aside in 1937 as Prince Edward Island National Park of Canada, and another lovely 3-mile (5-kilometer) stretch was added in 1998.

With its picturesque beaches, distinctive red sandstone cliffs, and massive sand dunes set against the deep blue waters of the Gulf of Saint Lawrence, the north shore of Prince Edward Island has been a popular vacation spot since the late 19th century.

The Spotted Sandpiper, *a local nester, is just one of a variety of shorebirds drawn to the island's barrier beaches.*

BIRDS TO LOOK FOR

Great Cormorant • Great Blue Heron • Canada Goose • Brant • American Black Duck • Ring-necked Duck • Red-breasted Merganser • Osprey • Northern Harrier • Piping Plover • Willet • Spotted Sandpiper • Caspian Tern • Common Tern • Arctic Tern • Black Guillemot • Bank Swallow

HABITAT

Prince Edward Island National Park offers a mix of habitats for both resident and migratory birds. Barrier beaches host an assortment of shorebirds, foraging along the water's edge during migration. Surf Scoters, White-winged Scoters, and other sea ducks swim offshore in the Gulf of Saint Lawrence. Mixed deciduous and coniferous woodlands hold an assortment of colorful warblers. In addition the ponds, salt marshes, and shallow bays provide breeding habitat for a variety of waterfowl.

One of the most striking habitats in the park is found on the sand dunes, many of which are huge and almost reminiscent of the vast dunes in a North African desert. Waves, water currents, and high winds are constantly at work on the dunes, creating a dynamic shoreline environment. The park is making a major effort to protect the long-rooted marram grass that helps to anchor the dunes in place. If these dunes become unstable, they will not adequately support vegetation and wildlife.

BIRD LIFE

The national park is the most popular place to birdwatch in the entire province of Prince Edward Island. That's not surprising, considering that more than 210 of the 330 species recorded on the island can be seen

Black Guillemots are known as "penguins of the north."

here. The park's official symbol is the Great Blue Heron, and it's easy to see dozens of these waders foraging in the water when driving through the park or walking the trails. They have a nesting colony nearby, but it is closed to the public during breeding season.

Approximately 25 pairs of Piping Plovers (almost 2 percent of the world's population) also nest on the sandy beaches in several areas of the park; these areas are also closed when the birds are nesting. A good place to watch waterfowl is Long Pond, where Mallards, American Black Ducks, American Wigeon, and many other ducks nest. Watch Northern Pintails dabbling for aquatic vegetation in the shallows, while Red-breasted Mergansers dive for fish in the deeper water and Ring-necked Ducks harvest tiny invertebrates from the muddy bottom of the pond. As summer progresses, it is possible to

spot some adult ducks being trailed by their lively ducklings.

Starting in early August, many migrating shorebirds stop on the park's beaches or around its ponds and marshes, resting en route from their arctic breeding grounds to their wintering areas far to the south. Hudsonian Godwits, Red Knots, Short-billed Dowitchers, Dunlins, Black-bellied Plovers, and tiny Sanderlings are just a few of the many species that are regularly seen during migration. One of the best areas to check for shorebirds is the marsh

The Ring-necked Duck's *cinnamon collar is difficult to see; look instead for its peaked head and white-ringed bill.*

between Covehead Harbor and Brackley Beach. Huge flocks of migrating swallows also roost along the beaches in August.

VISITING
Prince Edward Island National Park offers interesting birdwatching opportunities almost any time from late May through August. Many migrants pass through at the beginning and end of that period, and local breeding species can be seen throughout that time. But even in winter you can find Barrow's

Goldeneyes, Oldsquaws, and other northern ducks. July is the warmest month, but the moderating effects of the Gulf of Saint Lawrence help to maintain pleasant temperatures a little longer into the fall here than in other places at the same latitude.

HIGHLIGHTS

The Great Cormorants nesting west of Orby Head are well worth seeing. The colony is located approximately 3 miles (5 kilometers) west of the park entrance at North Rustico.

Site Map and Information

PRINCE EDWARD ISLAND
NATIONAL PARK

🚌 The park has seven entrances: six are located north of Charlottetown, off Highway 6 (Blue Heron Drive); one is located east of Charlottetown off Highway 313.

🗓 Daily with full services from late June through early September. (Entrance kiosks are open 11 a.m. to 5 p.m. from June 9 to June 22 and from 9 a.m. to 7 p.m. from June 23 through September 3.)

⬤ Never.

ℹ Prince Edward Island National Park of Canada, 2 Palmers Lane, Charlottetown, PE, Canada C1A 5V6. Cavendish and Brackley Visitor Centers are open from late May until mid- to late October. Greenwich Visitor Center is open from July to early October.

☎ (902) 672-6350; parkscanada.pch.gc.ca/pei

💲 $3 (CAN) adult; $2 per senior (over 65); $1.50 per youth (6–16); children (under 6) free; $7 per family.

♿ All Visitor Centers and the Reeds and Rushes Trail are wheelchair accessible. A beach wheelchair can be borrowed free of charge at Stanhope Campground. To reach TTY, call (902) 566-7061.

🏕 The park has 3 campgrounds—Robinson's Island, Stanhope, and Cavendish; call (800) 414-6765 for reservations.

👥 Guided tours are available with advanced reservation; call one of the Visitor Centers.

🛏 There are numerous hotels, motels, bed-and-breakfasts, and rental cottages in nearby Stanhope and Brackley Beach, and the historic Dalvay-by-the-Sea Hotel is within the park. For more information, call Prince Edward Island Tourism at (888) PEI-PLAY.

FORILLON NATIONAL PARK

At the farthest reach of Quebec's famed Gaspé peninsula, this park offers a majestic landscape of lofty cliffs, mountains, and sea and hosts over 225 species of birds.

Established in 1970, Forillon National Park encompasses some 95 square miles (246 square kilometers) of ruggedly beautiful forest, cliff, and seashore at the northeastern tip of the picturesque Gaspé peninsula. The peninsula actually forms the northeasternmost end of the Appalachian mountain system. The indigenous people, the Mi'kmaq, called it Gespeg – "the place where land ends" – thus the Europeanized name Gaspé.

The ocean environment is an ever-present part of Forillon National Park. The abundance of marine life attracts scores of seabirds, as well as gray and harbor seals and seven species of whales. The rocky escarpments, some rising hundreds of feet above the sea, provide both an awesome spectacle for visitors and prime nest sites for thousands of seabirds each summer.

The Belted Kingfisher *has a call that sounds like a big rattle.*

forest. Several rivers and streams flow through the park, and there are also five small lakes and numerous ponds, providing rich aquatic habitat for birds such as the Belted Kingfisher, Wood Duck, and American Black Duck. Some of the seacliffs support a number of arctic-alpine plants – remnants of the last ice age.

BIRD LIFE

More than 242 species of birds have been recorded at Forillon National Park, and at least 76 of them nest here. The greatest concentration of nesting seabirds is at Bon Ami Cape. Worn and weathered, the cliffs bear numerous narrow ledges, providing nest sites for thousands of Black-legged Kittiwakes. These small, dainty gulls are pelagic birds, coming to land only to breed each summer. They feed on small fishes, such as capelins and lancelets, which are numerous in the surrounding waters. The cliffs also host colonies of

HABITAT

Forillon boasts 10 distinct ecosystems: forest, lakes, streams, cliffs, alpine meadows, fallow fields, sand dunes, freshwater marshes, saltwater marshes, and seashore. The vast majority of the land in the park is forested at the lower levels with mixed woodlands and at the higher levels with coniferous woods typical of the boreal

BIRDS TO LOOK FOR

Double-crested Cormorant • American Black Duck • Northern Harrier • Rough-legged Hawk • Semipalmated Sandpiper • Purple Sandpiper • Herring Gull • Black-legged Kittiwake • Razorbill • Black Guillemot • Belted Kingfisher • Black-throated Green Warbler • Purple Finch

This grand coastal park draws Black-legged Kittiwakes, among other gulls.

Double-crested Cormorants, Herring Gulls, Black Guillemots, and Razorbills. Birdwatchers should also look for Peregrine Falcons along the cliffs of Forillon. In the late 1980s the Canadian Wildlife Service released 32 captive-bred Peregrine Falcons at the park, so there's definitely a chance of finding a breeding pair and their young here in summer.

Arctic Peregrine Falcons – as well as other migrating raptors such as Merlins, Sharp-shinned Hawks, Northern Harriers, and Rough-legged Hawks – also pass through Forillon during spring and fall migrations. Birdwatchers who visit at these times should choose a lofty vantage point – such as the spectacular observation tower on Mont Saint-Alban, which rises 928 feet (283 meters) above sea level – to watch for migrating raptors and other birds. The trail leading up

to this tower is worth experiencing, for its magnificent views of the cliffs and sea. In addition to raptors, numerous waterfowl, warblers, and finches also pass through Forillon during both migrations. The salt marsh at Penouille and L'Anse-au-Griffon valley are good places to look for migrants.

Forillon has nine developed hiking trails, which pass through a variety of bird-rich habitats and provide access to some beautiful viewpoints. Les Graves Trail, about five miles (eight kilometers) round-trip, leads to some nice coves with pebble beaches,

The American Black Duck *nests here by woodland lakes and streams.*

where birdwatchers can look for shorebirds such as Purple Sandpipers, Short-billed Dowitchers, Sanderlings, Least Sandpipers, and Semipalmated Sandpipers in spring, late summer, and fall. Les Cretes Trail is a long trip, but it leads through a wooded, mountainous area where hikers should watch and listen for nesting songbirds such as Purple Finches, Black-throated Green Warblers, and Red-breasted Nuthatches.

VISITING

To see migrants, visit Forillon in April and May or August through October. Resident landbirds and cliff-nesting seabirds are present all summer long. Visitors should go to the reception

centers at Penouille and L'Anse-au-Griffon or to the Interpretive Center near Cap-des-Rosiers to find out about the many services offered by the park.

During the summer the park staff provides a wide range of interpretive services, including films, slide shows, and lectures; guided hikes on some of the park's trails; and on-site talks about the varied habitats, wildlife, and birds, found at Forillon.

HIGHLIGHTS

Forillon National Park is one of the best places for sea kayaking. Cime Aventure (see Outfitters, below) offers guided wildlife-watching kayak tours and also rents kayaks.

Site Map and Information

FORILLON NATIONAL PARK

🚌 From Quebec City, drive east on Highway 132, following the shore of the St. Lawrence River about 375 miles (603 kilometers) in all to reach the park, at the northeastern tip of the Gaspé peninsula.

⬜ Daily, 24 hours, year-round.

⬤ Never, although bad weather conditions can close some roads.

ℹ️ Forillon National Park, 122 Gaspé Boulevard, Gaspé, Quebec G4X 1A9, Canada. Penouille Visitor Center is in the southern part of the park; L'Anse-au-Griffon is in the north. Hours vary; call ahead before visiting.

📞 (418) 368-5505; www.parkscanada.pch.gc/ca/forillon

💲 $3.75 (CAN) per adult.

♿ Some parts of the park offer alternative programs for people with disabilities. Prelude to Forillon has specially designed exhibits for people with physical or visual disabilities.

🏕️ The park has 4 commercial campgrounds as well as primitive campsites; call (418) 368-6050 for details.

🚣 For sea-kayaking tours contact Cime Aventure at (418) 892-5088.

🏨 Hotels and motels are available in the nearby villages of Cap-des-Rosiers, Cap-aux-Os, Riviére-au-Renard, and L'Anse-au-Griffon; contact the Gaspé Chamber of Commerce at (418) 638-3521 for listings.

PRINCE ALBERT NATIONAL PARK

Prince Albert National Park encompasses almost a million acres of Saskatchewan wilderness occupied by an impressive variety of birds and other wildlife.

W atching the landscape transform while driving through southern Saskatchewan to Prince Albert National Park is an enlightening experience. The scenery changes drastically, panning from vast agricultural areas with endless fields of grain, through picturesque aspen parkland, and finally into gently rolling hills dominated by evergreens, spruce bogs, and massive lakes. The park sits at the southern edge of the great boreal forest, which is home to a spectacular array of northern species, including interesting owls, woodpeckers, and other birds typical of the region.

Horned Grebes, *as well as Red-necked and Western, can be found in the park's many lakes, ponds, and wetlands.*

HABITAT

Prince Albert National Park lies in a transition zone where fescue grassland mixed with aspen parkland gives way to boreal forest in the northern half of the park. In fact, fully one-third of Canada's fescue grasslands – tufted perennial grasses that once formed a

---

BIRDS TO LOOK FOR

Horned Grebe • Red-necked Grebe • American White Pelican • Great Gray Owl • Boreal Owl • Black-backed Woodpecker • Olive-sided Flycatcher • Yellow-bellied Flycatcher • Gray Jay • Blackburnian Warbler • Bay-breasted Warbler • Blackpoll Warbler • White-winged Crossbill • Pine Siskin

---

major ecosystem in this country – exist in the southwestern section of the park. Because of the mixture of habitats, wildlife ranging from prairie species to those found only in the densest northern forests are both found within this park.

The park's terrain was formed thousands of years ago by huge glaciers that gouged the land, creating large bodies of water such as Kingsmere, Crean, and Waskesiu Lakes. This is still wild country, where on many nights campers lie awake watching the flickering lights of aurora borealis, while listening to the haunting tremolo calls of loons and the distant howls of wolves. Bison, woodland caribou, bear, moose, lynx, elk, and other wild creatures still roam freely in this fully protected wilderness environment.

BIRD LIFE

Lavallée Lake, in the northwestern section of the park, has the second-largest colony of American White Pelicans in the entire country, often

The Boreal Owl roosts in the thick foliage found at Prince Albert National Park.

numbering well over 15,000 birds. Although the immediate area of the colony is restricted to protect the birds and can be visited only with special permission, plenty of bird-rich areas exist throughout the park. More than 231 species of birds have been recorded here.

Prince Albert National Park is a promising place to look for northern forest specialties, such as Great Gray Owls, Boreal Owls, Boreal Chickadees, Black-backed Woodpeckers, Pine Siskins, White-winged Crossbills, and Gray Jays. Black-throated Green, Blackpoll, Bay-breasted, Blackburnian, Cape May, and Magnolia Warblers, as well as Olive-sided and Yellow-bellied Flycatchers, are found with ease in the central and northern areas of the

park. Look in the park's northern bogs for Northern Waterthrushes, Palm and Nashville Warblers, and Swamp Sparrows. The many lakes, ponds, and other wetland areas provide habitat for a wide range of birds, including Common Loons, Red-necked, Horned, and Western Grebes; and numerous duck species.

VISITING

Several hiking trails are available in Prince Albert National Park, providing access to a range of habitats. The Boundary Bog, Mud Creek Trails, and Narrows Peninsula are

Red-necked Grebes *breed on the shallow lakes. Listen for their* crick-crick *call and braying.*

particularly good for spring warbler watching. Namekus and Shady Lakes are great places to look for migrants during both spring and fall migrations.

The Information and Nature Centers are located in the village of Waskesiu Lake, at the southern end of the lake. The Information Center is a great place to begin a visit to this picturesque site. Pick up useful maps of foot, bicycle, cross-country ski, and canoe routes (bicycles and canoes can be rented nearby). From there, visit the Nature Center, where the knowledgeable staff will share the latest birdwatching information.

HIGHLIGHTS

One of the most interesting ways to go birdwatching at Prince Albert National Park is to travel by canoe. Canoes, which can be rented at the park, allow visitors access to areas that are difficult to reach on foot and provide close looks at loons and a variety of other waterfowl, as well as many mammals, from moose to beavers. Canoeing is best done in spring and early summer when the water level in the park's lakes is highest. (Remember to bring plenty of insect repellent.)

Site Map and Information

PRINCE ALBERT NATIONAL PARK

▣ The park is just 50 miles (80 km) north of the city of Prince Albert. Take Highway 2 north from Prince Albert and turn west on either Highway 263 (the scenic route) or farther north at Highway 264 to reach park entrances.

◻ Daily, 24 hours, year-round.

◉ Never.

■ Prince Albert National Park, Box 100, Waskesiu Lake, Saskatchewan S0J 2Y0, Canada. The Information Center is open daily from mid-May through early October and on Saturdays during the cross-country skiing season (approximately November through March). The rest of the year, it has reduced hours. The Nature Center is open daily from late June through the end of August, and on weekends in early June and in September.

▮ (877) 255-7267; www.parkscanada.pch.gc.ca/albert

⑤ A park entry permit can be purchased at any park entrance gate, campground kiosk, or at the Information Center.

& The park has a wide range of wheelchair-accessible services and facilities; contact the Information Center for details.

▲ Choices range from full-service RV parks with hookups to rustic unserviced sites to many backcountry hike-in sites. Commercial campgrounds are also available in the townsite of Waskesiu.

▥ Call the park's toll-free number for information about guiding services.

⊞ The scenic village of Waskesiu Lake, which is located inside the park, has hotels, motels, and rustic cottages available for visitors.

KLUANE NATIONAL PARK AND RESERVE

This park's high mountains, valley, and woodlands in the wilds of Yukon Territory are home to wolves, bears, and numerous species of birds.

To people throughout the world the Yukon has almost magical appeal – conjuring up images of rugged adventure, vast untamed country, and spectacular wildlife – and this is not an inaccurate picture. Lying between Canada's Northwest Territories on the east and the state of Alaska on the west, the Yukon holds tens of thousands of miles of pristine wilderness, high mountains, massive glaciers, alpine meadows, lush valleys, and clear rivers and lakes.

Gray-crowned Rosy-Finches *are fairly numerous in alpine regions.*

No place within the Yukon possesses more of these special features than Kluane National Park and Reserve, an approximately 8,500-square-mile (22,000-square-kilometer) park in the southwestern corner. The area was first set aside as a wildlife reserve in 1942, shortly after the Alaska Highway opened, but it wasn't until 1972 that the present Kluane National Park and Reserve was established.

HABITAT

Several of Canada's highest mountain peaks – including Mount Logan, the highest in the country – lie inside Kluane National Park and Reserve. These are covered by the world's largest nonpolar ice fields and boast huge glaciers that radiate into the high valleys.

From the lower valleys and slopes, covered with white spruce, aspen, and balsam poplar, to the alpine zone, to an open tundra area, which in summer is ablaze with colorful wildflowers, the park is home to an amazingly diverse group of plant and animal species. Moose are common in the wooded river valleys, and black bears, grizzly bears, and wolves also are seen regularly.

BIRDS TO LOOK FOR

Trumpeter Swan • Tundra Swan • Golden Eagle • Spruce Grouse • Willow Ptarmigan • Rock Ptarmigan • White-tailed Ptarmigan • Red-necked Phalarope • Mountain Bluebird • Varied Thrush • Yellow Warbler • Blackpoll Warbler • Wilson's Warbler • Smith's Longspur • Snow Bunting • Gray-crowned Rosy-Finch

BIRD LIFE

One hundred and eighty species of birds have been recorded at the park. Because 118 of them are confirmed nesters, birdwatchers have a good chance of seeing a variety of interesting species from June through mid-September.

The place to begin is the Dezadeash River Trail. This approximately four-mile (six-kilometer), self-guided trail

The Yellow Warbler can be easily spotted at this park in the early summer months.

starts at the Haines Junction Day-Use Area at the edge of the town and provides spectacular views of the Auriol Mountain Range. This trail, which is outfitted with platforms and benches, is probably the most productive birdwatching trail in the park and yet it's a very easy walk. Visitors in early summer won't go far before hearing the distinctive, slow warbling song of the Yellow-rumped Warbler – the park's most abundant woodland warbler.

But other warblers can be found easily at this time of year, such as the Blackpoll Warbler, the Orange-crowned Warbler, the Wilson's Warbler, and the Yellow Warbler. From late spring through summer, look also for Mountain Bluebirds, which are particularly easy to find in the grassy areas along the

The Varied Thrush *is blue-gray above with an orange breast; males feature a black breast band.*

river. Waterfowl such as Common and Barrow's Goldeneyes and Trumpeter Swans nest along the river.

All three species of ptarmigan – Willow, White-tailed, and Rock – can be seen in the southern end of the park. The most accessible place to spot them is along the Saint Elias Lake Trail, a relatively easy three- to four-hour walk that begins about 37 miles (60 kilometers) south of Haines Junction on the Haines Highway and leads to a small lake with a primitive campground. The trail starts in a wooded lower valley, so birdwatchers can often see Spruce Grouse en route to the high country. Ptarmigan are usually seen above the tree line. The Chilkoot Pass, where it intersects the Haines Highway south of the park, is another good location to look for ptarmigan.

Visitors should also look for shorebirds such as American Golden-Plover, Wandering Tattler, and Red-necked Phalarope, around the park's small lakes and tundra areas during spring migration. American Pipits, Varied Thrush, Snow Buntings, Gray-crowned Rosy-Finches, and Smith's Longspurs nest in high-country areas.

VISITING

Kluane National Park and Reserve has two visitor centers: one at Haines Junction and another at Sheep Mountain. Most visitors come to the park between mid-May and mid-September, when the weather is mildest. But in mid- to late April numerous migrating Trumpeter Swans and Tundra Swans congregate at the north end of Kluane Lake, a spectacle worth seeing. The park also has more than 155 miles (250 kilometers) of hiking trails, from boardwalk trails to primitive alpine routes.

HIGHLIGHTS

The Slims River Valley boasts one of the highest concentrations of nesting Golden Eagles in Canada. The visitor center at Sheep Mountain, which has a viewing platform and a spotting scope for public use, is a good place to see the eagles as they soar on warm air currents during the summer.

Site Map and Information

KLUANE NATIONAL PARK AND RESERVE

🚗 From Whitehorse, Yukon, drive approximately 100 miles (160 kilometers) west on the Alaska Highway; from Haines, Alaska, drive approximately 154 miles (249 kilometers) north on the Haines Road to reach Haines Junction and the main Visitor Center.

☐ Daily, 24 hours, year-round.

◾ The climate is mildest from June 15 through September 15, although it's possible to find good weather from May through the end of October. Always be prepared for cool mountain weather and storms.

ℹ Kluane National Park and Reserve, P.O. Box 5495, Haines Junction, Yukon Y0B 1L0, Canada. The Visitor Center at Haines Junction is open year-round, 8 a.m.–4:30 p.m. (except in summer, when it is open until 8 p.m.), while the one at Sheep Mountain is open from mid-May through mid-September, 8 a.m.–8 p.m.

☎ (867) 634-7250; www.parkscanada.pch.ca/kluane

⑤ $5 (CAN) per adult; $2.50 per youth (5–15); free for children (under 5); $12 per family.

♿ The two Visitor Centers and the Kathleen Lake Day-Use Area (which has a boardwalk and fishing dock) are wheelchair accessible.

🅰 Kathleen Lake Campground is on-site; no reservations taken.

🚶 Call Grayling Camp Enterprises at (867) 634-2099 to arrange a guide.

🛏 Motels are available in nearby Haines Junction. There are also motels along the Alaska Highway and the Haines Road, which skirt the park.

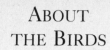

About the Birds

A closer look
at some featured birds.

Red-throated Loon *(Gavia stellata)*
The only loon capable of taking off from land, the Red-throated Loon nests on bare ground near the edges of shallow lakes, then flies to deep lakes to feed. It dives to 30 feet deep and catches fish with its thin, slightly upturned bill. In breeding plumage, the 25-inch-long bird has a gray head, brown back, white underparts, a distinctive chestnut patch on the front of the throat, and vertical white stripes on the back of the head. The young often ride on the parents' back. In winter the adults have gray heads, white cheeks and neck, and grayish backs with white spots. They breed from Alaska through northern Canada and winter along the Atlantic and Pacific Coasts and the Great Lakes. A few winter on the Gulf Coast, especially on impounded lakes. See sites 17, 36, 86.

Common Loon
(Gavia immer)
In the spring the eerie, yodeling call of the Common Loon echoes across remote lakes from Alaska through Canada and the northern U.S. These 32-inch-long birds require lakes large enough to stage their aerobatic courtship dance and deep and clear enough to allow them to dive for fish. During courtship, they dip their bills, splash dive, and dance across the water with wings outstretched. The young hatch on shoreline or floating nests and ride on the parents' backs. During breeding, these heavy-billed loons have glossy black heads and backs with white spots on the wings and sides; they are white below. Winter plumage is grayish black above and white below. Common Loons winter along the Atlantic, Pacific, and Gulf Coasts and the Great Lakes. Boating, lead ingestion

(from fishing sinkers), and acid rain in breeding areas have greatly reduced the population of Common Loons. See sites 11, 22, 25, 30, 35, 43, 83, 86, 92, 96.

Pied-billed Grebe
(Podilymbus podiceps)
The most widespread grebe in the New World, the Pied-billed Grebe breeds on freshwater lakes and marshes throughout the Western Hemisphere. Its winter range dips from British Columbia south through Texas and the southern states, and up the East Coast to New Jersey. This plump, 13.5-inch-long bird with a chickenlike beak is brown above, white below, and has almost no white wing patch. During breeding its dark bill ring and throat patch are prominent. Solid bones and the ability to squeeze air from their feathers, lungs, and air sacs help grebes forage underwater. The Pied-billed, like other grebes, exhibits the puzzling habit of eating its own feathers and even feeding them to its young. See sites 21, 33.

American White Pelican *(Pelecanus erythrorhynchos)*
Although gangly-looking on land, the White Pelican flies with graceful flaps of its wingspan (which spans 9 feet) and bobs like a cork high in the water when feeding. These birds never dive for fish. Instead, a group will form a line and thrash the water with their wings to drive fish into the shallows. Then they scoop them up in their pouchlike bills. During breeding the large orange beak grows a fibrous plate on the upper mandible. In flight the black outer wing feathers are prominent. White Pelicans nest on islands in remote lakes in the northwestern and north central U.S. and central Canada, and in bays on the Texas coast; they winter in central California,

Arizona, and the Gulf Coast. Though White Pelicans did not suffer the population crash from DDT poisoning that decimated many fish-eating birds in the 1960s, their numbers are greatly reduced. See sites 4, 5, 40, 42, 57, 60, 70, 72, 78, 82, 93, 99.

Brown Pelican *(Pelecanus occidentalis)*

These hunting fish soar 25 to 30 feet high, then plunge dramatically headfirst into the water, with their 3.5-foot wings folded back. A cushion of air cells beneath the skin of their heads protects them from injury. Although they were once killed by fishermen who feared competition, pelicans feed almost exclusively on noncommercial fish. They actually increase fish productivity by fertilizing the bays and stimulating plankton growth. During breeding the bird's white neck turns a rich chestnut and the white head feathers turn yellowish. They nest in bushes and low trees on protected islands and estuaries. Still listed as endangered in the west, Brown Pelicans are resident waterbirds of coastal California, the Gulf Coast, and the Atlantic north to Virginia. See sites 5, 58, 64, 65.

American Bittern
(Botaurus lentiginosus)

This stout, 28-inch-long heron depends on cryptic coloration for protection in its habitat of dense bulrush marshes, brackish sloughs, and salt marshes. A buff-tipped brown back, a front with buffy streaks, and a reedlike stance camouflage the bittern from both predators and its prey of small fish, frogs, crayfish, and snakes. When flushed, it flies a short distance on wings tipped with blackish flight feathers. It feeds mostly at dusk or night. It breeds continentally from central Canada to the southern U.S. In the winter, it retreats to the Pacific coast and the southern U.S.

from California to the Atlantic coast. Its numbers are diminishing with the increasing loss of wetland habitat. See sites 5, 20, 39, 44, 50, 53.

Great Blue Heron *(Ardea herodias)*

With a 6-foot wingspan, this largest and most dispersed of North American herons flies with slow, deep wing beats and its long neck held in a S-curve. Great Blues find suitable homes along the shores of rivers, lakes, bays, and marshes. This stately bird has blue-black upper parts; a black, white-streaked breast and belly; a gray to cinnamon neck; and a whitish head with long, black plumes during breeding. A white-colored morph with yellowish instead of blackish legs lives in extreme southern Florida. Great Blues feed by standing motionless or slowly stalking through the shallows. They breed singly or in small colonies from southeastern Alaska to Nova Scotia and throughout the U.S., and winter from British Columbia to Massachusetts and southward. See sites 8, 14, 15, 20, 41, 60, 77, 90, 97.

Great Egret *(Ardea alba)*

Its large size, yellow bill, and black legs and feet distinguish the 39-inch-tall Great Egret from other egrets. During breeding ornate plumes on its back extend beyond the tail. This wading bird feeds in shallow waters with head and body leaning forward to strike fish, frogs, snakes, and invertebrates. Great Egrets nest and roost communally with similar species in thickets and trees strong enough to support their bulky, stick nests. Their call is a loud, hoarse croak. They breed in the eastern half of the U.S. and the central Pacific Coast and winter from California to North Carolina. Plume hunters nearly decimated the species in the early 1900s, but by 1930 it had fully recovered. Now, loss of wetland habitat is its main threat. See sites 6, 19, 34, 42, 77.

Black-crowned Night-Heron
(Nycticorax nycticorax)
Colonies of these 25-inch-long night-feeding herons leave their day roosts at dusk to forage in brackish, salt, and freshwater marshes and sloughs. They stalk through shallow waters and snap up prey with short, stout bills. Unlike most herons, they hold their necks pulled in against their bodies so that the head and back form a continuous line. Adults have black bills, backs, and caps (with white plumes when breeding), white cheeks and underparts, and gray hindneck and wings. The brown-streaked juveniles reach adult plumage in the third year. The bird's loud, guttural croak is heard most often as it flies at dusk and after dark. This nearly cosmopolitan bird breeds from southern Canada throughout the U.S. and retreats to coastal areas in winter. See sites 3, 12, 19, 25, 29, 53, 83.

Roseate Spoonbill *(Ajaia ajaja)*
The only pink bird within its range in the U.S., the Roseate Spoonbill is a striking figure, whether wading in the shallows or flying overhead. It stands 32 inches tall with a wingspan of 52 inches, has a white neck, greenish bill, pink back and wings, a bright red shoulder patch, and an orange tail. Its distinctive spatula-shaped bill distinguishes it from escaped flamingos. The Roseate Spoonbill wades through tidal ponds and freshwater and brackish sloughs, swishing its bill back and forth in the murky water. A sensitive network of nerves in the bill detects minnows, shrimp, and other organisms and snaps it shut on contact. This member of the ibis family nests on coastal islands and lagoons in Texas and Louisiana

and on mangrove swamps in southern Florida, often with other wading birds. Plume hunters nearly drove this beautifully colored bird into extinction during the early 1900s, but the population rebounded with protection and is now stable. See sites 4, 5, 42, 58.

Wood Stork *(Mycteria americana)*
The bald, blackish head, 40-inch-long white body, and long, black bill distinguish the only true stork native to the U.S. (The jabiru, another stork species, lives in Mexico.) When the Wood Stork soars, often circling on thermals, the black wing tips and tail are prominent. This endangered bird requires swamps of bald cypress or red mangrove for nesting and brackish wetlands or marshes for feeding. It catchs small prey by wading slowly with an open bill in 6 to 10 inches of water. When the bill touches a fish, it snaps shut with one of the quickest reflexes known among vertebrates. Once nesting from Texas to Florida, Wood Stork breeding colonies now are confined to Florida, Georgia, and South Carolina. After breeding the birds disperse north, occasionally as far as Canada. They winter along the Gulf Coast. See sites 4, 5, 15, 16, 26, 34, 42, 65.

Snow Goose *(Chen caerulescens)*
This abundant 28-inch-long goose appears in two color morphs once considered separate species. The white morph is all white with black-tipped wings. The blue morph has a white head and a sooty gray body with variable white on the underparts. Both feature a pink bill with a black "grin" mark between the mandibles. The blue morph is most abundant in the Mississippi flyway. It breeds north of the Hudson Bay and winters on the Gulf Coast, mainly in Texas-Louisiana coastal marshes. The

white morph breeds across northernmost Canada and migrates to the Pacific, Gulf, and Atlantic Coasts. In the winter Snow Geese feed on marsh grasses and waste rice and grain in stubble fields. See sites 1, 3, 18, 22, 29, 30, 39, 42, 48, 57, 65, 76, 77, 80.

Trumpeter Swan *(Cygnus buccinator)*
Trumpeter Swans, the largest species of waterfowl in North America, reach 5 feet in length, have a wingspan of 7 feet, and weigh 23 pounds. European settlers moving west converted their habitat into farmland, making these waterfowl nearly extinct by the 1900s. Today they survive mainly in refuges and national parks in coastal Alaska and Canada and in the western U.S. This all-white swan is slightly larger than the Tundra Swan, has a flatter bill profile with no yellow nose spot, and utters a low-pitched, bugle-like yodeling call. Trumpeters pair after 3 years, maintaining a lifelong bond, and breed at 5 years. The 5-foot-wide nest of plant material is often built on top of a beaver or muskrat lodge. See sites 53, 60, 75, 78, 80, 81, 93, 100.

Tundra Swan *(Cygnus columbianus)*
Although it is the most common and widespread North American swan, the 52-inch-long Tundra Swan breeds almost exclusively north of the arctic circle in Alaska and Canada. It winters on the Pacific Coast and Great Basin in the West and along the Atlantic Coast from New Jersey to North Carolina. Adults are all white with black bills and legs; juveniles are gray. The graceful bird extends its long neck to pluck plants from fresh or brackish water. Tundra Swans are difficult to distinguish from Trumpeter Swans, but Tundras have a more rounded head and concave bill. A yellow spot in front of the eye may be visible. Also, their call, 3 mellow high-pitched whoops, sets them apart from the more raucous

Trumpeter Swan. See sites 20, 21, 22, 24, 30, 36, 53, 60, 72, 77, 78, 80, 96, 100.

Wood Duck *(Aix sponsa)*
One of North America's most vividly colored species, the 18-inch-long male Wood Duck is iridescent green, bronze, purple, and blue above with a long, slicked-back crest, white cheek markings, and red eyes and bill. The female is brownish above with speckled sides and white below. Wood Ducks prefer ponds, streams, and sloughs in open hardwood forests. They nest in tree cavities as high as 50 feet above the ground. Adults feed on acorns, leaves, insects, and a variety of water plants. These waterfowl nest in almost all of the lower 48 states and southern Canada in suitable habitat. They winter in the southern U.S. north to Maryland and along the Pacific Coast. See sites 6, 7, 9, 12, 15, 16, 21, 29, 33, 35, 55, 64, 70.

Gadwall *(Anas strepera)*
The most distinctive feature of this 20-inch-long duck is the male's black rump, which contrasts sharply with the predominately gray body. Males have brown heads, gray backs and sides, and white underparts. Females are mottled brown with white underneath. A white patch on the wings of both sexes is usually visible during swimming. Gadwalls dabble and tip up when feeding on bottom vegetation, but they also walk with ease in fields, where they feed on grain. This abundant duck favors freshwater marshes and meadows from southeastern Alaska and central Canada south through much of the U.S. Its nest is a grassy hollow on dry land. Gadwalls winter in the Pacific Northwest, the Southwest, and the Southern states to the Chesapeake Bay, especially in large impounded lakes. See sites 3, 18, 21, 30, 33, 44, 48, 55, 57, 76.

American Wigeon *(Anas americana)*

The male wigeon's white forehead – which appears bald – and a glossy, green streak behind the eye make the 19-inch-long brownish duck stand out in mixed flocks. The female has a grayish head and neck, brown back, and white belly. This surface-feeder tips up to feed on bottom plants. They do not dive but sometimes steal morsels of vegetation from the bills of emerging diving ducks. They also graze like geese for grass and grain. American Wigeons build down-lined nests on dry ground on islands in lakes, on open grasslands, or in woods from Alaska to the Hudson Bay and south into the western U.S. They winter on fresh and brackish bodies of water along the Pacific coast, through the Southwest and southern U.S., and along the Atlantic Coast. They often occur in mixed groups with other dabblers and diving ducks. See sites 1, 15, 16, 55, 67, 70, 72, 77, 80.

Green-winged Teal

(Anas crecca)

At 14.5 inches long, the Green-winged Teal is the smallest North American dabbling duck. The male has a dark cinnamon head with a broad green ear patch; a spotted, buffy breast; grayish back and sides; and a vertical white stripe in front of the wing. The female is mottled buff above and whitish below. Both show a green wing patch when swimming. They feed on bottom plants in freshwater ponds and marshes but also forage through woods far from water for acorns and berries. Green-winged Teal nest from above the arctic circle in Alaska across Canada and into the western U.S. They winter on unfrozen lakes from British Columbia through the western and southern U.S. into Mexico. They often fly in large, compact flocks that make twisting patterns in the sky. See sites 1, 3, 20, 39, 55, 66, 78, 80, 93.

Redhead *(Aythya americana)*

Male Redheads have reddish heads; black necks, wings, and tails; gray sides; and white bellies. Females are brown above and white below. A rounded head and a grayish, black-tipped bill distinguish the 19-inch-long Redhead from the similar-looking Canvasback. Redheads are excellent divers and feed on aquatic plants, fish, frogs, and insects. Their nests are built up out of the water on a base of vegetation and attached to surrounding plants. Females often lay eggs in the nests of neighboring Redheads or other species. Redheads winter in bays and estuaries on the Pacific, Gulf, and Atlantic Coasts and nest in cattail and bulrush marshes and swamps from central Canada through the western and midwestern U.S. Winter bird counts from California to the Chesapeake Bay indicate a stable population. See sites 38, 40, 50, 57, 60, 75, 78.

Harlequin Duck

(Histrionicus histrionicus)

These 16.5-inch-long sea ducks spend much of their winter lives in the rugged surf, foraging for barnacles and snails on wave-swept rocks. In the summer they retreat inland to nest in rocks, tree cavities, and burrows. There, they forage in rapid-flowing streams, often walking on the bottom to search submerged boulders for invertebrates. The colorful male is blue-gray with chestnut flanks and distinctive white patches on its head and body. The female is brownish with three white spots on her face. Harlequin Ducks nest from Alaska to the Pacific Northwest and in extreme northeastern Canada. They winter along the Pacific Coast from Alaska to California and on the Atlantic Coast from Maritime Canada to Virginia. See sites 43, 61, 73, 79, 82, 98.

Hooded Merganser
(Lophodytes cucullatus)

The distinctive male sports a fan-shaped black crest with a white central patch, a black back, rufous sides, and white underparts. The female is brown above and white below with a cinnamon crest patch. This uncommon, 18-inch-long duck of wooded streams and lakes nests in tree cavities from Alaska and British Columbia to the eastern half of Canada and the U.S. It winters south of the freeze line along the Pacific, Gulf, and Atlantic Coasts. Hooded Mergansers forage on the surface of freshwater ponds and marshes and dive for fish, crustaceans, and aquatic insects, which they grasp with toothlike serrations on their bills. Underwater, they swim rapidly using both wings and feet. They usually occur in pairs or small flocks. See sites 10, 21, 34, 53, 60, 76, 84, 96.

Ruddy Duck
(Oxyura jamaicensis)

With a stiff, fan-shaped tail, a black crown, bold white cheeks, a rusty red back, and a vivid blue bill during breeding season, the 15-inch-long Ruddy Duck warrants a second look. The female is brownish black above and gray below, with white cheeks. In winter both sexes are gray with white cheeks. The male is the only duck in America with an inflatable air sac in its neck. During its spectacular courtship dance, it cocks its tail over its back, puffs up its neck, bobs its head, splashes, and calls. These waterfowl nest across central Canada and into the western U.S. and winter in the Southwest and along Pacific, Gulf, and Atlantic Coasts. When alarmed, Ruddy Ducks dive instead of flying; they can sink with hardly a ripple. See sites 3, 26, 28, 40, 41, 44, 57, 67.

Osprey *(Pandion haliaetus)*

One of the widest-ranging birds in the world, the Osprey occurs in North America across Canada and along the Pacific and Atlantic Coasts and the Great Lakes. The 22-inch-long raptor is brown above, with a white head and dark mask, and white below with a brown-spotted breast. It requires large bodies of clear water for fishing and elevated nest sites. In many places it accepts artificial nest platforms. Ospreys hunt from 30 to 100 feet above the water and plunge in talons first. Special adaptations for catching fish include large, curved talons, reversible outer talons so that two point forward and two backward, and horny spines on the bottoms of the toes. In the winter the northern population retreats south to areas of unfrozen water. Ospreys are fairly common in their coastal range but still uncommon and local inland. See sites 2, 12, 20, 23, 45, 71, 82, 84, 90, 93, 97.

Mississippi Kite
(Ictinia mississippiensis)

The slender, 15-inch-long Mississippi Kite has a pale gray head that contrasts softly with its dark gray back and black wing tips and tail. The immatures have brown-streaked underparts and gray tail bars. Since the 1800s, when the Mississippi Kite was named, human settlement has forced this bird to shift from its humid forest habitat to the dry southwestern Great Plains. It frequents open woods and range land from Kansas to Virginia and south through the Gulf states; the highest nesting concentrations are in the Texas panhandle and Oklahoma. Kites are graceful fliers that feed primarily on large insects caught in flight. They often hover over farmers plowing their fields and follow livestock. They are gregarious; pairs often roost in the same tree and nest in colonies. See sites 16, 34, 40, 46, 55.

Bald Eagle *(Haliaeetus leucocephalus)*
When America adopted the Bald Eagle as the national symbol in 1782, as many as 100,000 nested in the lower 48 states. By 1963 only 417 pairs remained. After three decades of protection, the numbers rose to 5,748 nesting pairs, although the Bald Eagle is still on the the endangered species list. These majestic birds of prey with snow-white heads and tails live near large bodies of water throughout North America and feed on fish, waterfowl, and carrion. The dark brown immatures take 3 years to reach adult plumage. Though they are powerful fliers with 8-foot wingspans, Bald Eagles often hunt using the perch-and-pounce method from trees over water. Northern birds retreat south in the winter, especially to large, impounded lakes with abundant fish and waterfowl. See sites 3, 9, 20, 23, 28, 31, 33, 34, 35, 37, 38, 39, 40, 41, 45, 48, 51, 53, 56, 57, 76, 77, 78, 81, 84, 86, 88, 90, 92, 93, 96.

Northern Harrier *(Circus cyaneus)*
This 17- to 23-inch-long hawk is usually seen soaring low over marshes, pastures, tidal flats, and prairies in a relaxed flap-and-glide mode. Its long wings tilt up and its body rocks slightly as it searches for rodents, birds, and insects. The males are gray above with pale chests, black wing tips, and underparts flecked with cinnamon. The larger females are streaked cinnamon-brown above and streaked buffy white below. Both sexes have a conspicuous white rump patch. The Northern Harrier nests and roosts on the ground and seldom uses trees. It breeds across most of the U.S. and Canada and retreats to the southern half of its breeding range in the winter. Its numbers are diminished across its breeding range due to loss of marshlands. See sites 23, 25, 45, 46, 47, 71, 75, 78, 95, 97, 98.

Swainson's Hawk
(Buteo swainsoni)
The widespread, 21-inch-long Swainson's Hawk ranges over plains, prairies, and deserts in the western half of North America from Alaska to Texas. It hunts for grasshoppers and crickets from exposed limbs and fence poles. Its coloration varies from a sooty black dark morph to a light morph that is dark brown above and white below with a contrasting chestnut band across the breast. Both morphs feature banded tails. In the spring (March to May), and fall (August to November), Swainson's Hawks migrate up to 17,000 miles to South America in aggregations reaching thousands of individuals. They circle on thermals to gain altitude, then trail off in long lines, hardly flapping at all until they reach another thermal. See sites 54, 56, 57, 67, 71, 72, 82, 88.

Golden Eagle *(Aquila chrysaetos)*
Few animals impart a sense of domain as powerfully as a Golden Eagle soaring above a mountain valley. These high-flying raptors with 7-foot wingspans sweep low over open terrain when hunting rabbits, ground squirrels, and small mammals. A 40-inch-long, 10-pound eagle can lift and carry large prey to its nest. Adults are brown above and below with a golden tinge on the crown and neck. Immatures have white tails with a brown terminal band. Golden Eagles breed throughout the mountainous western half of North America and much of Canada. Pairs require a 20- to 60-square-mile nesting

and feeding territory. Northern birds move into the southwestern U.S. in the winter. Golden Eagles once were heavily persecuted by sheep and goat ranchers, but the numbers today are stable. See sites 15, 40, 45, 51, 54, 56, 57, 68, 71, 73, 74, 76, 81, 82, 93, 100.

Merlin *(Falco columbarius)*

This 12-inch-long, pigeon-sized falcon nests in the spruce-fir forest zone from Alaska across Canada and into the northern U.S. Males have white throats and blue-gray backs; females and immatures are brown above. Both sexes have rusty streaked underparts and a strongly barred tail. They also eat insects and small mammals. Merlins frequent woodland openings and edges of rivers and lakes, where they perch for long periods, looking for prey. They have a habit of flying low, then abruptly pumping their wings and swooping straight up to a perch. They winter in a variety of habitats along the Pacific, Gulf, and Atlantic Coasts and in the Great Plains. See sites 17, 23, 36, 43, 45, 66, 77, 87, 88.

Peregrine Falcon *(Falco peregrinus)*

These 16- to 20-inch-long streamlined falcons occur, but are uncommon, worldwide. They nest sparingly in Alaska, northern Canada, and as far south as the central U.S. Northern populations winter along the Gulf and Atlantic Coasts. Peregrines are dark gray above with barred, buffy underparts. A black cap forms a helmet around white cheeks and throat. With rapid thrusts of its powerful wings, the Peregrine Falcon dives as fast as 275 mph to catch or strike its prey in midair. Whether in mountains, forests, prairies, coastlands, or asphalt avenues, all this adaptable falcon requires is an abundant bird population and a cliff ledge, or reasonable substitute, for nesting. Increasingly, Peregrine Falcons nest on skyscrapers in cities across the nation. Once nearly extinct due to DDT poisoning, the population is slowly recovering. See sites 17, 22, 23, 30, 36, 45, 62, 80, 93.

Rock Ptarmigan *(Lagopus mutus)*

The dramatic seasonal color variation in the arctic environment requires an equally dramatic plumage change in the 3 species of ptarmigans. They molt white in the winter and barred brown in the summer. The 13-inch-long Rock Ptarmigan is distinguished by a black eye line in the winter and a black tail in all plumages. Rock Ptarmigans live in tundra and rocky uplands across arctic Canada and from Alaska south into mountainous British Columbia. They move to lower elevations when snow covers their primary food, willow and birch leaves and buds. See sites 61, 91, 100.

Sharp-tailed Grouse
(Tympanuchus phasianellus)

A speckled breast and a pointed tail with outer white feathers distinguish this 17-inch-long grouse from the Greater and Lesser Prairie-Chickens. In the spring 10 to 20 males at a time gather on elevated patches of ground, referred to as leks, for their courtship display. They challenge each other by rattling their wings and inflating purplish throat patches while making a booming sound. They strut and charge each other to establish their dominance. Females mate with the most aggressive males, then rear the chicks alone. The Sharp-tailed Grouse lives on prairies and brushland from Alaska through central Canada, the western Great Plains, and south into the Northern Rockies. In the winter they flock together in groups of 10 to 15 members. Though fairly common, their numbers, like those of other grouses, have been greatly reduced by game hunting. See sites 49, 50, 51, 56, 72, 88.

Northern Bobwhite
(Colinus virginianus)
The whistled call *(bob-white!)* of this chunky, 9-inch-long quail echoes across brushlands, prairies, and open woodlands from Wyoming through eastern Canada to Maine and south through the Gulf states to New Mexico. The Northern Bobwhite needs open grasslands in order to forage for seeds and insects and woody cover in which to roost and nest. The distinctive white throat and eye stripe of the male are buffy brown in the female. The brown back, rusty streaks on the sides, and barred breast help camouflage them. The birds pair off in the spring and form coveys of 10 to 30 in the fall. Bobwhite populations have declined greatly over the last 20 years, due perhaps to habitat loss and changing agricultural practices. See sites 3, 38, 46, 47, 49, 50.

Clapper Rail *(Rallus longirostris)*
The reclusive Clapper Rail is more often heard than seen. The harsh, staccato *kek kek kek* call is one of the most common sounds in dense salt marshes along the Atlantic and Gulf Coasts and southern California. The 14-inch-long, gray-brown bird has barred flanks and gray cheeks. It paces through the coastal marshes at low tide probing with its long, thin bill for crabs and other crustaceans. When startled, it does not fly, but retreats swiftly into tall vegetation. The similar King Rail, which prefers fresh water, has a cinnamon-colored breast and more distinct white bars on its sides and flanks. The Yuma Clapper Rail, found in the lower Colorado River valley in California and Arizona and in coastal southern California, is an endangered species. See sites 2, 26, 66.

American Coot *(Fulica americana)*
This abundant, ducklike member of the rail family dives like a grebe and tips up like a dabbling duck. The 15-inch-long, black-headed birds are slate gray with white bill. They forage in marshes for aquatic plants, and sometimes feed in stubble fields for grain. They communicate through a large repertoire of body postures and cackles, squawks, grunts, and whistles. Coots build floating nests anchored to dense vegetation in freshwater ponds, lakes, and marshes across the U.S. and Canada. In the winter, they frequent lakes, sloughs, brackish and saltwater estuaries, and shallow bays in the southern half of the U.S. and along the Gulf and Atlantic Coasts. Wintering populations on inland lakes provide an important food source for over wintering Bald Eagles. See sites 3, 30, 33, 38, 57.

Sandhill Crane *(Grus canadensis)*
With 3 stable western populations numbering about 650,000, the Sandhill Crane is the most numerous of all cranes in the world. The 4-foot-tall, stately gray bird has a 7-foot wingspan and bald, red skin on the forehead. It breeds from Alaska to the Hudson Bay, the Great Basin, and the Great Lakes area, and winters in California, New Mexico, and Texas. Each March up to 550,000 gather on sandbars in Nebraska's Platte River before continuing to the breeding grounds. Some cranes migrate as far as 7,000 miles each way. Two non-migratory populations survive in small numbers. In Mississippi, Sandhill Cranes require captive breeding to maintain the flock of 120 birds. In Florida this threatened crane numbers about 4,000 to 6,000 birds. See sites 1, 6, 38, 44, 48, 56, 67, 75, 76, 77, 81, 96.

Piping Plover *(Charadrius melodus)*
Beach development along the Atlantic shore has brought this 7-inch-long plover to near extinction. They nest in the narrow band between the dunes and the high-tide line. Colored light gray above

and white below, with a black band across the forehead and breast during breeding season, the birds are perfectly camouflaged in their sandy habitat. Their nest is a shallow depression in dry sand, sometimes lined with pebbles and broken shells. With the winter molt, the black breast band fades into two gray shoulder spots. The compact birds forage along the surf with the typical plover run-and-stop habit, eating fly larvae, crustaceans, and marine worms. Piping Plovers breed on lakes in central Canada and the Great Lakes region and on the Atlantic Coast south to Virginia. They winter along the coast from Texas to Florida and North Carolina. See sites 11, 13, 22, 40, 48, 50, 58, 90, 97.

American Avocet
(Recurvirostra americana)
The long-necked, long-legged American Avocet wades through shallow water, swishing its slender, upturned bill back and forth until it feels a fish, shrimp, or other crustacean. The 18-inch-tall wader is white above and below, with black wings featuring a prominent white wing bar. When breeding, its head and neck molt from gray to cinnamon buff. During courtship the pairs perform a stylized dance, with bills crossed and the male's wing stretched over the female. Avocets nest along shores of lakes, marshes, and estuaries from western Canada to California, the Great Basin, coastal Texas, and the middle Atlantic Coast. When disturbed, the alarmed birds circle and squawk loudly until the threat recedes. They winter along the coasts of California, Texas, and Louisiana. See sites 30, 50, 66, 67.

Greater Yellowlegs
(Tringa melanoleuca)
The Greater Yellowlegs earns its name from its long, brightly colored legs. In breeding plumage, it is mottled brown above and white below with brown streaks on neck, breast, sides, and flanks. When foraging, this 14-inch-long shorebird swishes its slightly upturned bill back and forth for minnows and crustaceans and picks insects off the surface. In flight the wings show uniform black and the white rump and tail are visible. Winter coloration is paler overall. The Greater Yellowlegs calls in triplets or more. It nests on open tundra across central Canada and winters from California to Texas and along the Gulf and Atlantic coasts. See sites 13, 18, 22, 24, 28, 80.

Upland Sandpiper
(Bartramia longicauda)
Unlike other sandpipers, which nest near water, this 12-inch-long bird nests in prairies, meadows, and rolling pastures from Alaska through central Canada and from the Midwest to the Atlantic Coast. Its dull yellow legs, buff-brown streaked back, throat, and breast, and pale underparts help camouflage it in its grassy habitat. Upland Sandpipers forage by alternately running and stopping like plovers. Their long necks and legs help them search through tall vegetation for beetles, grasshoppers, and other insects. They also perch on fences and stumps. After landing they typically hold their wings straight up for a few seconds. Migrants utter a fluttering, mellow whistle during their 7,000-mile nocturnal journey from South America. Uncommon today, the bird was killed in enormous numbers by market hunters in the 1880s, and modern agriculture has destroyed much of the bird's grassland habitat. See sites 41, 46, 47, 48, 49, 50.

White-rumped Sandpiper
(Calidris fuscicollis)
This 7.5-inch-long, 1.5-ounce sandpiper breeds in the high arctic and migrates through the U.S. on its 8,000-mile journey to Argentina. En route it rests and forages on muddy shores and sandbars of lakes and rivers and along the Gulf and Atlantic Coasts on tidal mud flats. During breeding it has a streaked brown back, white eye stripe, whitish head and breast with fine, brown streaks, and white underparts. In winter it molts gray above and white below, with scant breast markings. The white rump at the base of the black tail shows prominently in flight. It is 1 of 5 similar sandpipers (along with Least, Semipalmated, Baird's, and Western) called "peeps" because of their call when flushed. See sites 39, 40, 53, 91, 94.

Dunlin *(Calidris alpina)*
Flocks of these plump, 8-inch-long sandpipers race in and out with the waves as they probe the wet sand for crustaceans, small mollusks, and marine worms. They nest on high arctic tundra and winter in large numbers along the Pacific, Gulf, and Atlantic Coasts as far north as Long Island and southeastern Alaska. During breeding the rusty back and streaked white breast contrast with the black belly. In the winter they molt to gray above and white below, with a gray wash across the breast. Dunlins have a black bill, slightly downcurved at the tip, and display a narrow white stripe in the middle of their wings in flight. In the winter they congregate on mud flats and sand bars with mixed flocks of other sandpipers. See sites 1, 22, 24, 53, 80, 87, 91.

Wilson's Phalarope
(Phalaropus tricolor)
The 9-inch-long Wilson's Phalarope is the largest of its family

worldwide. Unlike the aquatic Red and Red-necked, which feed extensively in deep water, the Wilson's frequents inland ponds, sloughs, and wet meadows. It wades in shallow water and snaps up aquatic bugs, larvae, and beetles with its needlelike bill. Like other phalaropes, male Wilson's are 35 percent smaller than the females, and it is they who incubate the eggs. The nuptial female is gray above and white below, with a black face and neck stripe that turns cinnamon along the back. The males have a duller coloration. In winter, both are pale gray above and white below. Wilson's Phalaropes nest from British Columbia to the Great Lakes region and south into the western U.S. They winter in South America. See sites 40, 41, 50, 56, 65, 67.

Franklin's Gull *(Larus pipixcan)*
Once called prairie pigeons, the 14-inch-long Franklin's Gull frequents grasslands from central Canada into the Great Salt Lake region and the Great Plains. Like the Laughing Gull, it has a black head, gray back and wings, and white tail; however, its breast has a pale rosy wash and the black wing tips are bordered with white. In the winter, the black head feathers molt to a dusty cap. Immatures have a broad, black band across the white tail and take 3 years to reach adult plumage. Colonies of Franklin's Gulls

build floating nests in reed marshes. They forage plowed fields for grasshoppers and grubs and hover over ponds to catch dragonflies, aquatic insects, and small fish. They roost in lakes at night, and in winter, they migrate to South America. See sites 36, 37, 39, 44, 57, 72.

California Gull
(Larus californicus)
During breeding season this 21-inch-long gull ranges south from central Canada into the Great Basin. It has a white head, tail, and underparts; a yellow bill with red and black spots on the tip; a gray back; and gray wings with black tips bordered in white. The brown immatures take 4 years to reach adult plumage. The similar Ringed-bill Gull is smaller and has a black ring around the bill tip. California Gulls eat primarily insects in the summer. (In 1848, they saved early Mormons in Utah from a plague of grasshoppers.) They nest on bare ground in large colonies on islands or near alkaline lakes and marshes. In the winter they migrate to the Pacific Coast and change their diet to fish. See sites 65, 72, 82.

Caspian Tern *(Sterna caspia)*
With its heavy, blood-red bill pointed downward, the Caspian Tern hovers over the waves and dives head first after fish and shrimp. The largest tern, at 21 inches long, this stocky bird has a black forehead year-round, a slightly forked tail, and is light gray above and white below. In contrast, the Royal Tern has an orange bill, a more prominent crest, and a white forehead in the winter. Caspian Terns form loose flocks on the breeding grounds but are mostly seen in pairs or small groups. They nest in marshes and lakes in scattered locations across central Canada and the northern U.S. Along the Gulf and southeast Atlantic Coasts they breed on barrier islands in colonies with other terns and gulls. They winter coastally in southern California and on the Gulf and southeast Atlantic shores. See sites 4, 37, 70, 77, 82, 97.

Forster's Tern *(Sterna forsteri)*
This 14-inch-long, swallowlike tern gracefully swoops over lakes, marshes, lagoons, and salty bays. It maneuvers with its long, forked tail and rapid wing beats to catch flying insects and skims for small fish without getting wet. It also hovers above the water and dives for small fish. Like the Common Tern, the Forster's Tern is white overall with a gray back and wings, except its gray tail has white outer margins. The black cap during breeding reduces in the winter to an eye patch. Colonies of these birds nest in prairie marshes across central Canada and into the Great Basin and Great Plains states. It also nests on coastal islands from Texas to New Jersey, and winters along the Pacific, Gulf, and Atlantic Coasts. See sites 11, 37, 44, 60, 83, 96.

Black Guillemot
(Cepphus grylle)
The 13-inch-long ducklike Black Guillemot favors rugged coastlines, consisting of the northern Alaska coast and the Arctic coast of Canada through the Hudson Bay and south to Maine. It nests on rocky islands, inaccessible cliffs, and talus slopes. In the summer, a large white wing patch distinguishes this all-black member of the Alcid family, which includes Murres and other Alcids, it usually stays close to land and winters offshore from its nesting grounds. When diving for small fish or foraging on the ocean bottom for crustaceans and mollusks, it flaps its wings as though flying. It flies swift and close to the waves, with its red feet dangling behind. See sites 17, 89, 94, 97, 98.

Yellow-billed Cuckoo
(Coccyzus americanus)
The distinctive call of the Yellow-billed Cuckoo, a series of low, throaty clucks beginning rapid and becoming slower, announces its presence. The 12-inch-long, long-tailed cuckoo is brown above, white below, with a bold rufous wing patch. It has large, white spots on the underside of its black tail and the lower mandible of its black bill is yellow. This reclusive bird prefers undergrowth in open woodlands and thickets along streams, but has adapted to brushy roadsides, orchards, and city parks and neighborhoods with mature shade trees. They huddle motionless against inner branches and eye twigs and leaves for caterpillars and other insects. The Yellow-billed Cuckoo nests across most of the U.S. and winters in South America. See sites 4, 6, 12, 17, 41.

Barred Owl *(Strix varia)*
The round head with no ear tuffs, white underparts with bold brown bars across its chest, and brown streaks down its belly distinguish this 21-inch-long, gray-brown owl. Large brown eyes and yellowish bill set off a facial mask of brown concentric rings. The Barred Owl lives in deep, often wet woods and moves at dusk to open areas to hunt for rodents and other small animals. It can hear the squeak and scampering of a mouse from 50 yards away. Barred owls call frequently, even during the day, with a rhythmic who-cooks-for-you hoot. They range from British Columbia and the Pacific northwest through central Canada and the U.S. east of the Rockies. In the far West, its look-alike counterpart is the endangered Spotted Owl. See sites 1, 3, 12, 16, 33, 34.

Short-eared Owl *(Asio flammeus)*
This 15-inch-long, brown-streaked tawny owl, found worldwide, frequents the open countryside throughout North America. It has a round head with short ear tuffs that are seldom visible, a boldly streaked breast, and a streaked facial disk with black surrounding the yellow eyes. A prominent black mark on the underside of the wing joint shows during flight. From the arctic tundra to prairies, pastures, marshes, and coastal dunes, this bird of prey forages low over the ground with a buoyant flap-and-glide flight. It drops suddenly down on rodents and small animals and often hunts during the afternoon, dusk, and dawn. Short-eared owls nest and roost on the ground. In the winter, the northern birds retreat southward into the U.S. to find fields without snow cover. See sites 46, 47, 53, 67, 78, 80, 87, 93, 95, 96.

Northern Saw-whet Owl
(Aegolius acadicus)
This handsome, 8-inch-long owl is chocolate brown above with prominent white spots on its back and wings. The rich chestnut-striped underparts of the adult are solid brown in immatures. A black bill, yellow eyes, and white eyebrows highlight the facial disk in adults. Named because its rasping call sounds like a saw being sharpened, it prefers the interiors of dense coniferous forests, wooded swamps, and bogs. It ranges from southern Alaska, across central Canada to Nova Scotia, and south erratically from the Smoky Mountains through west Texas to the Pacific coast. With their swift, undulating flight, they forage through woods at dusk and before dawn for small animals. Saw-whet Owls perch in dense foliage. See sites 2, 9, 25, 32, 45, 52, 83, 88, 95.

Red-headed Woodpecker
(Melanerpes erythrocephalus)
With its flaming red head, black back, and white breast, this 9.5-inch-long woodpecker is unmistakable. In flight,

the bird flashes a white rump and white patches on the rear of its wings. The immatures have a buffy-brown head and neck. Red-headed Woodpeckers live in open deciduous forests and prairies with scattered groves and adapt to urban life where stands of mature trees remain. They forage in trees and on the ground for insects, about 50 percent of their diet, and acorns, seeds, and berries. Redheads live in wooded habitats east of the Rockies from southern Canada throughout the U.S. Their population began to decline in the early 1900s, primarily due to competition for nesting holes from European Starlings. See sites 12, 15, 33.

Pileated Woodpecker
(Dryocopus pileatus)
This 16.5-inch-long woodpecker earns its scientific name, which means cleaver of trees, from its powerful bill that can chisel off 3- to 6-inch wood chips. The prominent red crest and the white stripe from the bill down the neck distinguish the largest extant woodpecker in North America. (The Ivory-billed and Imperial Woodpeckers were larger, but they are most likely extinct.) In flight, the Pileated flashes large white patches on the forewings. Pileated Woodpeckers live in mixed coniferous and hardwood forests and in dense bottomlands along rivers and swamps in Pacific and central Canada and throughout the eastern U.S. from Texas to the Atlantic Coast. They strip off bark and bore deep into dead trees for ants, beetles, and other burrowing insects. Using their beaks, they excavate separate roosting and nesting cavities with triangular entrance holes and interiors about 8 inches across and 10 to 30 inches deep. See sites 6, 7, 21, 31, 55, 79, 86, 96.

Western Kingbird
(Tyrannus verticalis)
The black tail with white outer feathers distinguishes this 8.75-inch kingbird from similar gray-headed, black-backed, and yellow-bellied kingbirds within its range. The Western has an orange streak, usually concealed on its crown, and a lemon-yellow belly. Typical of flycatchers, the Western Kingbird darts out to catch flying insects, then returns to the same perch. It prefers open countryside with scattered trees and ventures into prairies and ranchland if fences and utility wires are available for perches. Western Kingbirds nest throughout the western U.S. and the Great Plains and into southern Canada. A small number winter on the Atlantic Coast from South Carolina to Florida; the rest migrate to Central America. The clearing of forests for pastureland has increased the range of this widespread bird. See sites 54, 70, 75.

Red-eyed Vireo *(Vireo olivaceus)*
In early April, migrating Red-eyed Vireos reach the Gulf Coast and spread out across the U.S., except for the Southwest, and into Canada north to the treeline. This 6-inch-long bird has a blue-gray crown with a white eyebrow bordered with black stripes, a ruby eye, olive uppers and white underparts, and no wing bars. Immatures have pale yellow on the flanks. It nests in open woodlands, along rivers, and in rural settings with mature trees. It also forages among shade trees in cities and parks. It searches for caterpillars and other insects in the canopy and lower foliage and often hangs upside down investigating leaves. An avid songster, the Red-Eyed Vireo sings throughout the summer after most birds lapse into silence. See sites 7, 21, 24, 25.

Gray Jay *(Perisoreus canadensis)*
Ranging from Alaska across Canada and into the western U.S. and high peaks of New York and New England, the 11.5-inch-long Gray Jay favors undisturbed coniferous forests. Colored smoky gray above and white below, it has a white face, forehead, and throat. These curious birds investigate campsites and cabins for the possibility of food and fearlessly approach humans for handouts, often feeding directly from the hand. They are omnivorous and cache food and other objects that catch their fancy in crevices in trees and rocks. Mouth glands secrete a sticky saliva used to glue together seeds and help them adhere to the hiding place. Gray Jays usually travel in pairs or family groups. They begin building a bulky nest in a stout tree while snow is still on the ground. Despite their boldness, Gray Jays do not adapt well to human settlement. See sites 10, 43, 79, 85, 90, 99.

Horned Lark *(Eremophila alpestris)*
The ground-dwelling Horned Lark walks and runs but never hops. The 7-inch-long bird is brown above and whitish below and has a black tail with white outer feathers that are prominent in flight. The white to yellow face and throat contrast with black whisker marks down the sides of the head and a black breast band. The males have black foreheads with feather tufts (or "horns") that are not always noticeable. The adaptable bird nests throughout North America from the arctic tundra to coastal plains and arid desert habitats, and winters in the lower 48 states. Horned Larks forage for seeds and insects on bare ground. During breeding the male proclaims his territory by flying as high as 800 feet where he circles and sings, then dives downward with wings folded. See sites 34, 47, 49, 57.

Tree Swallow *(Tachycineta bicolor)*
The iridescent blue or green-black back of the Tree Swallow glistens in the sun as the bird zips acrobatically overhead. The 6-inch-long bird has a white belly, and in flight, it shows triangular-shaped, not swept-back, wings. These swallows favor open habitats near woodlands, where they nest in tree cavities and forage over water. When natural cavities are scarce, they may be readily enticed to use nest boxes. The male courts the female with aerial gyrations. They mate in the air and plummet toward the earth, separating just before crashing. As one of the first migrants, Tree Swallows nest from Alaska to Newfoundland; however, they are absent completely in the southeastern U.S. as breeders. Virginia is the southern-most extent of their migration. See sites 13, 25, 53.

Boreal Chickadee *(Poecile hudsonicus)*
The towering trees of coniferous forests from Alaska through Canada and the extreme northern U.S. dwarf the 5.5-inch-long Boreal Chickadee. The tiny bird sports a brown cap, back, and sides; white cheeks and black bib; and whitish underparts. It flits restlessly through the treetops, scouring limbs for insects and larvae and picking seeds from cones. Boreal Chickadees travel in loose flocks while uttering a hoarse *tseek-a-day-day* call. Pairs nest in old woodpecker nests or cavities in dead wood. Both sexes share in caring for the young and may feed the nestlings as many as 360 times per day. Chickadees are unafraid of humans and will fly close to investigate

squeaking or shushing sounds. Though not migratory, the birds may move southward in the winter. See sites 10, 43, 61, 84, 85, 88, 92, 94.

Brown-headed Nuthatch
(Sitta pusilla)
Like other nuthatches, the 4.5-inch-long Brown-headed Nuthatch runs up, down, and around trunks and branches searching for bark insects and larvae. These year-round residents are endemic to the pinelands of the southeastern U.S., from Texas to Delaware. The bird has a brown cap covering the eye; white cheeks, throat, and nape of neck; gray back and wings; and white lower parts. Brown-headed Nuthatches travel in family groups and often forage with mixed flocks of chickadees and titmice. While feeding, these noisy birds keep in touch with a repeated double honking note. Pairs nest in old woodpecker cavities, in holes they excavate themselves, or in nest boxes. See sites 21, 26, 30, 55.

Winter Wren *(Troglodytes troglodytes)*
Only 4 inches long, the Winter Wren is one of the smallest songbirds in North America. Its small, rotund body is rusty brown above and buff below, with heavily barred flanks and tail. It has a slender bill and a stubby tail, usually held in a cocked upright position. These reclusive birds forage for insects in deep forests, dense thickets, and swamps among tangled undergrowth, rotting trunks, and fallen trees. They nest in the cavities of fallen trees or tangles of roots. Their song of warbles and trills can be heard most during nesting. Winter Wrens nest from Alaska to California, across Canada, and south into the southern Appalachians. They winter through much of their breeding range as well as the eastern half of the U.S. See sites 27, 30, 79, 89.

Mountain Bluebird
(Sialia currucoides)
The sight of the dazzling 7-inch-long turquoise Mountain Bluebird enlivens meadows, clearings, and open slopes from central Alaska through mountainous regions of Canada and the western U.S. The males are bright blue above and pale blue below with white bellies. The females are brownish gray, with a light wash of blue on their wings and rump. These thrushes dart from perches in trees or on boulders to catch flying insects, or they hover over the ground and then pounce on grasshoppers or other insects. They nest in natural tree cavities or old woodpecker nests and accept nesting boxes. For both summer and winter habitat, the Mountain Bluebird prefers cool, open country with trees nearby. It winters from southern British Columbia to Montana and south through California, Kansas, and Texas. See sites 51, 56, 68, 81, 82, 100.

Blackburnian Warbler
(Dendroica fusca)
The brilliant orange breast, throat, and facial marks and black eye mask of the male Blackburnian Warbler make it one of the most dramatic woodland birds. It has a yellow breast, black-streaked sides, black uppers with white lines, and black wings with a broad white patch. The female has duller facial markings and a small white wing bar. A canopy feeder, this 5-inch-long wood-warbler forages busily for insects throughout the tops of trees in mixed deciduous and coniferous woodlands. They nest from the Appalachian coniferous forests north to Nova Scotia and east into central Canada. The fiery-colored males perch on the tip of a tree or limb and sing with their breasts gleaming in the sun. This warbler winters in Latin America. See sites 37, 58, 60, 90, 99.

Cerulean Warbler
(Dendroica cerulea)

The blue back and white belly distinguish the male Cerulean Warbler from similar warblers. It has a narrow black band across the upper breast, black streaks on the sides, and two white wing bars. The females and fall immatures have olive-grayish uppers with no breast band, buffy white underparts, and a yellowish eye stripe. These 4.75-inch-long birds live in river-bottom hardwoods, swamps, and mixed upland forests near water. They forage for insects in the tallest treetops, making observation difficult. Migrants reach the Gulf Coast from South America by mid-April and nest from northeastern Texas through the Great Lakes and into New York. The Cerulean Warbler is common in scattered locations across its range. The male sings an accelerating series of buzzy notes incessantly during the April to July breeding season. See sites 1, 12, 20, 35.

Kentucky Warbler
(Oporornis formosus)

The dark olive-green back and black forehead and lack of white wing bars help conceal the ground-dwelling Kentucky Warbler in the shadows of the thickets and deep forests it favors. The 5.25-inch-long male has black sideburns, a yellow stripe over the eye, and bright yellow underparts. The female and immatures are duller. These birds walk quietly through bottomlands, moist ravines, and tangled undergrowth, with their tails bobbing up and down, looking for spiders, caterpillars, and other insects. They seldom venture high into trees. The migrants arrive in mid-April from Mexico and southward and nest from the Gulf states north to Nebraska and New York. They are especially common in the Mississippi River valley. See sites 8, 28, 33, 38.

Scarlet Tanager *(Piranga olivacea)*

No other North American bird has the bright red body and black wings of the male Scarlet Tanager. The females and nonbreeding males are dull green above and yellow below, with dark wings and tail. Males molting into winter plumage are red and yellow splotched. The 7-inch-long birds nest in deciduous and mixed woodlands and residential areas with mature trees. During spring migration, the male arrives first and sings from treetop perches to proclaim his territory. When the female arrives, he displays below her by spreading his dark wings to flash his brilliant red back. Scarlet Tanagers breed from Manitoba to New Brunswick and south through Oklahoma and South Carolina; and they winter in South America. See sites 7, 12, 14, 15, 19, 23, 24, 25, 27.

Lincoln's Sparrow
(Melospiza lincolnii)

The secretive Lincoln's Sparrow creeps through bogs and moist scrub and brush lands, staying close to the cover of tall grasses and thickets. The 5- to 6-inch-long bird has a gray back with black streaks and a whitish belly with a distinctive buffy breast band marked with fine, black streaks. The rusty crown has a gray stripe above the eye. When foraging for weed and grass seeds, the small bird scratches through leaves and dirt by kicking backward with both feet. When alarmed, it usually dashes away by foot instead of flying. Lincoln's Sparrows nest from northern Alaska to the mountains of the southwestern U.S. and across Canada and the northeastern U.S.

to the Atlantic. In the winter they retreat south to the Gulf states west to California. See sites 52, 68, 70.

Swamp Sparrow
(Melospiza georgiana)
True to its name, the Swamp Sparrow nests along the edges of freshwater or brackish swamps, marshes, and bogs filled with cattails, willow thickets, or dense brush. This 5.75-inch-long, rust-colored sparrow has a chestnut cap, gray hindneck, and white throat. It has dark gray cheeks with a grayish streak above the eye, a black-streaked back, unstreaked gray breast, and rufous wings. Winter adults are more buff-colored overall. Ideally adapted to its wet habitat in both coloration and feeding, the Swamp Sparrow forages for insects in reeds and wades through shallow water like a shorebird. It nests from Mackenzie to Newfoundland and south through Nebraska and Delaware, and winters from the Gulf states north to Nebraska and Massachusetts. See sites 3, 14, 32.

Indigo Bunting *(Passerina cyanea)*
Few birds are as striking as the solid blue, 5.5-inch-long male Indigo Bunting as it sings from a sunny perch. Because blue plumage in birds is not due to a pigment but to a reflected color, the bird appears gray in the shadows, an adaptive coloration for protection. The female and immatures have brown backs with no streaking and are buff below with faint breast streaks. The fall male is similar but with some mottled blue feathers. The first-spring male is mottled blue-brown above, blue-white below, and has brown wings. Indigo Buntings forage for seeds and berries in low branches, thickets, and on the ground. The reclusive female stays hidden in undergrowth. The birds nest from South Dakota to California and east across the U.S. and southern Canada

to Maine and the Gulf states. They winter in Central America. See sites 3, 7, 8, 23, 26, 39, 52, 88.

Eastern Meadowlark
(Sturnella magna)
The distinctive meadowlark makes its presence no secret. If the piping whistle of the 9.5-inch-long songster isn't enough, its lemon-yellow breast with a broad, black V can't be missed. In the treeless habitat that Eastern Meadowlarks prefer, the males perch on fence wires and poles and, with bill high and tail low, proclaim their territory with a loud 2-whistle song. The polygamous male may attract several females to his territory. The nest is a domed structure on the ground. These birds forage in grass and on bare ground for grasshoppers, crickets, and beetles and use their spadelike bills to dig for burrowing insects. They nest from Arizona and Texas north to South Dakota, and east through the U.S. and southern Canada. They winter, often in loose flocks, in the southern part of their breeding range. See sites 8, 11, 29.

Red Crossbill *(Loxia curvirostra)*
Using their hooked, crossed mandibles, Red Crossbills specialize in feeding on the cones of conifers. They pry apart the dense scales and pick out seeds with their tongues. The 6-inch-long birds also eat insects and the seeds of deciduous trees. While foraging, they often cling to limbs with their bills like parrots. The male has a brick-red body with a solid brown tail and wings. The female is yellowish olive, and juveniles are streaked olive above and streaked white below. Red Crossbills are resident nesters in coniferous forests from southern Alaska through the western U.S. and across Canada into the northeastern U.S. and the Appalachians. They are erratic migrants and often wander greatly. See sites 27, 82, 85.

INDEX

Index

350

PHOTO CREDITS

The scenic photographs of birds in their habitats, including the large section openers, are © Tom Vezo, with the exception of the following: page 81 © Frederick Truslow/VIREO; page 90 © Doug Wechsler/VIREO; pages 116–117 © David Dvorak Jr.; page 161 © Richard & Susan Day/VIREO; pages 208, 226 and 231 © Rick & Nora Bowers; page 229 © Eric Nishibayashi/VIREO; pages 326–327 © Tony Beck/VIREO. The silhouetted images of birds and other small photographs are copyrighted by the following photographers:

1: Kevin Karlson; 3: Kevin Karlson; 4–5: Ron Austing (top); all other photos © Tom Vezo; 6–7: Cyril Laubscher (top left); Ron Austing (bottom right); 8–9: Ron Austing (left), Kevin Karlson (center); Ron Austing (bottom right); 10–11: Ron Austing (bottom left); Tom Vezo (center); Ron Austing (left); 12: Tom Vezo; 13: Tom Vezo (top); Ron Austing (bottom); 14–15: Ron Austing (bottom); all other photos © Tom Vezo; 20: both photos © Tom Vezo; 20: Brian E. Small; 21: Ron Austing; 23: Ron Austing; 24: Ron Austing; 26: Ron Austing; 27: Dennis Avon; 29: Kevin Karlson; 30: Ron Austing; 32: Ron Austing; 33: Ron Austing; 35: Ron Austing; 36: Ron Austing; 38: Ron Austing; 39: Ron Austing; 41: Ron Austing; 42: Ron Austing; 44: Ron Austing; 45: Mike Dazenbaker; 47: Brian E. Small; 48: Ron Austing; 50: Ron Austing; 51: Ron Austing; 56: S. Maslowski; 57: Ron Austing; 59: Ron Austing; 60: Ron Austing; 62: Ron Austing; 63: Ron Austing; 65: Maslowski Photo; 66: Ron Austing; 68: Ron Austing; 69: Tom Vezo; 71: Ron Austing; 72: Ron Austing; 74 Ron Austing; 75: Kevin Karlson; 77: Ron Austing; 78: Ron Austing; 80: Ron Austing; 81: Tom Vezo; 83: Tom Vezo; 84: Tom Vezo; 86: Ron Austing; 87: Ron Austing; 89: Tom Vezo; 90: Ron Austing; 92: Ron Austing; 93: Ron Austing; 95: Ron Austing; 96: Tom Vezo; 98: Unknown; 99: Ron Austing; 101: Ron Austing; 102: Ron Austing; 104: Ron Austing; 105: Ron Austing; 107: Ron Austing; 108: Ron Austing; 110: Ron Austing; 111: Karl & Steve Maslowski; 113: Ron Austing; 114: Ron Austing; 118: Ron Austing; 119: Ron Austing; 121: Ron Austing; 122: Ron Austing; 124: Ron Austing; 125: Mike Dunning; 127: Frank Greenaway; 128: Ron Austing; 130: Ron Austing; 31: Ron Austing; 133: Mike Danzenbaker; 134: Ron Austing; 136: Kevin Karlson; 137: Ron Austing; 139: Ron Austing; 140: Ron Austing; 142: Kevin Karlson; 143: Brian E. Small; 145: Ron Austing; 146: Jane Burton; 148: Ron Austing; 149: Ron Austing; 151: Ron Austing; 152: Brian E. Small; 154: Ron Austing; 155: Ron Austing; 157: Brian E. Small; 158: Ron Austing; 160: Ron Austing; 161: Ron Austing; 163: Ron Austing; 164: Ron Austing; 166: Brian E. Small; 167: Maslowski Photo; 169: Ron Austing; 170: Brian E. Small; 172: Steve Maslowski; 173: Ron Austing; 175: Ron Austing; 176: Ron Austing; 178: Tom Vezo; 179: Tom Vezo; 181: Tom Vezo; 182: Brian E. Small; 184: Ron Austing; 185: Ron Austing; 187: Steve Maslowski; 189: Ron Austing; 190: Brian E. Small; 191: Brian E. Small; 193: Ron Austing; 194: Fred Alsop; 196: Mike Danzenbaker; 197: Kevin Karlson; 199: Kevin Karlson; 200: Tom Vezo; 204: Ron Austing; 205: Ron Austing; 207: Cyril Laubscher; 208: Ron Austing; 210: Ron Austing; 211: Tom Vezo; 213: Ron Austing; 214: Ron Austing; 216: Ron Austing; 217: Ron Austing; 219: Ron Austing; 220: Brian E. Small; 222: Cyril Laubscher; 223: Ron Austing; 225: Ron Austing; 226: Ron Austing; 228: Rob Reichenfeld; 229: Peter La Tourette/VIREO; 231: Ron Austing; 232: Mike Danzenbaker; 234: Ron Austing; 235: Cyril Laubscher; 237: Jerry Young; 238: Jane Miller; 240: Ron Austing; 241: Brian E. Small; 243: Ron Austing; 244: Karl & Steve Maslowski; 246: Ron Austing; 247: Ron Austing; 249: Ron Austing; 250: Karl & Steve Maslowski; 252: Ron Austing; 253: Ron Austing; 255: Ron Austing; 256: Ron Austing; 258: Ron Austing; 259: Cyril Laubscher; 261: Ron Austing; 262: Frank Greenaway; 264: Ron Austing; 265: Ron Austing; 267: Ron Austing; 268: Ron Austing; 272: Cyril Laubscher; 273: Ron Austing; 275: Ron Austing; 276: Tom Vezo; 278: Ron Austing; 279: Cyril Laubscher; 281: Ron Austing; 282: Ron Austing; 284: Tom Vezo; 285: Ron Austing; 287: Ron Austing; 288: Ron Austing; 290: Maslowski Photo; 291: Ron Austing; 293: Mike Danzenbaker; 294: Ron Austing; 296: Tom Vezo; 297: Kevin Karlson; 299: Ron Austing; 300: Ron Austing; 302: Ron Austing; 303: Frank Greenaway; 305: Brian E. Small; 306: Tom Vezo; 308: Ron Austing; 311: Ron Austing; 312: Ron Austing; 315: Ron Austing; 317: Ron Austing; 318: Ron Austing; 320: Tom Vezo; 321: Tom Vezo; 323: Brian E. Small; 324: Mike Danzenbaker; 328: Tom Vezo; 330: Ron Austing; 332: Ron Austing; 334: Brian E. Small; 337: Ron Austing; 338: Brian E. Small; 341: Ron Austing; 342: Ron Austing; 344: Ron Austing

Join the Network of Certified Backyard Wildlife Habitat Sites!

NATIONAL WILDLIFE FEDERATION®

The National Wildlife Federation's Backyard Wildlife Habitat™ (BWH) program can help you save a place for birds and other wildlife right in your own backyard while opening your eyes and heart to the natural world. BWH landscapes nature, wildlife, and at the same time, benefit the overall quality of the environment by improving air, water, and soil throughout the community. Habitat commercial and residential development has eliminated most natural areas.

All wildlife require four basic elements to survive: food; water; cover to protect against the elements and predators; and places to reproduce and bear young in safety. Combinations of these four elements are unique for each species, but you can plan a habitat that offers enough variation to attract the greatest number and variety of wildlife your area will support. Locally native plants are the main component of any BWH. Plants native to the soils and climate of your specific area provide the best overall food sources for wildlife and at the same time require less fertilizer, water, and pest control. Locally native flora and fauna have co-evolved, and native plants may support 10 to 50 times as many species of wildlife as non-native plants.

The first step in planning any BWH project is to identify the habitat elements that already exist. The best way to do this is to look at your yard from the wildlife's point of view. Is there a dying tree in the corner you were thinking of removing? The knotholes could provide a perfect home for a family of chickadees or another cavity-nesting bird. Is there a pile of brush that isn't very attractive? It could be tidied up and provide just the protection a mother rabbit needs to safely bear and raise her young.

Become familiar with the birds and other wildlife native to your region. Learn which species regularly migrate through your part of the country each year, and would benefit from "temporary room and board" provided in your yard or garden. Consider the size of the space you want to devote to your habitat project. Your planning and planting activities will vary with the habitat area you envision.

Having your yard certified as an official BWH site rewards you for the dedication you have shown to making a place for wildlife in your world. When your habitat is certified, you will receive a handsome, personalized Certificate of Achievement from the National Wildlife Federation®, recognizing your yard as part of the National Registry of nearly 28,000 BWH sites.

To find out how you can create your own certified BWH, visit the National Wildlife Federation web site at www.nwf.org The BWH kits are also available at all Wild Birds Unlimited stores. The backyard bird feeding specialists at Wild Birds Unlimited can help property owners meet the qualifications to certify their property. Visit www.wbu.com or call (800) 326-4WBU to find the store near you.